Learning
Microsoft®
PowerPoint 2013

Catherine Skintik

Prentice Hall

Boston • Columbus • Indianapolis • New York • San Francisco • Upper Saddle River
Amsterdam • Cape Town • Dubai • London • Madrid • Milan • Munich • Paris • Montreal • Toronto
Delhi • Mexico City • Sao Paulo • Sydney • Hong Kong • Seoul • Singapore • Taipei • Tokyo

Editor in Chief: Michael Payne
Product Development Manager: Laura Burgess
Director of Business & Technology Marketing:
 Maggie Moylan Leen
Marketing Manager: Brad Forrester
Marketing Coordinator: Susan Osterlitz
Marketing Assistant: Darshika Vyas
Production Project Manager: Kayla Smith-Tarbox
Operations Director: Alexis Heydt

Senior Operations Specialist: Maura Zaldivar-Garcia
Text and Cover Designer: Vanessa Moore
Media Project Manager, Production: Renata Butera
Editorial and Product Development: Emergent Learning, LLC
Composition: Vanessa Moore
Printer/Binder: Webcrafters, Inc.
Cover Printer: Lehigh-Pheonix Color
Text: 10/12 Helvetica

Credits and acknowledgements borrowed from other sources and reproduced, with permission, in this textbook are as follows: All photos courtesy of Shutterstock.com.

Microsoft® and Windows® are registered trademarks of the Microsoft Corporation in the U.S.A. and other countries. Screen shots and icons reprinted with permission from the Microsoft Corporation. This book is not sponsored or endorsed by or affiliated with the Microsoft Corporation.

Many of the designations by manufacturers and seller to distinguish their products are claimed as trademarks. Where those designations appear in this book, and the publisher was aware of a trademark claim, the designations have been printed in initial caps or all caps.

ISBN 10: 0-13-314861-0

ISBN 13: 978-0-13-314861-9

1 2 3 4 5 6 7 8 9 10 V064 16 15 14 13

Table of Contents

Introduction

Microsoft Office 2013 is Microsoft's suite of application software. The Standard version includes Word, Excel, Outlook, and PowerPoint. Other editions may also include Access, Publisher, OneNote, and InfoPath. This book covers PowerPoint (the presentation tool). Because Microsoft Office is an integrated suite, the components can all be used separately or together to create professional-looking documents and to manage data.

How the Book Is Organized

Learning Microsoft PowerPoint 2013 is made up of seven chapters. Chapters are comprised of short lessons designed for using Microsoft PowerPoint 2013 in real-life business settings. Each lesson is made up of six key elements:

- **What You Will Learn.** Each lesson starts with an overview of the learning objectives covered in the lesson.

- **Words to Know.** Key terms are included and defined at the start of each lesson, so you can quickly refer back to them. The terms are then highlighted in the text.

- **What You Can Do.** Concise notes for learning the computer concepts.

- **Try It.** Hands-on practice activities provide brief procedures to teach all necessary skills.

- **Practice.** These projects give students a chance to create presentations by entering information. Steps provide all the how-to information needed to complete a project.

- **Apply.** Each lesson concludes with a project that challenges students to apply what they have learned through steps that tell them what to do, without all the how-to information. In the Apply projects, students must show they have mastered each skill set.

- Each chapter ends with two assessment projects: **Critical Thinking** and **Portfolio Builder**, which incorporate all the skills covered throughout the chapter.

Working with Data and Solution Files

As you work through the projects in this book, you'll be creating, opening, and saving files. You should keep the following instructions in mind:

- For many of the projects, you will use data files. The data files can be accessed from the Companion Web site (www.pearsonhighered.com/learningseries). Other projects will ask you to create new documents and files and then enter text and data into them, so you can master creating documents from scratch.

- The data files are used so that you can focus on the skills being introduced—not on keyboarding lengthy documents.

- When the project steps tell you to open a file name, you open the data file provided.

- All the projects instruct you to save the files created or to save the project files under a new name. This is to make the project file your own and to avoid overwriting the data file in the storage location. Throughout this book, when naming files and folders, replace *xx* with your name or initials as instructed by your teacher.

- Follow your instructor's directions for where to access and save the files on a network, local computer hard drive, or portable storage device such as a USB drive.

- Many of the projects also provide instructions for including your name in a header or footer. Again, this is to identify the project work as your own for grading and assessment purposes.

- Unless the book instructs otherwise, use the default settings for text size, margin size, and so on when creating a file. If someone has changed the default software settings for the computer you're using, your exercise files may not look the same as those shown in this book. In addition, the appearance of your files may look different if the system is set to a screen resolution other than 1024 × 768.

Companion Web Site (www.pearsonhighered.com/learningseries)

The Companion Web site includes additional resources to be used in conjunction with the book and to supplement the material in the book. The Companion Web site includes:

- Data files for many of the projects.
- Glossary of all the key terms from the book.
- Microsoft Office Specialist (MOS) correlations.
- Puzzles correlated to the chapters in the book.

Navigating the Textbook and Supplemental Print Resources

Lesson 13

Drawing and Formatting Shapes

➤ What You Will Learn

Using Rulers, Guides, and Gridlines
Drawing Shapes
Moving and Sizing Shapes
Applying Fills and Outlines
Picking Up a Color with the Eyedropper
Applying Shape Effects and Styles
Adding Text to Shapes

WORDS TO KNOW

Gridlines
A regular grid of dotted lines displayed on a slide to help arrange objects.

Guides
Nonprinting vertical and horizontal lines you can use to align objects on a slide.

Sample
Pick up a color from an object or slide background.

Shape effects
Special effects such as glow, shadow, 3D rotation, and soft edges applied to drawn shapes.

Shape styles
Preset combinations of shape effects that can be applied as a single formatting action.

Snap
To change position to align precisely with a gridline.

Software Skills   Use PowerPoint's many drawing tools to help enhance a presentation. You might use rulers and guides or the grid to line up text or drawing objects, for example. Use shape tools to draw logos, illustrations, or other objects to add to slides. Then format shapes using fills, outlines, effects, and styles. Add text to a shape to use it as a visually interesting caption or label.

What You Can Do

Using Rulers, Guides, and Gridlines

- PowerPoint provides a vertical and horizontal ruler that you can show or hide at any time. Use the rulers to help you align objects on a slide.

- The ruler's origins (0 measurement on the ruler) change depending on whether you're using text or an object. The origin appears on the edge of the ruler when you're working with text and in the center point of the ruler when you're working with an object.

- As you move the mouse pointer, an indicator moves on each ruler showing your horizontal and vertical locations.

- **Guides** are alignment tools that help you line up objects and text. PowerPoint supplies one vertical and one horizontal guide that you can move and copy, as shown in Figure 13-1 on the next page.

Software Skills

Each lesson begins with an introduction to the computer skills that will be covered in the lesson.

Words to Know

Vocabulary terms are listed at the start of each lesson for easy reference and appear in bold in the text on first use.

What You Can Do

The technology concepts are introduced and explained.

Try It!

Short, hands-on activities give students the opportunity to practice the software features in a sample document.

Illustrations

Illustrations throughout the text can be used as guidelines for visual learners.

Try It!   Stacking Objects

1. Start PowerPoint, and open **P14Try** from the data files for this lesson.

2. Save the presentation as **P14Try_xx** in the location where your teacher instructs you to store the files for this lesson.

3. Click any of the shapes, and then click DRAWING TOOLS FORMAT > Selection Pane. The Selection pane opens.

4. In the Selection pane, click the eye symbol 👁 next to Oval 4. The circle disappears and the button changes to a blank. Click the blank button to make the circle reappear.

5. Click the circle to select it. Then hold down `SHIFT` and drag a corner selection handle on the circle to expand it so it is large enough to completely cover the star. Drag it to reposition it so it is directly over the star.

6. With the circle still selected, on the DRAWING TOOLS FORMAT tab, click the arrow to the right of the Send Backward button and click Send to Back.

7. Adjust the size and position of the circle so that the tips of the star barely touch the edges of the circle.

8. Click the pentagon, either on the slide or in the Selection pane.

9. Click the arrow to the right of the Bring Forward button and click Bring to Front.

10. Position the pentagon on top of the star, at its center.

11. Click DRAWING TOOLS FORMAT > Selection Pane to turn off the Selection pane. The design should look like that shown in the following figure.

12. Save the **P14Try_xx** file, and leave it open to use in the next Try It.

Select any object easily in this pane

Arrange and stack the pieces of the design

Grouping Objects

- You can **group** the objects within a drawing so that they can be treated as a single object. Grouping objects makes them easier to copy, move, or resize.

- You can ungroup objects when you want to work with the objects individually again.

- Some changes can be made to the individual elements of a grouped object without ungrouping it, such as changing the colors.

- To select the objects to be grouped, you can hold down `CTRL` as you click on each one, or you can drag a lasso around all the objects to be included. To lasso a group, drag the mouse pointer to draw an imaginary box around the items.

Teacher's Manual

The Teacher's Manual includes teaching strategies, tips, and supplemental material.

Lesson 38   Applying Advanced Picture Formatting

What You Will Learn

- ✓ **Understanding Picture Formats**
- ✓ **Formatting Different Types of Pictures**
- ✓ **Using a Picture As a Fill**
- ✓ **Using Advanced Cropping Techniques**

Words to Know

Bitmap image
Lossless compression
Lossy compression

Pixel
Vector image

Tips, Hints, and Pointers

- Discuss each of the skills listed in the What You Will Learn list and ask students if they have used any of these skills before.
- Inform students that they will use the skills covered in this lesson to complete the end-of-lesson Practice and Apply projects. Encourage them to ask questions if they are not sure about a topic covered or how to use a certain feature.
- **CUSTOMIZED INSTRUCTION: English Language Learners:** Have students make flashcards of the *Words to Know*, writing the term on one side and the definition on the other.

Understanding Picture Formats

- Begin by discussing some of the common picture file formats PowerPoint supports. A good place to start is with the difference between a bitmap image, which is composed of thousands of individual pixels, and a vector image, which is created from a series of mathematical curves.
- Explain that a user needs to understand these image types in order to select images that are in appropriate formats for the presentation.
- Discuss the common graphic file formats shown in Table 38-1 in the student text, pointing out the extension and key characteristics for each.
- Make sure students understand the role of compression when selecting a file type. File formats that use lossless compression will maintain their quality even after compression. File formats such as JPEG that use lossy compression

lose a bit of quality each time they are compressed.

Formatting Different Types of Pictures

- The real fun of working with pictures is formatting them using the options on the PICTURE TOOLS FORMAT tab. With a picture selected on a slide, display this tab and review the options it offers.
  - Use the options in the Adjust group to make changes to the picture's appearance. Review how to use the Corrections options to sharpen or soften or adjust brightness and contrast. Point out the Picture Corrections Options command at the bottom of the Corrections gallery. Clicking this command opens the Format Picture task pane with options for finer control over picture corrections. Explore the Color options to adjust color saturation, change color tone, recolor a picture, or make a color transparent. Be sure also to explore the options on the Artistic Effects gallery. Students who have worked with Adobe Illustrator or Photoshop will recognize some of these effects as similar to filters. Point out that the Change Picture option allows a user to replace the current picture with a different one. Use Reset Picture to restore a picture to its original appearance.
  - Apply some of the Quick Styles in the Picture Styles gallery for quick visual impact.

Tips, Hints, and Pointers

These items help explain the content and provide additional information for instructors to use in the classroom.

Customized Instruction

Support for English Language Learners, Less Advanced Students, More Advanced Students, and Special Needs Students is provided throughout.

Test Book with TestGen CD-ROM

Print tests include a pretest, posttest, and two application tests for each chapter in the student edition. Accompanying CD-ROM includes test-generator software so that instructors can create concept tests correlated to the chapters in the book.

Directions

Steps tell students what to do, without all of the how-to detail, so critical-thinking skills must be used.

PowerPoint 2013	Chapter 2: Working with Lists and Graphics
Application Test 2A	• **Work with Lists** • **Insert an Online Picture** • **Insert a Text Box** • **Draw and Format Shapes**
	• **Insert WordArt** • **Insert and Format a SmartArt Diagram**

✔ **Directions:**

Use PowerPoint to complete the project below. Carefully follow all directions and check your results.
(Time: 40 minutes. Point Scale: –5 per formatting error; –2 per typographical error.)

Halley Montgomery has reviewed your presentation and wants you to adjust some text and add graphic elements for greater visual interest. You will modify list formats and add graphics including an online picture, shape, text box, WordArt, and SmartArt.

Open and Save the Presentation

1. Start PowerPoint, and open **PTEST2A** from the data files.

2. Save the presentation as **P2A_xx** in the location where your teacher instructs you to store files.

Work with Lists

1. On slide 2, change the bullet characters to Checkmark Bullets from the Bullets gallery.

2. Change the color of the bullets to Red, Accent 5, and the size to 105% of text.

3. On slide 6, increase the indent for the last two bullet items to make them subordinate to the second subbullet.

4. On slide 7, select the bullets under the Repurposing abandoned factories bullet and change them to a numbered list.

5. Save the presentation.

Insert an Online Picture

1. On slide 3, insert an online picture. Use the keywords **building house** and then select a picture of a house under construction.

2. Resize the picture appropriately and position it on the right side of the slide.

3. Apply the same picture style to the online picture you applied to the picture on slide 5.

4. Save the presentation.

Insert a Text Box

1. On slide 4, insert a text box and type the following text: **See our Web site at www.montgomeryconstruction. com for pictures of our restoration and renovation projects.**

2. Resize the text box to be 1.4" high and 5" wide.

3. Apply the Intense Effect – Red, Accent 5 shape style to the text box, and use the Align Right alignment option to move it to the right side of the slide.

4. Position the text box vertically so that the bottom of the box is about an inch from the bottom of the slide.

5. Save the presentation.

Draw and Format Shapes

1. On slide 1, draw a rectangle 1" high by 2" wide.

2. Draw an oval 1" high by 1.3" wide.

3. Position the oval on top of the rectangle so that the two objects are centered and the side selection handles of the oval align with the top of the rectangle (see Illustration A).

Illustration A

4. On the DRAWING TOOLS FORMAT tab, click Merge Shapes and then Union to merge the shapes.

5. Resize the shape to be 1" high.

6. Add the text **Montgomery Construction**, and then use the Align Text command on the HOME tab to change vertical alignment to Bottom.

7. Apply the Intense Effect – Red, Accent 5 shape style and move the shape just above the aqua rectangle at the right side of slide 1.

Insert WordArt

1. Insert a new slide at the end of the presentation with the Blank layout.

2. Insert a Pattern Fill – Gray-25%, Text 2, Dark Upward Diagonal, Hard Shadow – Text 2 WordArt graphic with the text **We Build It Better!**

3. Change the font size of the graphic text to 66, and then resize the graphic to be 8.3" wide.

4. Align the graphic at the center and middle of the slide.

5. Save the presentation.

79

Solutions Manual

Contains final solution illustrations for all of the projects in the student textbook. Accompanying CD-ROM contains solution files in electronic format.

Solution Illustrations

Instructors can use the end-result illustrations to do a visual check of students' work.

Learning Microsoft® PowerPoint 2013

(Courtesy Goodluz/Shutterstock)

Using the Common Features of Microsoft Office 2013

Lesson 1
Microsoft Office 2013 Basics

- Analyzing Information Technology
- Analyzing Microsoft Office 2013
- Using the Mouse
- Using Touch Mode
- Using the Keyboard
- Analyzing Data Storage
- Navigating with Windows Explorer
- Creating and Deleting a Folder
- Starting a Microsoft Office Program, Creating a Blank File, and Exiting the Program

Lesson 2
Saving, Printing, and Closing Microsoft Office Files

- Identifying Common Microsoft Office Screen Elements
- Entering and Editing Text
- Correcting Errors
- Saving a File
- Printing a File
- Closing a File

Lesson 3
Working with Existing Files

- Opening an Existing File
- Saving a File with a New Name
- Viewing File Properties
- Using the Ribbon
- Using Access Keys
- Selecting Text
- Formatting Text

Lesson 4
Using Command Options

- Using the Quick Access Toolbar
- Using the Mini Toolbar
- Using Shortcut Menus
- Using Dialog Box Options
- Using Task Panes
- Formatting Pages

Lesson 5
Managing Program Windows

- Changing the View
- Using Window Controls
- Zooming
- Scrolling
- Using Multiple Windows
- Using the Microsoft Office Clipboard

Lesson 6
Using Microsoft Office Help

- Using Microsoft Office Help
- Searching for Help
- Using the Help Table of Contents
- Viewing Application Options
- Customizing the Ribbon
- Using AutoRecover and Autosave

Lesson 7
Managing Information Technology

- Copying Files and Folders
- Moving Files and Folders
- Compressing Files
- Recognizing Types of Business Documents
- Determining the Risks and Rewards of Developing an IT Strategy
- Identifying Needed Equipment and Supplies
- Establishing, Scheduling, and Following Maintenance Procedures

End-of-Chapter Activities

Lesson 1

Microsoft Office 2013 Basics

WORDS TO KNOW

Byte
A unit used to measure storage capacity. One byte equals about one character.

Communications technology
Technology that makes communication easier and more efficient.

Current file
The file currently open and active. Actions and commands affect the current file.

Folder
A location on disk where you can store files.

Hardware
Computers, printers, and other devices.

Hyperlink
Text or graphics that are linked to another location. When you click a hyperlink, the destination is displayed. Often referred to simply as "link."

Icon
A picture used to identify an element onscreen, such as a toolbar button.

➤ What You Will Learn

Analyzing Information Technology
Analyzing Microsoft Office 2013
Using the Mouse
Using the Keyboard
Navigating with Windows Explorer
Creating and Deleting a Folder
Starting and Exiting Microsoft Office Programs

Software Skills   Anyone trying to succeed in today's competitive business world benefits from an understanding of information technology. A good place to start is by learning how to use Microsoft® Office 2013, a suite of programs that may be used independently or together to create simple documents, such as letters and memos, as well as complex reports, data tables, and budget spreadsheets.

What You Can Do

Analyzing Information Technology

- **Information technology**, or IT, refers to the use of computers to collect, store, and distribute information.
- **Communications technology** is part of information technology. It refers to the use of technology to make communication easier and more efficient.
- Businesses rely on technology of many types to make sure employees have the tools they need to complete assignments, tasks, and other responsibilities.
- Technology purchases include **hardware** and **software**.
- At the very least, almost all businesses require a computer, a printer, a connection to the Internet, and software such as Microsoft Office for basic business applications, such as word processing, data management, and spreadsheet functions.
- Other IT needs depend on the type and size of business. Some common IT equipment includes **scanners** to convert printed material to digital format. Some businesses may use other input devices such as voice recognition software, digital cameras, touch screen monitors or tablet PCs, and microphones.

- Other technology a company might need includes projectors, bar code readers, cash registers, and video conferencing systems.
- Departments must evaluate the needs of each employee, research the available technologies and then purchase and install the appropriate systems. They must also be sure employees know how to use the new systems.
- Requirements vary from department to department and from company to company. For example, a large financial services company will have different technology needs than a small travel agency.
- When evaluating technology, consider the following:
  - Tasks you need to accomplish
  - Cost
  - Ease-of-use
  - Compatibility with existing systems
- You can learn more about hardware and software technology using the Internet, consulting a magazine or buyer's guide, or by visiting a retailer in your area to talk to a salesperson.

Analyzing Microsoft Office 2013

- Microsoft Office 2013 is a newest version of the popular Microsoft Office **software suite**.
- You use the Microsoft Office programs for many business tasks, including to create various types of documents, to communicate with co-workers and customers, and to store and manage information.
- The Microsoft Office 2013 software suite is available in different editions.
- Most editions include the following core Microsoft Office programs:
  - Microsoft® Word, a word processing program.
  - Microsoft® Excel®, a spreadsheet program.
  - Microsoft® PowerPoint®, a presentation graphics program.
  - Microsoft® Outlook®, a personal information manager and communications program.
- Some editions may include the following additional programs:
  - Microsoft® Access®, a database application.
  - Microsoft® Publisher, a desktop publishing program.
  - Microsoft® OneNote®, a note-taking and management program.
  - Microsoft® InfoPath™, an information gathering and management program.
- This book covers the most commonly used programs in the Microsoft Office 2013 suite: Word, Excel, Access, and PowerPoint.
- Microsoft Office 2013 runs with the Microsoft® Windows® 8 or Microsoft® Windows® 7 operating system.
- There may be slight differences in the programs depending on the operating system you are using.
- For example, features that involve browsing for storage locations are different depending on the operating system. This includes opening and saving a file, and selecting a file to insert.

Information technology (IT)
The use of computers to collect, store, and distribute information. Also the various technologies used in processing, storing, and communicating business and personal information.

Insertion point
The flashing vertical line that indicates where typed text will display.

Library
In Microsoft Windows 7 and above, a location where you can view files and folders that are actually stored in other locations on your computer system.

Menu
A list of commands or choices.

Mouse
A device that allows you to select items onscreen by pointing at them with the mouse pointer.

Mouse pad
A smooth, cushioned surface on which you slide a mouse.

Mouse pointer
A marker on your computer screen that shows you where the next mouse action will occur.

Object
Icon, menu, or other item that is part of an onscreen interface.

Random access memory (RAM)

Temporary memory a computer uses to store information while it is processing.

Read-only memory (ROM)

Fixed memory stored on a chip in a computer that provides startup and other system instructions.

Scanner

A device that converts printed documents into digital file formats.

Scroll

To page through a document in order to view contents that is not currently displayed.

Scroll wheel

A wheel on some mouse devices used to navigate through a document onscreen.

Software

Programs that provide the instructions for a computer or other hardware device.

■ In addition, there may be some visual differences in the way the programs look onscreen.

■ The procedures in this book assume you are using Microsoft Windows 8. Ask your teacher for information on procedures that may be different on systems using Windows 7.

Using the Mouse

■ Use your **mouse** to point to and select commands and features of Microsoft Office 2013 programs.

■ Most mouse devices work using light. Some older models work by sliding a tracking ball on your desk.

■ Notebook computers may have a touchpad or trackball to move the pointer on the screen in place of a mouse.

■ When you move the mouse on your desk, the **mouse pointer** moves onscreen. For example, when you move the mouse to the left, the mouse pointer moves to the left.

■ Hovering the pointer over an **object** such as an **icon** or menu name usually displays a ScreenTip that identifies the object.

■ When you click a mouse button, the program executes a command. For example, when you move the mouse pointer to the Save button and then click, the program saves the current document or file.

■ Clicking a mouse button can also be used to move the **insertion point** to a new location.

■ A mouse may have one, two, or three buttons. Unless otherwise noted, references in this book are to the use of the left mouse button.

■ Your mouse might have a **scroll wheel**. Spin the scroll wheel to **scroll**—move—through the file open on your screen.

Table 1-1	**Mouse Actions**
Point to.	Move mouse pointer to touch specified element.
Click.	Point to element then press and release left mouse button.
Right-click	Point to element then press and release right mouse button.
Double-click.	Point to element then press and release left mouse button twice in rapid succession.
Drag.	Point to element, hold down left mouse button, then move mouse pointer to new location.
Drop.	Release the mouse button after dragging.
Scroll	Rotate center wheel backward to scroll down, or forward to scroll up.
Pan	Press center wheel and drag up or down.
Auto-Scroll	Click center wheel to scroll down; move pointer up to scroll up.
Zoom	Hold down Ctrl and rotate center wheel.

- The mouse pointer changes shape depending on the program in use, the object being pointed to, and the action being performed. Common mouse pointer shapes include an arrow for selecting ⬚, an I-beam ⬚, and a hand with a pointing finger ⬚ to indicate a **hyperlink**.
- You should use a mouse on a **mouse pad** that is designed specifically to make it easy to slide the mouse.
- You can move the mouse without moving the mouse pointer by picking it up. This is useful if you move the mouse too close to the edge of the mouse pad or desk.

Software suite
A group of software programs sold as a single unit. Usually the programs have common features that make it easy to integrate and share data.

Storage
A computer device or component used to store data such as programs and files.

Stylus pen
A pen shaped device used to interact with a touch screen.

Subfolder
A folder stored within another folder.

Template
A document that contains formatting, styles, and sample text that you can use to create new documents.

Window
The area onscreen where a program or document is displayed.

| **Try It!** | **Using the Mouse** |

1 Start your computer if it is not already on. Log in to your user account, if necessary.

✓ *Ask your teacher how to log in to your user account.*

2 Click the Desktop tile on the Windows 8 Start screen.

✓ *If you are using Windows 7, skip step 2.*

3 Move the mouse pointer to point at the Recycle Bin icon.

4 Right-click the Recycle Bin icon. A shortcut menu displays (see picture at right).

5 On the shortcut menu, click Open. The Recycle Bin window opens and displays files and folders that have been deleted.

6 Click the Close button ▬✖▬ in the upper-right corner of the Recycle Bin window.

7 Double-click the Recycle Bin icon. This is another method of opening an object.

✓ *Some systems are set to open objects with a single click.*

8 Click the Close button ▬✖▬ in the upper-right corner of the Recycle Bin window.

**Right-click to display
a shortcut menu**

Using a Touch Screen

- If you are using the Windows 8 operating system on a device with a touch screen, you can use touch mode.
- With touch mode, you use your fingers or a stylus pen instead of a mouse.
- The basic gestures for interacting with a touch screen are tap and swipe.
- Tap means to gently touch the screen and then lift straight up. A tap is similar to a mouse click.
- Swipe means to slide your finger or pen across the screen.
- See Table 1-2 on the next page for more information on touch screen gestures.

Table 1-2   Touch Gestures

Tap.	Tap once on an item. This opens or selects the item that is tapped.
Press and hold.	Press down and hold for a few seconds. This selects an item (such as an icon), displays a ScreenTip, or opens a shortcut menu.
Pinch or stretch	Touch with two or more fingers and move the fingers closer (pinch) or apart (stretch). This displays different levels of information or zooms in or out.
Swipe to scroll	Drag across the screen. This scrolls in the direction you drag.
Swipe to select.	Quickly drag a short stroke in the opposite direction you would swipe to scroll. This selects an item.
Swipe from edge . . .	Start on an edge and swipe in. Results vary depending on the edge.

Try It!   Using a Touch Screen

1. Start your computer if it is not already on. Log into your user account, if necessary.

   ✓ *Ask your teacher how to log in to your user account.*

2. Swipe from right to left to scroll the Start screen.

3. Swipe from left to right to scroll back.

4. Tap the Desktop tile to display the desktop.

5. Press and hold the Recycle Bin icon.

6. Tap Open on the shortcut menu.

7. Tap the Close button ⊠ in the upper-right corner of the Recycle Bin window.

Using the Keyboard

- Use your keyboard to type characters, including letters, numbers, and symbols. The keyboard can also be used to access program commands and features.

- On a touch-enabled device, you can display a touch keyboard by tapping the Touch Keyboard button on the Taskbar.

- Function keys (F1–F12) often appear in a row above the numbers at the top of the keyboard. They can be used as shortcut keys to perform certain tasks.

- Modifier keys such as Shift [SHIFT], Alt [ALT], and Ctrl [CTRL] are used in combination with other keys or mouse actions to select certain commands or perform actions. In this book, key combinations are shown as: the modifier key followed by a plus sign followed by the other key or mouse action. For example, [CTRL] + [S] is the key combination for saving the **current file**.

- The 17-key keypad to the right of the main group of keyboard keys on an enhanced keyboard includes the numeric keys.

- Most notebook computers and portable devices integrate the numeric keys into the regular keyboard.

- When the Num Lock [NUM LOCK] feature is on, the keypad can be used to enter numbers. When the feature is off, the keys can be used as directional keys to move the insertion point in the current file.

- The Escape key [ESC] is used to cancel a command.

- Use the Enter key [ENTER] to execute a command or to start a new paragraph when typing text.

- Directional keys are used to move the insertion point.

- Editing keys such as Insert [INS], Delete [DEL], and Backspace [BACKSPACE] are used to insert or delete text.

- The Windows key [⊞] (sometimes called the Winkey or the Windows Logo key) is used alone to open the Windows Start **menu**, or in combination with other keys to execute certain Windows commands.

- The Application key [▤] is used alone to open a shortcut menu, or in combination with other keys to execute certain application commands.

- Some keyboards also have keys for opening shortcut menus, launching a Web browser, or opening an e-mail program.

Try It! — Using the Keyboard

1 Press ⊞ on your keyboard to open the Start screen.

✓ *On a touch-enabled device, tap the Touch Keyboard button on the Taskbar to display the keyboard.*

2 Press TAB twice to select the first tile.

3 Press the up- down-, left-, and right-arrow keys to select different tiles; stop when the Calendar tile is selected.

4 Press ENTER to open the Calendar app window.

5 Press ALT + F4 to close the window.

6 Press ESC to close the Start Screen and display the desktop.

Analyzing Data Storage

- Data **storage** is any device or component which can record and retain data, or information.
- Without storage, you would not be able to save files or access computer programs.
- Storage capacity is measured in bytes. One **byte** is equal to about one character.
- A typical hard disk drive today may have a capacity of 3 terabytes (TB) or more!
- The type of storage you have available depends on your computer system.
- Some common storage devices include the following:
  - Internal hard disk drive, which is a device mounted inside a computer, and used to store programs and data files.
  - External hard disk drive, which is similar to an internal hard disk drive except that it connects to the outside of the computer via a cable and a port, such as a Universal Serial Bus (USB).
  - Network drive, which is a hard disk drive attached to a network, Computers attached to the same network can access the information on the drive.
  - Flash drive, which is a small, portable device that can be attached to a USB port on the outside of a computer. A flash drive is convenient for transporting files from one computer to another.
  - Memory card, which is a small card that is usually inserted into a slot in a computer or other device, such as a digital camera or printer.
  - DVD, which is a disk that you insert into a DVD drive to record or read data. DVDs are often used for storing video, music, and pictures.
  - CD, which is an older form of storage disk.
  - Virtual drive, which is an area on a storage device that is identified as a separate drive.
  - Online storage, which allows you to save, access, and share data using storage space on the Internet. The data is protected from unauthorized access using a password. For example, SkyDrive, offered by Microsoft Corp., allows free access to up to 25 GB of online storage for saving and sharing files.
- Memory is also a type of storage. There are two types of computer memory:
  - **Read-only memory** (ROM) which is stored on a chip inside the computer. It provides the instructions your computer needs to start and begin operation, and it cannot be changed under normal circumstances,
  - **Random access memory** (RAM) is the temporary memory your computer uses to store information it is currently processing. Information stored in RAM is lost when then computer shuts down; you must save it on a storage device if you want to use it in the future.

Navigating with File Explorer

- You use File Explorer, a feature of the Windows 8 operating system, to navigate among your system components to find and use the information you need.

  ✓ *If you are using Windows 7, the navigation program is called Windows Explorer. The interface is slightly different. Ask your teacher for information on using Windows 7.*

- For example, you navigate to a storage device such as a disk drive to locate and open a file or program. You navigate to an output device such as a printer to perform maintenance, adjust settings, or use the device.

■ Windows comes with built-in **folders** that organize your computer components to make it easier to find the object you need. When you open a folder in File Explorer, its contents display in a **window** on your monitor.

■ For example, open the Computer folder window in File Explorer to display devices such as hard disk drives. Open the Libraries folder window to display **libraries** organized on your system. Open the Network window to display the devices connected to the same network as your system.

■ To select an item displayed in a window, click it. To open an item, double-click it.

✓ *This book assumes your system is set to open an object using a double click. If your system is set to open an object on a single click, you will use that method instead.*

✓ *This book assumes you are using a mouse. If you are using a touch-enabled device, you will use your finger or a pen instead.*

■ Every computer system has different components. For example, one system might have a DVD drive, and another system might not. One might connect to a networked printer, while another has a printer directly connected to a USB port. No matter what the system components might be, the methods for navigating are the same:

● Use the Back ⊙ and Forward ⊙ buttons to move through windows you have opened recently.

● Use the Recent Locations menu to go directly to a window you have opened recently.

● Click a location in the Address bar to open it.

● Click an arrow between locations in the Address bar to display a menu, then click a location on the menu to open it.

● Each window displays a navigation pane which provides links to common locations. Click a location in the Navigation pane to display its contents in the window.

Try It!   Navigating with File Explorer

1 If you have a removable storage device to use for storing your work in this class, connect it to your computer. For example, insert a removable disk in a drive, or connect a flash drive to a USB port.

2 If necessary, press ESC to switch from the Windows start screen to the desktop. Click the File Explorer icon 📁 on the Taskbar.

3 Click Computer in the Navigation pane of the File Explorer window to open the Computer window to view the storage devices that are part of your computer system.

OR

If you are storing your work for this class on a network location, click Network in the Navigation pane to open the Network window to view the components that are part of your computer network.

✓ *The Computer and Network components are specific to your system and may be different from those shown in the illustration.*

4 In the Content pane of the open window, double-click the location where you are storing your work for this class. For example, double-click the icon for the removable device you connected in step 1.

5 Click the Back button ⊙ above the navigation pane to display the previous storage location.

6 Click the Forward button ⊙ to move forward to the last window you had opened.

7 Click the Close button ✕ to close the window. If other windows are open, close them as well.

(continued)

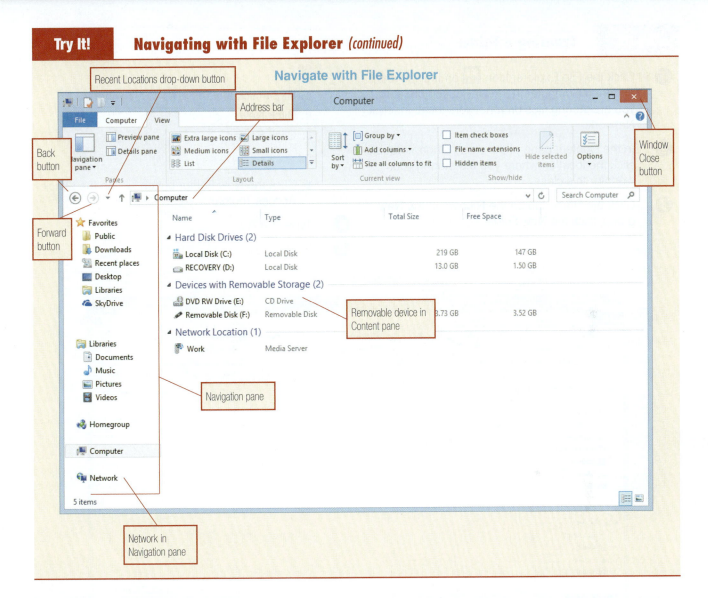

Try It! **Navigating with File Explorer** *(continued)*

Navigate with File Explorer

Creating and Deleting a Folder

- A folder is a named location on a storage device that you create using the Windows operating system.

- To create a folder, you specify where you want it on your computer system, and then give it a name.

- Folders help you keep your data organized, and make it easier to find the files you need when you need them.

- For example, you might store all the documents you use for planning a budget in a folder named Budget. You might store all the documents you use for a marketing project in a folder named Marketing Project.

- You can create a folder within an existing folder to set up layers of organization. A folder within another folder may be called a **subfolder**.

- You can delete a folder you no longer need. Deleting removes the folder from its current location and stores it in the Recycle Bin.

Try It!   Creating a Folder

1 Click the File Explorer icon 📁 on the Taskbar, and then Computer in the Navigation pane. If you are storing files on a network location, click Network.

2 In the Content pane of the open window, double-click the location where you are storing your work for this class.

3 Click the Home tab on the Ribbon. In the New group, click the New Folder button 📁 .

OR

a. Right-click a blank area of the window.

b. Click New.

c. Click Folder.

OR

■ Click the New Folder button 📁 on the Quick Access Toolbar.

4 Type **B01Try**.

5 Press ENTER .

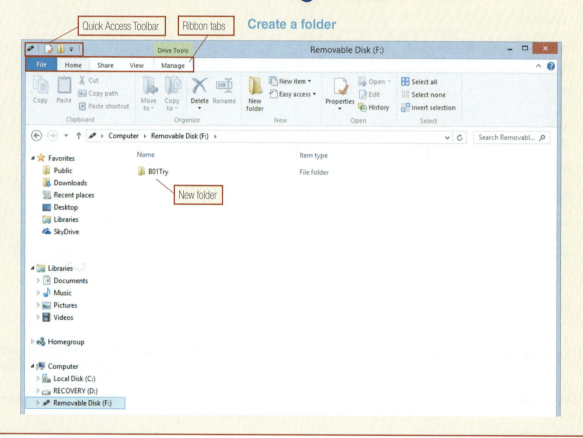

Quick Access Toolbar   Ribbon tabs   **Create a folder**

New folder

Try It!   Deleting a Folder

1 Right-click the **B01Try** folder.

2 Click Delete on the shortcut menu.

3 Click Yes to move the folder to the Recycle Bin.

4 Click the Close button ❌ in the storage location window to close File Explorer.

Starting a Microsoft Office Program, Creating a Blank File, and Exiting the Program

- To use a Microsoft Office 2013 program you must first start it so it is running on your computer.
- Use Windows to start a Microsoft Office program.
- The way you start a Microsoft Office program depends on your system configuration.
  - You will usually find the program's tile on your Windows Start screen. Click the tile to start the program.
  - If the program shortcut icon displays on your Windows desktop, you can click the Desktop tile on the Start screen, and then double-click the program icon.

- If the program icon has been added to the Taskbar, you can display the desktop and click the program icon on the Taskbar.
- If the program is not available on the Start screen or the desktop, you will find it on the Apps screen. The Apps screen lists all installed apps and programs alphabetically. Scroll to locate the Microsoft Office 2013 programs, then click the name of the program you want to open.
- When you start a Microsoft Office 2013 program, it displays a list of recently-used files and a gallery of available **templates**.
- Each program has a Blank template; click the Blank template to create a new blank file.
- When you are done using a Microsoft Office program, close it to exit. If you have a file open, the program prompts you to save, or to exit without saving.

Try It!   **Starting a Microsoft Office Program and Creating a Blank File**

① From the Windows 8 Start screen, click the Word 2013 program tile:

✓ *Depending on the number of tiles displayed, you may have to scroll to the right to locate the tile.*

OR

a. From the Windows 8 Start screen, click the Desktop tile.
b. On the Windows desktop, double-click the Word 2013 shortcut icon .

OR

- On the Taskbar, click the Word 2013 icon .

OR

a. Right-click a blank area of the Windows 8 Start screen.
b. Click the All apps button .
c. Scroll to the Microsoft Office 2013 programs.
d. Click Word 2013.

② Click the Blank document template.

Try It!   **Exiting a Microsoft Office Program**

① In the Microsoft Word program window, click the Close button ✕ at the right end of the program's title bar.

② If you have a file open, a dialog box displays. Click Save to save changes to the file and exit, or click Don't Save to exit without saving.

Lesson 1—Practice

You have just been hired as the office manager at Restoration Architecture, a growing firm that specializes in remodeling, redesign, and restoration of existing properties. In this project, you practice using your computer's operating system to create and name a folder. You also practice starting and exiting a Microsoft Office 2013 program.

DIRECTIONS

1. If you have a removable storage device to use for storing your work in this class, connect it to your computer. For example, insert a removable disk in a drive, or connect a flash drive to a USB port. (Close the AutoPlay dialog box without taking any action, if necessary.)

2. If necessary, press ESC to display the desktop. Click the **File Explorer** icon on the Windows Taskbar.

3. Click **Computer** in the navigation pane. The computer window opens. It displays the storage devices that are part of your computer system.

4. Follow your teacher's directions to navigate to and open the specific location where you will store the files and folders for this book.

5. Click the **View** tab on the Ribbon to display the commands on the View tab of the Ribbon.

6. In the Layout group, click **Medium icons** to select the way the items in the window display.

7. Click the Home tab and then click the **New folder** button to create a new folder.

8. Type **B01Practice_xx**.

   ✓ *Throughout this book, when naming files and folders, replace xx with your name or initials as instructed by your teacher.*

9. Press ENTER to name the new folder. The window should look similar to Figure 1-1 on the next page.

10. Double-click the new folder to open it.

11. Click the **Back** button ⊕ above the navigation pane to display the previous storage location.

12. Click the **Forward** button ⊕ to move forward to the **B01Practice_xx** folder window.

13. Click the **Close** button ⨯ to close the window.

14. Press ⊞ on your keyboard to display the Start screen.

15. Click the Excel 2013 tile:

   OR

   a. Right-click a blank area of the Start screen and click the **All apps** button ⊞.

   b. Scroll to locate the Microsoft Office 2013 programs.

   c. Click **Excel 2013**.

   ✓ *A quick way to locate a program from the Start screen is just to start typing its name. Windows displays a list of matching programs.*

16. Click the **Blank workbook** template.

17. Click the **Close** button ⨯ to exit Excel. Click **Don't Save** if prompted, to exit without saving the file.

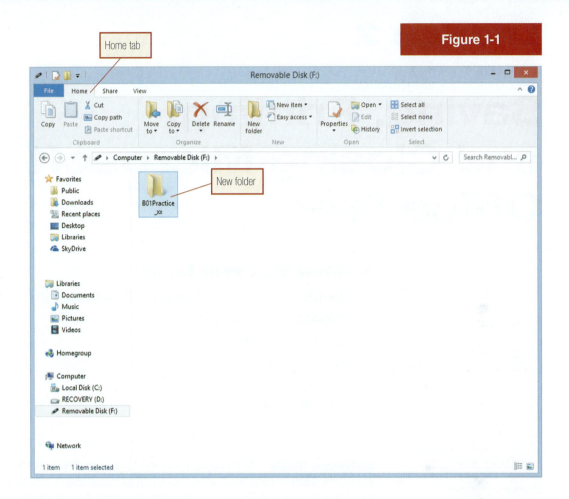

Figure 1-1

Lesson 1—Apply

In this project, you use your computer's operating system to navigate to a storage location where you create a subfolder. You then delete a subfolder and a folder and, finally, you practice starting and exiting Microsoft Office 2013 programs.

DIRECTIONS

1. Use File Explorer to navigate to and open the **B01Practice_xx** folder you created in Lesson 1—Practice

2. Create a new folder named **B01Apply_xx**.

3. Open the **B01Apply_xx** folder, then navigate back to the **B01Practice_xx** folder.

4. Navigate forward to the **B01Apply_xx** folder.

5. Navigate back to the **B01Practice_xx** folder.

6. Delete the **B01Apply_xx** folder.

7. Navigate back to the storage location where the **B01Practice_xx** folder is stored, and then delete the **B01Practice_xx** folder.

8. Close the File Explorer window.

9. Start Word 2013 and create a blank document.

10. Exit Word.

11. Start PowerPoint 2013 and create a blank presentation.

12. Exit PowerPoint.

Lesson 2

Saving, Printing, and Closing Microsoft Office Files

➤ ## What You Will Learn

Identifying Common Microsoft Office Screen Elements
Entering and Editing Text
Correcting Errors
Saving a File
Printing a File
Closing a File

WORDS TO KNOW

Backstage view
A feature of Microsoft Office 2013 from which you access file and program management commands.

Toolbar
A row of command buttons.

Software Skills   The programs in the Microsoft Office 2013 suite share common elements. That means that once you learn to accomplish a task in one program, you can easily transfer that skill to a different program. For example, the steps for saving a file are the same, no matter which program you are using.

What You Can Do

Identifying Common Microsoft Office Screen Elements

- When a program is running, it is displayed in a window on your screen.
- The program windows for each of the Microsoft Office applications contain many common elements.
- You will find more information about the individual program windows in the other sections of this book.
- Refer to Figure 2-1 on the next page to locate and identify these common window elements:
  - Ribbon. Displays buttons for accessing features and commands.
    - ✓ *Note that the way items display on the Ribbon may depend on the width of the program window. If your program window is wider than the one used in the figures, more or larger buttons may display. If your program window is narrower, fewer or smaller buttons may display. Refer to Lesson 3 for more information on using the Ribbon.*

- Ribbon tabs. Used to change the commands displayed on the Ribbon.
- Quick Access Toolbar. A **toolbar** that displays buttons for commonly used commands. You can customize the Quick Access Toolbar to display buttons you use frequently.
- Close button. Used to close the program window. It is one of three buttons used to control the size and position of the program window.
- Mouse pointer. Marks the location of the mouse on the screen.
- Scroll bar. Used with a mouse to shift the onscreen display up and down or left and right.
- Status bar. Displays information about the current document.

- Document area. The workspace where you enter text, graphics, and other data.

  ✓ *The appearance of the document area is different in each program.*

- ScreenTip. Displays information about the element on which the mouse pointer is resting.
- Title bar. Displays the program and file names.
- Zoom slider. Used to increase or decrease the size of the document onscreen.
- Help button. Used to start the program's Help system.
- View buttons. Used to change the document view.

Figure 2-1

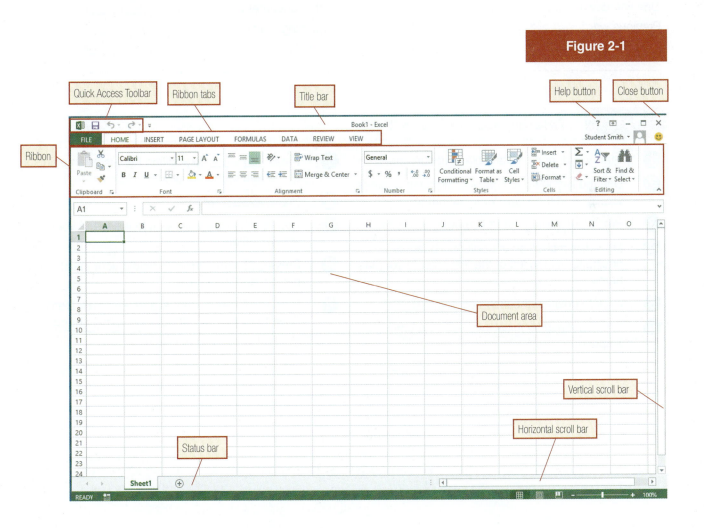

Entering and Editing Text

- Use your keyboard to enter or edit text in a file.
- Characters you type are inserted to the left of the insertion point.
- You position the insertion point using your mouse, touch device, or the directional keys on your keyboard.

- Press `BACKSPACE` to delete the character to the left of the insertion point.
- Press `DEL` to delete the character to the right of the insertion point.

  ✓ *When you are working in a program such as Access or Excel, text is entered into the selected cell. You learn about entering information in specific programs in each section of this book.*

Table 2-1	**Positioning the Insertion Point with the Keyboard**		
One character left	`←`	Up one paragraph	`CTRL` + `↑`
One character right	`→`	Down one paragraph	`CTRL` + `↓`
One line up	`↑`	Beginning of document	`CTRL` + `HOME`
One line down	`↓`	End of document	`CTRL` + `END`
Previous word	`CTRL` + `←`	Beginning of line	`HOME`
Next word	`CTRL` + `→`	End of line	`END`

Try It!   Entering and Editing Text

1. Start Word, and create a blank document.

2. Use the keyboard to type your first name, press `SPACEBAR` and then type your last name.

3. Press `ENTER` twice to start two new paragraphs.

4. Move the mouse so the pointer I-beam is positioned to the left of the first letter in your last name.

5. Click to position the insertion point.

6. Type your middle initial followed by a period and a space.

7. Press `CTRL` + `END` to position the insertion point at the end of the document.

8. Press `BACKSPACE` twice.

9. Position the insertion point to the left of your middle initial.

10. Press `DEL` three times to delete your initial, the period, and the space.

11. Click the Close button ✕ and then click Don't Save to exit Word without saving any changes.

Correcting Errors

- Press ESC to cancel a command or close a menu or dialog box before the command affects the current file.

- Use the Undo button ↰ on the Quick Access Toolbar to reverse a single action made in error, such as deleting the wrong word.

- Use the Undo drop-down list to reverse a series of actions. The most recent action is listed at the top of the list; click an action to undo it and all actions above it.

- Use the Redo button ↱ on the Quick Access Toolbar to reinstate any actions that you reversed with Undo.

- If the Undo button is dimmed, there are no actions that can be undone.

- If the Redo button is dimmed, there are no actions that can be redone.

- Sometimes when there are no actions to redo, the Repeat button ↻ is available in place of Redo. Use Repeat to repeat the most recent action.

Try It! Correcting Errors

1. Start Excel, and create a blank workbook file.

2. Use the keyboard to type your first name in the first cell (the rectangular area in the upper-left corner) and then press ENTER .

3. Click the Undo button ↰ on the Quick Access Toolbar. The previous action—typing your first name—is undone.

4. Click the Redo button ↱ on the Quick Access Toolbar. The undone action is redone.

5. Press the down arrow key ↓ three times to select the cell in the fourth row of column A.

6. Type today's date and press ENTER .

7. Click the Undo drop-down arrow ↰▾ to display the Undo menu. It should list two actions you could undo.

8. Press ESC . The menu closes without any action taking place.

9. Click the Close button ✕ and then click Don't Save to exit Excel without saving any changes.

Saving a File

- If you want to have a file available for future use, you must save it on a storage device.

- The first time you save a new file you must give it a name and select the location where you want to store it.

- Each Microsoft Office program is set to save files in a default storage location.

- You can select a different storage location on the Save As page in the program's Backstage view or in the Save As dialog box, or you can create and name a new folder using the New folder command on the menu bar in the Save As dialog box.

- After you save a file for the first time, you save changes to the file in order to make sure that you do not lose your work.

- Saving changes updates the previously saved version of the file with the most recent changes.

Try It!   Saving a File

1 Start Word, and create a blank document.

2 Click Save 🖬 on the Quick Access Toolbar.

OR

a. Click the FILE tab.

b. Click Save.

✓ *If the Save As dialog box displays, your computer was modified to skip the Backstage view. Skip step 3.*

3 On the Save As page in the Backstage view, click Computer, and then under Computer, click Browse 📂.

✓ *If the location where you want to store the file displays in the Backstage view, click it instead of clicking Browse.*

4 In the Save As dialog box, select the contents in the File name text box if it is not selected already.

✓ *To select the contents, drag across it with your mouse.*

5 Type **B02Try_xx**.

✓ *Remember to replace xx with your own name or initials, as instructed by your teacher. This will be the standard format for naming files throughout this book.*

6 Use the Navigation pane to navigate to the location where your teacher instructs you to store the files for this lesson. If necessary, click New folder on the menu bar to create and name a new folder.

✓ *If the Navigation pane is not displayed, click Browse Folders.*

7 Click Save or press ENTER .

8 Leave the **B02Try_xx** file open to use in the next Try It.

The Save As page in the Backstage view

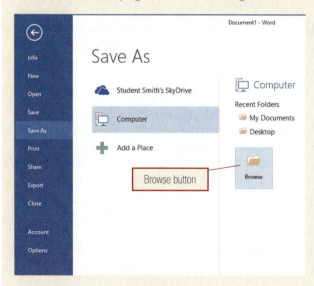

Save As dialog box

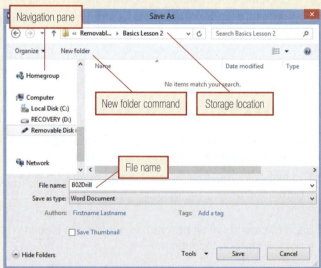

Saving Changes to a File

1 In the **B02Try_xx** file, type your first name, press SPACEBAR, type your last name, and then press ENTER .

2 Type today's date.

3 Click Save 💾 on the Quick Access Toolbar.

OR

a. Click FILE.

b. Click Save.

✓ *You can also press CTRL + S to save changes.*

4 Leave the **B02Try_xx** file open to use in the next Try It.

Printing a File

■ Printing creates a hard copy version of a file on paper.

■ In Microsoft Office 2013 programs you use the Print page in the **Backstage view** to preview and print a file.

■ You can also select printer settings such as the number of copies to print and which printer to use.

✓ *Printer setting options vary depending on the system configuration.*

■ Your computer must be connected to a printer loaded with paper and ink in order to print.

■ Ask your teacher for permission before printing.

✓ *Steps for printing in Access are different from printing in the other Microsoft Office programs. You learn how to print in Access in the Access section of this book.*

Printing the Current File

1 In the **B02Try_xx** file, click FILE.

2 Click Print.

3 **With your teacher's permission,** click the Print button 🖨 .

✓ *You can select settings such as the printer and number of copies to print before printing.*

4 Leave the **B02Try_xx** file open to use in the next Try It.

✓ *To return to the current file from the Backstage view, click the Back button ⬅ in the upper-left of the page.*

Closing a File

■ A file remains open onscreen until you close it.

■ If you try to close a file without saving, the program prompts you to save.

■ You can close a file without saving it if you do not want to keep it for future use.

■ You can use the Close button to close the file and exit the program; if there are multiple files open, the program remains running.

■ You can also use the FILE > Close command

✓ *In this book, the symbol > is used to indicate a series of steps. In this case, click the FILE tab and then click Close.*

Closing a File

1 With the **B02Try_xx** file open in Word, click the Close button ✕ .

OR

a. Click FILE.

b. Click Close.

✓ *If you have made changes since the last time you saved, click Save to save changes and close the file, or click Don't Save to close the file without saving. In Access, click Yes to save changes or click No to close without saving.*

Lesson 2—Practice

In this project, you practice the skills you have learned in this lesson to create, save, and print a file in Microsoft Word 2013.

DIRECTIONS

1. If you have a removable storage device to use for storing your work in this class, connect it to your computer. For example, insert a removable disk in a drive, or connect a flash drive to a USB port.
2. Start Word, and click the **Blank document template**.
3. Move the mouse pointer so it is resting on the **Save** button on the Quick Access Toolbar. The ScreenTip displays Save.
4. Point to the **Zoom** slider on the right end of the status bar.
5. Click the **INSERT** tab on the Ribbon.
6. Click the **FILE** tab.
7. Click **Save** > **Computer** > **Browse** to display the Save As dialog box.
8. Type **B02Practice_xx**.
9. Navigate to the location where your teacher instructs you to store the files for this lesson.

   ✓ *If necessary, create a new folder for storing the files.*
10. Click **Save** in the Save As dialog box to save the file.
11. In the new file, type your first name and your last name and press ENTER to start a new line.
12. Type today's date and press ENTER.
13. Type **Notes on using Microsoft Office 2013**.
14. Click the **Undo** button on the Quick Access Toolbar to undo the typing.
15. Click the **Redo** button to redo the action.
16. Click the **Save** button on the Quick Access Toolbar to save the changes to the file.
17. Click the **FILE** tab.
18. Click **Print**. Your screen should look similar to Figure 2-2.
19. **With your teacher's permission,** click the **Print** button to print the file.

    ✓ *If necessary, click the Printer drop-down arrow and select the printer your teacher wants you to use.*
20. Click the **FILE** tab, then click **Close** to close the file.
21. Exit Word.

Figure 2-2

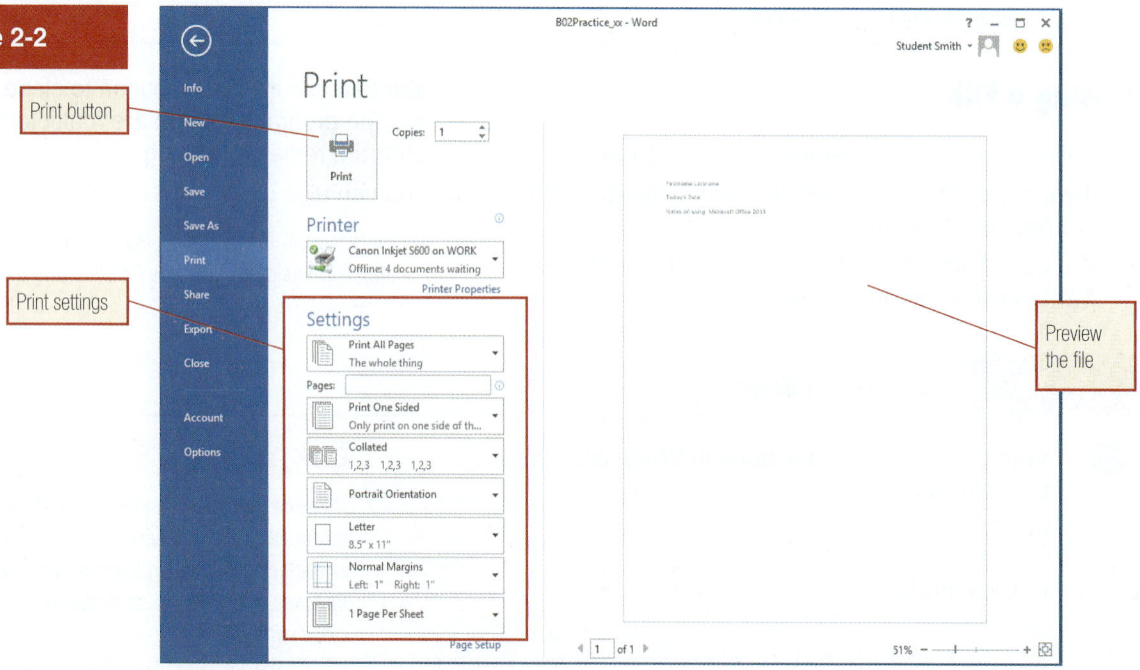

Lesson 2—Apply

As the new office manager at Restoration Architecture, you have been asked to analyze how the company might use Microsoft Office to achieve its business goals. In this project, you will use the skills you learned in this lesson to compare the Microsoft Office 2013 programs.

DIRECTIONS

1. Start Excel, and create a blank workbook.

2. Point to the following common elements in the Excel window: Zoom slider, Save button on the Quick Access Toolbar, View buttons, and the vertical scroll bar.

3. Click the **INSERT** tab on the Ribbon.

4. Click the **FILE** tab, and then click **Save**.

5. Click **Computer** > **Browse** 📁, and then type **B02ApplyA_xx**.

6. Navigate to the location where your teacher instructs you to store the files for this lesson, and then click **Save** to save the file.

7. In the new file, type your first name and your last name and press ENTER .

   ✓ In Excel, typing displays in the current, or selected, cell. Pressing ENTER enters the data in the cell and usually moves to the next cell down. If it does not move to the next cell down, press the down arrow key.

8. Type today's date and press ENTER

   ✓ Excel might apply date formatting to the entry. You learn more about formatting in a worksheet in the Excel section of this book.

9. Click **Undo** ↺ .

10. Click **Undo** ↺ again.

11. Click **Redo** ↻ twice.

12. Click the **Save** button 💾 on the Quick Access Toolbar to save the changes to the file.

13. Click the **FILE** tab, and then click **Print**.

14. **With your teacher's permission,** print the file.

15. Click the **Close** button × to close the file and exit Excel.

16. Start PowerPoint, and create a blank presentation.

17. Point to the following common elements in the PowerPoint window: Zoom slider, Save button on the Quick Access Toolbar, View buttons, and the Close button.

18. Click the **INSERT** tab on the Ribbon.

19. Click the **FILE** tab, and then click **Save**.

20. Click **Computer** > **Browse** 📁 and then type **B02ApplyB_xx**.

21. Navigate to the location where your teacher instructs you to store the files for this lesson, and then click **Save** to save the file.

22. In the new file, type your first name and your last name and press ENTER . Type today's date.

   ✓ In PowerPoint, typing displays in the current, or selected, placeholder. Pressing ENTER starts a new line.

23. Click **Undo** ↺ .

24. Click **Redo** ↻ .

25. Click the **Save** button 💾 on the Quick Access Toolbar to save the changes to the file.

26. Click the **FILE** tab, and then click **Print**.

27. **With your teacher's permission,** print the file.

28. Click the **Close** button × to close the file and exit PowerPoint.

Lesson 3

Working with Existing Files

WORDS TO KNOW

Access keys
Keys you can use to select or execute a command.

Command
Input that tells the computer which task to execute.

Contextual tab
A Ribbon tab that is only available in a certain context or situation.

Contiguous
Adjacent or in a row.

Dialog box launcher
A button you click to open a dialog box.

File properties
Information about a file.

Font
A complete set of characters in a specific face, style, and size.

Font color
The color of characters in a font set.

Font size
The height of an uppercase letter in a font set.

Font style
The slant and weight of characters in a font set.

Format
To change the appearance of text or other elements.

➤ What You Will Learn

Opening an Existing File
Saving a File with a New Name
Viewing File Properties
Using the Ribbon
Using Access Keys
Selecting Text
Formatting Text

Software Skills   You can open an existing file in the program used to create it. You can then use Microsoft Office program commands to save it with a new name so you can edit or format it, leaving the original file unchanged. Formatting improves the appearance and readability of text.

What You Can Do

Opening an Existing File

- To view or edit a file that has been saved and closed, open it again.
- Recently used files display when you first start a Microsoft Office program and on the Open page in the Backstage view; click a file to open it.
- You can use the Open dialog box to locate and open any file.

Try It!	**Opening an Existing File**
1 Start Excel. **2** At the bottom of the Recent list on the left side of the page, click Open Other Workbooks.	**3** Click Computer, and then click the location you want to open, or click the Browse button and navigate to the location where the data files for this lesson are stored.

(continued)

Gallery
A menu that displays pictures instead of plain text options.

Highlighted
Marked with color to stand out from the surrounding text.

KeyTip
A pop-up letter that identifies the access key(s) for a command.

Live Preview
A feature of Microsoft Office that shows you how a command will affect the selection before you actually select the command.

Noncontiguous
Not adjacent.

Select
Mark text as the focus of the next action.

Selection bar
A narrow strip along the left margin of a page that automates selection of text. When the mouse pointer is in the selection area, the pointer changes to an arrow pointing up and to the right.

Toggle
A type of command that can be switched off or on.

Try It!   **Opening an Existing File** *(continued)*

 Double-click **B03TryA** to open it.

OR

a. Click **B03TryA**.

b. Click Open.

 Click FILE > Close to close the file, but leave Excel open to use in the next Try It.

Open dialog box

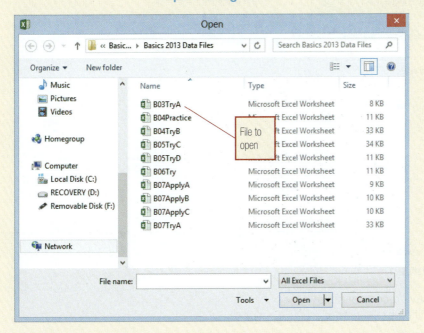

Try It!   **Opening a Recently Opened Document**

1 In Excel, click FILE.

2 In the list of Recent Workbooks, click **B03TryA**.

4 Leave the file open in Excel to use in the next Try It.

(continued)

Opening a Recently Opened Document *(continued)*

Open a Recent Workbook

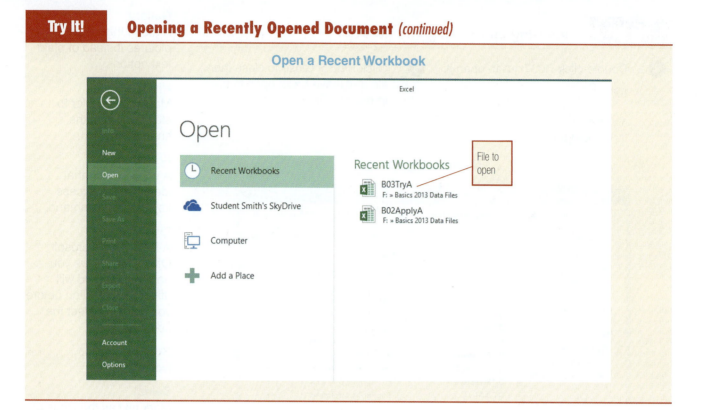

Saving a File with a New Name

- Use the Save As command to save a copy of a file in a different location or with a different file name.
- The original file remains unchanged.

Try It! **Saving a File with a New Name**

1. In Excel, with the **B03TryA** file open, click FILE.

2. Click Save As.

3. Click Computer and then click the location where you want to store the file, or click the Browse button 📂.

4. Type **B03TryB_xx** to rename the file.

5. Navigate to the location where your teacher instructs you to store the files for this lesson.

6. Click Save.

7. Close the file, and exit Excel.

Viewing File Properties

- You can view **file properties** on the Info tab in the Backstage view.
- File properties include information about the file, such as how big it is and when it was created or modified.

Try It! **Viewing File Properties**

1. Start PowerPoint.

2. Click Open Other Presentations.

3. Click Computer, then click the location you want to open, or click Browse 📂 and navigate to the location where the data files for this lesson are stored.

4. Double-click **B03TryB** to open it.

5. Click FILE. The Info page displays, with the Properties listed on the right.

6. Close the file, and exit PowerPoint.

Properties display on the Info page

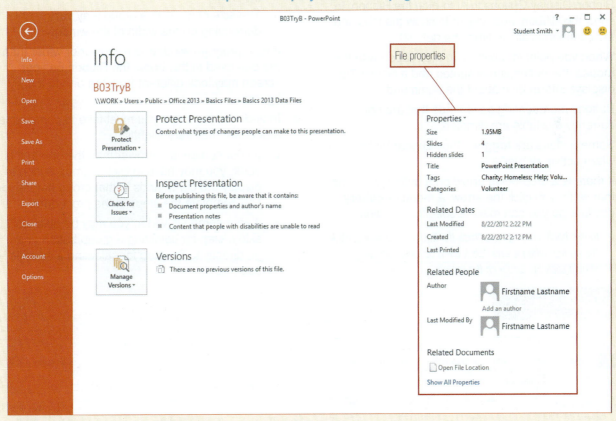

Using the Ribbon

- To accomplish a task in a Microsoft Office 2013 program, you execute **commands**. For example, Save is the command for saving a file.

- Most commands are available as buttons on the Ribbon. Refer to Figure 3-1 to identify parts of the HOME tab of the Ribbon.

- The Ribbon is organized into tabs based on activities, such as reviewing a file or inserting content. On each tab, commands are organized into groups.

- **Contextual tabs** are only available in certain situations. For example, if you select a picture, the PICTURE TOOLS tab becomes available. If you deselect the picture, the PICTURE TOOLS tab disappears.

- You can collapse the Ribbon to display only the tabs if you want to see more of a file, and expand it when you need to use the commands.

- In Word, Excel, and PowerPoint, you can change the Ribbon Display Options to Auto-hide the Ribbon, to show the Ribbon tabs only, or to show the tabs and the commands all the time (the default).

- When you point to a button on the Ribbon with the mouse, the button is highlighted and a ScreenTip displays information about the command.

- Buttons representing commands that are not currently available are dimmed.

- Some buttons are **toggles**; they appear highlighted when active, or "on."

- If there is a drop-down arrow on a button, it means that when you click the arrow, a menu or **gallery** displays so you can make a specific selection.

  ✓ *In this book, when it says "click the button" you should click the button; when it says "click the drop-down arrow" you should click the arrow on the button.*

- Sometimes, the entire first row of a gallery displays on the Ribbon.

- You can rest the mouse pointer on a gallery item to see a **Live Preview** of the way your document will look if you select that item.

- You can scroll a gallery on the Ribbon, or click the More button ⬇ to view the entire gallery.

- Some Ribbon groups have a **dialog box launcher** button ⌐ . Click the dialog box launcher to display a dialog box, task pane, or window where you can select additional options, or multiple options at the same time.

- Note that the way items display on the Ribbon may depend on the width of the program window.

  - If the window is wide enough, groups expand to display all items.

  - If the window is not wide enough, groups collapse to a single group button. Click the button to display a menu of commands in the group.

  - The size of icons in a group may vary depending on the width of the window.

- If your program window is narrower or wider than the one used in this book, the Ribbon on your screen may look different from the one in the figures.

- In addition, the steps you must take to complete a procedure may vary slightly.

  - If your screen is narrower than the one in this book, you may have to click a group button to display the commands in that group before you can complete the steps in the procedure.

  - If your screen is wider, you may be able to skip a step for selecting a group button and go directly to the step for selecting a specific command.

Figure 3-1

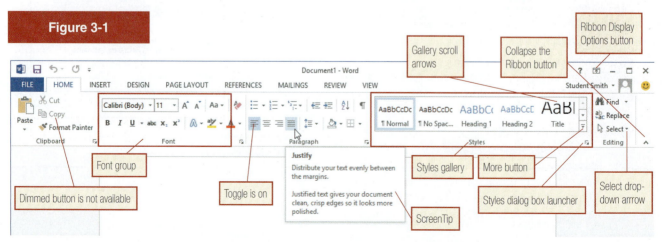

Try It! — Using the Ribbon

1. Start Word, and create a blank document.

2. Save the file as **B03TryC_xx** in the location where your teacher instructs you to store files for this lesson.

3. Point to the Center button ≡ on the Ribbon. The ScreenTip displays the button name, shortcut keys, and a description.

4. Click the Center button ≡. The insertion point moves to the center of the current line.

5. Type your first name, press ENTER , and then type your last name.

6. Press CTRL + ENTER , the shortcut key combination for starting a new page, and type today's date.

7. Click the VIEW tab on the Ribbon to make it active.

8. Click the Multiple Pages button ⊟⊟. This command changes the view to display two pages at the same time.

9. Click the One Page button ▤. This command changes the view to display one page at a time.

10. Save the changes to **B03TryC_xx**, and keep it open to use in the next Try It.

Try It! — Setting Ribbon Display Options

1. In **B03TryC_xx**, click the Collapse the Ribbon button ⌃. The Ribbon is hidden.

   ✓ CTRL + F1 *is the shortcut key combination for unpinning/ pinning the Ribbon.*

2. Click the INSERT tab. Clicking any tab expands the Ribbon temporarily so you can select a command.

3. Click the Pin the ribbon button ⌖ to keep the Ribbon displayed.

4. Double-click the VIEW tab. Double-clicking any tab is an alternative way to collapse/pin the Ribbon.

5. Click the Ribbon Display Options button ⊞ .

6. Click Show Tabs and Commands to expand the Ribbon and keep it displayed.

7. Save the changes to **B03TryC_xx**, and keep it open to use in the next Try It.

Using Access Keys

- Microsoft Office 2013 programs are designed primarily for use with a mouse or touch device.

- Some people prefer to select commands using the keyboard. In that case, you can press the Alt key to activate **access keys**.

- When access keys are active, **KeyTips** showing one or more keyboard letters display on the screen over any feature or command that can be selected using the keyboard.

- You press the letter(s) shown in the KeyTip to select the command or feature.

- If there is more than one access key for a command, you may press the keys in combination (at the same time) or consecutively (press the first key and then immediately press the next key).

- If a KeyTip is dimmed, the command is not available.

- The KeyTips remain active if you must press additional keys to complete a command.

- Once a command is executed, the KeyTips disappear.

- To continue using the keyboard, you must press the Alt key to activate the access keys again.

   ✓ *People accustomed to the shortcut key combinations in previous versions of Microsoft Office will be happy to know that they function in Microsoft Office 2013 programs as well. For example, you can still press CTRL + SHIFT + F to open the Font dialog box.*

Try It! Using Access Keys

1 With the **B03TryC_xx** file still displayed, press ⟨ALT⟩. The KeyTips for the Ribbon tabs display.

2 Press ⟨W⟩ to make the VIEW tab active. The KeyTips for the VIEW tab display.

3 Press ⟨2⟩ to change to Two Page view.

4 Press ⟨ALT⟩, ⟨W⟩, ⟨1⟩ to change to One Page view.

5 Press ⟨ALT⟩, ⟨W⟩, ⟨J⟩ to change the view to show the file at 100% magnification.

6 Press ⟨ALT⟩, ⟨H⟩ to make the HOME tab of the Ribbon active.

7 Press ⟨ESC⟩ twice to cancel the KeyTips.

8 Save the changes to **B03TryC_xx**, and keep it open to use in the next Try It.

KeyTips on the View tab

Selecting Text

- **Select** text in order to edit it or format it.
- You can select any amount of **contiguous** or **noncontiguous** text.
- You can also select non-text characters, such as symbols; nonprinting characters, such as paragraph marks; and graphics, such as pictures.
- By default, selected text appears **highlighted** onscreen.

- When you first select text, the Mini toolbar may display. Move the mouse pointer away from the selection to hide the Mini toolbar.
- When text is selected, any command or action affects the selection. For example, if text is selected and you press ⟨DEL⟩, the selection is deleted.
- To select text on a touch device, tap in the text and drag the selection handle. Refer to Table 3-1 for keyboard selection commands. Refer to Table 3-2 on the next page for mouse selection commands.

Table 3-1 Keyboard Selection Commands

To Select	Press
One character right	⟨SHIFT⟩ + ⟨→⟩
One character left	⟨SHIFT⟩ + ⟨←⟩
One line up	⟨SHIFT⟩ + ⟨↑⟩
One line down	⟨SHIFT⟩ + ⟨↓⟩
To end of line	⟨SHIFT⟩ + ⟨END⟩
To beginning of line	⟨SHIFT⟩ + ⟨HOME⟩
To end of document	⟨SHIFT⟩ + ⟨CTRL⟩ + ⟨END⟩
To beginning of document	⟨SHIFT⟩ + ⟨CTRL⟩ + ⟨HOME⟩
Entire document	⟨CTRL⟩ + ⟨A⟩

Table 3-2 Mouse Selection Commands

To Select	Do This
One word	Double-click word.
One sentence	CTRL + click in sentence.
One line	Click in **selection bar** to the left of the line.
One paragraph	Double-click in selection bar to the left of the paragraph.
Document	Triple-click in selection bar.
Noncontiguous text	Select first block, press and hold CTRL, then select additional block(s).

Try It! Selecting Text

1. In **B03TryC_xx**, press CTRL + HOME, the shortcut key combination to move the insertion point to the beginning of a Word document.

2. Position the mouse pointer to the left of the first character in your first name.

3. Hold down the left mouse button.

4. Drag the mouse across your first name to select it.

5. Click anywhere outside the selection to cancel it.

6. Double-click your last name to select it.

7. Press DEL. The selected text is deleted.

8. Save the changes to **B03TryC_xx**, and keep it open to use in the next Try It.

Formatting Text

- You can **format** text to change its appearance.
- Formatting can enhance and emphasize text, and set a tone or mood for a file.
- Microsoft Office 2013 programs offer many options for formatting text; you will learn more in the other sections of this book.

- Some common formatting options include:
  - **Font**
  - **Font size**
  - **Font style**
  - **Font color**
- You can change the formatting of selected text, or you can select formatting before you type new text.
- You can preview the way selected text will look with formatting by resting the mouse pointer on the formatting command on the Ribbon.

Try It!   **Formatting Selected Text**

1 In **B03TryC_xx**, double-click your first name to select it.

2 On the HOME tab, in the Font group, click the Bold button **B** .

3 On the HOME tab, in the Font group, click the Font Size drop-down arrow 11 ▾ to display a list of font sizes, and rest the mouse pointer on the number 28 to preview the text with the formatting.

4 Click 16 on the Font size drop-down list to change the font size to 16 points.

5 On the HOME tab, in the Font group, click the Underline button **u** .

6 On the HOME tab, in the Font group click the Italic button **I** .

7 Click anywhere outside the selection in the document to deselect the text.

8 Save the changes to **B03TryC_xx**, and keep it open to use in the next Try It.

Try It!   **Formatting New Text**

1 In **B03TryC_xx**, move the insertion point to the end of your first name and press ENTER to start a new line.

2 Type your middle name. (If you do not have a middle name, type any name.) Notice that the current formatting carries forward to the new line.

3 Press ENTER to start a new line. Click the Bold **B** , Italic **I** , and Underline **u** buttons to toggle those commands off.

4 Click the Font drop-down arrow Calibri (Body) ▾ and click Arial on the list of available fonts.

✓ *The list of fonts is alphabetical. Scroll down to find Arial.*

5 Click the Font Color drop-down arrow **A** ▾ and click Green.

6 Type your last name. The text displays in green 16-point Arial, without bold, italic, or underline formatting.

7 Close **B03TryC_xx**, saving the changes, and exit Word.

Select a font color

Lesson 3—Practice

As a public relations assistant at Voyager Travel Adventures, you are responsible for preparing press releases. In this project, you will open an existing press release file in Word and save it with a new name. You will then enter, edit, and format text to prepare it for distribution.

DIRECTIONS

1. If you have a removable storage device to use for storing your work in this class, connect it to your computer. For example, insert a removable disk in a drive, or connect a flash drive to a USB port.
2. Start Word.
3. Click **Open Other Documents**.
4. Click **Computer**, then click the location you want to open, or click **Browse** 📁, and navigate to the location where the data files for this lesson are stored.
5. Double-click the file **B03Practice** to open it.
6. Click the **FILE** tab, and then click **Save As**.
7. Click Computer, and then under **Computer**, click the **Browse** button 📁.
8. Type **B03Practice_xx** in the File name box.
9. Navigate to the location where your teacher instructs you to store the files for this lesson.
10. Click **Save**.
11. Select the headline: *Voyager Travel Adventures Announces Exciting Summer Tours*.
12. Click the **Bold** button ᴮ.
13. Click the **Font Size** drop-down arrow `11 ▾` and click **14**.

14. Select the text *Denver, Colorado – Today's Date –* and then click the **Italic** button *I*.
15. Select the text *Today's Date*, press `DEL` to delete it, and then type the actual date.
16. Press `CTRL` + `END` to move the insertion point to the end of the document, and press `ENTER` to start a new line.
17. Click the **Font** drop-down arrow `Calibri (Body) ▾` and click **Arial**.
18. Click the **Font Size** drop-down arrow `11 ▾` and click **12**.
19. Type **For more information contact:** and press `ENTER`.
20. Click the **Bold** button ᴮ.
21. Click the **Font Color** drop-down arrow 🅰 ▾ and click **Red**.
22. Type your full name. The file should look similar to Figure 3-2.
23. Save the changes to file.
24. Click the **FILE** tab. Click **Info**, if necessary, to view the file properties. Note the date and time the file was created and modified.
25. **With your teacher's permission**, print the file.
26. Close the file, saving changes, and exit Word.

Figure 3-2

FOR IMMEDIATE RELEASE:

Voyager Travel Adventures Announces Exciting Summer Tours

Denver, Colorado –Today's Actual Date– Voyager Travel Adventures, an adventure tour operator based in Denver, has announced three new travel opportunities for the coming summer months.

For more information contact:

Firstname Lastname

Lesson 3—Apply

In this project, you will open another press release and use the skills you have learned in this lesson to edit, format, and print the file.

DIRECTIONS

1. Start Word.
2. Open the file **B03Apply** from the location where the data files for this lesson are stored.
3. Save the file as **B03Apply_xx** in the location where your teacher instructs you to store the files for this lesson.
4. Change the font of the headline to Times New Roman and the font size to 16.
5. Replace the text *Today's Date* with the current date.
6. Position the insertion point at the end of the main paragraph and insert the paragraph shown in Figure 3-3, applying formatting as marked.
7. Move the insertion point to the end of the document, press ⌷ENTER⌷ , and type your full name in 12-point Times New Roman, bold, as shown in Figure 3-3.
8. Change the color of the first line of text to Light Blue and increase the font size to 12.

   ✓ *Use ScreenTips to identify the correct color.*
9. Save the changes.
10. **With your teacher's permission**, print the file.
11. Close the file, saving changes, and exit Word.

Figure 3-3

Lesson 4

Using Command Options

➤ What You Will Learn

Using the Quick Access Toolbar
Using the Mini Toolbar
Using Shortcut Menus
Using Dialog Box Options
Using Task Panes
Formatting Pages

Software Skills   As you have learned, to accomplish a task in a Microsoft Office 2013 program, you must execute a command. Most commands are available on the Ribbon, but you may also use toolbars, menus, dialog boxes, or task panes. To prepare a file for printing or other types of distribution you may have to change the page formatting, such as adjusting the margin width, or selecting a page size.

What You Can Do

Using the Quick Access Toolbar

- The Quick Access Toolbar displays in the upper-left corner of the program window.
- To select a command from the Quick Access Toolbar, click its button.
- By default, there are three buttons on the Quick Access Toolbar: Save, Undo, and Repeat. The Repeat button changes to Redo once you use the Undo command.
- Use the Customize Quick Access Toolbar button ⏷ to add or remove buttons for common commands, or use the Customize the Quick Access Toolbar options in the Word Options dialog box.
- The buttons on the Quick Access Toolbar are not available in the Backstage view.

WORDS TO KNOW

Dialog box
A window in which you select options that affect the way the program executes a command.

Landscape orientation
Rotating document text so it displays and prints horizontally across the longer side of a page.

Margins
The amount of white space between the text and the edge of the page on each side.

Portrait orientation
The default position for displaying and printing text horizontally across the shorter side of a page.

Scale
Adjust the size proportionately.

Shortcut menu
A menu of relevant commands that displays when you right-click an item. Also called a context menu.

Task pane
A small window that displays options and commands for certain features in a Microsoft Office program.

Try It!   Adding and Removing Quick Access Toolbar Buttons

1 Start Word, create a blank document, and save it as **B04TryA_xx** in the location where your teacher instructs you to store the files for this lesson.

2 Click the Customize Quick Access Toolbar button ⤓ to display a menu of common commands.

✓ *A check mark next to a command indicates it is already on the Quick Access Toolbar.*

3 Click Print Preview and Print on the menu. The button for Print Preview and Print is added to the Quick Access Toolbar.

4 Right-click the Paste button 📋 on the HOME tab of the Ribbon.

5 Click Add to Quick Access Toolbar.

6 Click the Customize Quick Access Toolbar button ⤓ to display a menu of common commands.

7 Click Print Preview and Print. The button is removed from the Quick Access Toolbar.

8 Right-click the Paste button 📋 on the Quick Access Toolbar.

9 Click Customize Quick Access Toolbar.

10 In the list on the right side of the Word Options dialog box, click Paste to select it.

11 Click the Remove button ⟨⟨ Remove ⟩, and then click OK.

12 Save the changes to **B04TryA_xx**, and keep it open to use in the next Try It.

Using the Mini Toolbar

■ The Mini toolbar displays when the mouse pointer rests on selected text or data that can be formatted.

■ Select a command from the Mini toolbar the same way you select a command from the Ribbon.

Try It!   Using the Mini Toolbar

1 In the **B04TryA_xx** document, type your first name, and then select it. The Mini toolbar displays.

2 Click the Bold button B on the Mini toolbar.

3 Save the changes to **B04TryA_xx**, and leave it open to use in the next Try It.

Formatting with the Mini toolbar

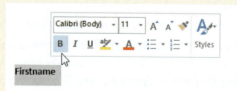

Using Shortcut Menus

■ When you right-click almost any element on the screen in any Microsoft Office 2013 program, a **shortcut menu** displays.

■ Shortcut menus include options relevant to the current item.

✓ *Shortcut menus are sometimes called context menus.*

■ Click an option on the shortcut menu to select it.

■ Alternatively, press the access key—the key that is underlined in the command name.

✓ *Sometimes, selecting an option on a shortcut menu opens a submenu, which is simply one menu that opens off another menu.*

■ If you right-click selected data, the Mini toolbar may display in addition to the shortcut menu. The Mini toolbar disappears when you select an option on the menu.

Try It!   **Using a Shortcut Menu**

1   In **B04TryA_xx**, click anywhere outside the selected text to deselect it.

2   Right-click the HOME tab of the Ribbon to display a shortcut menu.

3   Click Show Quick Access Toolbar Below the Ribbon on the shortcut menu. The Quick Access Toolbar moves below the Ribbon.

4   Right-click the status bar at the bottom of the Word window.

5   Click Zoom Slider on the shortcut menu to toggle the Zoom slider display off.

6   Click Zoom Slider on the shortcut menu again, to toggle the Zoom Slider display on.

7   Right-click the VIEW tab of the Ribbon to display a shortcut menu.

8   Click Show Quick Access Toolbar Above the Ribbon on the shortcut menu to move the toolbar back to its default position.

9   Leave the **B04TryA_xx** file open to use in the next Try It.

Use a shortcut menu to toggle screen elements off and on in Word

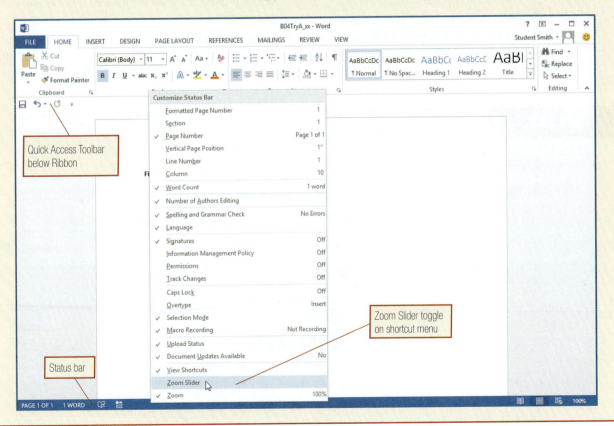

Using Dialog Box Options

- When you must provide additional information before executing a command, a **dialog box** displays.

- You enter information in a dialog box using a variety of controls (refer to Figures 4-1 and 4-2):

  - List box. A list of items from which selections can be made. If more items are available than can fit in the space, a scrollbar is displayed.

  - Palette. A display, such as colors or shapes, from which you can select an option.

  - Drop-down list box. A combination of text box and list box; type your selection in the box or click the drop-down arrow to display the list.

  - Check box. A square that you click to select or clear an option. A check mark in the box indicates that the option is selected.

  - Command button. A button used to execute a command. An ellipsis on a command button means that clicking the button opens another dialog box.

- Tabs. Markers across the top of the dialog box that, when clicked, display additional pages of options within the dialog box.

- Preview area. An area where you can preview the results of your selections before executing the commands.

- Increment box. A space where you type a value, such as inches or numbers, or use increment arrows beside the box to increase or decrease the value with a mouse. Sometimes called a spin box.

- Text box. A space where you type variable information, such as a file name.

- Option buttons. A series of circles, only one of which can be selected at a time. Click the circle you want to select it.

- To move from one control to another in a dialog box you can click the control with the mouse, or press TAB.

- Some dialog box controls have access keys which are underlined in the control name. Press ALT and the access key to select the control.

Figure 4-1

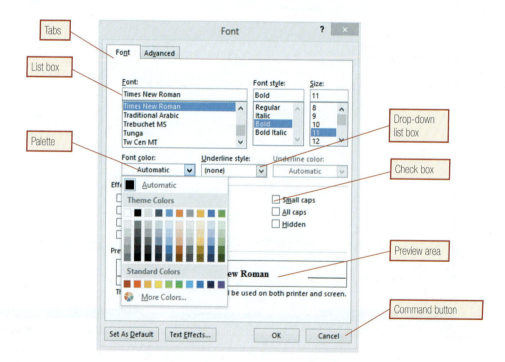

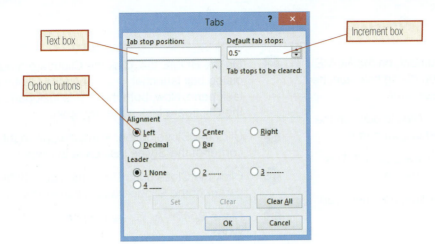

Figure 4-2

Try It!   **Using Dialog Box Options**

1 In **B04TryA_xx**, select your first name.

2 On the HOME tab, click the Font group dialog box launcher ⌐ to open the Font dialog box.

Font group on the Home tab

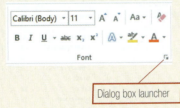

3 In the Font style list box, click Italic.

4 In the Size box, select 11 and then type **8**.

5 Click the Underline style drop-down arrow, and click the double underline that is second from the top.

6 In the Effects section, click the Small caps check box to select it.

7 Click the OK command button to apply the formatting to the selected text.

8 Deselect the text, then save the changes to **B04TryA_xx**, and leave it open to use in the next Try It.

Displaying Task Panes

- Some commands open a **task pane** instead of a dialog box. For example, if you click the Clipboard dialog box launcher, the Clipboard task pane displays.

- Task panes have some features in common with dialog boxes. For example, some have text boxes in which you type text as well as drop-down list boxes, check boxes, and options buttons.

- Unlike a dialog box, you can leave a task pane open while you work, move it, or close it to get it out of the way. You can also have more than one task pane open at the same time.

  ✓ *You learn how to accomplish tasks using task panes in the lesson in which that feature is covered. For example, in Basics Lesson 5 you learn how to use the Office Clipboard task pane to copy or move a selection.*

Try It!   **Displaying Task Panes**

1 In the **B04TryA_xx** document, on the HOME tab, click the Styles group dialog box launcher ⌐ to open the Styles task pane.

2 In the document window, click to position the insertion point at the end of your name.

3 In the Styles task pane, click Clear All. This clears the formatting from the text.

4 Press ENTER to start a new line, and then type your last name.

5 On the HOME tab, click the Clipboard group dialog box launcher ⌐ to open the Clipboard task pane. Now, both the Styles task pane and the Clipboard task pane are open.

6 Click the Close button × in the upper-right corner of the Styles task pane to close it.

7 Click the Close button × in the upper-right corner of the Clipboard task pane to close it.

8 Close **B04TryA_xx**, saving changes, and exit Word.

Open multiple task panes

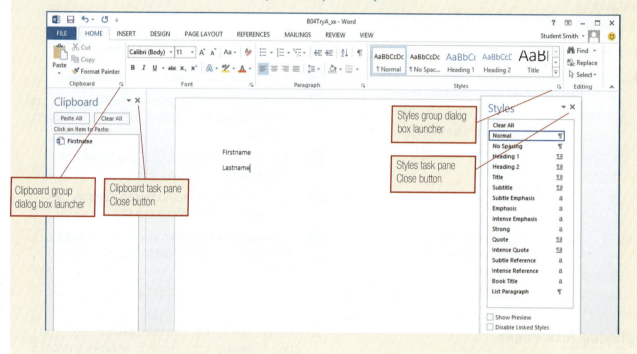

Formatting Pages

- Before you print or otherwise distribute a file, you may need to adjust the page formatting.

- Use the Print options in the Backstage view to select basic page formatting settings.

- In Access, use the options on the Print Preview tab.

- You can select an orientation, a paper size, and **margin** widths. You can also select to **scale** the file, if necessary, to fit on the selected paper size.

- Orientation is either portrait or landscape.

- Select **Portrait orientation**—the default—when you want data displayed across the shorter length of a page.

- Select **Landscape orientation** when you want data displayed across the wider length of a page.

✓ *You will learn about more advanced page formatting settings, such as setting custom margins and adjusting the alignment, in the program sections of this book.*

- You can select from a list of preset margins, including Normal, Wide, and Narrow. Margins are measured in inches.

Try It!   **Formatting Pages**

1 Start Excel, and open **B04TryB** from the data files for this lesson. Save the file as **B04TryB_xx** in the location where your teacher instructs you to store the files for this lesson.

2 Click the FILE tab, and then click Print. In the preview, you see that not all columns fit on the first page.

3 Click the Margins down arrow and click Narrow on the menu. This changes the width of the margins to 0.75" on the top and bottom and 0.25" on the left and right. Now, only the Total column is still on page 2.

4 Click the Scaling down arrow and click Fit Sheet on One Page. Now all columns fit, but they are quite small.

5 Click the Orientation down arrow and click Landscape Orientation to provide more room across the page.

6 Click the Margins down arrow and click Normal to increase the width of the margins.

7 Close **B04TryB_xx**, saving changes, and exit Excel.

Formatting pages before printing

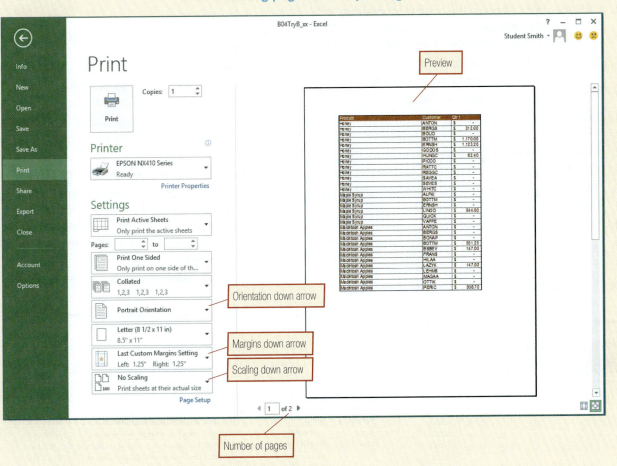

Lesson 4—Practice

As the store manager for Whole Grains Bread, a bakery, you must prepare a contact list of your employees for the franchise owner. In this project, you will use Excel to complete and format the contact list.

DIRECTIONS

1. Start Excel, open the file **B04Practice** from the data files for this lesson, and save it as **B04Practice_xx** in the location where your teacher instructs you to store the files for this lesson.

2. Double-click on the word *Position* (in cell A2). This positions the insertion point in the cell.

3. Select the word *Position*. The Mini toolbar displays.

4. Cick the **Bold** button в on the Mini-toolbar.

5. Click the next cell down the column, containing the text *Clerk*, and drag down to the cell in row 12, containing the text *Manager*. This selects the cells.

6. On the HOME tab, click the **Font group dialog box launcher** ⌐ to open the Font dialog box.

7. In the Font style list box, click **Italic**.

8. Click the **Underline** drop-down arrow and click **Double**.

9. Click **OK** to close the dialog box and apply the formatting.

10. Click cell **B12**—the blank cell to the right of the text *Manager* and below the text *Kevin*.

11. Type your own first name, and then press TAB.

12. Type your last name, and then press TAB.

13. Type today's date, and then press TAB.

14. Type your e-mail address, and then press TAB.

15. Right-click your e-mail address to display a shortcut menu

16. On the shortcut menu, click **Remove Hyperlink**. This removes the hyperlink formatting from your e-mail address. The data in your file should look similar to Figure 4-3.

17. Click the **Customize Quick Access Toolbar** button ⌐ and click **Print Preview and Print** to add the Print Preview and Print button to the Quick Access Toolbar.

18. Click the **Print Preview and Print** button ⌐ on the Quick Access Toolbar to display the Print tab in Backstage view.

19. Click the **Orientation** down arrow and click **Landscape Orientation** to change the page formatting to Landscape orientation.

20. Click the **Margins** down arrow and click **Normal** to change the page formatting to the default Normal margin widths.

21. **With your teacher's permission**, print the file.

22. Click the Back button to close Backstage view, click the **Customize Quick Access Toolbar** button ⌐, and click **Print Preview and Print** to remove the Print Preview and Print button from the Quick Access Toolbar

23. Close the file, saving all changes, and exit Excel.

Figure 4-3

	A	B	C	D	E	F	G
					student@school.edu		
1							
2	**Position**	First Name	Last Name	Date Hired	Email	Telephone	
3	*Clerk*	Karen	Smith	5/8/2014	karen.smith@wgbreads.net	555-555-5551	
4	*Clerk*	William	Brown	1/17/2014	william.brown@wgbreads.net	555-555-5552	
5	*Baker*	Jorge	Hernandez	9/22/2013	jorge.hernandez@wgbreads.net	555-555-5553	
6	*Baker*	Lisa	McAnn-Dinardo	10/11/2013	lisa.mcann.dinardo@wgbreads.net	555-555-5554	
7	*Baker*	Amil	Muhammed	6/1/2012	amil.muhammed@wgbreads.net	555-555-5555	
8	*Baker*	Peter	Shepherd	5/22/2012	peter.j.shepherd@wgbreads.net	555-555-5556	
9	*Stock*	Jackson	Little	7/13/2014	jackson.little@wgbreads.net	555-555-5557	
10	*Assistant Manager*	Angela	Greene	8/23/2003	angela.greene@wgbreads.net	555-555-5558	
11	*Assistant Manager*	Kevin	Duchesne	9/22/2012	kevin.duchesne@wgbreads.net	555-555-5559	
12	*Manager*	Firstname	Lastname	9/18/2015	student@school.edu	555-555-5560	
13							

Lesson 4—Apply

The Whole Grains Bread franchise owner has asked for the employee list in a Word document. In this project, you will open an existing Word file and then revise, format, and print the document.

DIRECTIONS

1. Start Word.

2. Open the file **B04Apply** from the data files for this lesson, and save it as **B04Apply_xx** in the location where your teacher instructs you to store the files for this lesson.

3. Display the Print options in the Backstage view and change to Landscape Orientation.

4. Set the margins to Normal.

5. Close the Backstage view.

6. Select all data in the document, and use the Mini toolbar to increase the font size to **12** points.

7. Display the Quick Access Toolbar below the Ribbon.

8. Type your name, today's date, and your e-mail address into the appropriate cells in the document.

9. Use a shortcut menu to remove the hyperlink formatting from your e-mail address.

10. Select the line of text above the table, and use the Styles task pane to clear all formatting, then close the Styles task pane.

11. With the first line of text still selected, open the Font dialog box, and apply **Bold, Green, 14-point** formatting. When you deselect the text, your screen should look similar to Figure 4-4.

12. **With your teacher's permission**, print the file.

13. Return the Quick Access Toolbar to its position above the Ribbon.

14. Close the file, saving changes, and exit Word.

Figure 4-4

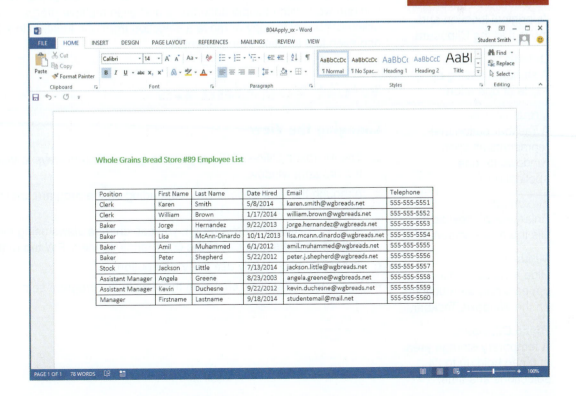

Lesson 5

Managing Program Windows

WORDS TO KNOW

Active window
The window in which you are currently working.

Cascade
Arrange windows so they overlap, with the active window in front. Only the title bars of the nonactive windows are visible.

Copy
To duplicate a selection. The original remains unchanged.

Cut
To delete a selection from its original location and move it to the Clipboard.

Default
A standard setting or mode of operation.

Group button
A Taskbar button that represents all open windows for one application.

Maximize
Enlarge a window so it fills the entire screen.

Minimize
Hide a window so it appears only as a button on the Windows Taskbar.

Office Clipboard
A temporary storage area that can hold up to 24 selections at a time.

➤ **What You Will Learn**

Changing the View
Using Window Controls
Zooming
Scrolling
Using Multiple Windows
Using the Microsoft Office Clipboard

Software Skills   Controlling the way Microsoft Office 2013 programs and documents are displayed on your computer monitor is a vital part of using the programs successfully. For example, you can control the size and position of the program window onscreen, and you can control the size a document is displayed. In addition, you can open more than one window onscreen at the same time, so that you can work with multiple documents and even multiple programs at once. Use the Office Clipboard to copy or move a selection from one location in a file to another, and even to a location in a different file.

What You Can Do

Changing the View

- The Microsoft Office 2013 programs provide different ways to view your data in the program window.
- Although the view options vary depending on the program, most offer at least two different views.
- In Word, Excel, and PowerPoint, you can change views using the View shortcut buttons on the status bar or the commands on the VIEW tab of the Ribbon.
- In Access, you usually use the Views button.
- You learn more about changing the view in the program sections of this book.

<table>
<tr><td>**Try It!**</td><td colspan="2">**Changing the View**</td></tr>
</table>

① Start Excel and create a blank workbook file.

② Click the VIEW tab.

③ In the Workbook Views group, click the Page Layout button 📄 to change from Normal view to Page Layout view. In Excel, Page Layout view displays the header and footer areas and rulers.

④ On the status bar, click the Normal view button ⊞.

⑤ Leave the file open to use in the next Try It.

Page Layout view in Excel

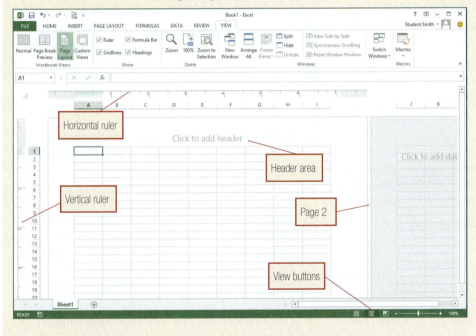

Using Window Controls

- When you start a Microsoft Office 2013 program, it opens in a program window using **default** settings.
- You can control the size and position of the program window.
  - You can **maximize** the window to fill the screen.
  - You can **minimize** the window to a Taskbar button.
  - You can **restore** a minimized window to its previous size and position.
  - You can **restore down** a maximized window to its previous size and position.
  - In Word, Excel, and PowerPoint, you can Auto-hide the Ribbon to display the window in Full Screen Mode.

Paste
To insert a selection from the Clipboard into a document.

Restore
Return a minimized window to its previous size and position on the screen.

Restore down
Return a maximized window to its previous size and position on the screen.

Scroll
Shift the displayed area of the document up, down, left, or right.

Tile
Arrange windows so they do not overlap.

Zoom
Adjust the magnification of the content displayed on the screen. This does not affect the actual size of the printed document.

Zoom in
Increase the size of the document as it is displayed onscreen.

Zoom out
Decrease the size of the document as it is displayed onscreen.

■ Use the Control buttons located on the right end of the title bar to control a program window.

    – Minimize

    ▫ Maximize

    ▫ Restore Down

    ✓ *Restore Down is only available in a maximized window.*

■ You can also use the program's control menu to Maximize, Minimize, or Restore the window.

Try It!   Using Window Controls

1 In the Excel window, click the Minimize button – . When the program window is minimized, it displays as a button on the Windows Taskbar.

2 Click the Excel program icon on the Windows Taskbar to restore the window to its previous size and position.

3 In the Excel window, click the Maximize button ▫ .

    ✓ *If the Maximize button is not displayed, the window is already maximized. Continue with step 4.*

4 Click the Restore Down button ▫ to restore the window to its previous size and position.

5 Exit Excel without saving any changes.

Zooming

■ In Word, Excel, and PowerPoint, you can adjust the **zoom** magnification setting to increase or decrease the size a program uses to display a file onscreen.

    ✓ *The Zoom options may be different depending on the program you are using.*

■ There are three ways to set the zoom:

    ● The Zoom slider on the right end of the program's status bar

    ● The commands in the Zoom group of the VIEW tab on the Ribbon

    ● The Zoom dialog box

■ **Zoom in** to make the data appear larger onscreen. This is useful for getting a close look at graphics, text, or data.

    ✓ *When you zoom in, only a small portion of the file will be visible onscreen at a time.*

■ **Zoom out** to make the data appear smaller onscreen. This is useful for getting an overall look at a document, slide, or worksheet.

■ You can set the zoom magnification as a percentage of a document's actual size. For example, if you set the zoom to 50%, the program displays the document half as large as the actual, printed document would appear. If you set the zoom to 200%, the program displays the document twice as large as the actual printed file would appear.

■ Other options may be available depending on your program.

    ● In Word, you can select from the following preset sizes:

        ■ Page Width. Word automatically sizes the document so that the width of the page matches the width of the screen. You see the left and right margins of the page.

- Text width. Word automatically sizes the document so that the width of the text on the page matches the width of the screen. The left and right margins may be hidden.

- One Page (or Whole page). Word automatically sizes the document so that one page is visible on the screen.

- Multiple Pages. Word automatically sizes the document so that multiple pages are visible on the screen.

- Many pages. Word automatically sizes the document so that the number of pages you select can all be seen onscreen.

✓ Some options may not be available, depending on the current view. Options that are not available will appear dimmed.

- In Excel you can Zoom to Selection, which adjusts the size of selected cells to fill the entire window.

- In PowerPoint you can Fit to Window, which adjusts the size of the current slide to fill the entire window.

Try It! **Zooming Using the Slider**

1. Start Word, and open **B05TryA** from the data files for this lesson. Save the file as **B05TryA_xx** in the location where your teacher instructs you to store the files for this lesson.

2. Drag the Zoom slider to the left to zoom out, or decrease the magnification. At 10% magnification, the document page is so small you cannot view the content.

3. Drag the Zoom slider to the right to zoom in, or increase the magnification. At 500% magnification, the document page is so large you can only view a small portion of the content.

4. Click the Zoom Out button at the left end of the Zoom slider. Each time you click, the magnification zooms out by 10%.

5. Click the Zoom In button at the right end of the Zoom slider. Each time you click, the magnification zooms in by 10%.

6. Leave the **B05TryA_xx** file open to use in the next Try It.

Zoom out to 10%

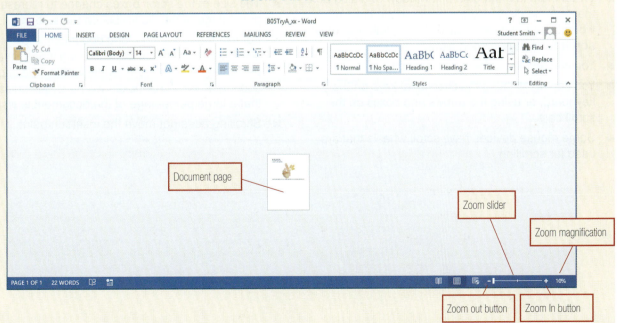

Try It!   **Zooming Using the View Tab**

1. With the **B05TryA_xx** file open, click the VIEW tab on the Ribbon and locate the Zoom group of commands.

2. Click the 100% button in the Zoom group. The magnification adjusts to display the document at its actual size.

3. Click the Zoom button in the Zoom group to open the Zoom dialog box.

4. Click the 75% option button and then click OK to apply the change and close the dialog box.

5. Click the Zoom button in the Zoom group again, and use the Percent increment arrows to set the zoom magnification to 150%.

   ✓ *In Excel, set the percentage in the Custom box.*

6. Click OK.

7. Save the changes to **B05TryA_xx**, and leave it open to use in the next Try It.

Zoom using the Zoom group on the View tab

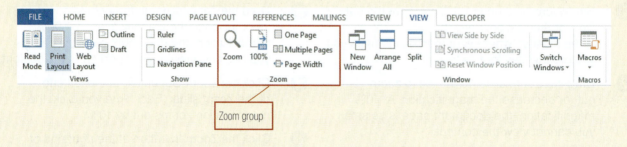

Scrolling

- When there is more data in a window or dialog box than can be displayed onscreen at one time, or when the zoom magnification is set high, you must **scroll** to see the hidden parts.

- You can scroll up, down, left, or right.

- You can scroll using the directional keys on the keyboard, or using the arrows and boxes on the scroll bars.

- Some mouse devices have scroll wheels that are used for scrolling.

- If you are using a touch device, you scroll by swiping left, right, up, or down.

- The size of the scroll boxes change to represent the percentage of the file visible on the screen.

- For example, in a very long document, the scroll boxes will be small, indicating that a small percentage of the document is visible. In a short document, the scroll boxes will be large, indicating that a large percentage of the document is visible.

- Scrolling does not move the insertion point.

Try It!   Scrolling

1 In the **B05TryA_xx** file, click the down scroll arrow ⊡ at the bottom of the vertical scroll bar on the right side of the window. The content in the window scrolls down.

✓ *If you have a wide screen, you may have to increase the zoom for the vertical scroll bar to display.*

2 Drag the vertical scroll box about halfway to the bottom of the scroll bar to scroll down in the file until you can see the line of text below the picture.

3 Click the right scroll arrow ⊡ at the right end of the horizontal scroll bar above the status bar at the bottom of the window to scroll to the right so you can see the entire line of text.

4 Drag the vertical scroll box all the way to the top of the scroll bar to scroll to the top of the document page.

5 Save the changes to **B05TryA_xx**, and leave it open to use in the next Try It.

Tools for scrolling in a document

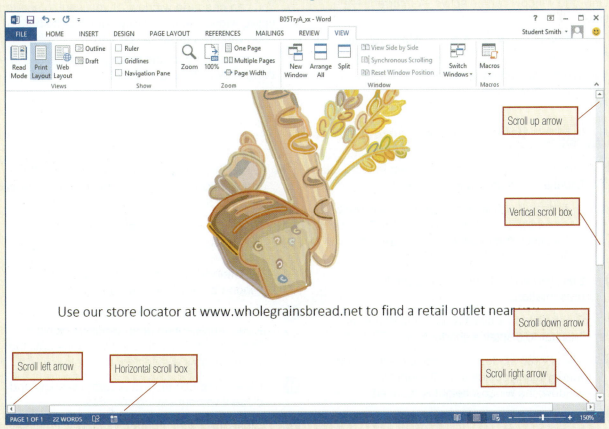

Using Multiple Windows

- You can open multiple program windows at the same time.

- You can also open multiple document windows in Word, PowerPoint, and Excel.

- Each open window is represented by a button on the Windows Taskbar.

- If there is not room on the Taskbar to display buttons for each open window, Windows displays a **group button**.

   ✓ *The Taskbar may not be visible onscreen if Windows is set to hide the Taskbar, or to display windows on top of the Taskbar. To see the Taskbar, move the mouse pointer to the edge of the screen where it usually displays.*

- Only one window can be active—or current—at a time.

- The **active window** is the one in which you are currently working.

- You can switch among open windows to make a different window active.

- You can **tile** windows if you want to see all of them at the same time. Tiled windows do not overlap; they are arranged side by side or stacked so you see the full width of each window across the screen. The active window has a brightly colored border.

- The more windows you have open, the smaller they display when tiled.

   - If necessary in smaller windows, the program may hide or condense common screen elements such as the Quick Access Toolbar and Ribbon and display only a program icon on the left end of the title bar.

   - You can click the program icon to display a shortcut menu of commands including Maximize, Minimize, and Close.

- You can **cascade** windows if you want to see the active window in its entirety, with the title bars of all open windows displayed behind it.

- You can also open and arrange multiple files in Word, PowerPoint, and Excel.

Try It!   **Using Multiple Program Windows**

1 With the **B05TryA_xx** file still open in Word, start Excel and create a blank workbook.

   ✓ *To display the Windows desktop, move the mouse to the lower-right corner of the display, and click. To display the Windows 8 Start screen, move the mouse to the lower-left corner of the display and click.*

2 Start PowerPoint and create a blank presentation.

3 Right-click on a blank area of the Windows Taskbar to display a shortcut menu.

4 Click Show windows stacked to tile the three windows so you see the full width of each window; the window height is reduced.

5 Right-click on a blank area of the Windows Taskbar.

6 Click Cascade windows to overlap the three program windows; the active window displays on top.

7 Right-click on a blank area of the Windows Taskbar.

8 Click Show windows side by side to tile the three windows so you see the full height of each window; the window width is reduced.

9 Click at the beginning of the text in the **B05TryA_xx** document window. Now, the **B05TryA_xx** window is active. Notice the insertion point in the window, and that the window's border displays brighter.

10 Press and hold ALT and press TAB. A bar of icons representing open windows displays. Press TAB to move through the icons until the Excel window is selected, then release ALT.

11 Click in the PowerPoint program window and close it without saving changes.

12 Close the Excel program window without saving changes.

13 Maximize the Word program window.

14 Save the changes to **B05TryA_xx**, and leave it open to use in the next Try It.

(continued)

Try It!   Using Multiple Program Windows *(continued)*

Arrange multiple windows side by side

Try It!   Arranging Multiple Files in Word

1 With the **B05TryA_xx** window open, click FILE > Open.

2 Open **B05TryB** from the data files for this lesson. Now, both files are open in Word at the same time.

3 Rest the mouse pointer on the Word icon on the Taskbar to view thumbnails of all open Word files.

4 Click the **B05TryA_xx** thumbnail to make that window active.

5 Click the VIEW tab on the Ribbon.

6 In the Window group, click the Arrange All button ⊟ . The two open files are tiled in the program window.

> ✓ *If nothing happens when you click Arrange All, you may have to Restore Down the B05TryA_xx window.*

7 Close both files, without saving any changes, and exit Word.

Try It!   Arranging Multiple Files in Excel

1 Start Excel and maximize the window, if necessary. Open **B05TryC** from the data files for this lesson.

2 Click FILE > Open, and then open **B05TryD** from the data files for this lesson. Both files are now open in Excel.

3 Click the VIEW tab on the Ribbon.

4 In the Window group, click the Arrange All button ⊟ . The Arrange Windows dialog box opens.

5 Click the Horizontal option button and then click OK to tile the open files one above the other (stacked).

6 Click in the **B05TryC** window to make it active.

7 Click VIEW > Arrange All ⊟ again to open the dialog box, click the Vertical option button, and then click OK. The files are tiles side by side.

8 Close both files, without saving any changes, and exit Excel.

Try It!   Arranging Multiple Files in PowerPoint

1 Start PowerPoint and maximize the window, if necessary. Open **B05TryE** from data files for this lesson.

2 Click FILE > Open, and then open **B05TryF** from the data files for this lesson. Both files are now open in PowerPoint.

3 Click the VIEW tab on the Ribbon.

4 In the Window group, click the Cascade button 🗗 to overlap the windows with the active window on top.

5 In the Window group, click the Switch Windows button 🖭 to display a list of open windows. A check mark displays beside the active window.

6 Click **B05TryE** on the Switch Windows drop-down list to make it active.

7 Click the VIEW tab, then, in the Window group, click the Arrange All button 🖻 to tile the windows side by side.

8 Close both files, without saving changes, and exit PowerPoint.

Using the Microsoft Office Clipboard

- Use the Microsoft **Office Clipboard** with the Cut, Copy, and Paste commands to copy or move a selection from one location to another.
- The **Copy** command stores a duplicate of the selection on the Office Clipboard, leaving the original selection unchanged.
- The **Cut** command deletes the selection from its original location, and stores it on the Office Clipboard.
- You can then use the **Paste** command to paste the selection from the Office Clipboard to the insertion point location in the same file or a different file.
- By default, the last 24 items cut or copied display in the Office Clipboard task pane.
- You can paste or delete one or all of the items.

- You can turn the following Office Clipboard options off or on (a check mark indicates the option is on):
  - Show Office Clipboard Automatically. Sets the Clipboard task pane to open automatically when you cut or copy a selection.
  - Show Office Clipboard When Ctrl+C Pressed Twice. Sets Word to display the Clipboard task pane when you press and hold CTRL and then press C on the keyboard twice.
  - Collect Without Showing Office Clipboard. Sets the Clipboard task pane so it does not open automatically when you cut or copy data.
  - Show Office Clipboard Icon on Taskbar. Adds a Clipboard icon to the Show Hidden Icons group on the taskbar.
  - Show Status Near Taskbar When Copying. Displays a ScreenTip with the number of items on the Clipboard when you cut or copy a selection.

Try It!   Using the Microsoft Office Clipboard

1 Start Word and maximize the window, if necessary. Open **B05TryG** from the location where the data files for this lesson are stored, and save it as **B05TryG_xx** in the location where your teacher instructs you to store the files for this lesson.

2 On the HOME tab click the Clipboard group dialog box launcher 🗅 to display the Clipboard task pane.

3 In the document, select the text *Whole Grains Bread*.

(continued)

Try It!   Using the Office Clipboard *(continued)*

4 Right-click the selection and click Copy. The selected text is copied to the Office Clipboard. Notice that it remains in its original location in the document, as well.

5 In the document window, click on the picture to select it. (A selection box displays around a selected picture.)

6 Right-click the selection and click Cut. The selection is deleted from the document, and displays in the Clipboard task pane.

7 In Word, open **B05TryH** from the location where the data files for this lesson are stored. The Clipboard task pane is still displayed.

8 Save the file as **B05TryH_xx** in the location where your teacher instructs you to store the files for this lesson. Make sure the insertion point is at the beginning of the document, and then press ENTER to insert a blank line. Press the up arrow key ⬆ to move the insertion point to the blank line.

9 In the Clipboard task pane, click the picture of the bread. It is pasted into the document at the insertion point location. It also remains on the Clipboard so you can paste it again, if you want.

10 Right-click the picture of the runner in the document and click Copy to copy it to the Clipboard. Now, there are three selections stored on the Clipboard.

11 Save the changes to **B05TryH_xx**, and close it. **B05TryG_xx** is still open.

12 Position the insertion point at the end of the document and press ENTER to insert a new line.

13 Click the picture of the runner in the Clipboard task pane. It is pasted into the document. Even though the original file is closed, you can still paste a selection that is stored on the Clipboard. Save the changes to the file and leave it open to use in the next Try It.

Try It!   Deleting Selections from the Office Clipboard

1 With **B05TryG_xx** still open, click the Options button at the bottom of the Clipboard task pane. A menu of settings that affect the Clipboard displays. A check mark indicates that an option is selected.

2 In the Clipboard task pane, rest the mouse pointer on the picture of the runner, and click the down arrow that displays.

3 Click Delete on the drop-down menu. The selection is removed from the Clipboard, but it remains in place in the document.

4 Rest the mouse pointer on the picture of the bread in the Clipboard task pane, click the down arrow that displays, and click Delete.

5 Rest the mouse pointer on the text *Whole Grains Bread*, click the down arrow, and click Delete. Now, the Office Clipboard is empty.

✓ *Click Clear All at the top of the Clipboard task pane to quickly delete all selections.*

6 Close the Clipboard task pane.

7 Close **B05TryG_xx**, saving changes, and exit Word.

Lesson 5—Practice

You are a marketing assistant at Voyager Travel Adventures, a tour group operator. In this project, you will practice managing program windows and using the Office Clipboard to copy a picture of kayaking from a PowerPoint presentation to a Word document.

DIRECTIONS

1. Start Word, and create a blank document.
2. Save the file as **B05PracticeA_xx** in the location where your instructor tells you to store the files for this lesson.
3. Click the **VIEW** tab.
4. In the Zoom group, click the **100%** button to set the zoom to 100% magnification.
5. On the first line of the document, type the text **Kayak in the Land of the Midnight Sun** and then press ENTER .
6. Click the **HOME** tab.
7. Select the text, and then change the font to Times New Roman and the font size to 28 points.
8. Move the insertion point to the end of the document, set the font size to 12 points, and type: **Join Voyager Travel Adventures on a 10-day sea kayaking trip in one of the most beautiful and exciting places on earth! Experience the thrill of seeing whales, bears, and other wildlife up close, while enjoying a comfortable base camp and first-class dining.**
9. Press ENTER and then save the changes.
10. Click the **VIEW** tab on the Ribbon, and then, in the Document Views group, click the **Read Mode** button to change to Read Mode view.
11. Click the **Print Layout** button on the status bar to change back to Print Layout view.
12. Click the **Zoom In** button on the Zoom slider as many times as necessary to increase the zoom magnification to 150%.
13. Save the changes to the file, and then click the **Minimize** button – to minimize the Word program window.
14. Start PowerPoint and maximize the window if necessary. Open the file **B05PracticeB** from the location where the data files for this lesson are stored.

15. Click the **Word** button on the Windows Taskbar to restore the Word program window.
16. Right-click a blank area of the Windows Taskbar and click **Show windows Side by Side** to view both the Word and PowerPoint windows.

   ✓ *If you have other windows open, they will be arranged as well. Minimize them, and then repeat step 16.*

17. Click the **Maximize** button in the PowerPoint window.
18. Click the **HOME** tab, if necessary, and then click the **Clipboard group dialog box launcher** .
19. In the list of slides on the left side of the PowerPoint window, right-click **slide 2**—Kayaking in Alaska.
20. Click **Copy** on the shortcut menu to copy the selection to the Clipboard.
21. Close the PowerPoint window without saving any changes.
22. Click the **Maximize** button in the Word window.
23. Click the **HOME** tab and then click the **Clipboard group dialog box launcher** to open the Clipboard task pane. The picture copied from the presentation in step 20 should display.
24. Make sure the insertion point is at the end of the **B05PracticeA_xx** document, and then click **Kayaking in Alaska** in the Clipboard task pane to paste the selection into the Word document.
25. Click the **Zoom Out** button on the Zoom slider until the magnification is set to 80%.
26. Rest the mouse pointer on the picture in the Clipboard task pane, click the **down arrow** that displays, and click **Delete**.
27. Click the **Close** button × in the Clipboard task pane.
28. **With your teacher's permission**, print the file.
29. Close the file, saving changes, and exit Word.

Lesson 5—Apply

In this project, you will use the skills you have learned in this lesson to cut a picture from a Word document and paste it into a PowerPoint presentation, and cut a picture from a PowerPoint presentation and paste it as an illustration in a Word document.

DIRECTIONS

1. Start Word, and open **B05ApplyA** from the data files for this lesson.

2. Save the file as **B05ApplyA_xx** in the location where your teacher instructs you to store the files for this lesson.

3. Zoom out to 80% so you can see all content in the document.

4. Display the Clipboard task pane.

5. Cut the picture from the document to the Clipboard.

6. Start PowerPoint and maximize the window, if necessary.

7. Open **B05ApplyB** from the location where the data files for this lesson are stored. Save it as **B05ApplyB_xx** in the location where your teacher instructs you to store the files for this lesson.

8. Display the Clipboard task pane, if necessary.

9. Click slide 3 in the list of slides to make that slide active. On the slide in the main area of the window, right-click the picture and click **Cut**.

10. Click the dotted line bordering the placeholder for content on the slide to select it, as shown in Figure 5-1 on the next page.

11. In the Clipboard task pane, click the picture you cut from the Word document to paste it on to the slide.

12. Close the Clipboard task pane and save the changes to the PowerPoint presentation.

13. Make the Word program window active, and then arrange the PowerPoint presentation and the Word document side by side.

14. Arrange them stacked.

15. Minimize the PowerPoint presentation window.

16. Maximize the Word window.

17. Paste the picture you copied from the PowerPoint presentation on to the last line of the Word document.

18. Close the Clipboard task pane and zoom out so you can see the entire document.

19. **With your teacher's permission**, print the file.

20. Close the file, saving all changes, and exit Word.

21. Maximize the PowerPoint window.

22. Close the file, saving changes, and exit PowerPoint.

Figure 5-1

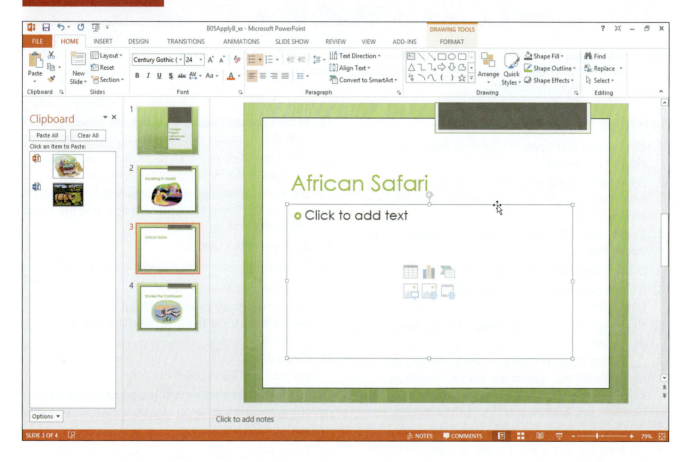

Lesson 6

Using Microsoft Office Help

➤ What You Will Learn

Using a Help Program
Searching for Help
Viewing Application Options
Customizing the Ribbon
Using AutoRecover and AutoSave

Software Skills Each Microsoft Office 2013 program comes with Help information that you can access and display in a window while you work. Use the Help program to get help about using a specific command, search for help topics, or link to additional resources on the Microsoft Office Web site. Each program also has optional settings you use to control how the program operates. For example, you can specify how often the program should automatically save an open file.

What You Can Do

Using Microsoft Office Help

- Each Microsoft Office program has its own Help program.
- You can start Help by clicking the Help button **?** which displays in the upper-right corner of the program window, or in a dialog box.
- Help opens in a window that you can keep open while you work.
- By default, the Help Home page displays links to popular searches and program basics.
- When the mouse pointer touches a link, it changes to a hand with a pointing finger.
- Click a link to display a list of related articles or specific Help information.
- Links may be graphics, or text. Text links are formatted in blue so they stand out from the surrounding text.

WORDS TO KNOW

AutoRecover
A feature in some Microsoft Office 2013 programs that automatically saves files at a set interval so that in the event of a system failure the files may be recovered.

Read-only mode
A mode in which the open file can be viewed but not edited.

■ Use the buttons on the Help window toolbar to control the Help display.

- Back ⬅. Displays the previously viewed page.
- Forward ➡. Returns to a viewed page.
- Home ⌂. Displays the Help Home page.
- Print 🖨. Prints the current page.
- Change Font Size A˙. Displays an option to change the size of the characters in the Help window.
- Keep Help on Top ⚲. Sets the Help window to always display on top of other windows.

■ At the bottom of most Help pages there is a question asking if you found the information helpful. If you are connected to the Internet, click Yes, No, or I don't know to display a text box where you can type information that you want to submit to Microsoft.

■ Most Microsoft Office Help information is available online. If you do not have Internet access, you may not be able to take full advantage of the Help program.

Try It!   Using Office Help

1 Start Access.

2 Click the Help button ? in the upper-right corner of the window

3 Click the first link under Popular searches.

4 Click the first link in the list that displays.

5 Click the Back button ⬅ on the toolbar to display the previously viewed page.

6 Click the Home button ⌂ on the toolbar to display the Help Home page.

7 Close the Help program window, and exit Access.

Searching for Help

■ You can search for a Help topic from any Help page.

■ Simply type the term or phrase for which you want to search in the Search box, and then click the Search button 🔍.

■ A list of topics that contain the term or phrase displays in the Help window.

■ Click a topic to display the Help information.

Try It!   Searching for Help

1 Start PowerPoint.

2 Click the Help button ? to to start the Help program.

3 Click in the Search box, and type **Print**.

4 Click the Search button 🔍. A list of topics related to the term *Print* displays.

5 Click the topic Create and print handouts to display that article.

6 Close the Help window, and exit PowerPoint.

Viewing Application Options

- Each of the Microsoft Office programs has options for controlling program settings.

- The settings depend on the program, although some are the same for all of Microsoft Office. For example, you can enter a user name, set a default storage location for files, and control the way the programs open read-only files.

- You view and set program options in the program's Options dialog box, which is accessed from the Backstage view.

Try It!   **Viewing Application Options**

1. Start Excel and create a blank workbook. Maximize the window, if necessary.

2. Click FILE and then click Options to open the Excel Options dialog box. The General options display. Note the options under Personalize your copy of Microsoft Office.

3. Click Save in the list on the left side of the dialog box to display the Save options. Locate the default local file location, which is where Office files are saved by default.

4. Click Proofing to display the Proofing options. This is where you select options for spelling, including foreign languages.

5. Click Cancel to close the dialog box without making any changes.

6. Leave Excel open to use in the next Try It.

Customizing the Ribbon

- In Microsoft Office 2013 applications, you can customize the Ribbon by adding commands you use frequently or removing commands you rarely use.

- You can create new groups on a Ribbon tab, and you can even create a completely new tab with new groups.

- Commands for customizing the Ribbon are on the Customize Ribbon tab of the Options dialog box in each application.

Try It!   **Customizing the Ribbon**

1. In Excel right-click anywhere on the Ribbon and click Customize the Ribbon.

2. On the right side of the dialog box, under Main Tabs, click to clear the check mark to the left of Insert, then click OK to apply the change and close the Excel Options dialog box. Notice on the Ribbon that the Insert tab no longer displays.

3. Click FILE > Options to open the Excel Options dialog box.

4. Click Customize the Ribbon.

5. Under Main tabs, click to select Home and then click the New Tab button. Excel creates a new tab with one new group.

6. Click to select New Tab (Custom), click the Rename button, and type **WORKBOOK**. Click OK.

7. Click to select New Group (Custom), click the Rename button, and type **Management**. Click OK.

8. In the upper-left of the dialog box, click the Choose commands from drop-down arrow and click File Tab.

(continued)

Try It!   Customizing the Ribbon *(continued)*

9 In the list of commands, click Close, and then click the Add button.

10 In the list of commands, click New, and then click the Add button.

11 In the list of commands, click Save As, and then click the Add button.

12 Click OK to close the Excel Options dialog box, then click the WORKBOOK tab on the Ribbon to view the new group of commands.

13 Right-click anywhere on the Ribbon and click Customize the Ribbon.

14 Click the Reset button and then click Reset all customizations.

15 Click Yes in the confirmation dialog box and then click OK. Leave Excel open to use in the next Try It.

Custom tab on the Ribbon

Using AutoRecover and AutoSave

- By default the **AutoRecover** feature in Word, Excel, and PowerPoint is set to automatically save open files every ten minutes.

- If you close a file that has been autosaved without saving changes, the autosaved version will be available on the Info tab in the Backstage view.

  - If you were working in a new, unsaved file, click the Manage Versions button to recover a draft version from the UnsavedFiles folder.

  - If you were working in a file that had been saved, but not since your most recent changes, it will be listed under Versions; click a version to open it.

- An autosaved file opens in **read-only mode**, which means you must save it with a new name, or replace the existing file with the same name if you want to edit it.

- AutoRecovered files are stored for up to four days or until you edit the file, and then deleted.

- If a program closes unexpectedly due to a system failure or power outage, the Document Recovery task pane may display the next time you start the program.

- Up to three autosaved versions of the file(s) you were working on before the program closed are listed in the task pane. You may select the version you want to save, and delete the others.

Try It!   Setting AutoRecover and AutoSave Options

1 In Excel, open **B06Try** from the location where the data files for this lesson are stored, and save it as **B06Try_xx** in the location where your teacher instructs you to store the files.

2 Click the FILE tab to display the Backstage view.

3 Click Options > Save to display the Save options in the Excel Options dialog box.

4 Use the Save AutoRecover information every increment arrows to set the time to 1 minute.

5 Verify that there is a check mark in the Keep the last autosaved version if I close without saving check box.

  ✓ *A check mark indicates the option is selected. If it is not, click the check box to select it.*

6 Verify that there is no check mark in the Disable AutoRecover for this workbook only check box.

7 Click OK to apply the changes and close the dialog box. Leave **B06Try_xx** open in Excel to use in the next Try It.

Try It!   **Opening an Autosaved File**

1 In the **B06Try_xx** file, click on cell B6, where the total sales figure displays, if it is not already selected.

2 Press ⌴DEL⌴ to delete the information.

3 Wait at least one minute without saving the file.

4 Click FILE > Close > Don't Save.

✓ *Notice the text in the file delete confirmation dialog box indicating that a recent copy of the file will be temporarily available.*

5 Open the **B06Try_xx** file in Excel.

6 Click FILE > Info. Under Versions, a list of autosaved versions of the file displays including versions closed without saving.

7 Under Versions, click the file that was automatically saved when you closed without saving. Notice the information bar that indicates that it is a recovered file that is temporarily stored on your computer. Notice also that the contents of cell B6 has been deleted.

8 Close both versions of the file without saving changes. Leave Excel open to use in the next Try It.

Open an autosaved file

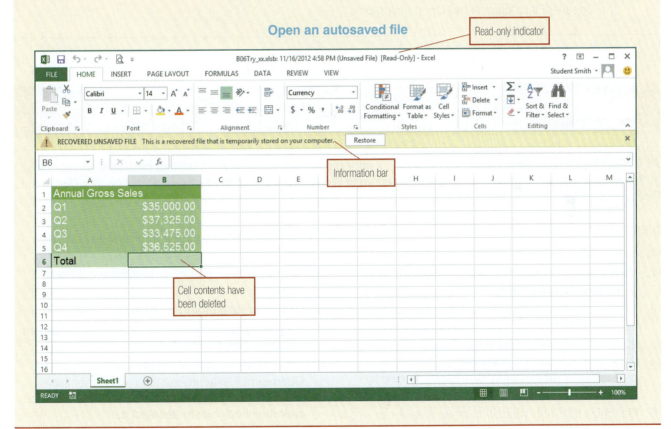

Try It! Opening a Draft Version of an Unsaved File

1. In Excel, create a new blank workbook. Maximize the window, if necessary.

2. Type your first name, press `ENTER`, type your last name, and press `ENTER`.

3. Wait at least a minute without saving the file.

4. Close the file without saving.

5. Click FILE to display the Open page in the Backstage view.

6. At the bottom of the Recent Workbooks list on the right side of the window, click Recover Unsaved Workbooks to display the contents of the UnsavedFiles folder in the Open dialog box.

7. Click the unsaved file at the bottom of the list, and then click Open to open it in Excel.

8. Close the file without saving the changes.

9. Click FILE > Options > Save to display the Save tab of the Excel Options dialog box.

10. Change the Save AutoRecover information setting back to 10 minutes.

11. Click OK to apply the changes and close the dialog box. Exit Excel.

Lesson 6—Practice

As a new employee at Restoration Architecture, it's important to learn how to troubleshoot problems on your own. In this project, you will practice using the Help system in Word to locate and print information about the Document Recovery feature.

DIRECTIONS

1. Start Word.

2. Click the **Help** button **?** in the upper-right corner of the program window to start the Help program.

3. Type **autorecover** in the Search text box, and then click the **Search** button to display a list of articles about recovering files.

4. Click **Turn on AutoRecover and AutoSave to protect your files in case of a crash.** to display that article.

5. Maximize the **Help** window to make it easier to read the content.

6. Click the link to **My Office program did not open a recovered file** to display that article.

7. **With your teacher's permission**, click the **Print** button and print the article.

8. Click the **Back** button to display the previous page.

9. Click the **Home** button to display the Home page.

10. Close the Help program window.

11. Click **Blank document** to create a new document, and then click **FILE** > **Options**.

12. Under Start up options, verify that the option to Open e-mail attachments and other uneditable files in reading view is no selected. If it is selected, click the check box to deselect it.

13. Click **OK** to close the Word Options dialog box.

14. Exit Word.

Lesson 6—Apply

In this project, you will use the skills you have learned in this lesson to search the Help program in Word for information about formatting text with superscript and subscript.

DIRECTIONS

1. Start Word, and open the file **B06Apply** from the data files for this lesson.
2. Save the file as **B06Apply_xx** in the location where your teacher instructs you to store the files for this lesson.
3. Create a custom Ribbon tab named **DOCUMENT**, with a group named **Management**. Add the New, Close, Save As, and Print buttons to the group.
4. On the first line of the file, type your first name and last name. Press ENTER and type today's date, and then press ENTER to insert a blank line.
5. Start the Help program.
6. Search for information about how to format text with superscript and subscript.
7. Set the Help window to remain on top of other windows, and then use the information in the Help article to apply superscript to the *nd* and *rd* in the sentence.
8. Use the information in the Help article to apply subscript to the *2* in *H_2O*.
9. Close the Help program window. The **B06Apply_xx** document should look similar to Figure 6-1.
10. Save the changes to the document.
11. **With your teacher's permission**, print the file.
12. Reset all Ribbon customizations.
13. Close the file, saving changes, and exit Word.

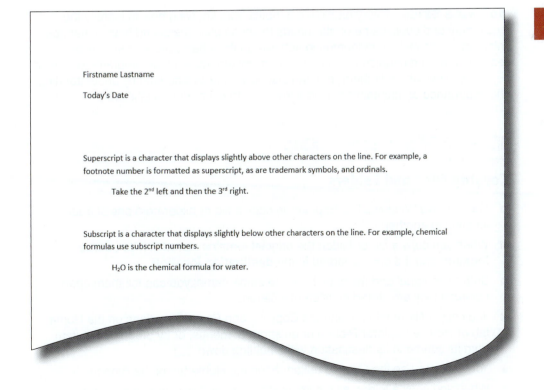

Figure 6-1

Firstname Lastname

Today's Date

Superscript is a character that displays slightly above other characters on the line. For example, a footnote number is formatted as superscript, as are trademark symbols, and ordinals.

Take the 2nd left and then the 3rd right.

Subscript is a character that displays slightly below other characters on the line. For example, chemical formulas use subscript numbers.

H_2O is the chemical formula for water.

Lesson 7

Managing Information Technology

WORDS TO KNOW

Business document
A professional document used to communicate information within a company, or between one company and another.

Compress
Minimize the size of something.

Destination location
The location where a folder or file is stored after it is moved.

Extract
Remove, or separate from.

IT strategy
A plan that identifies how information technology will be put in place over time to help an organization achieve its overall business goals.

Source location
The original location where a folder or file is stored.

Technology infrastructure
The computer systems, networking devices, software, and other technologies used to collect, store, and distribute information.

➤ What You Will Learn

Copying Files and Folders
Moving Files and Folders
Compressing Files
Recognizing Types of Business Documents
Determining the Risks and Rewards of Developing an IT Strategy
Identifying Needed Equipment and Supplies
Establishing, Scheduling, and Following Maintenance Procedures

Software Skills   Every employee benefits from knowing how to identify the equipment and supplies he or she needs to accomplish tasks and how to manage information technology resources to achieve goals. A basic place to start is by learning how to recognize types of business documents and the programs you need to create, view, and edit them. You can also save money and time by understanding the importance of maintaining IT equipment so that it performs efficiently.

What You Can Do

Copying Files and Folders

- You can use Windows File Explorer to copy a file or folder from one storage location to another.

- When you copy a file or folder, the original remains stored in it its **source location** and the copy is stored in the **destination location**.

- Both the original and the copy have the same name; you can tell them apart because they are stored in different locations.

- You copy a file or folder using the Copy 🗐 and Paste 📋 buttons on the Home tab of the File Explorer Ribbon or on shortcut menus, or by dragging the item from its source to its destination while holding down CTRL.

- You can also use the Copy to button 📑 on the Home tab of the Ribbon,

- When you copy a folder, all the items stored in the folder are copied as well.

- If you try to copy a folder or file to a location that already contains a folder or file with the same name, Windows offers three options:
  - Replace the file in the destination. Select this option to replace the existing file with the copy.

- Skip this file. Select this option to cancel the command.
- Compare info from both files. Select this option to display information about both files. You can choose to replace one file or to keep both.

Try It! Copying Files and Folders

1 From the Windows desktop, click the File Explorer button 📁 on the Taskbar and navigate to the location where your teacher instructs you to store the files for this lesson.

2 Create a new folder named **B07Try_Copy_xx**, and open it.

3 Without closing the File Explorer window, right-click the **File Explorer** button 📁 on the Taskbar and click **File Explorer** on the shortcut menu to open a second File Explorer window. In the second window, navigate to the location where the data files for this lesson are stored.

4 Click a blank area of the Windows Taskbar and click Show windows side by side to arrange the two windows so you can see the contents of both.

5 In the location where the data files are stored, right-click the Excel file named **B07TryA** and click Copy on the shortcut menu.

6 Right-click a blank area in the **B07Try_Copy_xx** folder and click Paste on the shortcut menu.

7 Press and hold CTRL and drag the **B07TryB** Word file from the data files storage location to the **B07Try_Copy_xx** folder.

8 Drop the file and release CTRL when the ScreenTip displays *Copy to B07Try_Copy_xx*.

9 On your screen, you can see the two copied files in the **B07Try_Copy_xx** folder. The originals are still in the original location.

10 Maximize the **B07Try_Copy_xx** folder, and click the Back button ← to return to the location where you are storing the files for this lesson.

11 Click the **B07Try_Copy_xx** folder to select it, and click Home > Copy to 📋 > Desktop.

12 Navigate to the desktop, locate the **B07Try_Copy_xx** folder, and open it.

13 Navigate back to the desktop and delete the **B07Try_Copy_xx** folder.

14 In File Explorer, navigate to the location where you are storing the files for this lesson. Notice that the original **B07Try_Copy_xx** folder is still there. Leave both File Explorer windows open to use in the next Try It.

(continued)

Try It!   **Copying Files and Folders** *(continued)*

Copy by dragging

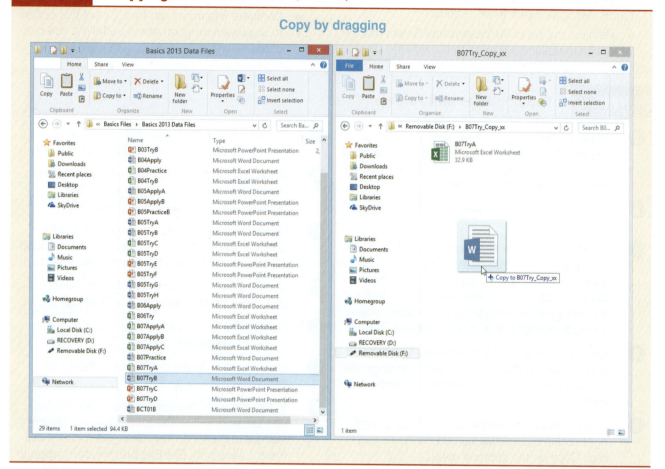

Moving Files and Folders

- You can move a file or folder from one storage location to another.
- When you move a file or folder, it is deleted from its source location and is stored in the destination location.
- You move a file or folder using the Cut ✂ and Paste 📋 buttons on the Home tab of the File Explorer Ribbon or on shortcut menus, or by dragging it to the destination.
- You can also use the Move to button 📁 on the Home tab of the Ribbon.

- When you move a folder, all the items stored in the folder are moved as well.
- If you try to move a folder or file to a location that already contains a folder or file with the same name, Windows offers three options:
  - Replace the file in the destination. Select this option to replace the existing file with the one you are moving.
  - Skip this file. Select this option to cancel the command.
  - Compare info for both files. Select this option to display information about both files. You can choose to replace one file or to keep both.

Try It! — Moving Files and Folders

1. In the File Explorer window open the **B07Try_Copy_xx** folder.

2. Right-click the **B07TryA** file, and click Cut on the shortcut menu.

3. Click the Back button ← to display the location where you are storing the files for this lesson, right-click a blank area and click Paste on the shortcut menu. The file is deleted from its previous location and pasted into the new location.

4. In the current window, create a new folder named **B07Try_Move_xx**.

5. Drag the **B07TryA** file on to the **B07Try_Move_xx** folder.

6. Release the mouse button when the ScreenTip displays *Move to B07Try_Move_xx*. The file is deleted from its original location, and pasted into the **B07Try_Move_xx** folder.

7. Click the **B07Try_Move_xx** folder, and click Home > Move to 📁 > Desktop.

8. Navigate to the desktop and open the **B07Try_Move_xx** folder. Note that the file was moved as well.

9. Click the Back button ←, click to select the **B07Try_Move_xx** folder on the desktop, and click Home > Cut ✂.

10. Navigate to the location where you are storing the files for this lesson, and click Home > Paste 📋.

11. Open the **B07Try_Copy_xx** folder, and leave File Explorer open to use in the next Try It.

Compressing Files

- **Compress**, or zip, a file to minimize its size, making it easier to store or transmit.
- You use Windows to compress files.
- When you compress a file, you create a compressed, or zipped, folder in which the file is stored.
- By default, the compressed folder has the same name as the compressed file, but you can rename it, if you want.
- You can compress multiple files together into one folder.
- You can even compress entire folders.
- To use the compressed files, you must extract them from the folder.
- When you **extract** the files, you copy them from the compressed folder to a destination location. By default, the location is a new folder with the same name as the compressed folder, but you can select a different location.
- The Zip command is on on the Share tab of the File Explorer Ribbon and on shortcut menus; the Extract command is on the Compressed Folder Tools Extract tab of the Ribbon and on shortcut menus.

Try It! — Compressing Files

1. Arrange the **B07Try_Copy_xx** window and the window for the location where the data files for this lesson are stored side by side.

2. Press and hold CTRL and drag the **B07TryC** file to copy it from the location where the data files are stored to the **B07Try_Copy_xx** folder.

(continued)

Try It!   **Compressing Files** (continued)

3 In the **B07Try_Copy_xx** window, click to select the **B07TryC** file, then click Share > Zip on the Ribbon. Windows zips the file into a compressed folder. The new folder name is selected so you can type a new name.

4 Type **B07Try_compressed_xx**, and press ENTER . Notice that the compressed folder has fewer kilobytes (KB) than the original file. Kilobytes are a measurement of size.

5 In the location where the data files are stored, right-click the **B07TryD** file and click Copy on the shortcut menu.

6 Right-click the **B07Try_compressed_xx** folder and click Paste on the shortcut menu. This copies the **B07TryD** file into the compressed folder.

7 Double-click the **B07Try_compressed_xx** folder to open it and view its contents. It contains both the **B07TryC** and **B07TryD** files.

8 Click the Back button ⊖ and maximize the File Explorer window in which the **B07Try_compressed_xx** folder is stored. Leave it open to use in the next Try It.

A compressed file is smaller than the original

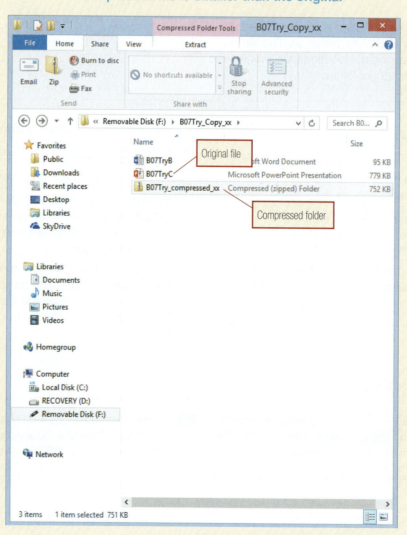

Try It!   **Extracting Compressed Files**

1 In File Explorer, click to select the **B07Try_ compressed_xx** folder, and then click Extract all 📁 on the Extract tab of the Ribbon. Windows displays the name of the default folder where it will store the extracted files.

2 Select just the text *compressed* in the folder name and then type **extracted** to change the name to **B07Try_extracted_xx**.

3 Click Extract. Windows creates a new folder in the current location and copies the files to it. By default, it opens the new folder in a separate window. You can see the extracted files.

✓ *If the window does not open by default, double-click the B07Try_extracted_xx folder to open it.*

4 Close all open File Explorer windows.

Recognizing Types of Business Documents

■ Some common **business documents** used by most companies include letters, memos, fax covers, marketing presentations, training slide shows, invoices, purchase orders, press releases, agendas, reports, and newsletters.

■ Certain businesses—or departments within a larger company—may have specialized documents. For example, a law office or legal department produces legal documents such as wills, contracts, and bills of sale.

■ In additional, individuals create personal business documents such as letters, research papers, and resumes.

■ Each Microsoft Office program is designed for creating specific types of business documents.

- Microsoft Word is used for text-based documents, such as letters, memos, and reports.
- Microsoft Excel is used for numeric or financial documents, such as invoices, sales reports, and graphic analysis.
- Microsoft PowerPoint is used for slide shows and presentation graphics.
- Microsoft Access is used to store and search data and create forms, tables, and reports based on that data.

■ Most business documents have standard formats, which means each type of document includes similar parts.

■ You will learn about the standard formats for different types of documents throughout the lessons in this book.

Determining the Risks and Rewards of Developing an IT Strategy

■ An **IT strategy** is a road map or plan that identifies how information technology will be put in place over time to help an organization achieve its overall business goals.

■ A successful IT strategy prepares a business for future growth and puts the technology in place that a company needs to make the best use of available resources, solve problems, and compete.

■ Companies that take the time and make the effort to include IT in their overall business plans are more likely to implement successful IT strategies.

- Different businesses have different IT needs.
- A small business might require only a desktop computer, an all-in-one printer/scanner device, and an Internet connection.
- A large business might require hundreds of desktop PCs, notebook and tablet computers, one or more internal networks, corporate servers, a telephone system, printers, scanners, and copier machines, projection systems, and more.

■ Some businesses might require specialized IT tools.

- A construction company might require rugged portable devices that can withstand extreme weather or rough conditions.
- A design firm might require high-end computer-aided design software, while an investment firm requires high-end financial applications.

- A successful IT strategy takes into consideration factors such as the current needs of the company, how to best use systems currently in place, and how to implement new technologies that support the business.

- It also takes into consideration the cost of new equipment, maintenance, and training, as well as the physical environment in which IT will be installed. For example, a small business must consider if there is space to install new computer systems. A large company might need to install a climate control system for a new data center.

- There are two primary risks of locking in to a particular IT strategy: a plan that is too advanced, and a plan that is not advanced enough.

  - If a company puts a plan in place that is more advanced than it can support, it wastes money on unnecessary technology that employees do not know how to use.

  - If a company puts a plan in place that is not advanced enough, the company may lose ground to its competition or find that it has to spend money to upgrade systems sooner than expected.

- When an IT strategy balances the needs, costs, and corporate goals, the risks are minimized and the rewards are achievable.

Identifying Needed Equipment and Supplies

- Almost every business has a **technology infrastructure**, which is the computer systems, networking devices, software, and other technologies used to collect, store, and distribute information.

- No matter how large or small a business may be, it is vital that someone monitor, manage, and maintain the technology infrastructure in order to keep the business running.

  - In a small organization, each employee might be responsible for his or her own technology. That might mean changing the ink in a desktop printer.

  - In larger organizations, the employees in the IT department are responsible for the IT systems.

- Performing an inventory of the current IT situation is a good first step in developing an IT strategy. Knowing what is already in place and how well it meets current needs helps define future needs.

- Researching and budgeting for an IT project is much like planning any project. You can check pricing online, get bids from various consultants and vendors, or use a combination of those techniques.

- When budgeting for IT systems, it is important to factor in the costs of ongoing support, maintenance, and training.

Establishing, Scheduling, and Following Maintenance Procedures

- Technology systems require maintenance to operate properly. In a large company, maintenance is a constant need. A dedicated staff of technicians responds to employee requests, services hardware, and upgrades software, or outside technicians are hired to provide service.

- In a small company, maintenance might be as basic as keeping a computer keyboard clean, installing a virus protection program, and changing the ink in the printer, when necessary.

- All systems will be more reliable and effective if maintenance is performed on a regular basis.

- Establishing maintenance schedules enables you to plan and perform maintenance appropriately, provide notice to users when maintenance is due, and budget for ongoing maintenance costs.

- Many maintenance tasks can be automated, including data backup, virus scans, and program updates.

- Manufacturers provide maintenance procedures for all equipment and programs. If the user does not follow the manufacturer's recommended maintenance procedures, warranties and service contracts become void, and the company becomes responsible for costs associated with damage and repair.

- In addition, qualified IT professionals are able to diagnose and solve problems individually and as a team to keep the systems running efficiently.

Lesson 7—Practice

You have been hired by the Michigan Avenue Athletic Club to set up policies for purchasing and maintaining information technology equipment and supplies. In this project, you use Word to create a memo to the office manager asking him to conduct an inventory of hardware currently owned by the club, the software programs currently in use, and the current maintenance schedules. You also ask him to provide you with a list of needed equipment and supplies. You will create a folder and a compressed folder where you can store the related files.

DIRECTIONS

1. Start Word.
2. Open the file **B07Practice** from the data files for this lesson, and save it as **B07Practice_xx** in the location where your teacher instructs you to store the files for this lesson.
3. Replace the text *Student's Name* with your own first and last name.
4. Replace the text *Today's Date* with the current date.
5. Press CTRL + END to move the insertion point to the last line of the document and type the following paragraph:

   Tom, as a first step in developing policies for purchasing and maintaining the club's IT equipment and supplies, I need to know what we have and what we need. Please take an inventory of the hardware we currently own, the software we currently use, and the maintenance schedule currently in place. I would also like a list of any equipment and supplies we need.

6. Press ENTER and type the following paragraph:

   I would like to receive this information by the end of the week. Thanks so much for your assistance. Let me know if you have any questions.

7. Save the document. It should look similar to Figure 7-1 on the next page.
8. **With your teacher's permission**, print the file.
9. Close the file and exit Word.
10. Open File Explorer and navigate to the desktop.

11. Create a folder named **B07Practice_xx** on the desktop.
12. Right-click the **B07Practice_xx** folder and click **Cut** on the shortcut menu. This cuts the folder from the desktop and stores it on the Clipboard.
13. Navigate to the location where your teacher instructs you to store the files for this lesson.
14. Right-click a blank area of the window, and click **Paste** on the shortcut menu to paste the folder from the Clipboard into the selected storage location.
15. Right-click the **B07Practice_xx** Word file, and click **Copy** on the shortcut menu.
16. Right-click the **B07Practice_xx** folder, and click **Paste** on the shortcut menu. This copies the file into the folder. The original file remains stored in its current location.
17. Right-click the original **B07Practice_xx** Word file, click Send to, and then click Compressed (zipped) folder. The file is sent to a compressed folder with the default name **B07Practice_xx**.
18. Type **B07Practice_xx_compressed** to rename the folder, and press ENTER to rename the compressed folder.
19. Right-click the original **B07Practice_xx** Word file, and click **Delete** on the shortcut menu.
20. Click **Yes** to delete the file. Now, you have a regular folder named **B07Practice_xx**, which contains the Word memo file, and a compressed folder named **B07Practice_xx_compressed**, which contains a compressed version of the Word memo file.
21. Leave File Explorer open to use in the Apply project.

Figure 7-1

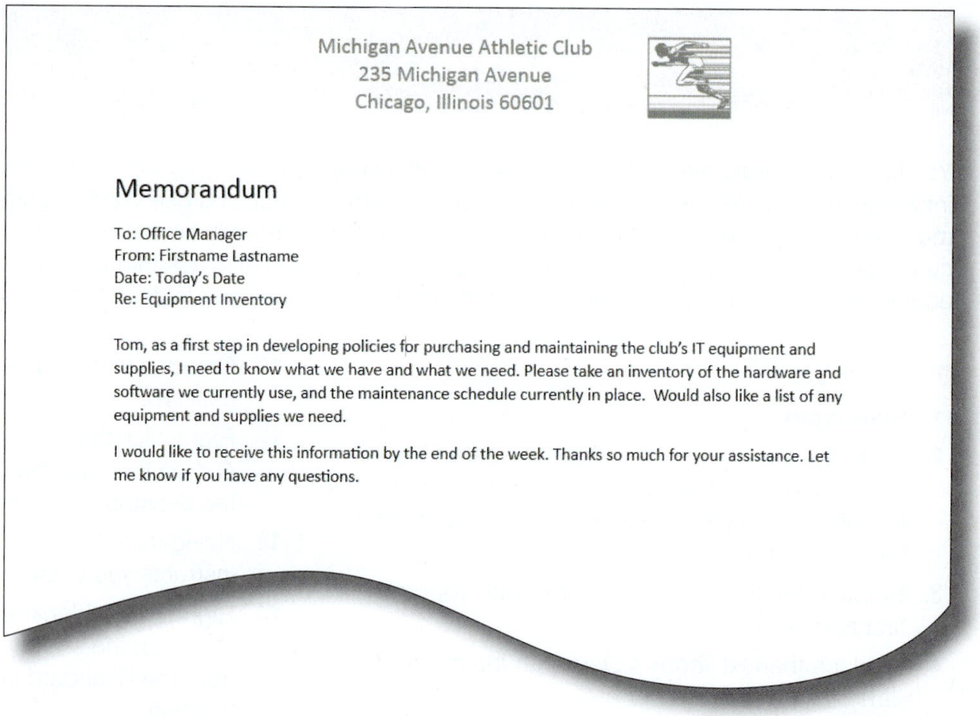

Michigan Avenue Athletic Club
235 Michigan Avenue
Chicago, Illinois 60601

Memorandum

To: Office Manager
From: Firstname Lastname
Date: Today's Date
Re: Equipment Inventory

Tom, as a first step in developing policies for purchasing and maintaining the club's IT equipment and supplies, I need to know what we have and what we need. Please take an inventory of the hardware and software we currently use, and the maintenance schedule currently in place. Would also like a list of any equipment and supplies we need.

I would like to receive this information by the end of the week. Thanks so much for your assistance. Let me know if you have any questions.

Lesson 7—Apply

In this project, you use the skills you learned in this lesson to copy, move, and compress files.

DIRECTIONS

1. In File Explorer, in the location where your teacher instructs you to store the files for this lesson, create a new folder named **B07Apply_xx**.

2. Copy **B07ApplyA** from the location where the data files for this lesson are stored to the **B07Apply_xx** folder.

3. Copy **B07ApplyB** from the location where the data files for this lesson are stored to the **B07Apply_xx** folder.

4. Copy **B07ApplyC** from the location where the data files for this lesson are stored to the **B07Apply_xx** folder.

5. Compress the **B07Apply_xx** folder and its contents into a compressed folder named **B07Apply_xx_compressed**.

6. Move the **B07Practice_xx** regular folder into the **B07Apply_xx_compressed** compressed folder.

7. Open the **B07Apply_xx_compressed** compressed folder.

8. Extract all files from **B07Apply_xx_compressed** into a folder named **B07Apply_xx_extracted**.

9. Close all open File Explorer windows.

End-of-Chapter Activities

➤ Basics Chapter 1—Critical Thinking

Create an IT Strategy

You are responsible for developing a list of ways a group, organization, or business might use Microsoft Office 2013 as part of an IT strategy. Start by selecting the group. It might be a club, team, or organization to which you belong, the place where you work, or any business of your choice. Research its goals, current IT infrastructure, and requirements. You can do this by talking to the people responsible for the information technology and taking notes, and also by observing the information technology in use. Then, use Microsoft Office 2013 and the skills you have learned in this chapter to develop your list.

DIRECTIONS

1. Create a folder named **BCT01_xx** in the location where your teacher instructs you to store the files for this chapter.
2. Start the Microsoft Office 2013 program you want to use to create the list. For example, you might use Word or Excel.
3. Create a blank file and save the file as **BCT01A_xx** in the **BCT01_xx** folder.
4. Type your name in the file.
5. Type the date in the file.
6. Type a title for your list and format the title using fonts, font styles, and font color.
7. Type the list of ways the group, organization, or business might use Microsoft Office 2013 as part of an IT strategy.
8. Save the changes to the file.
9. Start Word, if necessary, and open **BCT01B**. Save it as **BCT01B_xx** in the **BCT01_xx** folder.
10. Type your name on the first line of the file and the date on the second line. Then, move the insertion point to the blank line above the picture, and type a paragraph explaining the list you typed in step 7.

11. Save the changes to the file.
12. **With your teacher's permission**, print the file. If necessary, adjust page formatting such as orientation, scale, and margins so its fits on a single page. It should look similar to Illustration 1A on the next page.
13. Copy the picture in the file to the Clipboard, and then close the file, saving all changes.
14. Make the **BCT01A_xx** file active, and paste the picture at either the beginning or end of the file.
15. Save the changes, and, **with your teacher's permission**, print the file. If necessary, adjust page formatting such as orientation, scale, and margins so it fits on a single page. It should look similar to Illustration 1B on the next page.
16. Close the file, saving changes, and exit all programs.
17. Compress the **BCT01_xx** folder into a compressed folder named **BCT01_xx_compressed**.

Firstname   Lastname
Today's Date
<u>Ways the Marching Band Might Use Microsoft Office 2013</u>

Use Microsoft Word to create memos to band members, letters to parents, and fundraising letters to send to neighborhood businesses.
Use Microsoft Excel to create worksheets tracking income and expenses, to create a budget, and to create graphs illustrating the data.
Use Microsoft Access to set up and maintain a database of members, parents, volunteers, and community supporters.
Use Microsoft Publisher to create postcard mailings, flyers, and even brochures.
Use Microsoft PowerPoint to create an informational presentation.
Use Microsoft Outlook for communication.

Firstname Lastname

Today's Date

Explanation of My List

I think the marching band could benefit from using all of the Microsoft Office 2013 programs. It will be faster to use Microsoft Word to create all text-based documents such as letters and memos. Old files can be reused and updated, and it is easier to make corrections. It also looks professional. Microsoft Excel automates calculations so it is easier to keep track of income and expenses and to identify ways to save and spend. It makes it easy to create charts that illustrate the data which might help the band convince the school committee to increase funding. By creating databases in Microsoft Access the band can easily keep track of the people and equipment it has. The databases can be used to generate mass mailings and reports. With Microsoft Publisher, the band can create professional quality publications. Microsoft Office makes it easy to create and store email messages, to schedule appointments and meetings, and to keep track of tasks that must be accomplished. With Microsoft PowerPoint, the band can create a presentation to use at back-to-school night and other times to provide information and even a little marketing.

➤ Basics Chapter 1—Portfolio Builder

Create a Memo

Voyager Travel Adventures is opening a new office. You have been asked to make a list of IT equipment and supplies needed to get the office up and running. In this project, you will create a folder for storing your work. You will start Microsoft Office 2013 programs and create, save, and print files. You will also open and save existing files, use the Office Clipboard to copy a selection from one file to another, and prepare a file for distribution. Finally, you will compress the files.

DIRECTIONS

1. On the Windows desktop, create a new folder named **BPB01_xx**.

2. Move the folder to the location where your teacher instructs you to store the files for this chapter.

3. Start Microsoft Word, and create a new blank document. Save the file in the **BPB01_xx** folder with the name **BPB01A_xx**.

4. On the first line of the document, type today's date. Press ENTER and type your full name. Press ENTER and type the following:

   I recommend the following IT equipment to get the new Voyager Travel Adventures office up and running:

5. Press ENTER and type the following list, pressing ENTER at the end of each line to start a new line.

   4 personal computers running Microsoft Windows 8, with Microsoft Office 2013

   2 notebook computers to be shared as necessary, also running Microsoft Windows 8, with Microsoft Office 2013

   2 tablet PCs

   Wireless network devices

   1 printer

   1 printer/fax/copier all-in-one

   1 external hard drive for backing up data

   Internet telephone system

6. Save the changes to the document.

7. Format the date in bold and increase the font size to 14, then format your name in bold italic, and increase the font size to 12.

8. Start the Help program and locate information about how to format a bulleted list.

9. Use the Help information to apply bullet list formatting to the list of equipment.

   If you cannot find information about bullet list formatting, select the items in the list, and then click the Bullets button ☰ ▾ in the Paragraph group on the HOME tab of the Ribbon.

10. Save the changes to the file.

11. Start Microsoft Excel and open the file **BPB01B** from the data files for this chapter. Save the file in the **BPB01_xx** folder as **BPB01B_xx**.

12. Copy the picture in the Excel file to the Clipboard.

13. Arrange the Excel and Word windows side by side.

14. Make the Word window active and display the Clipboard task pane.

15. Exit Excel without saving any changes, and maximize the Word window.

16. Paste the picture on to the last line of the document, and then delete it from the Clipboard.

17. Close the Clipboard task pane.

18. Save the changes to the Word document.

19. Change the margins for the document to Wide.

20. **With your teacher's permission**, print the document. It should look similar to Illustration 1C on the next page.

21. Close the file, saving changes, and exit Word.

22. Navigate to the location where you are saving the files for this lesson.

23. Compress the entire **BPB01_xx** folder into a compressed folder named **BPB01_xx_ compressed**.

24. If you have completed your session, close all open windows and log off your computer account.

Illustration 1C

Today's Date

Firstname Lastname

I recommend the following IT equipment to get the new Voyager Travel Adventures office up and running:

- 4 personal computers running Microsoft Windows 8, with Microsoft Office 2013
- 2 notebook computers to be shared as necessary, also running Microsoft Windows 8 and Microsoft Office 2013
- 2 tablet PCs
- Wireless network devices
- 1 printer
- 1 printer/fax/copier all-in-one
- 1 external hard drive for backing up data
- Internet telephone system

(Courtesy Konstantin Chagin/Shutterstock)

Getting Started with Microsoft PowerPoint 2013

Lesson 1
Getting Started with PowerPoint

- About PowerPoint
- Starting PowerPoint
- Using a Storyboad to Plan a Presentation
- Saving and Closing a Presentation
- Opening an Existing Presentation
- Exploring the PowerPoint Window
- Entering Text Using Placeholders
- Applying a Theme
- Checking Spelling in a Presentation
- Previewing a Presentation

Lesson 2
Working with Slides

- Customizing the Quick Access Toolbar
- Viewing PowerPoint Options
- Inserting New Slides
- Selecting Slide Layout
- Moving from Slide to Slide
- Changing List Levels
- Printing a Presentation

Lesson 3
Working with Headers, Footers, and Notes

- Reusing Slides from Other Presentations
- Adding Notes
- Changing Slide Size and Orientation
- Inserting Headers and Footers
- Working with Presentaion Properties

Lesson 4
Inserting and Formatting Pictures

- Inserting a Picture from a File
- Formatting Pictures Using the PICTURE TOOLS FORMAT Tab
- Formatting Pictures Using the Format Task Pane

Lesson 5
Formatting Text

- Finding and Replacing Text and Fonts in a Presentation
- Selecting Text and Placeholders
- Changing the Appearance of Text Using Fonts, Font Sizes, Styles, and Colors
- Copying Text Formatting
- Using Undo and Redo
- Clearing Formatting

Lesson 6
Aligning Text

- Aligning Text
- Adjusting Line Spacing
- Adjusting Paragraph Spacing and Indents
- Moving and Copying Text
- Using AutoFit Options
- Adjusting and Formatting Placeholders

Lesson 7
Displaying the Presentation Outline

- Displaying the Presentation Outline
- Viewing a Presentation in Reading View
- Viewing a Presentation in Grayscale or Black and White

Lesson 8
Arranging Slides

- Copying, Duplicating, and Deleting Slides
- Arranging Multiple PowerPoint Windows
- Copying Slides from One Presentation to Another
- Rearranging Slides

Lesson 9
Adding Slide Transitions

- Identifying Guidelines for Using Graphics, Fonts, and Special Effects in Presentations
- Evaluating and Selecting Appropriate Sources of Information
- Adding Slide Transitions
- Controlling Slide Advance

End-of-Chapter Activities

Getting Started with PowerPoint

➤ What You Will Learn

About PowerPoint

Starting PowerPoint

Using a Storyboard to Plan a Presentation

Saving and Closing a Presentation

Opening an Existing Presentation

Exploring the PowerPoint Window

Entering Text Using Placeholders

Applying a Theme

Checking Spelling in a Presentation

Previewing a Presentation

WORDS TO KNOW

Normal view
PowerPoint's default view that displays the Slide pane and the Thumbnail pane.

Placeholders
Designated areas in PowerPoint layouts that can be used to easily insert text, graphics, or multimedia objects.

Presentation
A set of slides or handouts that contains information you want to convey to an audience.

Storyboard
A series of drawings used to illustrate the sequence of action or outline of a presentation.

Theme
Formatting feature that applies a background, colors, fonts, and effects to all slides in a presentation.

Software Skills   PowerPoint's many features make it easy to create both simple and sophisticated presentations. One way to create a new slide show is to start with a Blank Presentation from the template choices that display when PowerPoint opens. Once a presentation is open, you can enter text and apply a theme to give it a consistent design.

What You Can Do

About PowerPoint

- PowerPoint is a presentation graphics program that lets you create slide shows you can present using a computer projection system or publish online as a slideshow.

- A **presentation** can include handouts, outlines, and speaker notes as well as slides.

- PowerPoint slides may contain text and various other types of content, such as clip art, pictures, videos, tables, or charts.

- You can create all the slide content in PowerPoint or import data from other Microsoft Office programs such as Word and Excel to create slide content.

Starting PowerPoint

- To use PowerPoint 2013 you must first start it so it is running on your computer.
- You use Microsoft Windows to start PowerPoint.

- When PowerPoint starts, it displays a selection of templates for you to choose from. You can start with a blank presentation or one of the other presentation designs.

Try It!   **Starting PowerPoint**

1 Start Windows 8.

   ✓ *If you are using Windows 7, ask your instructor for directions.*

2 In the application tiles at the right side of the Windows 8 Start screen, click PowerPoint 2013.

   ✓ *If PowerPoint 2013 does not appear among the apps displayed on the Start screen, right-click, click All apps ⊞ near the lower-right corner of the screen, scroll to the right to see the Microsoft Office 2013 applications, and click PowerPoint 2013.*

OR

1 If Windows 8 is already running, point to the lower-left corner of the screen and click to display the Start screen.

2 Locate PowerPoint 2013 as directed previously.

OR

1 From the Windows 8 Start screen, click Desktop.

2 You may then have an option to click a PowerPoint shortcut icon 🖻 on the desktop or the taskbar.

3 With PowerPoint open, click Blank Presentation to start a new presentation.

4 Leave the blank presentation open to use in the next Try It.

Using a Storyboard to Plan a Presentation

- Before starting PowerPoint and beginning a new presentation, you may find it helpful to create a storyboard to plan what you want to say and show in the presentation.
- A **storyboard** is a series of images that represent the slides you intend to create.
- The slide images might include slide titles, rough notes about the text you want to appear on each slide, and suggestions for supporting graphics, video, or audio files.
- The simplest way to create a storyboard is to sketch the slide images on paper. If you are using a tablet computer with an input stylus, you can draw your storyboard right on the screen to store it digitally.

- You may also want to storyboard using a two-column table in a word processing program such as Microsoft Word 2013. You can quickly type the text you plan to use for your slides in the left column, and after printing, sketch in the right column next to each slide's text the graphics you need for that slide.

   ✓ *An advantage to storyboarding with Word is that you can then copy the text to PowerPoint so you don't have to retype it.*

- You can also use this planning process to decide what kinds of slides you will need, such as a title slide, blank slides on which you intend to draw shapes, slides in which you will have content in two columns, and so on.

Saving and Closing a Presentation

- PowerPoint supplies the default title *Presentation* and a number (for example, *Presentation1*) in the title bar of each new presentation. You should change this default title to a more descriptive title when you save a new presentation so that you can work on it again later.

- By default, a new presentation is saved in XML format, the standard for Office 2010 and Office 2013 applications, giving the file an extension of .pptx.

- If you wish to use a presentation with earlier versions of PowerPoint, you can save the file in PowerPoint 97-2003 Presentation format. You can also save the presentation in several other formats, such as PDF or XPS, or as a template or show.

✓ *You will save presentations as templates and shows in later lessons.*

- Close a PowerPoint presentation the same way you close other Microsoft Office documents and spreadsheets.

- Use the Close button in the upper-right corner of the window to close a presentation. If only one presentation is open, clicking this button closes both the presentation and PowerPoint.

- To close a presentation and leave PowerPoint open, use the Close command on the FILE menu.

Try It!   **Saving and Closing a Presentation**

1. Click Save 🖫 on the Quick Access Toolbar.

   OR

   a. Click FILE.
   b. Click Save.

2. Click Computer and then click Browse 📂. Navigate to the location where your teacher instructs you to store the files for this lesson.

3. In the File name box, type **P01Try_xx**.

   ✓ *Replace xx with your initials or full name, as instructed by your teacher.*

4. Click Save or press ⌷ENTER⌷ .

5. Click FILE and then click Close.

6. Leave PowerPoint open to use in the next Try It.

Opening an Existing Presentation

- Open an existing presentation to modify, add, or delete material.

- PowerPoint makes it easy to open presentations on which you have recently worked by listing them in the Recent Presentations list that displays when you click Open on the FILE tab.

- If you do not see the presentation on this list, you can click the place where you stored the file (your SkyDrive or Computer) and access a recent folder.

- Or click Browse to display the Open dialog box to navigate to the presentation you want to open.

Try It!   **Opening an Existing Presentation**

1. Click FILE > Open.

2. Click **P01Try_xx** in the Recent Presentations list.

3. Leave **P01Try_xx** open to use in the next Try It.

Exploring the PowerPoint Window

- PowerPoint, like other Microsoft Office 2013 applications, displays the Ribbon interface that groups commands on tabs across the top of the window below the title bar.

- The status bar displays information about the presentation, such as the slide number and view options.

- A presentation opens by default in **Normal view**, which displays the Slide pane and the Thumbnail pane. You can also toggle on the Notes pane by clicking the Notes button on the status bar.

  - Use the Slide pane to insert and modify slide content.

  - Use the Notes pane to add text for personal reference, such as material you want to remember to cover during the presentation.

  - The Thumbnail pane shows a small version of all slides in the presentation and can be used to quickly select slides or reorganize them.

Try It!　　**Exploring the PowerPoint Window**

1. In the **P01Try_xx** file, move your mouse pointer over each window element shown in the figure.

2. Leave the **P01Try_xx** file open to use in the next Try It.

The PowerPoint window

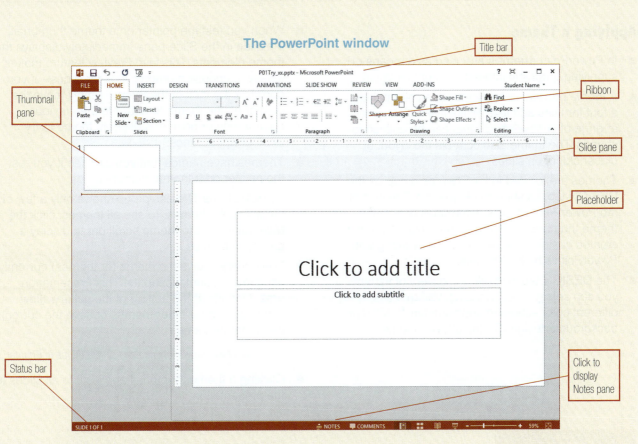

Entering Text Using Placeholders

- PowerPoint displays **placeholders** to define the arrangement and location of text and other objects you can add to slides.

- The title slide you see when creating a new presentation has two placeholders: one for the title and one for the subtitle.

- Different types of slides in a presentation have different types of placeholders in which you can insert lists, pictures, tables, charts, or videos.

- To insert text in a placeholder, click inside the placeholder. PowerPoint selects the box and displays a blinking insertion point that shows where text will appear when typed. Begin typing to insert the desired text.

Try It!	Entering Text Using Placeholders

1 In the **P01Try_xx** file, click once in the title placeholder to select it and position the insertion point.

2 Type **Premier Soccer Club** in the title placeholder.

3 Click the Click to add subtitle placeholder. Type **Top Travel Soccer Competition for Boys and Girls**.

4 Save the **P01Try_xx** file and leave it open to use in the next Try It.

Applying a Theme

- In PowerPoint, **themes** are used as a means of supplying graphical interest for a presentation.

- A theme provides a background, a color palette, a font for titles and text, distinctive bullets, and a range of special effects that can be applied to shapes. The theme also controls the layout of placeholders on slides.

- Themes are located in the Themes group on the DESIGN tab, as shown in Figure 1-1. The size of the PowerPoint window determines how many theme thumbnails display in the group. If you have created custom themes, they display along with PowerPoint's built-in themes.

- The DESIGN tab also offers a gallery of variants you can select for each theme. Variants supply different color schemes and sometimes different background designs for the chosen theme.

- When you rest the pointer on a theme thumbnail, the slide in the Slide pane immediately displays the theme elements. This Live Preview feature makes it easy to choose a graphic look for slides—if you don't like the look of the theme, simply move the pointer off the theme to return to the previous appearance or point at a different theme to try another appearance.

- Themes have names that you can see if you rest the pointer on a theme thumbnail.

- By default, the Themes group shows only a few of the available themes. To see all themes, click the More button in the theme scroll bar to display a gallery of themes.

- The gallery shows the theme (or themes) currently used in a presentation in the This Presentation area. Options at the bottom of the gallery allow you to search for other themes or save the current theme for future use.

  ✓ *You will learn how to change and save a theme in Chapter 3.*

- Clicking a theme thumbnail applies it to all slides in the presentation.

Figure 1-1

Try It!   **Applying a Theme**

1 In the **P01Try_xx** file, click the DESIGN tab.

2 Click the More button ⊡ to display all themes.

3 Point to several themes in the gallery to see them previewed in the presentation.

4 Click the Facet theme to apply it to the presentation.

5 Choose the variant at the far right of the Variants gallery, with the dark background.

6 Save the **P01Try_xx** file, and leave it open to use in the next Try It.

Checking Spelling in a Presentation

- PowerPoint provides two methods of spell checking in your presentation: automatic and manual.

- Automatic spell checking works while you're typing, displaying a wavy red line under words PowerPoint doesn't recognize. Right-click a wavy underline to see a list of possible correctly spelled replacements.

- To check spelling manually, use the Spelling button on the REVIEW tab. The process of checking spelling in a presentation using the Spelling dialog box is similar to that in other Microsoft Office applications.

Try It!   **Checking Spelling in a Presentation**

1 In the **P01Try_xx** file, click the subtitle text and select the entire subtitle.

2 Type **The Top Travil Soccer Clubb for Boys and Girls**.

> ✓ *Note: "Travil" and "Clubb" should be typed incorrectly for purposes of the Try It.*

3 Right-click on *Travil* to see a list of suggested spellings. Click Travel to replace with the correct spelling.

4 Click the REVIEW tab, and then click Spelling ✓.

5 Click Change in the Spelling task pane to replace the misspelled word *Clubb* with Club.

6 Click OK.

7 Save the **P01Try_xx** file, and leave it open to use in the next Try It.

Previewing a Presentation

- Use Slide Show view to see how your presentation will look to your audience.

- Previewing a presentation allows you to check wording, graphics, and other attributes such as transitions and animations.

> ✓ *You apply transitions in later in this chapter and animations in Chapter 3.*

- You can start a slide show from the first slide using the Start From Beginning button on the Quick Access Toolbar or the From Beginning button on the SLIDE SHOW tab, or by pressing F5. To start from the slide currently displayed in the Slide pane, click the Slide Show button in the status bar or the From Current Slide button on the SLIDE SHOW tab.

- Click the left mouse button in Slide Show view to move from slide to slide. If your computer has a touch screen, you can tap the screen to advance slides.

- Click ESC to end a slide show on any slide.

Try It!   **Previewing a Presentation**

1 In the **P01Try_xx** file, click the Slide Show button near the right side of the status bar. The presentation's title slide displays in Slide Show view.

2 Click the left mouse button to display the End of slide show screen, and then click again to exit Slide Show view and return to Normal view.

3 Close the **P01Try_xx** file, saving changes, and exit PowerPoint.

Lesson 1—Practice

Wynnedale Medical Center has contacted you to create a presentation to announce the opening of their new laser eye surgery unit. In this project, you create a new presentation, add text to placeholders, apply a theme, and check your spelling.

DIRECTIONS

1. Start PowerPoint, and create a new blank presentation.

2. Click **FILE** > **Save As**. Navigate to the location where your teacher instructs you to store the files for this lesson. Type **P01Practice_xx** in the File name text box, then click **Save**.

3. Click on the title placeholder and type the text **Wynnedale Medical Center**.

4. Click on the subtitle placeholder and type the text **Laser Eye Surgery Unit**.

5. Click the **DESIGN** tab, then click the **More** button to see the gallery of themes.

6. Click the **Slice** theme to apply it, and then select the light orange variant. Your slide should look like Figure 1-2 on the next page.

7. Click **REVIEW** > **Spelling** to check spelling in the presentation.

8. Click Ignore All to skip changing the spelling of Wynnedale, then click OK.

9. Click the Slide Show button on the status bar to preview the presentation.

10. Click the left mouse button twice to end the show and return to Normal view.

11. Close the file, saving changes, and exit PowerPoint.

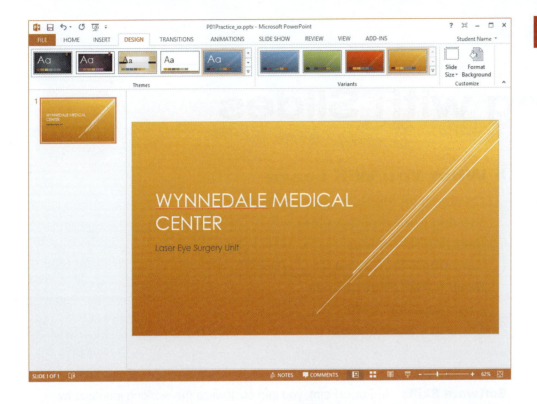

Figure 1-2

Lesson 1—Apply

In this project, you create another version of the Wynnedale Medical Center presentation. You add text to placeholders, apply a theme and variant, and check spelling.

DIRECTIONS

1. Start PowerPoint, if necessary.
2. Open **P01Apply** from the data files for this lesson.
3. Save the presentation as **P01Apply_xx** in the location where your teacher instructs you to store the files for this lesson.
4. Click in the subtitle placeholder, click following the word *Unit*, press ENTER , and type the following text: **Find out if Laser Surgery is right for you**
5. Apply the **Ion** theme to the presentation. Apply the blue variant.
6. Check and correct the spelling, and then preview the presentation in Slide Show view.
7. Close the presentation, saving changes, and exit PowerPoint.

Lesson 2

Working with Slides

➤ What You Will Learn

Customizing the Quick Access Toolbar
Viewing PowerPoint Options
Inserting New Slides
Selecting Slide Layout
Moving from Slide to Slide
Changing List Levels
Printing a Presentation

WORDS TO KNOW

Active slide
The slide currently selected or displayed.

Handouts
Printed copies of the presentation for the audience to refer to during and after the slide show.

Slide layout
Prearranged sets of placeholders for various types of slide content.

Software Skills   In PowerPoint, you can customize the working interface by adjusting the appearance of the Quick Access Toolbar and by selecting from among a number of PowerPoint options. You can quickly and easily add new slides to a presentation. After adding new slides, you can change the slide layout and change the level of an item in a bulleted list. It's easy to move from one slide to the other, and you can also preview your slide show before printing it or presenting it.

What You Can Do

Customizing the Quick Access Toolbar

- The Quick Access Toolbar in the upper-left corner of the program window displays four commands by default: Save, Undo, Redo (which becomes Repeat after you perform an action), and Start From Beginning.

- Use the Customize Quick Access Toolbar button to add or remove buttons for common commands. You can also choose to add commands from Ribbon tabs.

- You can change the position of the Quick Access Toolbar to move it below the Ribbon.

Try It!   Customizing the Quick Access Toolbar

1 Start PowerPoint, and open **P02Try** from the data files for this lesson.

2 Save the presentation as **P02Try_xx** in the location where your teacher instructs you to store the files for this lesson.

3 Click the Customize Quick Access Toolbar button ☰ to display a menu of common commands.

✓ *A check mark next to a command indicates it is already on the Quick Access Toolbar.*

4 Click Print Preview and Print on the menu. The button for Print Preview and Print is added to the Quick Access Toolbar.

5 Right-click the Copy button ▣ on the HOME tab of the Ribbon.

6 Click Add to Quick Access Toolbar.

7 Click the Customize Quick Access Toolbar button ☰ and click Show Below the Ribbon.

8 Right-click the Copy button ▣ on the Quick Access Toolbar.

9 Click Remove from Quick Access Toolbar.

10 Click the Customize Quick Access Toolbar button ☰ and click Show Above the Ribbon.

11 Save the **P02Try_xx** file, and leave it open to use in the next Try It.

Viewing PowerPoint Options

■ PowerPoint's PowerPoint Options dialog box offers a number of options for controlling program settings.

■ In this dialog box, you will find general options for adjusting the user interface and personalizing PowerPoint, as well as options for making corrections, saving, choosing a default language, and controlling editing tools.

■ The PowerPoint Options dialog box also allows you to customize the Ribbon or the Quick Access Toolbar.

Try It!   Viewing PowerPoint Options

1 In the **P02Try_xx** file, click FILE and then click Options to open the PowerPoint Options dialog box. The General options display. Note the options under Personalize your copy of Microsoft Office.

2 Click Save in the list on the left side of the dialog box to display the Save options. Locate the default local file location, which is where Office files are saved by default.

3 Click Proofing to display the Proofing options.

4 Click Cancel to close the dialog box without making any changes.

5 Leave the **P02Try_xx** file open to use in the next Try It.

Inserting New Slides

- Most presentations consist of a number of slides. Use the New Slide button on the HOME tab to add a slide to a presentation.

- If you simply click the New Slide button, PowerPoint adds the kind of slide you are most likely to need. With the default title slide displayed, for example, PowerPoint will assume the next slide should be a Title and Content slide.

- If the **active slide**—the currently displayed slide—uses a layout other than Title Slide, PowerPoint inserts a new slide with the same layout as the one currently displayed.

- A new slide is inserted immediately after the active slide.

Try It!   Inserting New Slides

1. In the **P02Try_xx** file, click HOME > New Slide 📄.

2. Press CTRL + M to add another slide.

3. Save the **P02Try_xx** file, and leave it open to use in the next Try It.

Selecting Slide Layout

- To specify a particular layout for a slide, click the down arrow on the New Slide button to display a gallery of slide layout choices.

- A **slide layout** arranges the standard objects of a presentation—titles, charts, text, pictures—on the slide to make it attractive. Each layout provides placeholders for specific types of content.

- Slide layout choices depend on the slide design. Some slide designs offer more layouts than others, but all offer standard layouts such as Title Slide, Title and Content, Two Content, Comparison, and Blank, among others.

- The New Slide gallery also provides options to Duplicate Selected Slides, add new Slides from Outline, and Reuse Slides.

- You can change the layout of any slide using the Layout command. This command displays the same gallery of choices as the New Slide gallery.

- When you specify a new layout, slide content you have already added to the slide adjusts as necessary to fit the new layout.

Try It!   Selecting Slide Layout

1. In the **P02Try_xx** file, on the HOME tab, in the Slides group, click the New Slide button 📄 down arrow. A gallery of available slide types appears.

2. Click the Two Content slide.

3. Click New Slide 📄 > Duplicate Selected Slides.

4. Click HOME > Layout 📄 Content with Caption to change the layout.

5. Save the **P02Try_xx** file, and leave it open to use in the next Try It.

The New Slide gallery

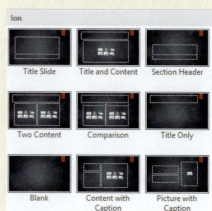

Moving from Slide to Slide

■ Most presentations include multiple slides. You will need to move from slide to slide in Normal view to enter text and modify the presentation.

■ PowerPoint offers a variety of ways to select and display slides. Click in the scroll bar or drag the scroll box to display slides, or use the Previous Slide and Next Slide buttons at the bottom of the scroll bar to move through the slides.

■ You can also select slides by clicking them in the Thumbnail pane.

■ If you are working in a tablet, you can use standard touch screen gestures to move from slide to slide. To go to the next slide, flick upward on the current slide in the Slide pane. To move to the previous slide, flick downward. To select a specific slide, tap it in the Thumbnail pane.

Try It!   Moving from Slide to Slide

1 In the **P02Try_xx** file, click slide 3 in the Thumbnail pane.

2 Click the Next Slide button ⬇.

3 Press `PG UP` twice.

4 Click in the scroll bar three times. You should now be on slide 5, as shown by the highlighted slide in the Thumbnail pane.

5 Save the **P02Try_xx** file, and leave it open to use in the next Try It.

Changing List Levels

■ Slide text content consists mostly of list items that may or may not be formatted with bullets, depending on the theme. First-level list items are supplied on content placeholders. PowerPoint supplies formatting for five list levels. Each subordinate level uses a smaller font size than the previous level.

✓ If the list is bulleted, the same bullet symbol is used for all levels.

■ Create subordinate list levels as you type by pressing `TAB` at the beginning of a line. You can also use the Increase List Level button in the Paragraph group on the HOME tab to apply subordinate level formatting.

■ To return to a higher list level, press `SHIFT` + `TAB` or use the Decrease List Level button.

Try It!   Changing List Levels

1 In the **P02Try_xx** file, click slide 2 in the Thumbnail pane.

2 Click in the title placeholder and type **Tryouts Begin Next Week**.

3 Click in the content placeholder and type **Club tryouts start Wednesday, June 8** and press `ENTER`.

4 Press `TAB`. Type **4 p.m. for under-11** and press `ENTER`.

5 Type **5 p.m. for all others** and press `ENTER`.

6 Click HOME > Decrease List Level ⬅ and type **Please be prompt!**

7 Save the **P02Try_xx** file, and leave it open to use in the next Try It.

(continued)

Try It!   **Changing List Levels** *(continued)*

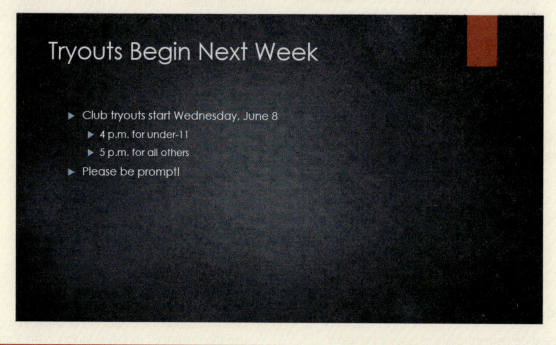

Two list levels on a slide

Printing a Presentation

- Printing PowerPoint materials is similar to printing pages in other Microsoft Office programs, with a few exceptions.

- A presentation can be printed in various formats: as slides, notes pages, **handouts**, or as an outline. You choose the settings for these formats by clicking the FILE tab and then clicking the Print tab, shown in the illustration in the following Try It.

- Among the options you can choose are:
  - Which slides to print, number of copies to print, and whether hidden slides should be printed.
  - What material (slides, notes pages, handouts, or outline) to print. If you choose to print notes pages, any notes you have typed in the Notes pane will print on the page with the slide.
  - If handouts are to be printed, how many slides per page and the order in which the slides display on the page.
  - Whether the material should be scaled (sized) to fit the page or framed by a box.
  - Whether comments and markup annotations should be printed.
  - Whether to print in grayscale, color, or black and white. You might choose to print in black and white or grayscale to preserve your printer's color ink or toner, or to allow you to concentrate on the text rather than the slide design.

- Printing a presentation can help you prepare to deliver the presentation. You may find it easier to judge the flow of information when you can see the entire presentation on one or two pages.

Try It!   **Printing a Presentation**

1. In the **P02Try_xx** file, click Print Preview and Print ⧉ on the Quick Access Toolbar. You should see a screen that looks like the following figure.

2. At the bottom of the preview area, click the Previous Page arrow ◀ to preview slide 1.

3. Click Color, then select Grayscale.

4. Click Full Page Slides, then select 2 Slides in the Handouts area of the gallery.

5. Click Grayscale, then select Color.

6. Click Print All Slides, then select Print Current Slide.

7. **With your teacher's permission**, click Print.

8. On the Quick Access Toolbar, right-click Print Preview and Print ⧉ and click Remove from Quick Access Toolbar.

9. Close the **P02Try_xx** file, saving changes, and exit PowerPoint.

The Print tab

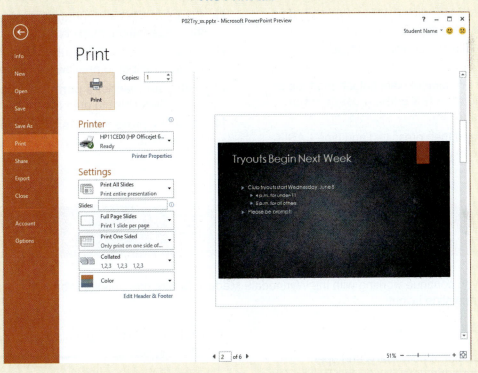

Lesson 2—Practice

In this project, you continue to work with the Wynnedale Medical Center presentation. You will add more content to the presentation using slides with different layouts.

DIRECTIONS

1. Start PowerPoint, if necessary, and open **P02Practice** from the data files for this lesson. Save the presentation as **P02Practice_xx** in the location where your teacher instructs you to store the files for this lesson.

2. Click on slide 3 to display it in the Slide pane.

3. On the HOME tab, click the **New Slide** 🌄 drop-down arrow, then click **Two Content**.

4. Click in the title placeholder and type **Laser Eye Surgery Facts**.

5. Click in the left content placeholder and type the first bullet item, **LASIK is the most common refractive surgery**.

6. Press ENTER and then press TAB and type **LASIK corrects near-sightedness and astigmatism**.

7. Press ENTER and type the next bullet item, **Uncorrected vision may be 20/40 or better after surgery**.

8. Press ENTER and then press SHIFT + TAB to move back to a higher list level.

9. Type **Other options include PRK and LASEK**.

10. Click **HOME** > **Layout** 🖽 > **Title and Content**.

11. Click **REVIEW** > **Spelling** 🗸 to check spelling in the presentation, then click OK.

12. Click **Start From Beginning** 🖵 on the Quick Access Toolbar to preview the presentation.

13. **With your teacher's permission,** click **FILE** > **Print**. Click **Print** to print the presentation.

14. Close the presentation, saving changes, and exit PowerPoint.

Lesson 2—Apply

In this project, you continue working with the Wynnedale Medical Center presentation. You add a slide, adjust list levels, and change slide layout.

DIRECTIONS

1. Start PowerPoint, if necessary, and open **P02Apply** from the data files for this lesson. Save the presentation as **P02Apply_xx** in the location where your teacher instructs you to store the files for this lesson.

2. Move to slide 2 and increase the list level of the last two bullet items to indent them.

3. Insert a new slide following slide 2 and then change the layout to Two Content.

4. Click in the title placeholder and type **A First Look at Laser Surgery**

5. Click in the left content placeholder and type the following items:

   Safe, fast, and reliable

   Covered by most insurance carriers

   The key to clear vision

6. Click in the right content placeholder and type the following items:

   Relative lack of pain

   Almost immediate results (within 24 hours)

7. Apply the **Ion Boardroom** theme to the presentation, and then move through the slides to see how the new theme has changed the appearance of slides. Your presentation should look like the one shown in Figure 2-1 on the next page.

8. Check the spelling and preview the presentation.

9. **With your teacher's permission,** print the presentation as handouts with 9 slides vertical.

10. Close the presentation, saving changes, and exit PowerPoint.

Figure 2-1

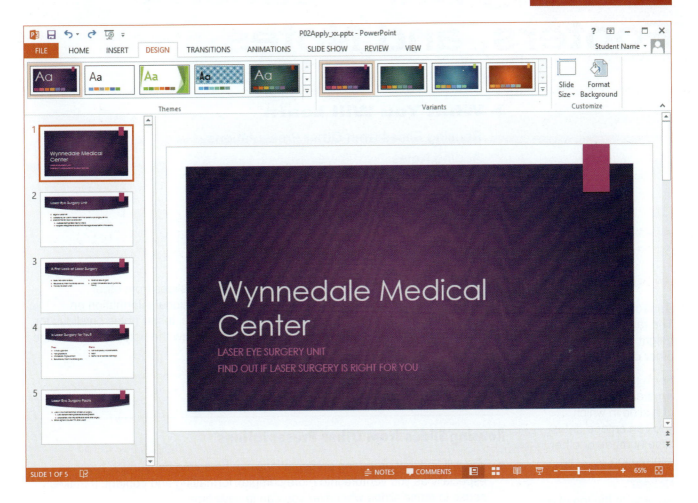

Lesson 3

Working with Headers, Footers, and Notes

➤ **What You Will Learn**

Reusing Slides from Other Presentations
Adding Notes
Changing Slide Size and Orientation
Inserting Headers and Footers
Working with Presentation Properties

WORDS TO KNOW

Aspect ratio
The ratio of width to height in a screen or other output device.

Footer
An area at the bottom of a slide in which you can enter a date, slide number, or other information.

Header
An area at the top of a slide in which you can enter a date or other information that repeats for each page.

Landscape orientation
A slide or printout is wider than it is tall.

Portrait orientation
A slide or printout is taller than it is wide.

Properties
Categories of information about a presentation.

Software Skills   PowerPoint makes it easy to reuse slides from other presentations. Footers, dates, and numbers provide additional information on slides to help users navigate and work with presentations. Insert notes on slides for supplemental information you want to cover, and then view the notes in Notes Page view.

What You Can Learn

Reusing Slides from Other Presentations

■ You will find that preparing presentations can be a time-consuming process, especially as you venture into more complex formatting and content. It makes sense to reuse slides whenever you can to save time.

■ Borrowing slides from other presentations can also help to ensure consistency among presentations, an important consideration when you are working with a number of presentations for a company or organization.

■ You can find the Reuse Slides command on the New Slide drop-down list. This command opens the Reuse Slides task pane where you can specify the presentation file to open. The slides are then displayed in the task pane. To see the content more clearly, rest the pointer on a slide in the current presentation. To insert a slide, simply click it.

■ By default, slides you insert this way take on the formatting of the presentation they're inserted into (the destination presentation).

■ If you want to retain the original formatting of the inserted slides, click the Keep source formatting check box at the bottom of the Reuse Slides task pane.

Try It! Reusing Slides from Other Presentations

1 Start PowerPoint, and open **P03TryA** from the data files for this lesson.

2 Save the presentation as **P03TryA_xx** in the location where your teacher instructs you to store the files for this lesson.

3 Click slide 4 in the Thumbnail pane to select it.

4 Click HOME > New Slide 📑 drop-down arrow, then click Reuse Slides.

5 In the Reuse Slides pane, click Browse and then click Browse File. Navigate to the location where the data files for this lesson are stored and open **P03TryB**. The slides from this presentation appear in the Reuse Slides pane, as shown in the figure at the right.

6 Point to the first slide to view the slide content in a larger format. Point to each of the slides to see their content as well.

7 Click *June Calendar* to insert it into the destination presentation.

✓ *Note that the inserted slide takes on the theme and formatting of the destination presentation.*

8 Click on the remaining four slides in the Reuse Slides pane to insert them in the presentation.

9 Click the Close button × on the Reuse Slides pane to close the pane.

10 Save the **P03TryA_xx** file, and leave it open to use in the next Try It.

The Reuse Slides pane

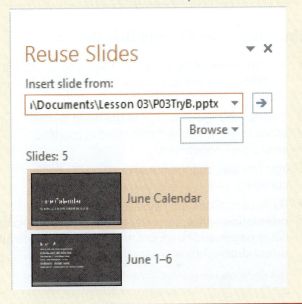

Adding Notes

■ You can enter notes to which you want to refer during a presentation using either the Notes pane in Normal view or Notes Page view.

■ Click the NOTES button in the status bar to display the Notes pane below the slide in the Slide pane.

■ Use the Notes Page command on the VIEW tab to display the slides in Notes Page view. In this view, you can type notes in the Notes placeholder beneath the slide.

■ You can preview or print slides in Notes Page layout to see the notes you entered below each slide.

Try It! Adding Notes

1 In the **P03TryA_xx** file, click slide 5 in the Thumbnail pane.

2 Click VIEW > Notes Page 📄.

3 Click in the Notes placeholder and type **Tell them about what's coming up in June.**

4 Click VIEW > Normal 📄, and then click NOTES 📄 on the status bar.

5 Press PG UP . Click in the Notes pane of slide 4 and type **Remind them that membership is free.**

(continued)

Try It!   **Adding Notes** *(continued)*

6. Click the NOTES button ☰ to hide the Notes pane.

7. Click FILE > Print. Click Full Page Slides, then click Notes Pages in the Print Layout section of the gallery.

8. Click the Next Page arrow ▶ at the bottom of the Preview pane to see the next slide and its note.

9. Click the Back button ⬅ to return to the presentation.

10. Save the **P03TryA_xx** file, and leave it open to use in the next Try It.

Changing Slide Size and Orientation

- In PowerPoint 2013, slides are displayed by default in Widescreen format because many output devices display the 16:9 **aspect ratio** by default.

- You can change slide size to Standard to view slides in the 4:3 aspect ratio used in previous versions of PowerPoint.

- You can also change the orientation of slide content.

- By default, slides are displayed in **landscape orientation**—they are wider than they are tall—and notes pages and handouts are displayed in **portrait orientation**—they are taller than they are wide.

- In some instances, you may want to reverse the usual orientation of slides to display them in portrait orientation.

  ✓ *If your presentation includes graphics, they may become distorted when orientation is changed.*

- You can change orientation in the Slide Size dialog box.

- Use this dialog box to select a size that will work best for a particular paper size, for 35mm slides, for overheads, or even for a custom size that you specify in the Width and Height boxes.

- When you change size or orientation, PowerPoint may display a dialog box that asks you if you want to maximize the size of the content or scale it to ensure it will fit in the new slide size.

Try It!   **Changing Slide Size and Orientation**

1. In the **P03TryA_xx** file, click DESIGN > Slide Size ☐ and click Standard (4:3).

2. In the Microsoft PowerPoint dialog box, click the Maximize button. The slide layout changes to display content in the 4:3 aspect ratio.

3. Click DESIGN > Slide Size ☐ Custom Slide Size.

4. In the Slide Size dialog box, click Portrait in the Slides area, and then click OK.

5. In the Microsoft PowerPoint dialog box, click the Maximize button.

6. Scroll through the slides to see how the layout has changed to fit the portrait orientation.

7. Click DESIGN > Slide Size ☐ > Custom Slide Size.

8. Click the Slides sized for drop-down arrow and select Widescreen, and then select Landscape in the Slides area under Orientation. Click OK.

9. Click Ensure Fit.

10. Save the **P03TryA_xx** file, and leave it open to use in the next Try It.

Inserting Headers and Footers

- You can add several types of information that repeat for each slide to help organize or identify slides.
  - Use a slide **footer** to identify a presentation's topic, author, client, or other information.
  - Add the date and time to a slide footer so you can tell when the presentation was created or updated.
  - Include a slide number in the footer to identify the slide's position in the presentation.

- Use the Header and Footer dialog box to specify these options. Note that you can choose a fixed date or a date that updates each time the presentation is opened. You can also choose to not display the information on the title slide, apply the information only to the current slide, or apply it to all slides.

- If you are working with notes pages or handouts, you can use the options on the Notes and Handouts tab to add a **header** in addition to date and time, page number, and footer.

Try It!   **Inserting Headers and Footers**

1. In the **P03TryA_xx** file, click INSERT > Header & Footer 📄.

   The Header and Footer dialog box

   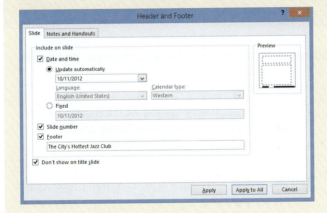

2. Click the Slide tab in the Header and Footer dialog box, if necessary, then click Date and time.

3. Click Slide number and Don't show on title slide.

4. Click Footer, and type **The City's Hottest Jazz Club**. The dialog box should look like the one shown in the illustration at the left.

5. Click the Notes and Handouts tab, then click Header and type **The City's Hottest Jazz Club**.

6. Click Apply to All. Click through the slides to view the footers.

7. On slide 5, click VIEW > Notes Page 🔲 to view the notes page headers and footers.

8. Save the **P03TryA_xx** file, and leave it open to use in the next Try It.

Working with Presentation Properties

- **Properties** are categories of information about a presentation, such as the name of the person who created the file, when the file was modified, and the file's size.

- Properties are stored with the presentation and display on the Info tab in the Backstage view.

- Some of a presentation's properties update automatically as you work with the file. You can also change properties to provide more information about the presentation.

- You can work with properties on the Info tab, in the Document Information Panel, or in the Properties dialog box.

Try It!   Working with Presentation Properties

1 In the **P03TryA_xx** file, click FILE to display the Info tab in Backstage view.

2 In the Preview pane, under Properties, click the Title to select it and type **Embers Presentation**.

3 At the bottom of the properties list, click Show All Properties to see all the properties for the presentation.

4 Click the Properties drop-down arrow and click Show Document Panel. The panel opens above the Slide pane in Normal view.

5 In the Subject box, type **Information on Club**.

6 In the Status box, type **In progress**.

7 Click the Document Properties drop-down arrow and click Advanced Properties.

8 Click the Summary tab, and then click the Statistics tab.

9 Click OK, and then click the Close Document Information Panel button ⊗ .

10 Close the **P03TryA_xx** file, saving changes, and exit PowerPoint.

Lesson 3—Practice

In this project, you will add existing slides to a new travel adventures presentation. You will add notes and footer information and change slide size and orientation.

DIRECTIONS

1. Start PowerPoint, if necessary, and open **P03PracticeA** from the data files for this lesson. Save the presentation as **P03PracticeA_xx** in the location where your teacher instructs you to store the files for this lesson.

2. Click on slide 3 to display it in the Slide pane.

3. Click **HOME** > **New Slide** 📑 drop-down arrow. Then click **Reuse Slides**.

4. In the Reuse Slides pane, click **Browse** and then click **Browse File**. Navigate to the location where the files for this lesson are stored and open **P03PracticeB**.

5. Point to the second slide to view the slide content in a larger format. Click **Adventure Travel Packages** to insert it into the destination presentation.

   ✓ Note that the inserted slide takes on the theme and formatting of the destination presentation.

6. Click the **Close** button ⊗ on the Reuse Slides pane to close the pane.

7. Click slide 2, then click the **NOTES** button 📄 on the status bar to display the Notes pane.

8. Click in the Notes pane and type **Be sure to mention special group rates.**

9. Click **VIEW** > **Notes Page**, and then press ⏷ PG DN to display slide 3.

10. Click in the Notes placeholder of slide 3 and type **Also tell them about special rates on the Web site.**

11. Click **VIEW** > **Normal** 📰 .

12. Click **INSERT** > **Header & Footer** 📄 .

13. Click the **Slide** tab in the Header and Footer dialog box, then click **Date and time**.

14. Click **Slide number** and **Don't show on title slide**.

15. Click **Footer** and type **Everywhere You Want to Go**. Click **Apply to All** 📋 .

16. Click **DESIGN** > **Slide Size** ▭ > **Standard (4:3)**, and then click **Maximize**.

17. Scroll through the slides to see the new layout.

18. Click **DESIGN** > **Slide Size** 🔲 > **Widescreen**.
19. Click **REVIEW** > **Spelling** to check spelling in the presentation, then click **OK**.
20. Click **Start From Beginning** on the Quick Access Toolbar to preview the presentation.

21. **With your teacher's permission,** click **FILE** > **Print**. Select **Full Page Slides**, then click **Notes Pages**. Click **Color** and then click **Grayscale**. Then click **Print** to print the presentation.
22. Close the presentation, saving changes, and exit PowerPoint.

Lesson 3—Apply

In this project, you return to the Wynnedale Medical Center presentation. You reuse slides from another presentation, insert notes, add footers, and change the slide size.

DIRECTIONS

1. Start PowerPoint, if necessary, and open **P03ApplyA** from the data files for this lesson. Save the presentation as **P03ApplyA_xx** in the location where your teacher instructs you to store the files for this lesson.

2. Move to slide 4, and then choose to reuse slides from another presentation. Browse to **P03ApplyB**, and insert both slides from the presentation. Close the Reuse Slides pane.

3. Move to slide 5 and note that the picture overlaps the title area. Reapply the **Two-Content** layout.

4. Add the following note to slide 5: **Compare surgery cost to the cost of glasses or contacts.** Add the following note to slide 6: **Make sure potential patients know that the surgery is painless.**

5. Add the following footers to all slides except for the title slide: **Date and time**, **Slide number**, and **Clear Vision in a Day** footer text.

6. Change the slide size to **Standard (4:3)** and ensure fit. Your presentation should look like the one in Figure 3-1 on the next page.

7. Check the spelling and then preview the presentation in Slide Show view.

8. **With your teacher's permission,** print the presentation.

9. Close the presentation, saving changes, and exit PowerPoint.

Figure 3-1

Lesson 4

Inserting and Formatting Pictures

➤ What You Will Learn

Inserting a Picture from a File

Formatting Pictures Using the PICTURE TOOLS FORMAT Tab

Formatting Pictures Using the Format Task Pane

Software Skills   You can insert your own pictures in a presentation and then use tools on the PICTURE TOOLS FORMAT tab and the Format task pane to adjust the picture's appearance and apply special effects.

What You Can Do

Inserting a Picture from a File

- You can use your own pictures of specific locations, events, or people to illustrate your slides.

- You can scan your own pictures into the computer using a scanner. Using the scanner and computer, you can save the scanned image to the folder where you store your photos. If your picture is already in digital form, you only need to save it to the desired folder.

- Use the Pictures icon in any content placeholder or the Pictures button on the INSERT tab to place your own picture file on a slide. This command opens the Insert Picture dialog box so you can navigate to and select the picture you want to insert.

WORDS TO KNOW

Crop
Remove a portion of a picture that you don't want.

Scale
Specify a percentage of original size to enlarge or reduce the size of an object.

Try It!   Inserting a Picture from a File

1 Start PowerPoint, and open **P04TryA** from the data files for this lesson.

2 Save the presentation as **P04TryA_xx** in the location where your teacher instructs you to store the files for this lesson.

3 Go to slide 2 and click the Pictures 🖼 icon in the content placeholder.

4 Navigate to the location where files for this lesson are stored, select the **P04TryB_picture** image, then click Insert.

5 Press CTRL + M to add a new slide, and type **The Haystack at Cannon Beach** in the title placeholder.

6 Click in the content placeholder, then click INSERT > Pictures 🖼. Navigate to the location where files for this lesson are stored, select the **P04TryC_picture** image, and then click Insert.

7 Save the **P04TryA_xx** file, and leave it open to use in the next Try It.

Formatting Pictures Using the PICTURE TOOLS FORMAT Tab

- Once you have inserted a picture, you can resize it by dragging a corner handle, or reposition it by dragging it to a new location.

- Use the tools on the PICTURE TOOLS FORMAT tab to modify and enhance a picture. Options on this tab allow you to create interesting and unusual picture effects as well as specify a precise size.

- Use the tools in the Adjust group to change brightness or contrast. You can also recolor a picture using the current theme colors or apply an artistic effect such as Paint Strokes or Marker.

- You can also use the Reset Picture option to remove any formatting or resizing to restore the picture to its original appearance.

- The Picture Styles group lets you apply a number of interesting styles to your pictures. You can also select border options or apply standard effects such as shadows or reflections.

- The Size group allows you to **crop** a picture to remove portions of the picture you don't need. You can restore the hidden portion of the picture by using the Crop tool again.

- The Size group also supplies width and height settings that allow you to precisely size a picture.

- You can quickly access picture styles and the Crop tool by right-clicking a picture to display shortcut formatting options.

Try It!   Formatting Pictures Using the PICTURE TOOLS FORMAT Tab

1 In the **P04TryA_xx** file, click slide 2 and click the picture.

2 Click the upper-right corner handle and drag it up and to the right about 0.5" to enlarge the picture.

3 Click PICTURE TOOLS FORMAT > Corrections ☀ and then click the far-right image in the Sharpen/Soften row.

4 Click PICTURE TOOLS FORMAT > Color 🖼 and select Saturation: 200% in the Color Saturation row.

5 Click PICTURE TOOLS FORMAT and select Soft Edge Rectangle from the Picture Styles gallery.

6 Click PICTURE TOOLS FORMAT > Crop 🖼 to activate the crop tool. Click the bottom middle handle and drag it up to remove most of the trees from the picture.

(continued)

Formatting Pictures Using the PICTURE TOOLS FORMAT Tab *(continued)*

7 Click Crop again to complete the crop. Drag the picture down to center it vertically on the slide.

8 Click slide 3 and click the picture. Click PICTURE TOOLS FORMAT > Picture Effects > Soft Edges > 25 Point.

9 Click PICTURE TOOLS FORMAT > Artistic Effects , then select Glow Diffused.

10 Save the **P04TryA_xx** file, and leave it open to use in the next Try It.

Click and drag to move a picture on the slide

Seattle Skyline

Click to add text

Formatting Pictures Using the Format Task Pane

- The galleries on the PICTURE TOOLS FORMAT tab allow you to easily apply standard formats to a picture. For more formatting options, use the Format task pane.

- You can display this task pane by clicking any Options command at the bottom of a format gallery, or by right-clicking the picture and selecting Format Picture.

  ✓ *If you have a picture selected, the task pane name is Format Picture. If you have a shape selected, the task pane name is Format Shape.*

- The Format Picture task pane (see Figure 4-1 on the next page) has four icons below the title you can use to display settings for fill and line, effects, size and properties, and picture adjustments.

- Clicking an icon displays a list of options in the task pane for making more detailed adjustments to the graphic than you can make with the PICTURE TOOLS FORMAT tab commands.

- Clicking the Size & Properties icon, for example, displays options not only for changing height and width, but also options to **scale** the picture to a percentage of its original size, rotate it, change its resolution, and position it precisely.

- Because it stays open as you work and allows you to switch among categories of options with the click of an icon, the Format task pane can be the most efficient way to format graphic objects.

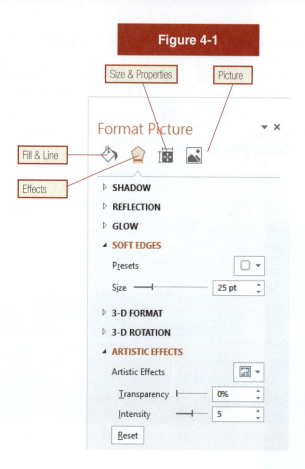

Figure 4-1

Try It!   **Formatting Pictures Using the Format Task Pane**

① In the **P04TryA_xx** file, click slide 2 and select the picture.

② On the PICTURE TOOLS FORMAT tab, in the Adjust group, click the Reset Picture drop-down arrow and click Reset Picture & Size. The picture is uncropped and restored to its original formats.

③ Right-click the picture and click Format Picture to display the Format Picture task pane.

④ Click the Picture icon , and then click the PICTURE CORRECTIONS heading to display options for correcting the picture.

⑤ Drag the Contrast slider to the right until the Contrast box displays 30%.

⑥ Click the Size & Properties icon and click SIZE to expand options.

⑦ In the Height box, type **5.3**.

⑧ Click the down arrow in the Scale Height box to reduce the picture to 95% of its original size.

✓ *Notice that the Scale Width value changes at the same time to maintain the correct proportion of height to width.*

⑨ Expand the POSITION heading. Click in the Horizontal position box and type **5.3**. Click in the Vertical position box and type **1**.

⑩ Click the Effects icon and click the SHADOW heading to expand it.

⑪ Click the Presets button to display a gallery of shadow variations, and then click Offset Diagonal Bottom Left. Then drag the Distance slider to the right to increase the distance to 10 pt.

⑫ Close the Format Picture task pane.

⑬ Close the **P04TryA_xx** file, saving changes, and exit PowerPoint.

Lesson 4—Practice

A local environmental group, Planet Earth, has asked you to prepare a presentation they can show on Earth Day. In this project, you begin the presentation by inserting and formatting a picture.

DIRECTIONS

1. Start PowerPoint, if necessary, and open **P04PracticeA** from the data files for this lesson. Save the presentation as **P04PracticeA_xx** in the location where your teacher instructs you to store the files for this lesson.

2. Display slide 2 and click on the **Pictures** icon 🖼 in the content placeholder to the right of the Preserving Planet Earth text.

3. Navigate to the location where files for this lesson are stored and select the **P04PracticeB_picture** image, then click **Insert**.

4. Click **PICTURE TOOLS FORMAT** > **Corrections** ☀ and then click the image to the right of the current image in Brightness and Contrast to increase the image brightness by 20%.

   ✓ *The current brightness/contrast setting has a light orange outline around it.*

5. Right-click the picture and click Format Picture to open the Format Picture task pane.

6. Click the **Picture** icon 🖼 and expand PICTURE CORRECTIONS if necessary, and then drag the Contrast slider to the right to change the contrast to **25%**.

7. Expand the CROP heading in the Format Picture task pane, if necessary, and change the Crop position height to **3.75"**. Then close the Format Picture task pane.

8. On the **PICTURE TOOLS FORMAT** tab, type **3.9"** in the Height box 🔳.

9. Right-click the picture to display the shortcut options, click the **Picture Quick Styles** button 🖼, and click **Reflected Rounded Rectangle**.

10. Click **REVIEW** > **Spelling** ✓ to check spelling in the presentation, then click **OK**.

11. Click **Start From Beginning** 📺 on the Quick Access Toolbar to preview the presentation.

12. **With your teacher's permission,** click **FILE** > **Print**. Click **Print All Slides**, then select **Print Current Slide** and click **Print**.

13. Close the presentation, saving changes, and exit PowerPoint.

Lesson 4—Apply

In this project, you continue working on the Planet Earth presentation. You insert a second picture and format it with picture effects.

DIRECTIONS

1. Start PowerPoint, if necessary, and open **P04ApplyA** from the data files for this lesson. Save the presentation as **P04ApplyA_xx** in the location where your teacher instructs you to store the files for this lesson.

2. Insert the **P04ApplyB_picture** image in slide 3. Notice that the picture does not display entirely.

3. Display the Format Picture task pane, click the **Picture** icon 🖼, and display the Crop settings.

4. Change the Offset Y value to **1"**.

5. Increase the image brightness by 20%.

6. Recolor the image to **Aqua, Accent color 2 Dark**.

7. Apply the **Pencil Sketch** Artistic Effect to the image. Your slide should look like the one in Figure 4-2 on the next page.

8. Check the spelling and preview the presentation.

9. **With your teacher's permission,** print the presentation.

10. Close the presentation, saving changes, and exit PowerPoint.

Figure 4-2

THE GATHERING STORM | Recent events have endangered wildlife in our oceans and threatened habitats on land.

Lesson 5

Formatting Text

➤ What You Will Learn

Finding and Replacing Text and Fonts in a Presentation
Selecting Text and Placeholders
Changing the Appearance of Text Using Fonts, Font Sizes,
    Styles, and Colors
Copying Text Formatting
Using Undo and Redo
Clearing Formatting

Software Skills   Although themes and theme fonts are designed to produce a pleasing appearance, you may sometimes wish to modify the appearance of text by changing font, font style, size, or color. Use the Format Painter to copy formatting from one slide to another.

What You Can Do

Finding and Replacing Text and Fonts in a Presentation

■ As with other Microsoft Office 2013 applications, you can search for specific text in a PowerPoint presentation and replace it with new text. You can use the Find and Replace buttons in the Editing group of the HOME tab to do this.

■ You can also use the Replace Fonts command to find and replace text fonts throughout a presentation. Just indicate the font you want to replace, and the new font you want to use.

WORDS TO KNOW

Format Painter
A tool that lets you copy text formatting from one text selection and apply it to any other text in the presentation.

1 Start PowerPoint, and open **P05Try** from the data files for this lesson.

2 Save the presentation as **P05Try_xx** in the location where your teacher instructs you to store the files for this lesson.

3 Click HOME > Find 🔍 and type **walkathon** in the Find dialog box. Click Find Next.

4 Click Replace and type **Walkathon** in the Replace dialog box. Click Replace to change the selected text. Click Find Next to locate the instance of walkathon in the Notes pane, and then click Find Next again.

5 Click OK and then click Close.

6 Click HOME > Replace 🔤 > Replace Fonts. Click the Replace drop-down arrow and select Tw Cen MT Condensed.

7 Click to select Calibri in the With list box, click Replace, then click Close.

8 Save the **P05Try_xx** file, and leave it open to use in the next Try It.

Selecting Text and Placeholders

■ Manipulating text in a presentation requires you to know some basics about selecting text and placeholders to ensure you are working efficiently.

■ As in a word processing document, you can select text by dragging the insertion point over it, highlighting the selected text. You can also double-click a single word to select it.

    ✓ *If you are using a touch screen, double-tap text to select it.*

■ As you are working with text in a placeholder, the placeholder displays a dashed line, sizing handles, and a rotation handle.

■ You can also select the placeholder by clicking its outline with the four-headed pointer. The selected placeholder has a solid outline.

■ While a placeholder is selected, any change you make using text tools will apply to all text in the placeholder.

■ When you want to make a change to all text in a placeholder, it is speedier to select the placeholder rather than drag over the text to select it.

1 In the **P05Try_xx** file, go to slide 2, then click and drag to select **Homeless** in the slide title. Note the dashed line, sizing handles and rotation handle shown in the following figure.

Placeholder tools with selected text

2 Click in the content placeholder, move the mouse pointer over the placeholder outline until it changes to a four-headed pointer, then click to select the slide content placeholder.

3 Double-click the word **homeless** in the second bullet to select it.

4 Move the mouse arrow slightly over the selected word to make the Mini toolbar appear. This toolbar can be used to change formatting of the selected text.

5 Save the **P05Try_xx** file, and leave it open to use in the next Try It.

Changing the Appearance of Text Using Fonts, Font Sizes, Styles, and Colors

- PowerPoint's themes guarantee a presentation with a sophisticated design, and that includes the appearance of text. You can, however, easily customize text appearance to emphasize it or to make your presentation more readable, interesting, or unique.

- Text appearance attributes include font family, size, color, style, and special effects. You can also change the case of text to control use of uppercase and lowercase letters.

- To change text attributes:
  - Select text or a placeholder and then use the options in the Font group on the HOME tab of the Ribbon. Commands in this group allow you to change font, font size, font style, and font color. You can also increase or decrease font size by set increments and clear formatting to restore default appearance.

  - Use the Mini toolbar that appears near selected text to modify text appearance as well as adjust paragraph features such as alignment, and indents.

- You can open the Font dialog box by clicking the Font group's dialog box launcher to change multiple attributes at one time and then apply them all at once.

- Note that effects such as superscript and subscript that are not available on Ribbon buttons are available in this dialog box.

- The Character Spacing option on the HOME tab and in the Font dialog box allows you to control the amount of space between characters from very tight to very loose, or you can set a specific spacing amount.

Try It!   **Changing the Appearance of Text Using Fonts, Font Sizes, Styles, and Colors**

1. In the **P05Try_xx** file, display slide 5 and click the content placeholder.

2. Double-click **Walkathon** in the second bullet, then click the Font dialog box launcher. Click Equalize Character Height, then click OK.

3. Select the title placeholder. Click HOME > Font drop-down list, then click Tw Cen MT Condensed in the Theme Fonts section of the Font drop-down list.

4. Click HOME > Font Color and then select Brown, Accent 5 from the Theme Colors.

5. Click HOME > Text Shadow.

6. With the title placeholder still selected, click HOME > Character Spacing > Loose.

7. With the title placeholder still selected, click HOME > Font Size drop-down list > 66.

8. Save the **P05Try_xx** file, and leave it open to use in the next Try It.

Copying Text Formatting

- You can quickly copy and apply text formatting in PowerPoint by using the **Format Painter**.

- You can copy text and object formatting and apply it to one or multiple text blocks or objects.

- To copy formatting to multiple objects, double-click the Format Painter. Then click the button again to turn off the feature.

Try It!　Copying Text Formatting

1 In the **P05Try_xx** file, click slide 5, if necessary, and click the title placeholder.

2 Click HOME > Format Painter 🖌️.

3 Click the title placeholder in slide 4 to apply the formatting.

4 Save the **P05Try_xx** file, and leave it open to use in the next Try It.

Using Undo and Redo

- PowerPoint contains an Undo feature, as in other Microsoft Office applications, which reverses the most recent action or a whole series of previous actions.

- The Redo button allows you to redo actions after you undo them, if you change your mind.

- You can find the Undo and Redo buttons on the Quick Access Toolbar.

Try It!　Using Undo and Redo

1 In the **P05Try_xx** file, click slide 4 and click Undo ↶ in the Quick Access Toolbar.

2 Now click Redo ↷ in the Quick Access Toolbar.

3 Click the Undo drop-down list arrow to see a list of the most recent actions you can undo. Click Text Shadow. Notice that all the subsequent actions are also undone.

4 Save the **P05Try_xx** file, and leave it open to use in the next Try It.

Clearing Formatting

- Use the Clear All Formatting button on the HOME tab to remove font formatting you have applied directly to text.

- You can also use the Reset button to clear formatting you have added to text and return the position, size, and formatting of the slide placeholders to the default settings.

Try It!　Clearing Formatting

1 In the **P05Try_xx** file, go to slide 5.

2 Select the title placeholder and then in the Font group, click the Clear All Formatting button 🧹. All formats you applied to the title text are removed.

　✓ *The font replacement, however, is not removed.*

3 Click Reset 🖻. Notice that the content placeholder formatting returns to the default settings, and the Equalize Character Height effect is removed from *Walkathon*.

4 Close the **P05Try_xx** file, saving changes, and exit PowerPoint.

Lesson 5—Practice

Whole Grains Bread, a company that sells fresh-baked breads and other bakery items at various locations around your area, wants you to help them create a presentation to display at a trade show. In this project, you explore ways to improve the appearance of text in the presentation.

DIRECTIONS

1. Start PowerPoint, if necessary, and open **P05Practice** from the data files for this lesson. Save the presentation as **P05Practice_xx** in the location where your teacher instructs you to store the files for this lesson.

2. Click **HOME** > **Find** and type **Breads, baguettes, and bagels** in the Find dialog box. Click **Find Next**.

3. Click **Replace** and type **Breads and baguettes** in the Replace with text box. Click **Replace All**.

4. Click **OK**. Click **Close**.

5. Click **HOME** > **Replace** > **Replace Fonts**. Click the **Replace** drop-down arrow and select **Century Gothic** from the list of fonts used in the presentation.

6. Click to select **Franklin Gothic Book** in the With list box, click **Replace**, then click **Close**.

7. Click to select slide 3, then select the title placeholder.

8. Click **HOME** > **Font** drop-down list, then click **Century Gothic (Headings)** in the Theme Fonts section of the Font drop-down list.

9. Click **HOME** > **Font Color** drop-down list and then select **Dark Red, Accent 1** from the Theme Colors.

10. Click **HOME** > **Character Spacing** > **Loose** and then click **HOME** > **Font Size** drop-down list > **40**. Click **HOME** > **Text Shadow**.

11. Double-click **HOME** > **Format Painter**. Click the title placeholder in slide 4. Use the Format Painter to apply the title placeholder formatting to all the remaining slides. Then click **Format Painter** again to turn off the feature.

12. Click slide 5 and click **Undo** in the Quick Access Toolbar. Then click **Redo**.

13. Click **Reset**, then click **Undo**. Your slide should look like the one shown in Figure 5-1.

14. Click **REVIEW** > **Spelling** to check spelling in the presentation, then click OK.

15. Preview your presentation in Slide Show view.

16. **With your teacher's permission,** click **FILE** > **Print**. Select **Print All Slides**, then click **Print** to print the presentation.

17. Close the presentation, saving changes, and exit PowerPoint.

Figure 5-1

Lesson 5—Apply

In this project, you work on a presentation that delivers information about acceptable use policies. You modify text formats to improve the presentation's appearance.

DIRECTIONS

1. Start PowerPoint, if necessary, and open **P05Apply** from the data files for this lesson. Save the presentation as **P05Apply_xx** in the location where your teacher instructs you to store the files for this lesson.

2. Replace the **Garamond** font with **Calibri** throughout the presentation.

3. Replace the word **teacher** with **instructor** throughout the presentation.

   ✓ *Be sure to check capitalization and punctuation throughout after replacing.*

4. On slide 2, change the title font to **40 point**. Change the font color to Theme Color **Red, Accent 2**, and apply the **Shadow** effect.

5. Copy this text formatting to the titles of all the slides in the presentation, except the title slide.

6. On slide 2, change the bullet list font to **22 point**. Change the font color to Theme Color **Olive Green, Accent 6**. On slide 6, copy the formatting to the first-level bullet only, not to the sub-bullets.

7. On slide 6, use Undo or the Reset button to remove copied formatting from the sub-bullets.

8. On slide 6, format the sub-bullet font as **20 point, Olive Green, Accent 6**. Your slide should look like the one shown in Figure 5-2.

9. Check the spelling and preview the presentation.

10. **With your teacher's permission,** print the presentation.

11. Close the presentation, saving changes, and exit PowerPoint.

Figure 5-2

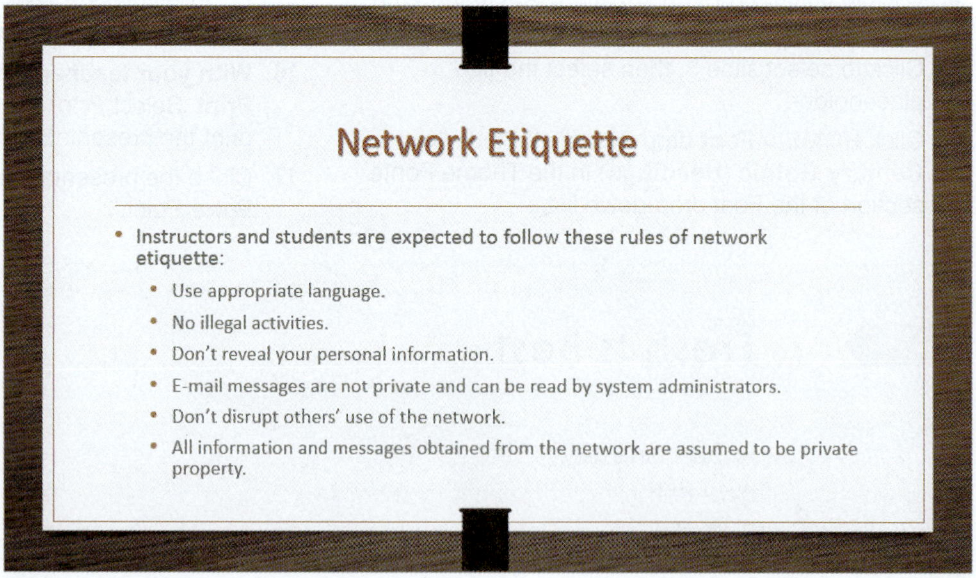

Network Etiquette

- Instructors and students are expected to follow these rules of network etiquette:
  - Use appropriate language.
  - No illegal activities.
  - Don't reveal your personal information.
  - E-mail messages are not private and can be read by system administrators.
  - Don't disrupt others' use of the network.
  - All information and messages obtained from the network are assumed to be private property.

Lesson 6

Aligning Text

➤ What You Will Learn

Aligning Text

Adjusting Line Spacing

Adjusting Paragraph Spacing and Indents

Moving and Copying Text

Using AutoFit Options

Adjusting and Formatting Placeholders

Software Skills   Other ways to modify the appearance of text on a slide include changing text alignment and tweaking paragraph spacing. Move or copy text from slide to slide just as you would in a document. You can also move, resize, copy, or delete any placeholder on a slide or any object on a slide.

What You Can Do

Aligning Text

- Themes control the alignment of text in placeholders. You can left-align, center, right-align, or justify text in any placeholder to add interest or enhance text appearance.

- You can change alignment of any paragraph of text in a text placeholder without affecting other paragraphs of text. In a title placeholder, however, changing alignment of one paragraph realigns all paragraphs in that placeholder.

- Use buttons in the Paragraph group on the HOME tab to align text. You can also use the Mini toolbar to apply left, center, or right alignment or use the Paragraph dialog box, discussed in the next section, to specify alignment.

- You can also click the Align Text button in the Paragraph group on the HOME tab to adjust the vertical alignment of text within a placeholder. Settings options are Top, Middle, and Bottom.

WORDS TO KNOW

AutoFit
PowerPoint feature designed to reduce font size to fit text in the current placeholder.

Try It!   Aligning Text

1 Start PowerPoint, and open **P06TryA** from the data files for this lesson.

2 Save the presentation as **P06TryA_xx** in the location where your teacher instructs you to store the files for this lesson.

3 Go to slide 6 and click on the text placeholder underneath the slide title.

4 Click HOME > Align Left ≡.

5 Click HOME > Justify ≡.

6 Double-click on any word in the title placeholder, then move the arrow over the Mini toolbar and click Align Right ≡.

7 Click HOME > Paragraph dialog box launcher ⌐. Click Centered in the Alignment drop-down list, then click OK.

8 Go to slide 3 and click on the text placeholder. Click HOME > Align Text ⊞ > Middle.

9 Save the **P06TryA_xx** file, and leave it open to use in the next Try It.

Adjusting Line Spacing

- You can also change the spacing between lines of text in a placeholder.

- Use the Line Spacing button to apply line spacing options similar to those you would use in Word: 1.5, 2.0, and so on. Line spacing affects all lines of a paragraph.

- With the insertion point in a single paragraph in a placeholder, the new line spacing option applies only to that paragraph. To adjust line spacing for all items in a placeholder, select them or select the placeholder.

- From the Line Spacing drop-down list, you can click Line Spacing Options to open the Paragraph dialog box for more customized line spacing options.

- In the Paragraph dialog box, you can specify Single, Double, Exact, Multiple, or 1.5 lines of spacing.

- If you choose Exact or Multiple spacing, you can specify the exact amount of space you want between lines or the number of lines of space you want between lines by using the At text box in the Paragraph dialog box.

Try It!   Adjusting Line Spacing

1 In the **P06TryA_xx** file, click slide 2 and click in the second line of text in the text placeholder.

2 Click HOME > Line Spacing ↕≡▾ > 2.0.

3 Click HOME > Line Spacing ↕≡▾ > 1.5.

4 Click HOME > Line Spacing ↕≡▾ > Line Spacing Options.

5 In the Paragraph dialog box, click Exactly in the Line Spacing drop-down list, then type **32** in the At text box and click OK.

6 Click in the third line of text in the text placeholder. Click HOME > Line Spacing ↕≡▾, then roll the arrow over all the line spacing options to see the effect on the paragraph.

7 Move the arrow away from the drop-down list without changing the spacing.

8 Click to select the entire text placeholder. Click HOME > Paragraph dialog box launcher ⌐.

9 In the Paragraph dialog box, click Exactly in the Line Spacing drop-down list, then type **32** in the At text box and click OK.

10 Save the **P06TryA_xx** file, and leave it open to use in the next Try It.

Adjusting Paragraph Spacing and Indents

- Adjust paragraph spacing between bullets or other paragraphs to make text easier to read or to control space on a slide.

- For greater control over paragraph spacing, use the Paragraph dialog box. You can choose alignment and indention settings as well as specify a space before and/or after each paragraph and choose a line spacing option.

Try It!   Adjusting Paragraph Spacing and Indents

1. In the **P06TryA_xx** file, click slide 2 and click the text placeholder to select it.

2. Click HOME > Paragraph dialog box launcher ⌐.

3. In the Paragraph dialog box, click in the Before text text box in the Indentation area and type **0.5"** to change the indentation.

4. Click in the By text box and type **0.5"** and click First line in the Indentation drop-down list.

5. Click in the Before text box in the Spacing area and type **10 pt**. Click OK.

6. Save the **P06TryA_xx** file, and leave it open to use in the next Try It.

Moving and Copying Text

- As you review a slide or presentation, you may rearrange the text to make it easier to follow.

- You can move text using drag-and-drop or cut-and-paste methods.

- Use the drag-and-drop method to move text to a nearby location, such as within the same placeholder or on the same slide.

- When you move text, a vertical line moves with the mouse to help you position the text.

- Use the cut-and-paste method to move text between two locations that are some distance apart, such as from one slide to another or from one presentation to another.

Try It!   Moving and Copying Text

1. In the **P06TryA_xx** file, click slide 5 and select the text in the second line in the content placeholder.

2. Click and drag the text in the second line down beneath the next item, *Volunteer your services*.

3. Open the file **P06TryB** from the location where the files for this lesson are stored.

4. In the **P06TryA_xx** file, click slide 6, then click HOME > New Slide 📄 > Title and Content.

5. In the **P06TryB** file, click slide 1 and select the text in the title placeholder. Press CTRL + C.

6. Go to slide 7 of the **P06TryA_xx** file, click in the title placeholder, then press CTRL + V.

7. Save the **P06TryA_xx** file, and leave it open to use in the next Try It. Leave the **P06TryB** file open to use in the next Try It as well.

Using AutoFit Options

- If you enter more text than a placeholder can handle—such as a long slide title or a number of list entries—PowerPoint will by default use **AutoFit** to fit the text in the placeholder. AutoFit reduces font size or line spacing (or both) to fit the text into the placeholder.

- You can control AutoFit options using the AutoFit Options button that displays near the lower-left corner of a placeholder.

Try It!   Using AutoFit Options

1 In the **P06TryB** file, click slide 1 and select all three bullets of text in the text placeholder. Press CTRL + C.

2 In the **P06TryA_xx** file, go to slide 7 and click in the text placeholder, then press CTRL + V.

3 In the **P06TryB** file, click slide 2 and select all four bullets of text in the text placeholder. Press CTRL + C.

4 In the **P06TryA_xx** file, go to slide 7 and click in the text placeholder after the three paragraphs of text you previously inserted, then press CTRL + V. Note that PowerPoint has used AutoFit to fit the text in the placeholder.

5 Click AutoFit Options ✳ > Change to Two Columns.

6 Click Undo ↶ to reverse the change.

7 Click AutoFit Options ✳ > Split Text Between Two Slides.

AutoFit to Two Columns

THE POWER OF GIVING

We are so grateful for the incredible support our organization has received from the community.

We truly appreciate your investing in this outreach project, which, in turn, is an investment in the lives of those who come to us in need.

One young homeless man entered our doors a little over a year ago. He was living on the streets of our city, and describes his former life as one filled with

darkness and despair.

With the help of your donations, he has completed our recovery program and now says he has hope.

His future looks bright as opportunities have been presented to him which will bring further stability to his new life.

Thanks for your part in his recovery.

We truly appreciate your support!

8 Save the **P06TryA_xx** file, and leave it open to use in the next Try It. Also leave the **P06TryB** file open to use in the next Try It.

Adjusting and Formatting Placeholders

■ You can move or size any text or object placeholder to make room on the slide for other objects such as text boxes or images.

■ You can also delete any placeholder to remove it from a slide, or copy a placeholder to use on another slide or in another presentation.

■ To move, copy, size, or delete a placeholder and everything in it, select the placeholder so that its border becomes a solid line.

   • To move the placeholder, drag it by its border or use cut-and-paste to remove it from one slide and paste it on another.

   • To copy the placeholder, use copy-and-paste. A pasted placeholder appears in the same location on the new slide as on the original slide.

   • Delete a placeholder by simply pressing Delete while it is selected.

   • To resize a placeholder, drag one of the sizing handles at the corners and centers of the sides of the placeholder box.

■ You can format a placeholder in various ways to add visual interest to a slide. Use a Quick Style, for example, to apply color and other effects to an entire placeholder.

■ You can also apply a fill, outline, or other shape effect to a placeholder, using the DRAWING TOOLS FORMAT tab, the Format Shape task pane, or a right-click shortcut formatting option.

Try It! Adjusting and Formatting Placeholders

1 In the **P06TryA_xx** file, go to slide 8, if necessary, then click HOME > New Slide 📋 > Title and Content.

2 In the **P06TryB** file, go to slide 3 and click to select the title placeholder. Press CTRL + C .

3 In the **P06TryA_xx** file, go to slide 9, then click to select the title placeholder. Press CTRL + V .

4 Click the bottom center sizing handle and drag it up to resize the title placeholder.

5 In the **P06TryB** file, go to slide 3 and click to select the text placeholder. Press CTRL + C .

6 In the **P06TryA_xx** file, go to slide 9, then click to select the text placeholder. Press CTRL + V .

7 Click the right center sizing handle of the text placeholder and drag it left to the center of the slide to resize the text placeholder.

8 Go to slide 4 and click to select the text placeholder. Click the center top sizing handle of the text placeholder and drag it down slightly to move the text away from the title.

9 Click HOME > Quick Styles 🖋, then move the arrow over the various Quick Styles in the palette to see how they look in the text placeholder. Click on the Quick Style of your choice to apply it.

10 Right-click the title placeholder, and then click Format Shape on the shortcut menu to display the Format Shape task pane.

11 Click the LINE heading to expand it, click the Solid line option, click the Color drop-down arrow and select Orange, Accent 2, and then click the Width up arrow until the width is 2 pt.

12 Close the Format Shape task pane and deselect the placeholder to see the line format.

13 Save the **P06TryA_xx** file, and close the file. Close the **P06TryB** file without saving and exit PowerPoint.

Lesson 6—Practice

In this project, you work on the presentation for Wynnedale Medical Center by modifying list items, text alignment, text, and the position and size of placeholders.

DIRECTIONS

1. Start PowerPoint, if necessary, and open **P06PracticeA** from the data files for this lesson. Save the presentation as **P06PracticeA_xx** in the location where your teacher instructs you to store files for this lesson.

2. Go to slide 6 and click the text placeholder. Click **HOME** > **Align Left** ≡ .

3. Go to slide 5 and click the text placeholder. Click **HOME** > **Align Text** 🔲 > **Top**.

4. Now click **HOME** > **Line Spacing** ↕≡ ▾ > **1.5**.

5. Go to slide 2 and click the text placeholder. Click **HOME** > **Line Spacing** ↕≡ ▾ > **1.5**.

6. Go to slide 6 and click the text placeholder. Click **HOME** > **Line Spacing** ↕≡ ▾ > **1.5**.

7. Go to slide 3 and click the left text placeholder. Click **HOME** > **Paragraph** dialog box launcher ⌐ .

8. In the Paragraph dialog box, click in the **Before text** text box in the Indentation area and type **0.5"** to change the indentation.

9. Click in the **By** text box, type **0.3"**, and leave the indentation option set at Hanging. Click **OK**.

10. Click the right text placeholder. Click **HOME** > **Paragraph** dialog box launcher ⌐ .

11. In the Paragraph dialog box, click in the **Before text** text box in the Indentation area and type **0.5"** to change the indentation.

12. Click in the **By** text box, type **0.3"**, and leave the indentation option set at Hanging. Click **OK**.

13. Go to slide 7 and click the picture. Drag the picture to align with the title placeholder at the left.

   ✓ *You will see a vertical dashed line when the picture aligns with the title. You learn about layout guides in Chapter 2.*

14. Click the center left sizing handle of the text placeholder and drag it to the right to resize the placeholder and display all text. Your slide should look similar to the one in Figure 6-1.

15. Click **FILE** > **Open** > **Computer** and navigate to the location where the files for this lesson are stored. Open **P06PracticeB**.

16. Select the text in the text placeholder. Press CTRL + C .

17. Go to slide 6 in the **P06PracticeA_xx** file, click after the last text bullet, press ENTER , then press CTRL + V .

18. Click to select the text placeholder, then click the bottom center sizing handle and drag it down to expand the text placeholder. PowerPoint AutoFits the text to the new placeholder size.

19. Select the text in the placeholder, then click **HOME** > **Line Spacing** ⬆≡ ⬇ > **1.0**.

20. Click **REVIEW** > **Spelling** ᴬᴮᶜ✓ to check spelling in the presentation.

21. Click **Start From Beginning** 🖳 on the Quick Access Toolbar to preview the presentation.

22. **With your teacher's permission,** click **FILE** > **Print**. Select **Print All Slides**, then click **Print** to print the presentation.

23. Close the presentations, saving changes, and exit PowerPoint.

Figure 6-1

► In most cases, vision clears immediately, or within 24 hours of surgery. The patient should be able to return to normal activities in a day and feel no discomfort or side effects from the surgery.

Lesson 6—Apply

In this project, you work with a presentation for Whole Grains Bread. You adjust paragraph and line spacing, copy and move text, adjust the size and position of placeholders, and format placeholders to add visual interest.

DIRECTIONS

1. Start PowerPoint, if necessary, and open **P06Apply** from the data files for this lesson. Save the presentation as **P06Apply_xx** in the location where your teacher instructs you to store the files for this lesson.

2. On slide 1, center the title and subtitle.

3. On slide 2, change the paragraph indent of the four bullet items under *Breads* and the three bullet items under *Sweet specialties* to: **0.55"** indentation before text.

4. On slide 3, position the insertion point after the first bullet item, press ENTER , and type **Franchises available**. Move the last bullet item on the slide to be the first bullet item.

5. On slide 4, copy the first item and paste it at the end of the list. Add an exclamation point at the end of the word *Quality* in the last item. Then change the word *Four* in the slide title to **Five**.

6. Change the line spacing for all items in the text placeholder to **1.5**.

7. On slide 5, delete the *Turbinado sugar* and *Gourmet sea salt* items and then drag the bottom of the placeholder upwards to redistribute the items so the *Fair trade* item is positioned in the right column. Your slide should look like the one shown in Figure 6-2.

8. On slide 6, select the text placeholder on top of the photo and delete it.

9. Select the photo and drag it to the right, to center it between the paragraph of text and the edge of the slide.

10. Right-align the text in the placeholder to the left of the photo.

11. Copy the subtitle placeholder from slide 1 and paste it on slide 6. Move it below the photo and resize the placeholder to be the same width as the photo. Click the **Bullets** button on the HOME tab to remove bullet formatting if necessary.

12. Apply a Quick Style to the placeholder. You may need to change the text color to make it stand out against the Quick Style formatting.

13. Select the placeholder that contains the paragraph of text to the left of the picture and adjust its size until it is as tall as the picture and aligns at the bottom with the placeholder below the picture.

14. Display the Format Shape task pane, expand the FILL heading, and click the **Gradient fill** option. Then close the task pane.

15. Check the spelling and preview your presentation.

16. **With your teacher's permission,** print the presentation.

17. Close the presentation, saving changes, and exit PowerPoint.

Figure 6-2

Fresh Is Best!

- Locally grown herbs
- Whole grain flours
- Fresh creamery butter
- Free range eggs
- Locally produced honey

- Fair trade coffee and chocolate
- Certified organic fruits and vegetables
- Local and imported cheeses

Lesson 7

Displaying the Presentation Outline

➤ What You Will Learn

Displaying the Presentation Outline
Viewing a Presentation in Reading View
Viewing a Presentation in Grayscale or Black and White

WORDS TO KNOW

Grayscale
A way of displaying the current slide so that you can see how it will appear when printed on a black and white printer.

Software Skills   Use PowerPoint views to work with the outline when doing detailed editing work and to view a finished presentation. You may want to view a presentation in black and white or grayscale to concentrate on text or see how the presentation would look printed on a black-only printer.

What You Can Do

Displaying the Presentation Outline

■ It is sometimes easier to edit a presentation that has lots of text using the presentation outline.

■ To display the outline, click Outline View on the VIEW tab.

■ The outline of the presentation displays in the Thumbnail pane. You can cut, copy, and edit text here as you would within slide placeholders.

■ To create a new slide in the outline, click to the right of the numbered slide icon and press ENTER .

■ After typing the slide title, press ENTER and then TAB to begin typing list items.

Try It! — Displaying the Presentation Outline

1 Start PowerPoint, and open **P07Try** from the data files for this lesson.

2 Save the presentation as **P07Try_xx** in the location where your teacher instructs you to store the files for this lesson.

3 Click VIEW > Outline View 🖾. The outline displays in the Thumbnail pane.

✓ Note the slide icon to the right of the slide number in the Thumbnail pane. The active slide icon is orange.

4 Read the presentation by scrolling through the outline using the scroll bar at the right of the Thumbnail pane.

5 Click at the end of each list item in the outline (not including the titles of the slides) and insert a period.

✓ Note that the slide displayed in the Slide pane changes as you click on list items of subsequent slides. Outline view is good for this kind of detailed editing work.

6 Save the **P07Try_xx** file, and leave it open to use in the next Try It.

Viewing a Presentation in Reading View

- Reading view can be used instead of full-screen Slide Show view to see how a presentation will appear when you deliver it to an audience.

- Reading view includes a simple control menu you can use to copy slides and move around the presentation.

- Reading view is also useful for someone who wants to display your presentation on his or her computer, rather than on a large screen with Slide Show view.

Try It! — Viewing a Presentation in Reading View

1 In the **P07Try_xx** file, click Reading View 🖾 on the status bar.

2 Click Next ▶ and Previous ◀ to scroll through the presentation.

3 Click Menu 🗉 > Go to Slide > 4 Fair Use of Material.

4 Click Menu 🗉 > Full Screen.

5 Click the left mouse button to advance to the next slide.

6 Right-click to display the shortcut menu, then click End Show.

7 Click Normal 🖾 on the status bar to return to Normal view.

8 Save the **P07Try_xx** file, and leave it open to use in the next Try It.

Viewing a Presentation in Grayscale or Black and White

- If you plan on printing your presentation with a printer that has only black ink or toner, or you need to conserve colored inks, you may want to view the slides in a **grayscale** or black and white mode to see how the slides will look when printed.

- Click Grayscale on the VIEW tab to display a GRAYSCALE tab to the left of the HOME tab. This tab contains a variety of settings for viewing your slides in grayscale.

- Selecting Black and White on the VIEW tab displays the BLACK AND WHITE tab.

- Redisplay the presentation in color by clicking the Back To Color View button in either the GRAYSCALE or the BLACK AND WHITE tabs.

Try It!   Viewing a Presentation in Grayscale or Black and White

1 In the **P07Try_xx** file, click VIEW > Normal 🖼 to turn off Outline view and restore Normal view.

2 Click VIEW > Grayscale ▨ .

3 Click in the title of slide 1.

4 Click GRAYSCALE > Light Grayscale ▨ .

5 Click GRAYSCALE > Inverse Grayscale ▨ .

6 Click VIEW > Black and White ▨ .

7 Click BLACK AND WHITE > Black with Grayscale Fill ▨ .

8 Click BLACK AND WHITE > Back To Color View ▨ .

9 Close the **P07Try_xx** file, saving changes, and exit PowerPoint.

Lesson 7—Practice

In this project, you begin work on a presentation for a community aid organization. You edit text in Outline view and view the finished presentation in Reading view. You also display the presentation in grayscale to see how it will look when printed in one color.

DIRECTIONS

1. Start PowerPoint, if necessary, and open **P07Practice** from the data files for this lesson. Save the presentation as **P07Practice_xx** in the location where your teacher instructs you to store the files for this lesson.

2. Go to slide 1 and click **VIEW > Outline View** 🖼.

3. Click after *services* in the third bullet of slide 4, then press ⌨ENTER .

4. In the new fourth bullet, delete **or** and capitalize the word **every** to start the new bullet.

   ✓ *Note the changes as they appear in the slide displayed in the Slide pane.*

5. Delete the period at the end of the final bullet.

6. Click **Reading View** 🖼 on the status bar.

7. Click **Next** ⊙ and **Previous** ⊙ to scroll through the presentation.

8. Click **Menu** 🖺 > **Go to Slide** > **3 Giving Can Mean...**.

9. Click **Menu** 🖺 > **Full Screen**.

10. Click the left mouse button to advance to the next slide.

11. Right-click to display the shortcut menu, then click **End Show**.

12. If necessary, click **Normal** 🖺 on the status bar, and then click **VIEW > Normal** 🖼 to close the Outline view and to return to Normal view.

13. Go to slide 1 and click in the title placeholder.

14. Click **VIEW > Grayscale** ▨ . Click all of the options on the GRAYSCALE tab to see how the view changes.

15. Click **Back To Color View** ▨ .

16. Click **REVIEW > Spelling** ᴬᴮᶜ✓ to check spelling in the presentation. Click **OK**.

17. **With your teacher's permission,** click FILE > **Print**. Select **Print All Slides**, then click **Print** to print the presentation.

18. Close the presentation, saving changes, and exit PowerPoint.

Lesson 7—Apply

In this project, you work on a presentation for Voyager Travel Adventures. You work with the presentation outline to edit text, and then you preview the presentation using several different view options.

DIRECTIONS

1. Start PowerPoint, if necessary, and open **P07Apply** from the data files for this lesson. Save the presentation as **P07Apply_xx** in the location where your teacher instructs you to store files for this lesson.

2. Display the presentation in Outline view.

3. On slide 2, add the text shown in Figure 7-1.

   ✓ *You can press* ENTER *in the outline to enter a new bullet in the list, and press* TAB *to decrease the level of an item within the outline.*

4. View the presentation in Reading view, then return to Normal view.

5. View the presentation in black and white.

6. Check the spelling.

7. **With your teacher's permission,** print the presentation.

8. Close the presentation, saving changes, and exit PowerPoint.

Figure 7-1

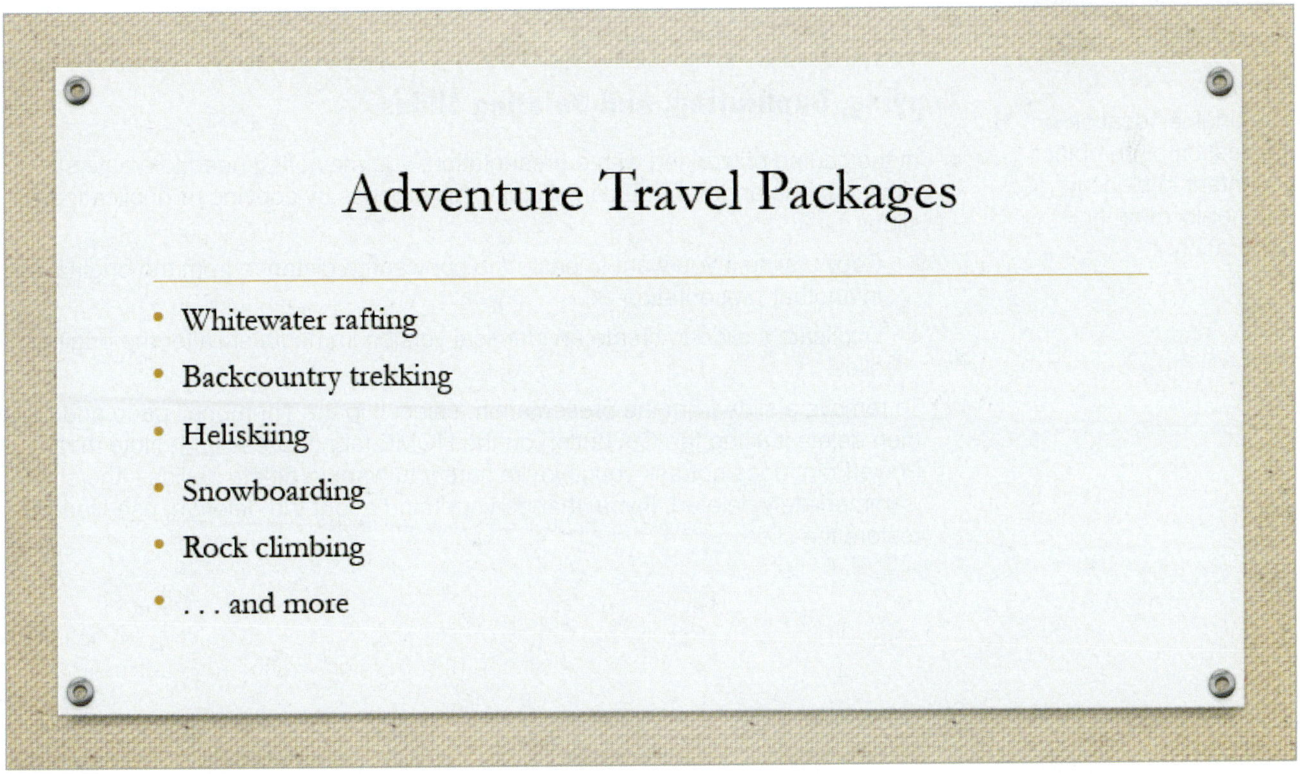

Adventure Travel Packages

- Whitewater rafting
- Backcountry trekking
- Heliskiing
- Snowboarding
- Rock climbing
- . . . and more

Lesson 8

Arranging Slides

➤ What You Will Learn

Copying, Duplicating, and Deleting Slides
Arranging Multiple PowerPoint Windows
Copying Slides from One Presentation to Another
Rearranging Slides

WORDS TO KNOW

Destination
The location or application in which you place an object that was originally in another location or application.

Source
The original location or application of an object you intent to place in another location or application.

Software Skills   As you work on a presentation, you often need to copy or delete slides. You may sometimes need to view two presentations at the same time. You can arrange multiple PowerPoint windows to work with two presentations. Rearrange slides in either the Thumbnail pane or Slide Sorter view.

What You Can Do

Copying, Duplicating, and Deleting Slides

- In the course of working with a presentation, you may often need to create slides similar to one another. You can simplify this process by copying or duplicating slides.
  - Copy a slide if you want to paste the copy some distance from the original or in another presentation.
  - Duplicate a slide to create an identical version immediately after the original slide.
- To remove a slide from the presentation, select it in the Thumbnail pane and then delete it using the Cut button on the HOME tab, or press ⌈DEL⌋ . Note that PowerPoint does not ask you if you're sure you want to delete a slide—the slide is immediately deleted. If you change your mind about the deletion, use Undo to restore the slide.

Try It! **Copying, Duplicating, and Deleting Slides**

1 Start PowerPoint, and open **P08TryA** from the data files for this lesson.

2 Save the presentation as **P08TryA_xx** in the location where your teacher instructs you to store the files for this lesson.

3 Click slide 3.

4 Click HOME > Copy 📋.

5 Click in the space between slides 4 and 5 in the Thumbnail pane, and then click Paste 📋.

✓ *Note that a horizontal line appears in the space between the two slides when you click there.*

6 Click slide 8, then click HOME > Copy 📋 > Duplicate.

7 With slide 8 selected, click HOME > Cut ✂.

8 Save the **P08TryA_xx** file, and leave it open to use in the next Try It.

Arranging Multiple PowerPoint Windows

- When you are working on a presentation, you may want to pull in content from another presentation.

- If you are not sure which slides you want to reuse, you may want to display the other presentation at the same time as your current presentation so you can easily work with the content of both presentations.

- Use commands in the Window group on the VIEW tab to open a new window showing your current presentation or arrange several open presentations side by side.

- Click the presentation you want to work with to make it active.

- To return to viewing only a single presentation, click its Maximize button.

Try It! **Arranging Multiple PowerPoint Windows**

1 In the **P08TryA_xx** file, click VIEW > New Window 🗗 to open a new version of the current presentation. Note that the title bar designates the original presentation as **P08TryA_xx.pptx:1** and the new window as **P08TryA_xx.pptx:2**.

2 Click the Close button ✕ for **P08TryA_xx.pptx:2**.

3 Open **P08TryB** from the data files for this lesson.

4 Click VIEW > Arrange All ⊟. The new presentation displays in the left half of the screen, and the original presentation displays in the right half of the screen.

5 Leave both presentations open for the next Try It.

Copying Slides from One Presentation to Another

- You can use the Copy and Paste commands to copy a slide from a **source** presentation to a **destination** presentation.

- As when copying within a presentation, you position the insertion point in the destination presentation where you want the slide from the source presentation to appear and then click Paste.

- If you have both presentations arranged onscreen, you can simply drag a slide from the source presentation to the destination presentation.

- As when you use the Reuse Slides command, slides you drag from a source presentation to a destination presentation will automatically display the theme of the destination presentation.

Try It!   **Copying Slides from One Presentation to Another**

1 In the **P08TryB** file, click slide 2 in the Thumbnail pane, and click HOME > Copy.

2 In the **P08TryA_xx** file, click below slide 3 to position the horizontal line, and then click HOME > Paste.

3 Click the **P08TryB** file to make it active and click slide 3.

4 Drag slide 3 to the **P08TryA_xx** file and drop it below slide 9.

5 Close the **P08TryB** file, and then click the **P08TryA_xx** file's Maximize button.

6 With slide 10 displayed, click HOME > Reset to restore the table to its proper place in this slide design.

7 Save the **P08TryA_xx** file, and leave it open to use in the next Try It.

Rearranging Slides

- Another task you must frequently undertake when working with slides is to rearrange them. Slide Sorter view is your best option for moving slides from one place in a presentation to another.

- Rearrange slides in Slide Sorter view by simply dragging a slide to a new location.

- You can also rearrange slides in the Thumbnail pane in Normal view, using the same dragging technique. This is an easy process in a presentation that has only a few slides, but for a large presentation, Slide Sorter view is the better choice because you can see more slides at a time without scrolling.

Try It!   **Rearranging Slides**

1 In the **P08TryA_xx** file, click slide 5 in the Thumbnail pane and drag it above slide 2, so it becomes the second slide in the presentation.

2 Select slide 4 and press DEL.

3 Click the Slider Sorter view button in the status bar.

4 Click slide 6 and drag it to the position between slides 2 and 3.

5 Click slide 6 and press DEL.

6 Click slide 7 and drag it before slide 4.

7 Click slide 7 and drag it to follow slide 4.

8 Close the **P08TryA_xx** file, saving changes, and exit PowerPoint.

Lesson 8—Practice

In this project, you work on a presentation for Restoration Architecture, a local architecture firm. You will modify the presentation by copying slides within the presentation and from another presentation, and rearranging and deleting slides.

DIRECTIONS

1. Start PowerPoint, if necessary, and open **P08PracticeA** from the data files for this lesson. Save the presentation as **P08PracticeA_xx** in the location where your teacher instructs you to store the files for this lesson.

2. Click **Slide Sorter** ⊞, then click slide 11.

3. Click **HOME** > **Copy** 🗐 > **Duplicate**.

4. Click and drag slide 12 before slide 5.

5. Click and drag slide 11 before slide 5.

6. Click **FILE** > **Open** and navigate to the location where the files for this Lesson are stored. Open **P08PracticeB**.

7. In the **P08PracticeB** file, click **VIEW** > **Arrange All** ⊟ .

8. Hold the CTRL key down while you click to select slides 1, 2, and 3 in the Thumbnail pane.

9. Drag the three selected slides to **P08PracticeA_xx** and drop the slides to the left of slide 6.

10. Click the **P08PracticeB** file's Close button ✕ , and then click the **Maximize** button in the **P08PracticeA_xx** file.

11. Click slide 15, then press DEL . Your presentation should look like the one shown in Figure 8-1.

12. Preview the presentation to check the order of slides.

13. **With your teacher's permission,** click **FILE** > **Print**. Select **Full Page Slides** > **6 Slides Horizontal**, then click **Print** to print the presentation.

14. Close the presentation, saving changes, and exit PowerPoint.

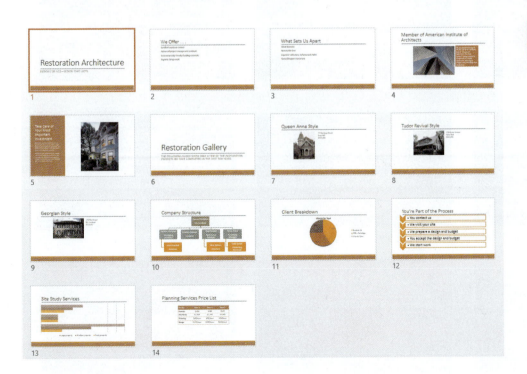

Figure 8-1

Lesson 8—Apply

In this project, you start on a strategic planning presentation. You copy and delete slides, and rearrange slides to improve the flow of information.

DIRECTIONS

1. Start PowerPoint, if necessary, and open **P08ApplyA** from the data files for this lesson. Save the presentation as **P08ApplyA_xx** in the location where your teacher instructs you to store the files for this lesson.

2. In the Thumbnail pane, move slide 2 to follow slide 3.

3. Change to Slide Sorter view.

4. Duplicate slide 4.

5. Double-click slide 5 to return to Normal view and change the title of slide 5 to **Additional Options**.

6. Open **P08ApplyB** and display it side by side with **P08ApplyA_xx**.

7. Drag the slide from **P08ApplyB** to follow slide 5 in **P08ApplyA_xx**.

8. Maximize **P08ApplyA_xx**. Change to Slide Sorter view again to view the sequence of the slides, which should look like that shown in Figure 8-2.

9. Check the spelling and preview the presentation.

10. **With your teacher's permission,** print the presentation.

11. Close both presentations, saving changes, and exit PowerPoint.

Figure 8-2

Lesson 9

Adding Slide Transitions

➤ What You Will Learn

Identifying Guidelines for Using Graphics, Fonts, and Special Effects in Presentations

Evaluating and Selecting Appropriate Sources of Information

Adding Slide Transitions

Controlling Slide Advance

Software Skills   PowerPoint allows you to add transitions to make your slides more visually interesting during a presentation. After you set up the transitions, you can rehearse the show to make sure you have allowed enough time for the audience to view slide content.

WORDS TO KNOW

Advance slide timing
A setting that controls the amount of time a slide displays on the screen.

Transitions
The visual effects used when one slide moves off of the screen and another moves onto the screen.

What You Can Do

Identifying Guidelines for Using Graphics, Fonts, and Special Effects in Presentations

- When working with graphic information such as a PowerPoint presentation, keep in mind that you should avoid overloading a presentation with too many graphics, fonts, and special effects.

- Make sure all graphics you use, including images and shapes, fit with the color scheme of the slide or presentation, and serve a purpose for conveying your message.

- PowerPoint themes make it easy to provide visual interest with colors and fonts that are combined in a pleasing way. You can modify fonts to emphasize key information or provide additional visual appeal to a presentation.

- Make sure that all text stands out against placeholder backgrounds and is large enough to be readable. Also, make sure you're using text effects such as bold, italic, and underline in an appropriate way. And don't get too carried away with special effects such as drop shadows.

- PowerPoint also provides a wide variety of slide transitions and special effects to provide interest and movement as you present a slide show. Again, make sure that the effects you use are appropriate to the visual theme and the message of the presentation.

- In most cases, simpler, more subtle transition effects will prove to be most effective, and won't detract from the message you're delivering.

Evaluating and Selecting Appropriate Sources of Information

- When doing research for a project or presentation, it's important to evaluate and select appropriate sources of information, whether the source is print, electronic, video, or a person you interview.

- Use Internet search engines and bookmarks to locate and access information. Basic and advanced search techniques will help you pinpoint exactly what you need to find using search engines, directories, biographical dictionaries, and other research tools.

- Be sure to evaluate the accuracy and validity of the information you find by understanding the author's point of view, credentials, and any potential bias that might come as a result of his or her position.

- Finding information on the Internet often gives a source more credibility than it may deserve. It's important to be able to decide what is someone's opinion, and what is a fact backed up by research and data.

- As always, cite the sources of the information, and request permission to use if necessary.

Adding Slide Transitions

- PowerPoint provides **transitions** that you can use to make the slide show more interesting. You can apply transitions in either Normal view or Slide Sorter view using tools on the TRANSITIONS tab.

- The Transition to This Slide gallery offers almost 40 different transitions. Clicking a transition previews the transition on the current slide in either Normal or Slide Sorter view.

- The Transition to This Slide gallery organizes transition effects by Subtle, Exciting, and Dynamic Content.

- The TRANSITIONS tab offers several other important options. You can:
  - Choose an effect option to control the direction of the transition or how it appears.
  - Select a sound effect or sound clip to accompany the transition.
  - Choose a duration for the transition effect.
  - Choose how to advance slides: by clicking the mouse or automatically after a specific time lapse. This option is discussed further in the next section.
  - Apply settings to all slides at the same time.
  - After you have applied a transition, you can use the Preview button to review all effects you have applied to the slides.

- You can use multiple transitions in a presentation, or apply the same transition to all slides for a more formal presentation.

Try It!   **Adding Slide Transitions**

1. Start PowerPoint, and open **P09Try** from the data files for this lesson.

2. Save the presentation as **P09Try_xx** in the location where your teacher instructs you to store the files for this lesson.

3. With slide 1 selected, click TRANSITIONS, then click Reveal.

   ✓ Note that a star with lines appears to the left of the slide thumbnail in the Thumbnail pane to indicate a transition has been applied.

4. Go to slide 2 and then click Fade from the Transition to This Slide gallery.

5. Go to slide 3, click the Transition to This Slide More button ⬇, and then click Flash from the Transition to This Slide gallery.

6. Go to slide 4, click the Transition to This Slide More button ⬇, and then click Random Bars from the Transition to This Slide gallery.

7. Go to slide 5, click the Transition to This Slide More button ⬇, and then click Ripple from the Exciting effects.

8. Go to slide 6, then click Fly Through from the Dynamic Content section of the Transition to This Slide gallery.

(continued)

Try It!   **Adding Slide Transitions** *(continued)*

9   Go to slide 1, then click TRANSITIONS > preview ▣. Click Slide Sorter ▦, then click each slide and Preview the transition.

10   Double-click slide 1 to return to Normal view, then click Sound 🔊 > Drum Roll. Click Apply To All ▣.

11   Click SLIDE SHOW > From Beginning ▣ to view the transitions with the sound. Click to exit the slide show.

12   Try experimenting with the different Effect Options by clicking TRANSITION > Effect Options ▣.

13   You can also try changing the duration of transitions by entering times in the duration text box, or clicking the up or down arrows to increase or decrease the time.

14   Save the **P09Try_xx** file, and leave it open to use in the next Try It.

Controlling Slide Advance

- By default, you advance slides in a presentation manually by clicking the mouse button or a keyboard key. If you do not want to advance slides manually, you can have PowerPoint advance each slide automatically.

- **Advance slide timing** defines the amount of time a slide is on the screen before PowerPoint automatically advances to the next slide.

- You can set advance slide timing on the TRANSITIONS tab for individual slides or for all slides in a presentation. Set advance slide timing in seconds or minutes and seconds.

- Even if you set advance timings for your slides, you can also choose to advance a slide manually.

- The advance slide timing for each slide is indicated in Slide Sorter view by a number below the slide.

Try It!   **Controlling Slide Advance**

1   In the **P09Try_xx** file, click Slide Sorter ▦.

2   Click slide 1, then click TRANSITIONS > Advance Slide After and type 5.

3   Click Apply To All ▣.

4   Click Sound 🔊 > No Sound, then click Apply To All ▣.

5   Click SLIDE SHOW > From Beginning ▣ to view the transitions without the sound. Click to exit the slide show.

6   Close the **P09Try_xx** file, saving changes, and exit PowerPoint.

Lesson 9—Practice

In this project, you continue to work on the presentation for the community aid organization by adding appropriate slide transitions.

DIRECTIONS

1. Start PowerPoint, if necessary, and open **P09Practice** from the data files for this lesson. Save the presentation as **P09Practice_xx** in the location where your teacher instructs you to store the files for this lesson.

2. Go to slide 1 and click **TRANSITIONS**, then click **Wipe** from the Transition to This Slide gallery.

3. Go to slide 2 and click **Wipe** from the Transition to This Slide gallery.

4. Go to slide 3 and click **Cover** from the Transition to This Slide gallery.

5. Go to slide 4 and click **Flip** from the Transition to This Slide gallery.

6. Go to slide 5 and click **Doors** from the Transition to This Slide gallery.

7. Go to slide 6 and click **Conveyor** from the Transition to This Slide gallery.

8. Go to slide 7 and click **Shape** from the Transition to This Slide gallery.

9. Go to slide 1, click **Slide Sorter** ⊞, then click each slide to preview the transition.

10. Click **Normal** ▣, go to slide 1, then click **Sound** 🔊 > **Chime**.

11. Click **TRANSITIONS** > **Effect Options** ▣ > **From Left**.

12. Click **Advance Slide After**, then type **5** in the text box. Click **Apply To All** ⤇ .

13. Click **SLIDE SHOW** > **From Beginning** 📺 to view the transitions. Click to exit the slide show.

14. **With your teacher's permission,** click **FILE** > **Print**. Select **Full Page Slides** > **6 Slides Horizontal**, then click **Print** to print the presentation.

15. Close the presentation, saving changes, and exit PowerPoint.

Lesson 9—Apply

In this project, you continue to work on the laser surgery unit presentation. You add slide transitions to give the slides more visual interest.

DIRECTIONS

1. Start PowerPoint, if necessary, and open **P09Apply** from the data files for this lesson. Save the presentation as **P09Apply_xx** in the location where your teacher instructs you to store the files for this lesson.

2. Apply several different slide transitions to the slides. View the slides in Slide Show view to see the transitions.

3. Apply the **Laser** sound to the first slide and the last slide.

4. Choose to advance all slides after 5 seconds.

5. View the presentation as a slide show, without clicking the mouse to advance each slide.

6. Check the spelling.

7. **With your teacher's permission,** print the presentation.

8. Close the presentation, saving changes, and exit PowerPoint.

End-of-Chapter Activities

➤ PowerPoint Chapter 1—Critical Thinking

Managing Computer Software and Maintenance

You work for Tech for All and have been asked to create a presentation that can be used to give clients a basic understanding of software and how to maintain a computer system. To complete this project, you will need to do research on the Internet and then create the presentation using the information you find.

You will need to locate information on the generally accepted categories of software—such as system software, programming software, and application software—and the uses of each type of software.

You will also need to locate information on how to maintain a computer system's software and hardware to keep the system working efficiently.

DIRECTIONS

1. Begin by doing your research on the Internet, evaluating each source as you explore its information to make sure the source is reputable and reliable. Take notes from your sources, recording the notes in a word processing document if desired.

2. When you have completed your research, create a storyboard for the presentation. You may sketch slide images on paper or use a word processing document to develop the storyboard.

3. Start a new presentation, and save it as **PCT01_xx** in the location where your teacher instructs you to store the files for this chapter.

4. Apply a theme and variant of your choice.

5. Insert the title **Managing Computer Software and Maintenance**, and in the subtitle placeholder, type **A Presentation by** and then insert your first and last name.

6. If necessary, use an AutoFit option to fit the title in the title placeholder.

7. Insert slides to record the information from your storyboard. Use different slide layouts as necessary to present your information clearly and in a visually appealing way.

8. If desired, use the Outline view to input your information. Adjust list levels as necessary to indicate items that are subordinate to other items.

9. Add notes to some slides to remind yourself of information you want to cover during the presentation.

10. Adjust font, font style, font size, and font color formatting as necessary to add visual interest to slides. You may also replace fonts on all slides if desired. Use the Format Painter to make sure formats are applied consistently throughout the presentation.

11. Adjust text alignment and line spacing as necessary. If text on any slides exceeds the depth of the content placeholder, use an AutoFit option to fit the text or divide it into columns or onto additional slides.

12. Adjust the position or size of placeholders, if necessary, and apply fill or line formatting to at least one placeholder in the presentation.

13. Insert the date and time, slide number, and an appropriate footer on all slides except the title slide.

14. Check spelling.

15. View the slides in Slide Sorter view and rearrange them as necessary.

16. Add slide transitions and an automatic advance timing to all slides.

17. Preview the presentation and then make any necessary corrections and adjustments.

18. Deliver the presentation to your class. Ask for comments on how the presentation could be improved.

19. After you have made all necessary corrections, view the presentation in Grayscale.

20. **With your teacher's permission**, print the presentation in Grayscale in Notes Page layout so you have a printed record of the notes you added to slides.

21. Close the presentation, saving changes, and exit PowerPoint.

➤ PowerPoint Chapter 1 — Portfolio Builder

Franchise Sales Presentation

As a new sales manager for Whole Grains Bread, you have been asked by one of the sales representatives if you can help him spruce up his presentation for customers and potential franchisees. Follow the guidelines below to add stronger introductory slides to the presentation, additional photos and text formatting, as well as a new theme and transitions.

DIRECTIONS

1. Start PowerPoint, if necessary, and open **PPB01A** from the data files for this chapter. Save the presentation as **PPB01A_xx** in the location where your teacher instructs you to store the files for this chapter.

2. Apply a theme from the themes available on the DESIGN tab. Pick one that you think is appropriate for the audience. Change the variant if desired. Adjust placement of the objects on slide 4 if necessary, and reset slide 6 to move the table into its proper position.

3. Insert three new slides before slide 1. Make the first new slide a **Title** slide, the second new slide a **Two Content** slide, and the third new slide should be a **Title and Content** slide.

4. On slide 1, type **Whole Grains Bread** in the title placeholder. In the subtitle placeholder, enter **Fresh to You Each Day**.

5. On slide 2, type **A Variety of Baked Goods** in the title placeholder. In the left content placeholder, type the following bullets:
   - **Breads**
     - **Croissants**
     - **Bagels**
     - **Muffins**
     - **Rolls**

6. On slide 2, in the right content placeholder, type the following bullets:
   - **Sweet specialties**
     - **Pastries**
     - **Cookies**
     - **Cakes**

7. On slide 3, type **Fresh Is Best!** in the title placeholder. In the content placeholder, type the following bullets:
   - **Locally grown herbs**
   - **Whole grain flours**
   - **Fresh creamery butter**
   - **Free range eggs**
   - **Locally produced honey**
   - **Fair trade coffee and chocolate**
   - **Certified organic fruits and vegetables**
   - **Local and imported cheeses**

8. Change the title and text fonts throughout the presentation to a font, font size, and font color of your choice. Check all slides for text alignment and fit within placeholders after making the change.

9. Open **PPB01B** from the data files for this chapter.

10. Change the slide size of all slides in this presentation to **Widescreen**.

11. Arrange the two presentations side by side. Drag slide 1 from **PPB01B** to follow slide 8 of **PPB01A_xx**. Drag slides 2 and 3 from **PPB01B** to follow slide 4 of **PPB01A_xx**.

12. Close **PPB01B** without saving changes.

13. Find all instances of **Great Grains** and replace them with **Whole Grains**.

14. Insert **PPB01C_picture** on a slide of your choice; resize and position appropriately. Add picture styles and formatting to the photo you inserted and the photo on slide 9.

15. Change the footer to show only your full name.

16. Add a note to slide 8 that say **Remind seminar audiences that franchises are going fast!**

17. On slide 11, move the Soup information above the Sandwich information.

18. In Slide Sorter view, delete slide 10. Move slides 10 and 11 to follow slide 4. Move slide 9 in front of slide 4. Duplicate the new slide 4, and move the copy to the end of the presentation.

19. Add slide transitions, sounds, and timings of your choosing.

20. View the presentation in Reading View. After viewing each slide, make any necessary corrections or adjustments.

21. Check spelling, and, **with your instructor's permission,** print one copy of your presentation.

22. Deliver the presentation to your class.

23. Close the presentation, saving changes, and exit PowerPoint.

Chapter 2

(Courtesy Konstantin Chagin/Shutterstock)

Working with Lists and Graphics

Lesson 10

Working with Lists

➤ What You Will Learn

Applying or Removing Bullets
Changing a Bulleted List to a Numbered List
Modifying the Bulleted List Style

WORDS TO KNOW

Picture bullet
A graphic specifically designed to be used as a bullet character.

Software Skills   You can add or remove bullets from list items, or change a bullet character to customize a list style. You can also change any list to a numbered list when items should appear in a particular order.

What You Can Do

Applying or Removing Bullets

■ In previous versions of PowerPoint, all list items were bulleted. In PowerPoint 2013, however, some themes format list items without bullets.

■ When you want to customize the lists in a presentation, you may want to add bullets to list items that do not have them, or remove bullets from lists that do have them.

■ You can apply or remove bullets from list items with the Bullets button on the HOME tab. This button is an on/off toggle for the Bullets feature.

✓ *The Bullets button also has a drop-down list for selecting a different bullet character. You will learn how to switch characters later in this lesson.*

Try It!   **Applying or Removing Bullets**

1 Start PowerPoint, and open **P10TryA** from the data files for this lesson.

2 Save the presentation as **P10TryA_xx** in the location where your teacher instructs you to store the files for this lesson.

3 Display slide 2 and click in the third bullet item.

4 Click HOME > Bullets ≔ ▾. The bullet character is toggled off.

5 Click HOME > Bullets ≔ ▾. The bullet character is toggled back on again.

6 Save the **P10TryA_xx** file, and leave it open to use in the next Try It.

Changing a Bulleted List to a Numbered List

- Numbered lists are almost identical to bulleted ones except they use consecutive numbers rather than using the same character for each paragraph.

- Use a numbered list when the order of the items is significant, such as in step-by-step instructions.

  ✓ *Avoid using numbered lists when the order is not significant, because the audience may erroneously read significance into it.*

Try It!   Changing a Bulleted List to a Numbered List

1 In the **P10TryA_xx** file, display slide 6.

2 Drag across the entire bulleted list to select it.

OR

Click to move the insertion point into the bulleted list and press `CTRL` + `A` to select all.

3 Click HOME > Numbering ≣ ▾ . The list becomes numbered.

4 Save the **P10TryA_xx** file, and leave it open to use in the next Try It.

Modifying the Bulleted List Style

- There are two ways of modifying a bulleted list's style. You can manually edit the individual paragraphs or lists that you want to specifically affect, or you can change the overall style for bulleted lists on the slide master.

  ✓ *You will work with the slide master in Chapter 4.*

- A wide variety of bullet characters are available, including symbols and pictures. You can select a bullet character from any font installed on your PC, or you can use any picture file to create **picture bullets**.

- Changes to the default bullet are made in the Bullets and Numbering dialog box.

Try It!   Modifying the Bulleted List Style

1 In the **P10TryA_xx** file, display slide 2.

2 Click anywhere in the bulleted list and press `CTRL` + `A` to select all.

3 On the HOME tab, in the Paragraph group, click the down arrow on the Bullets button ≣ ▾ , opening its menu.

4 Click the small round bullets on the menu. The bullets change.

5 With the bulleted list still selected, click the down arrow on the Bullets button ≣ ▾ again.

6 Click Bullets and Numbering to open the Bullets and Numbering dialog box.

7 Click the Customize button. The Symbol dialog box opens.

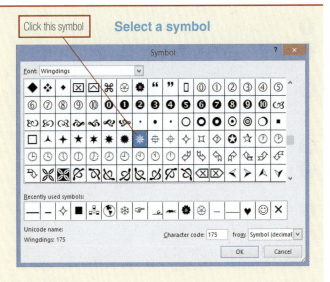

Click this symbol   **Select a symbol**

(continued)

Try It!   **Modifying the Bulleted List Style** *(continued)*

8   If the Wingdings font is not already selected in the Font list, open the Font list and click Wingdings.

✓ *You can choose any character from any font as a bullet symbol. Wingdings is a font designed specifically for this purpose, but other fonts may have interesting bullet characters, too.*

9   Click a fancy star symbol in Symbol dialog box. and click OK.

10   Click the up increment arrow next to the Size text box to increase the size of the bullet to 110%.

11   Open the Color button's ![palette icon] palette and click the Red, Accent 6 color from the theme colors.

12   Click OK. The bullets on the slide change.

13   Save the **P10TryA_xx** file, and leave it open to use in the next Try It.

Select a color

Try It!   **Using a Picture As a Bullet Character**

1   In the **P10TryA_xx** file, display slide 3.

2   Click anywhere in the list and press CTRL + A to select all.

3   On the HOME tab, in the Paragraph group, click the down arrow on the Bullets button ![bullets icon], opening its menu.

4   Click Bullets and Numbering.

5   Click Picture. The Insert Pictures dialog box opens.

6   Click the Browse button to the right of the From a file option and then navigate to the data files for this lesson.

7   Click **P10TryB_picture** and click Insert.

8   With the list still selected, click the down arrow on the Bullets button ![bullets icon] and click Bullets and Numbering.

9   Click the up increment arrow next to the Size box to change the bullet size to 100%. Click OK.

10   Close the **P10TryA_xx** file, saving changes, and exit PowerPoint.

Lesson 10—Practice

At Wynnedale Medical Center, the manager for whom you have created a presentation has commented that she does not like the bullet character in the draft presentation. You will apply several different bullet characters and customize them to give the manager options to choose among. You will also show her what list items would look like without bullets.

DIRECTIONS

1. Start PowerPoint, if necessary, and open **P10Practice** from the data files for this lesson.

2. Save the presentation as **P10Practice_xx** in the location where your teacher instructs you to store the files for this lesson.

3. Change the footer text on all slides (except the title slide) to your first and last name.

4. Click slide 2, select the first three bullet items, and then, on the HOME tab, click the drop-down arrow on the **Bullets** button ⧉ ˅.

5. Select the **Hollow Square Bullets** style.

6. Select the two subordinate bullet items, click the drop-down arrow on the **Bullets** button ⧉ ˅, and select **Filled Square Bullets**.

7. With the two subordinate bullet items still selected, click the drop-down arrow of the **Bullets** button ⧉ ˅ and click **Bullets and Numbering**.

8. Click the up increment arrow to change the bullet size to 110% of text. Click the **Color** button 🪣 ˅ and click **Red, Accent 3**. Click **OK**.

9. Display slide 4. Select the bullet items under Pros and click **HOME** > **Bullets** ⧉ ˅ to turn off bullet formatting. Make the same change for the list under Cons.

10. Display slide 6, and then select all bullet items in the content placeholder.

11. Click **HOME** > **Bullets** ⧉ ˅ > **Bullets and Numbering**.

12. Click **Customize**. The Symbol dialog box opens.

13. Open the Font drop-down list and click **Zapf Dingbats**.

    ✓ *If you do not have this font, choose Wingdings.*

14. Click a check mark symbol.

15. Click **OK** to close the Symbol dialog box.

16. Click **OK** to close the Bullets and Numbering dialog box.

17. Click slide 7, click the bullet item in the content placeholder, and click **Bullets** ⧉ ˅ to turn off bullet formatting.

18. Preview the presentation to view the new bullet styles.

19. **With your teacher's permission**, print slide 2 of the presentation.

    ✓ *Refer to Lesson 2 in Chapter 1 for information on printing slides.*

20. Close the presentation, saving changes, and exit PowerPoint.

Lesson 10—Apply

The Wynnedale laser surgery presentation has a new look with a new theme. In this project, you will work with list formats to give your manager additional options to choose among.

DIRECTIONS

1. Start PowerPoint, if necessary, and open **P10ApplyA** from the data files for this lesson.

2. Save the presentation as **P10ApplyA_xx** in the location where your teacher instructs you to store the files for this lesson.

3. Replace the slide footer with your first and last names, displayed on all slides.

4. On slides 2 and 5, change the bullet character for the subordinate bullet items to **Hollow Round Bullets** in a color different from the current one.

5. On slide 4, apply the picture bullet **P10ApplyB_picture** to the lists beneath Pros and Cons. Your slide should look like Figure 10-1.

6. Close Master view.

7. Remove the bullet from the paragraph on slide 7.

8. Convert the bullet points on slide 6 to a numbered list, and then change the color of the numbers in the Bullets and Numbering dialog box.

9. Preview the presentation to view the new list formats.

10. **With your teacher's permission**, print the presentation as handouts (6 slides per page).

11. Close the presentation, saving changes, and exit PowerPoint.

Figure 10-1

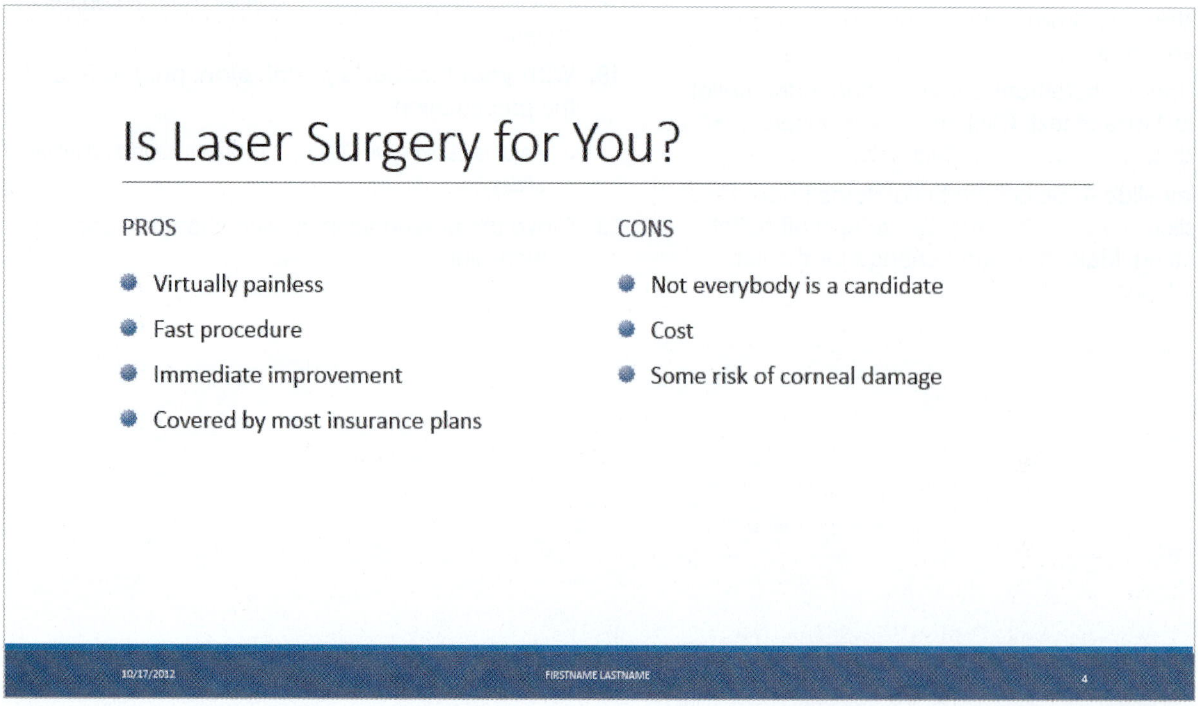

Is Laser Surgery for You?

PROS

- Virtually painless
- Fast procedure
- Immediate improvement
- Covered by most insurance plans

CONS

- Not everybody is a candidate
- Cost
- Some risk of corneal damage

10/17/2012   FIRSTNAME LASTNAME   4

Lesson 11

Inserting Online Pictures

➤ What You Will Learn

Inserting Online Pictures
Resizing and Positioning Online Pictures
Formatting a Clip Art Illustration
Removing the Background from a Picture

Software Skills   Clip art can be a tremendous asset to you as you create presentations. Your copy of PowerPoint includes free access to a huge library of ready-made drawings on Microsoft's Web site. You can access them through the Online Pictures feature in PowerPoint.

What You Can Do

Inserting Online Pictures

- **Clip art** can be used in any Office application, but it is especially suitable for PowerPoint because of the graphical focus of most slides.

- You use the Online Pictures command on the INSERT tab to open the Insert Pictures dialog box. Here you have options to search Office.com's clip art files, use Bing to search the Web for an image, look on your SkyDrive for images, or insert an image from Flickr.

  ✓ *If you use Bing, be aware that you may find copyrighted pictures when you search. Do not insert copyrighted pictures in your slides without first determining whether you need permission to do so. You will be reminded when searching the Web with Bing that some search results are licensed.*

- You can find clip art by searching for specific **keywords**. Each clip art image has one or more keywords assigned to it that describe it. For example, a picture of a dog might include the keywords *dog, pup, canine, animal,* and *pet*.

- If the slide contains an open content placeholder, you can place the clip art using the Online Pictures button in the placeholder. You can also insert clip art on any slide without using a placeholder.

- Unlike in previous Office versions, Office 2013 does not give you the option of searching only for clip art or only for photos.

- Search results from your keywords display both photos and the illustrations that are usually called clip art.

WORDS TO KNOW

Clip art
Generic, reusable drawings of common people, places, things, and concepts.

Keyword
A descriptive word attached to an image, used for searching and indexing the image library.

Try It!   Inserting Online Pictures

1 Start PowerPoint, and open **P11Try** from the data files for this lesson.

2 Save the presentation as **P11Try_xx** in the location where your teacher instructs you to store the files for this lesson.

3 Click slide 3 in the Thumbnail pane.

4 In the empty content placeholder, click the Online Pictures icon. The Insert Pictures dialog box opens.

5 In the text box to the right of Office.com Clip Art, type **helping hand** and click the Search button.

6 Click the picture that shows a reaching hand (at the end of the first row of search results), and then click Insert. The clip appears in the placeholder.

7 Click slide 4 in the Thumbnail pane.

8 Click INSERT > Online Pictures to open the Insert Pictures dialog box.

9 Type **donation** in the search box and click Search.

10 Click the first result, a jar of money, and click Insert.

11 Save the **P11Try_xx** file, and leave it open to use in the next Try It.

Resizing and Positioning Online Pictures

■ When you insert a clip art image in a placeholder, the placeholder determines the image's size and position.

■ When you insert an image without a placeholder, the image appears in the center of the slide, at a default size.

■ Resize and position an online image using the same options you learned in Lesson 4 when inserting pictures from files:

● Resize an image by dragging a corner handle or by specifying an exact size using the Size controls on the PICTURE TOOLS FORMAT tab.

● Position an image by dragging it to the desired location or by specifying an exact position using the Format Picture task pane.

Try It!   Resizing and Positioning Online Pictures

1 In the **P11Try_xx** file, on slide 4, click the image to select it (if not already selected). Selection handles appear around it.

2 Click the upper-left corner handle and drag diagonally toward the lower-right of the image about 1" to resize the image.

3 Click PICTURE TOOLS FORMAT > Shape Height and type **4"**.

4 Drag the image to the right of the list items in the content placeholder.

5 Right-click the picture and click Format Picture to display the Format Picture task pane.

6 Click the Size & Properties icon, and click the POSITION heading to expand it.

7 Type **7"** in the Horizontal position box and **1.6"** in the Vertical position box. Close the Format Picture task pane.

8 Save the **P11Try_xx** file, and leave it open to use in the next Try It.

(continued)

<table>
<tr><td>**Try It!**</td><td>**Resizing and Positioning Online Pictures** (continued)</td></tr>
</table>

Reposition the clip art on the slide

Formatting a Clip Art Illustration

- If you select an illustration rather than a photo from the Insert Picture search results, you can format the illustration in many of the same ways as a photo.
  - Resize and position an illustration using the same options as for a picture.
  - Use tools on the PICTURE TOOLS FORMAT tab to correct color or apply picture styles or effects.

- You can also ensure that the illustration blends well with your slide design by recoloring the image using the current theme colors.
- You can even make a color transparent to allow the theme background to become part of the image, for a more unified look.

<table>
<tr><td>**Try It!**</td><td>**Formatting a Clip Art Illustration**</td></tr>
</table>

1. In the **P11Try_xx** file, display slide 5.

2. Click INSERT > Online Pictures 🖼 to open the Insert Pictures dialog box.

3. In the Search box, type **job search** and click the Search button 🔍 .

4. Click the clip art illustration at the end of the first row, the two people looking at a resume, and then click Insert.

5. Resize the image to 3.2" high and wide, and position it in the upper-right corner of the slide.

6. Click PICTURE TOOLS FORMAT > Color 🖼 , and choose Dark Blue, Background color 2 Light at the far left of the bottom row of the Recolor gallery.

7. Click PICTURE TOOLS FORMAT > Color 🖼 > Set Transparent Color.

8. Click the transparent color pointer on the light blue background area of the illustration. The background color is removed, allowing the slide background to appear in the illustration.

9. Save the **P11Try_xx** file, and leave it open to use in the next Try It.

Removing the Background from a Picture

- In some photos, the background detracts from the main image. Using a graphics program, you can cut out the part of the image you want to use.

- PowerPoint also provides this capability, so you can remove a photo's background without leaving PowerPoint.

- PowerPoint makes a guess about what part of the image is background and covers it with pink shading.

- You can fine-tune where the dividing lines are between the foreground and background of the image if PowerPoint does not guess them correctly.

- Use the Mark Areas to Keep tool to drag over parts of the image that should not be removed. Use the Mark Areas to Remove tool to drag over parts of the image you don't want.

Try It!   **Removing the Background from a Picture**

1. In the **P11Try_xx** file, display slide 3.

2. Click the picture to select it, and then click PICTURE TOOLS FORMAT > Remove Background 🖼. Most of the image is covered with pink shading to indicate it will be removed.

3. You do not want the arm in the image to be removed, so click BACKGROUND REMOVAL > Mark Areas to Keep ⊕.

4. The pointer changes to a pencil pointer. Drag the pointer from the palm of the hand diagonally along the arm. PowerPoint removes the pink shading from the arm, indicating that this portion of the image will not be discarded.

5. Click Keep Changes ✓.

6. Close the **P11Try_xx** file, saving changes, and exit PowerPoint.

Lesson 11—Practice

In this project, you continue to work with the Wynnedale Medical Center presentation. You will select appropriate online images and insert them in the presentation to enhance its appearance.

DIRECTIONS

1. Start PowerPoint, if necessary, and open **P11Practice** from the data files for this lesson.

2. Save the presentation as **P11Practice_xx** in the location where your teacher instructs you to store the files for this lesson.

3. Change the slide footer to display your first and last name on all slides.

4. Click slide 2, and click **INSERT** > **Online Pictures** 🖼.

5. Click in the search box and type **eye chart**.

6. Select a picture from the search results and click **Insert**. Then drag the picture to place it to the right of the bulleted list.

7. Click slide 6 to display it.

8. Click the **Online Pictures** placeholder icon.

9. Click in the search box and type **dollar bill**. Click the **Search** button 🔍 or press ⏎.

10. Click any of the found clips to insert it on the slide.

    ✓ *Try to find a clip that fits the content of the list as well as possible.*

11. Preview the presentation to see the new images in place.

12. **With your teacher's permission**, click **FILE** > **Print**. Select **Print All Slides**, and then click **Print** to print the presentation.

13. Close the presentation, saving changes, and exit PowerPoint.

Lesson 11—Apply

In this project, you continue to work with the Wynnedale presentation to add online images. You will also remove the background from an image.

DIRECTIONS

1. Start PowerPoint, if necessary, and open **P11Apply** from the data files for this lesson.

2. Save the presentation as **P11Apply_xx** in the location where your teacher instructs you to store the files for this lesson.

3. Change the footer to your first and last name.

4. Display slide 5 and use the keywords **woman sunglasses** to insert the picture shown in Figure 11-1.

5. Size the clip art **5.7"** high, and move it to the right of the list.

6. Use Remove Background to begin the process of removing the blue background.

7. Adjust the outline inside the picture by dragging the left, right, and bottom center handles to the edge of the picture, as shown in Figure 11-1, to identify more of the picture as foreground.

8. Remove the picture background and adjust the size and position of the image as necessary to fit on the slide.

9. On slide 7, use the Online Pictures icon in the placeholder and the keywords **blue sky** to locate an appropriate image.

10. Preview the presentation and make any necessary corrections and adjustments.

11. **With your teacher's permission**, print the presentation as handouts, 6 slides per page.

12. Close the presentation, saving changes, and exit PowerPoint.

Figure 11-1

Drag the inner selection handle outward

Lesson 12

Inserting Symbols and Text Boxes

➤ **What You Will Learn**

Inserting Symbols
Inserting and Formatting a Text Box
Using Multiple Columns in a Text Box

WORDS TO KNOW

Symbol
A typographical character that is neither a letter nor a number. Some symbols can be typed on a keyboard, and others must be inserted.

Text box
A non-placeholder container for text that you can position anywhere on a slide.

Software Skills   Not all characters are available for insertion by typing on the keyboard. Some characters such as ® and © are available only as symbols. In this lesson, you will learn how to insert symbols in a presentation. You will also learn how to create text boxes that are not a part of a slide layout, and to format the text in multiple columns in a single text box.

What You Can Do

Inserting Symbols

■ **Symbols** are characters that are neither alphabetic nor numeric. Most of them cannot be typed from the keyboard. Symbols can include decorative characters, foreign language characters, and mathematical or punctuation characters.

■ You can insert symbols from the Symbols dialog box. You have a choice of fonts there. You can choose normal text, which uses the same font as the default used for list paragraphs in the presentation, or some other font.

✓ *If you want decorative characters instead, you can choose a font such as Zapf Dingbats or Wingdings, both of which are specifically designed for symbol use.*

Try It! Inserting Symbols

1 Start PowerPoint, and open **P12Try** from the data files for this lesson.

2 Save the presentation as **P12Try_xx** in the location where your teacher instructs you to store the files for this lesson.

3 Display slide 1, and click to place the insertion point immediately after the word *Giving* in the title.

4 Click INSERT > Symbol Ω. The Symbol dialog box opens.

5 If (normal text) does not appear in the Font box, open its drop-down list and select (normal text).

6 Scroll through the symbols, and click the TM (trademark) symbol.

7 Click Insert.

8 Click Close. The symbol appears in the title.

9 Save the **P12Try_xx** file, and leave it open to use in the next Try It.

The Symbol dialog box

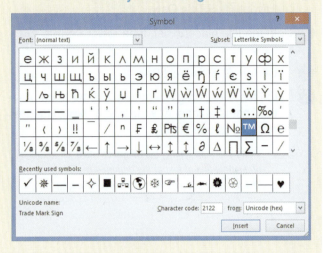

Inserting and Formatting a Text Box

■ A **text box** is a container for text that you can position anywhere on a slide. It is not a placeholder, and not part of a slide layout. Like other slide objects, text boxes are inserted from the INSERT tab.

■ There are two ways to use the Text Box tool. After clicking the Text Box button you can:

● Click on the slide and start typing. This creates a text box in which the text does not wrap; the text box just keeps getting wider to accommodate your text.

● Drag on the slide to define the size and shape of the text box, and then click inside it and start typing. This creates a text box in which text wraps to multiple lines automatically.

■ You can resize a text box as you would any other object, by dragging the selection handles.

■ You can format a text box as you would any other object. This includes adding a border, shading, and special effects. Use the tools in the Drawing group on the HOME tab, or use the DRAWING TOOLS FORMAT tab. You can also right-click the border of the text box and use the shortcut format tools, or display the Format Shape task pane to apply formats.

✓ *Lesson 13 covers object formatting in detail. The same basic formatting commands work for all types of objects, including drawn shapes and text boxes.*

■ In addition to applying shape formats in the Format Shape task pane, you can display text options that allow you to control how the text appears in the text box (alignment, margins, and so on).

Try It!   **Inserting a Text Box**

1 In the **P12Try_xx** file, in the Thumbnail pane, click between slides 6 and 7, and press ENTER, creating a new slide there.

2 With the new slide displayed, click HOME > Layout ▦ > Title Only.

3 In the title placeholder, type **What People Are Saying**.

4 Click INSERT > Text Box ▣.

5 On the slide, drag the mouse pointer to create a box that is at least 4" wide and 3" high. Use the rulers to gauge size.

  ✓ *When you start typing, the height snaps back to the size of a single line of text at the default size. This is normal. The text box will expand vertically as you type.*

6 Type the text shown below. To manually insert a line break between the end of the quotation and the person's name, press SHIFT + ENTER.

7 Save the **P12Try_xx** file, and leave it open to use in the next Try It.

Type this text in the box

"Without the support of good people in our community who want to make a difference, our family would not have been able to stay together last year when I was unable to find work."
—Trisha K.

Try It!   **Formatting a Text Box**

1 In the **P12Try_xx** file, click the outer border of the text box. This selects the box itself, and not the text inside.

2 On the DRAWING TOOLS FORMAT tab, click the More button ▾ in the Shape Styles group to open the Shape Styles gallery.

3 Click the second style in the bottom row.

4 Click DRAWING TOOLS FORMAT > Edit Shape ▨▾ > Change Shape and click a rounded rectangle.

5 Right-click the text box and then click Format Shape to display the Format Shape task pane.

6 Click the Effects icon ◌, expand the REFLECTION heading, click Presets, and click the first reflection type in the Reflection Variations section.

7 Expand the 3-D ROTATION heading, click Presets, and click the second sample in the first row of the Perspective section. When you are finished, the text box should look like that shown in the figure on the right. Close the Format Shape task pane.

8 Save the **P12Try_xx** file, and leave it open to use in the next Try It.

The formatted text box

"Without the support of good people in our community who want to make a difference, our family would not have been able to stay together last year when I was unable to find work."
—Trisha K.

Using Multiple Columns in a Text Box

- You can place text in multiple columns in a single text box. This gives a different look than placing two text boxes side-by-side, and makes it easier to move text between columns after making edits.

- Use the Columns dialog box, accessed from the Columns drop-down list, to select the number of columns and space between them.

Try It!   **Using Multiple Columns in a Text Box**

1 In the **P12Try_xx** file, click New Slide 📄 to create a new Title Only slide to become slide 8 in the presentation.

2 In the title placeholder, type **In the News**.

3 Click INSERT > Text Box 🔤.

4 On the slide, drag the mouse pointer to create a box that runs from the 4" mark on the ruler at the left to the 4" mark on the right.

> ✓ *The height you drag does not matter because PowerPoint will make the box as tall as needed for the content.*

5 Type the following paragraphs into the new text box:

In a recent study at Purdue University, it was shown that the return on investment (ROI) for investing in job skills training programs for people living below the poverty line is approximately 5:1. That means for every one dollar invested, you can expect a return of five dollars.

How is this money generated? When you train people who are currently receiving government assistance, they can get jobs and stop needing those payments. In addition, they begin paying income taxes, sales taxes, and property taxes as income rises and property is purchased.

6 Click HOME > Add or Remove Columns ▦ ▾ > Two Columns.

7 Click HOME > Add or Remove Columns ▦ ▾ > More Columns. The Columns dialog box opens.

8 In the Spacing text box, type **0.2"**.

9 Click OK.

10 Close the **P12Try_xx** file, saving changes, and exit PowerPoint.

The Columns dialog box

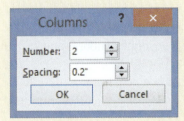

Lesson 12—Practice

In this project, you will add a copyright notice to the first slide of the Wynnedale presentation, break the text into columns, and format the text box.

DIRECTIONS

1. Start PowerPoint, if necessary, and open **P12Practice** from the data files for this lesson.

2. Save the presentation as **P12Practice_xx** in the location where your teacher instructs you to store the files for this lesson.

3. With slide 1 displayed, click **INSERT > Text Box** 🄰. Click at the top center of the slide and type your full name.

4. Click **INSERT > Text Box** 🄰.

5. Drag to create a 7" wide text box at the lower-right corner of the slide.

6. In the text box, type **Copyright** and press SPACEBAR once.

7. Click **INSERT > Symbol** Ω.

8. Click the Copyright symbol © and click **Insert**. Then click **Close**.

9. Press SPACEBAR again.

10. Type **2014**, press ENTER , type **Wynnedale Medical Group, LLC. All Rights Reserved.**

11. Press ENTER , and type **For information on how to obtain this presentation to show to your group, contact Wynnedale Medical Center.**

12. Press CTRL + A to select all the text in the text box.

13. On the **HOME** tab, in the Font group, open the **Size** drop-down list and click **10**.

14. Click **HOME > Add or Remove Columns** ☰ ▾ > **Two Columns**.

15. On the **DRAWING TOOLS FORMAT** tab, click in the **Shape Height** box 🔲 1" and change the text box height to **0.6"**. Click in the **Shape Width** box 🔲 1" and change the text box width to **6.7"**.

16. Right-click the text box, click the **Shape Quick Styles** button, and click **Colored Fill - Plum, Accent 1**.

17. Adjust the position of the text box if necessary to fit exactly in the lower-right corner of the slide.

18. Click Slide Show 🖵 on the status bar to preview your changes to slide 1. Then press ESC to end the slide show.

19. Close the presentation, saving changes, and exit PowerPoint.

Lesson 12—Apply

You continue to fine-tune the Wynnedale presentation. You will add customer testimonials to a page, using manually placed text boxes that you format in colorful ways.

DIRECTIONS

1. Start PowerPoint, if necessary, and open **P12Apply** from the data files for this lesson.

2. Save the presentation as **P12Apply_xx** in the location where your teacher instructs you to store the files for this lesson.

3. On slide 1, insert a text box at the top of the slide, and type your full name.

4. Move to slide 7 and create the text boxes shown in Figure 12-1 on the next page.

   a. Draw each text box and add the text shown in the figure. (You may need to change the font color initially to black to see what you are typing.)

   b. Italicize the names of the people and insert an em dash symbol to left of each name.

   c. On the **DRAWING TOOLS FORMAT** tab, use four different colors of presets from the bottom row of the palette of Shape Styles.

5. Adjust the width and height of each text box as necessary to display the text attractively.

6. Move the text boxes on the slide as desired to create an interesting layout. Figure 12-1 shows one layout option.

7. Check the spelling and preview the slide in Slide Show view.

8. **With your teacher's permission**, print the presentation as handouts, six slides per page.

9. Close the presentation, saving changes, and exit PowerPoint.

Figure 12-1

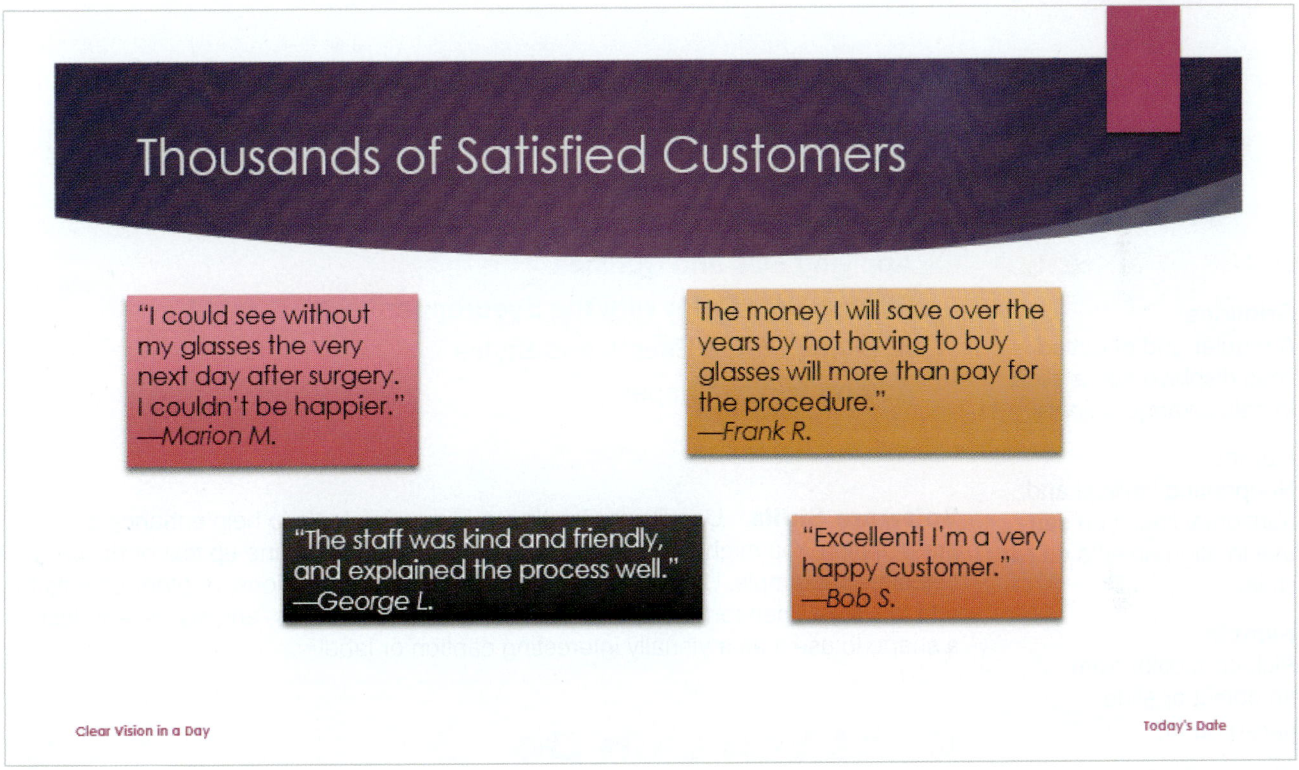

Thousands of Satisfied Customers

"I could see without my glasses the very next day after surgery. I couldn't be happier." —Marion M.

The money I will save over the years by not having to buy glasses will more than pay for the procedure." —Frank R.

"The staff was kind and friendly, and explained the process well." —George L.

"Excellent! I'm a very happy customer." —Bob S.

Clear Vision in a Day

Today's Date

Lesson 13

Drawing and Formatting Shapes

➤ What You Will Learn

Using Rulers, Guides, and Gridlines
Drawing Shapes
Moving and Sizing Shapes
Applying Fills and Outlines
Picking Up a Color with the Eyedropper
Applying Shape Effects and Styles
Adding Text to Shapes

WORDS TO KNOW

Gridlines
A regular grid of dotted lines displayed on a slide to help arrange objects.

Guides
Nonprinting vertical and horizontal lines you can use to align objects on a slide.

Sample
Pick up a color from an object or slide background.

Shape effects
Special effects such as glow, shadow, 3D rotation, and soft edges applied to drawn shapes.

Shape styles
Preset combinations of shape effects that can be applied as a single formatting action.

Snap
To change position to align precisely with a gridline.

Software Skills   Use PowerPoint's many drawing tools to help enhance a presentation. You might use rulers and guides or the grid to line up text or drawing objects, for example. Use shape tools to draw logos, illustrations, or other objects to add to slides. Then format shapes using fills, outlines, effects, and styles. Add text to a shape to use it as a visually interesting caption or label.

What You Can Do

Using Rulers, Guides, and Gridlines

- PowerPoint provides a vertical and horizontal ruler that you can show or hide at any time. Use the rulers to help you align objects on a slide.
- The ruler's origins (0 measurement on the ruler) change depending on whether you're using text or an object. The origin appears on the edge of the ruler when you're working with text and in the center point of the ruler when you're working with an object.
- As you move the mouse pointer, an indicator moves on each ruler showing your horizontal and vertical locations.
- **Guides** are alignment tools that help you line up objects and text. PowerPoint supplies one vertical and one horizontal guide that you can move and copy, as shown in Figure 13-1 on the next page.

- PowerPoint's **gridlines** display as a grid of dotted lines over the entire slide. Like guides, they can help you line up objects or position them attractively on the slide.

- By default, objects **snap** to the grid as they are drawn or positioned on the slide, even if the gridlines are not currently displayed. If you find you want to position an object more exactly, you can turn off the snapping feature or hold down ALT while dragging to temporarily disable the snapping feature.

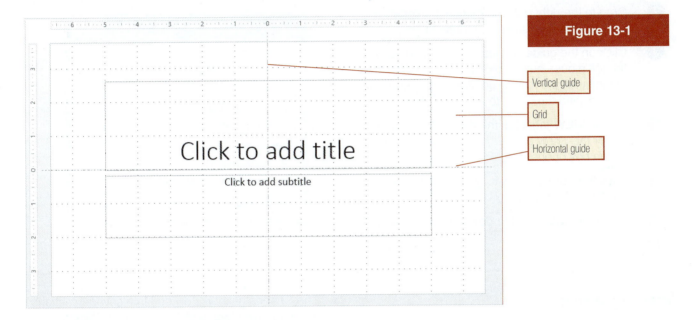

Figure 13-1

Vertical guide

Grid

Click to add title

Click to add subtitle

Horizontal guide

Try It!   Turning on Rulers, Gridlines, and Guides

1. Start PowerPoint, and start a new blank presentation.

2. Save the presentation as **P13Try_xx** in the location where your teacher instructs you to store the files for this lesson.

3. Click the VIEW tab.

4. If the Ruler check box is not already marked, click to mark it.

5. If the Gridlines check box is not already marked, click to mark it.

6. If the Guides check box is not already marked, click to mark it.

7. Save the **P13Try_xx** file, and leave it open to use in the next Try It.

Try It!   **Adjusting Grid and Guide Settings**

1 In the **P13Try_xx** file, position the mouse pointer over the dashed vertical guide and click and hold the left mouse button.

✓ *The mouse pointer changes to show 0.00.*

2 Drag to the right until the mouse pointer shows 1.50, and then release the mouse button.

3 Click on the guide you just moved, hold down the left mouse button, press CTRL, and drag to the left until the mouse pointer shows 3.00. You have copied the guide to a new location.

4 On the VIEW tab, click the dialog box launcher ⌐ for the Show group. The Grid and Guides dialog box opens.

5 Click the Snap objects to grid check box if it is not already marked.

6 Open the Spacing drop-down list and click 1/16".

7 Click OK.

8 Save the **P13Try_xx** file, and leave it open to use in the next Try It.

The Grid and Guides dialog box

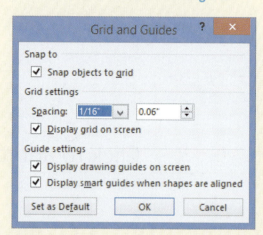

Drawing Shapes

- Use the shapes in the Shapes gallery to draw basic objects such as lines, rectangles, and circles as well as more complex shapes such as stars, banners, and block arrows.

- The Shapes gallery is available on the INSERT tab, as well as on the HOME tab, and on the DRAWING TOOLS FORMAT tab when a drawing object is selected.

- The Shapes gallery is divided into several sections that organize shapes of various kinds. Click a shape and then drag on the slide to draw it. You control the size as you draw.

- If you click on the slide instead of dragging, you get a default-sized shape.

- You can hold down SHIFT as you drag to constrain the shape to its original aspect ratio. If you draw an oval while holding down SHIFT, it's a perfect circle; if you draw a rectangle, it's a perfect square.

Try It!   **Drawing Shapes**

1 In the **P13Try_xx** file, click HOME > Layout ▦ > Blank to switch to a blank layout with no placeholders.

2 Click INSERT > Shapes ▨. In the Stars and Banners section, click the five-pointed star.

3 Hold down SHIFT and draw a star in the center of the slide, approximately 4" × 4".

✓ *Each square in the grid is 1".*

4 Click INSERT > Shapes ▨. In the Basic Shapes section, click the oval.

5 Hold down SHIFT and draw a circle to the left of the star, approximately 3" in diameter.

6 With the circle still selected, click the Line shape in the gallery in the Insert Shapes group.

7 Hold down SHIFT and draw a straight horizontal line above the star.

8 Save the **P13Try_xx** file, and leave it open to use in the next Try It.

Moving and Sizing Shapes

- You can move, size, copy, and delete drawing objects just like any other PowerPoint object.
  - To move a shape, drag it.
    - ✓ *You can also display the Format Shape task pane and use the Position settings in the Size & Properties settings.*
  - To size a shape, drag one of its selection handles.

- ✓ *You can also enter a precise height and width on the DRAWING TOOLS FORMAT tab, in the Size group, or on the Format Shape task pane.*
- To delete a shape, select it and press ⌈DEL⌋.
- To nudge an object (move it in small increments), hold down ⌈CTRL⌋ while pressing an arrow key in the direction you want it to move.

- Some shapes also have one or more yellow diamond resize handles that you can use to adjust the appearance of the shape.

Try It!   **Moving and Sizing Shapes**

1 In the **P13Try_xx** file, click the circle to select it.

2 Hold down ⌈SHIFT⌋ and drag the shape's lower-right corner selection handle, to shrink the circle to approximately 2" in diameter.

3 On the DRAWING TOOLS FORMAT tab, click in the Shape Height box ⌈↕1"⌋ and type **2.5"**.

4 Click in the Shape Width box ⌈↔1"⌋ and type **2.5"**.

5 Drag the circle to the upper-right corner of the slide.

6 Right-click the circle and click Format Shape. The Format Shape task pane displays.

7 Click the Size & Properties icon ⌈▦⌋, and click the POSITION heading to expand it.

8 In the Horizontal position box, type **0.5"**.

9 In the Vertical position box, type **0.5"**.

10 Close the Format Shape task pane.

11 Click INSERT > Shapes ⌈▱⌋ and in the Block Arrows section, click the Up Arrow shape.

12 Drag on the slide to place a block arrow to the right of the star, approximately 4" high and 2" wide.

- ✓ *Two yellow diamonds appear on it: one on the arrowhead and one on the arrow shaft.*

13 Drag the diamond on the arrowhead upward to change the shape of the arrowhead.

14 Drag the diamond on the arrow shaft to the right to change the width of the shaft.

15 Save the **P13Try_xx** file, and leave it open to use in the next Try It.

Modify the arrow by dragging the yellow diamonds

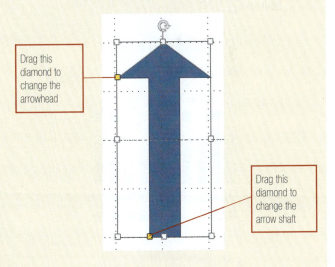

Drag this diamond to change the arrowhead

Drag this diamond to change the arrow shaft

Applying Fills and Outlines

- By default, shapes are formatted with the current theme colors. The fill is the Accent 1 color in the theme (the fifth color), and the outline is a related color.

- On the DRAWING TOOLS FORMAT tab, you can use the Shape Fill and Shape Outline drop-down lists to format a shape differently from the default.

- You can also right-click the shape and use the Fill and Outline shortcut buttons, or choose Format Shape to open the Format Shape task pane, where a wider variety of formatting options are available.

Applying Fills and Outlines

1 In the **P13Try_xx** file, click the star to select it.

2 On the DRAWING TOOLS FORMAT tab, click the Shape Fill ⬧ drop-down arrow, opening its menu.

3 Click the yellow square under Standard Colors.

4 Click the Shape Outline ✎ drop-down arrow, opening its menu.

5 Click More Outline Colors.

6 In the Colors dialog box, click the Standard tab.

7 Click an orange hexagon, and then click OK.

8 Right-click the star and click the Outline shortcut button ✎.

9 Click Weight and then click 3 pt.

10 Right-click the horizontal line and click Format Shape on the shortcut menu to open the Format Shape task pane. Click the Fill & Line icon ⬧ if necessary.

11 Click the LINE heading to expand it. Click the Width up arrow until the width is 5 pt, and then click the Dash type button, opening its menu. Choose the Square Dot dash style (the third style on the list).

12 Close the Format Shape task pane.

13 Save the **P13Try_xx** file, and leave it open to use in the next Try It.

Select a fill color

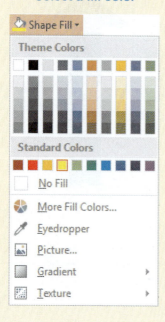

Select an outline color

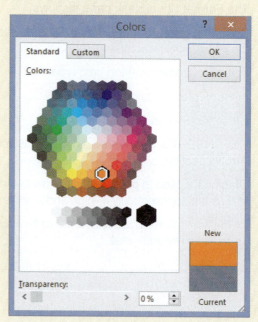

Picking Up a Color with the Eyedropper

- In PowerPoint 2013, you can use a new feature, the Eyedropper, to pick up a color from one object to use as the fill or outline color in another object.

- You can pick up a color from a photo or clip art illustration, for example, to fill a shape or placeholder. Using the Eyedropper to apply colors allows you to build unity among slide objects. Unity is one of the standard principles of design.

- As you move the Eyedropper over a slide and its contents, the Eyedropper **samples** the color under the pointer and shows you the exact color values using the RGB color mode.

  ✓ *RGB, or Red Green Blue, is the color mode used for images that appear onscreen, such as PowerPoint slide objects.*

Try It!	Picking Up a Color with the Eyedropper

1. In the **P13Try_xx** file, click INSERT > Online Pictures.

2. In the Clip Art search box, type **job search** and click the Search button.

3. Select the illustration of two people looking at a resume and click Insert. Use the grid as a reference as you drag the upper-right corner handle to enlarge the image to about 3" high and wide. Move the illustration to the lower-left corner of the slide.

4. Click the circle on the slide to select it and then click DRAWING TOOLS FORMAT > Shape Fill to display the Shape Fill menu.

5. Click Eyedropper. The pointer changes to the shape of an eyedropper, and a thumbnail attached to the pointer displays the color the Eyedropper is currently sampling.

6. Click the light-green background of the illustration with the Eyedropper. The circle fills with the same color.

7. With the circle still selected, click DRAWING TOOLS FORMAT > Shape Outline to display the Shape Outline menu.

8. Click Eyedropper, and then click the brown color of the man's hair. Click DRAWING TOOLS FORMAT > Shape Outline > Weight > 6 pt.

9. Save the **P13Try_xx** file, and leave it open to use in the next Try It.

Applying Shape Effects and Styles

- **Shape effects** are special formatting options you can apply to PowerPoint objects. You have already used some of these effects in formatting pictures and text boxes.

- The available effects include shadows, reflections, soft edges, bevels, and 3D rotation. After opening the Shape Effects menu, you point to a submenu name and then click one of the presets from the submenu that appears.

  ✓ *The shape effect you choose does not affect the color or border of the object. However, some effects hide the shape's outline.*

- Each of the effect submenus has an Options command at the bottom that opens the Format Shape task pane with the corresponding options selected. For example, the Shadow Options command opens the task pane to the SHADOW settings.

- You have also previously applied **shape styles**, combinations of color, outline, and shape effects you add to an object with a single click.

- Shape styles automatically use the colors of the current theme. You can apply a shape style and then manually change the color if you like.

Try It!   **Applying Shape Effects and Styles**

1 In the **P13Try_xx** file, click the circle to select it.

2 Click DRAWING TOOLS FORMAT > Shape Effects 🔲 > Preset and click the second preset in the first row of the Presets section.

3 Click Shape Fill 🔲, click Eyedropper, and click the woman's orange garment in the illustration.

   ✓ *Notice that the effect remains, even though you have changed the color.*

4 Click Shape Effects 🔲 > Bevel > Riblet (the second effect in the third row of the Bevel section).

5 Click the star to select it.

6 On the DRAWING TOOLS FORMAT tab, in the Shape Styles group, click the More button 🔽 to open the Shape Styles gallery.

7 Click the style in the lower-right corner of the gallery.

   ✓ *Notice that the shape outline is removed because this shape style does not include an outline.*

8 Click the block arrow shape. Click the More button 🔽 to open the Shape Styles gallery again.

9 Click the first style in the fourth row of the gallery.

10 Right-click the shape, click Format Shape to open the Format Shape task pane, click the Effects icon ⬠, and expand the GLOW heading.

11 Click the Presets button and then click Gold, 18 pt glow, Accent color 4.

12 Save the **P13Try_xx** file, and leave it open to use in the next Try It.

Adding Text to Shapes

■ You can add text to any filled shape. Simply click on the shape and start typing. PowerPoint handles line length and text wrap. This allows you, in effect, to have any shape of text box you want, not just rectangular.

■ You can edit and format text in a shape just as you would edit text in a text box. For a special effect, you can change text direction so that text reads from top to bottom or bottom to top.

Try It!   **Adding Text to a Shape and Rotating the Text**

1 In the **P13Try_xx** file, click the block arrow to select it.

2 Type **Check out our specials**. The text appears in the shaft of the arrow, with only a few characters per line.

3 Right-click the block arrow and click Format Shape.

4 In the Format Shape task pane, click TEXT OPTIONS.

5 Click the Textbox icon 🔠 to display TEXT BOX settings.

6 Open the Text direction drop-down list and click Rotate all text 270°.

7 Close the task pane. The text now runs vertically in the shape.

8 Close the **P13Try_xx** file, saving changes, and exit PowerPoint.

Lesson 13—Practice

A friend who works for Kelly Greenery, a landscaping company, has asked you to create a presentation he can run at a garden show. You will begin work on the presentation by creating and formatting shapes on a slide to which you have already added a clip art photo.

DIRECTIONS

1. Start PowerPoint, if necessary, and open **P13Practice** from the data files for this lesson.

2. Save the presentation as **P13Practice_xx** in the location where your teacher instructs you to store the files for this lesson.

3. On slide 1, click **INSERT** > **Text Box** 📇. Click at the bottom of the slide and type your full name.

4. On the VIEW tab, mark the **Guides** check box and the **Gridlines** check box, if necessary.

5. Display slide 2. Position the mouse pointer over the vertical guide, hold down the left mouse button, and drag to the left until the mouse pointer displays **1.75**.

6. With the mouse pointer still on the vertical guide, press ⌈CTRL⌋ and drag a copy of the vertical guide to the right until the mouse pointer displays **5.00**.

7. Click **INSERT** > **Shapes** ▽. Click the Wave shape in the Stars and Banners section.

8. Drag on the slide above the tulips illustration to create a banner that extends from the left edge of the slide to the 1.75 guide you positioned in step 5.

9. Click **INSERT** > **Shapes** ▽. Click the Up Arrow shape in the Block Arrows section.

10. Drag on the slide to the right of the tulips to create a block arrow from the bottom edge of the slide to the horizontal guide at the middle of the slide. The arrow should be about **2.3"** wide and **3.75"** tall.

11. Use the grid to draw an oval **5** inches wide and **3** inches high.

12. Position the shapes as follows:

    a. Move the block arrow so that its point is at the intersection of the left vertical guide and the horizontal guide.

    b. Move the oval so that its right edge snaps to the right vertical guide and it is vertically centered on the horizontal guide.

13. Change fill and outline formats as follows:

    a. Select the banner and click **DRAWING TOOLS FORMAT** > **Shape Fill** 🎨. Click **Eyedropper** and sample an area on one of the tulip leaves, as shown in Figure 13-2 on the next page.

    b. Right-click the oval, click the **Fill** shortcut button, and then click **Orange, Accent 2** from the theme colors.

    c. Right-click the block arrow and click **Format Shape** on the shortcut menu. Expand the FILL heading, click **Color** 🎨, and click **More Colors**. Click the Standard tab, and click the dark pink color that is second from the right in the third row from the bottom of the color chart. Click **OK**.

    d. With the block arrow still selected, click **LINE**, click Color 🎨 and then click **Gold, Accent 4** from the theme colors. Click the **Width** up arrow until the width is **6 pt**.

14. Select the green banner and type **KELLY GREENERY**. Change the font to **Algerian** and the font size to **60**.

15. On the **DRAWING TOOLS FORMAT** tab, click **Shape Effects** ▭ > **Bevel** and click the first option in the first row, Circle.

16. Select the block arrow and type **TULIPS**. In the Format Shape task pane, click **TEXT OPTIONS**, click the **Textbox** icon 📇, click the **Text direction** arrow, and click **Stacked**.

17. **With your teacher's permission**, print the slides.

18. Close the presentation, saving changes, and exit PowerPoint.

Figure 13-2

RGB(148,210,78)
Green

Lesson 13—Apply

In this project, you continue working on the Kelly Greenery presentation. You will adjust shape formats, add text to a shape, and insert a new shape with additional information.

DIRECTIONS

1. Start PowerPoint, if necessary, and open **P13Apply** from the data files for this lesson.

2. Save the presentation as **P13Apply_xx** in the location where your teacher instructs you to store the files for this lesson.

3. Create a text box at the bottom of slide 1 and type your name in it.

4. Turn off display of the gridlines and guides.

5. Remove the fill and the outline from the text box on slide 1.

6. On slide 2, make the following adjustments to the green banner shape:

   a. Drag upward on the adjustment handle near the upper-left corner of the object to make the shape less curvy.

   b. Resize it to be about 3" high and 5" wide and move it to the top of the slide.

   c. Use the Eyedropper to sample a different fill color, either a darker green or one of the other colors from the tulip picture.

   d. Left-align the text in the shape.

7. Boldface the text in the block arrow, change font color to black, and increase the font size as much as possible without having the text set in two columns.

   ✓ *Change Character Spacing to Very Tight to fit text at a larger font size.*

8. Apply a Glow effect to the block arrow. Click **More Glow Colors** on the Glow gallery and use the Eyedropper to sample a glow color from one of the tulip flowers.

9. Type the text **Buy Your Spring Bulbs Soon!** in the orange oval. Increase text size as much as possible while still fitting all words in the shape.

10. Insert a Down Arrow Callout shape above the orange oval and insert the text **On Sale Through October**.

11. Apply a fill color, outline color, effect, and/or style of your choosing, and adjust the font size as necessary. Figure 13-3 shows the completed slide.

12. **With your teacher's permission**, print the presentation.

13. Close the presentation, saving changes, and exit PowerPoint.

Figure 13-3

Lesson 14

Positioning and Grouping Shapes

➤ What You Will Learn

Stacking Objects
Grouping Objects
Combining Shapes to Create a New Shape
Rotating and Flipping Objects
Duplicating Objects
Aligning and Distributing Objects

WORDS TO KNOW

Group
To combine multiple shapes or other objects into a collective unit that can be controlled as a single object.

Rotate
Turn an object on a central axis to a new orientation.

Stack
To overlap objects, and control the order in which overlapping objects appear.

Software Skills   Many of the drawings you create with the Shapes tools in PowerPoint will consist of multiple shapes that overlap each other. When a graphic consists of several pieces, you need to know how to combine and position them to make a cohesive whole.

What You Can Do

Stacking Objects

- As you create objects on a slide, they **stack** from the "back" (the first object created) to the "front" (the last object created). You can think of this process as a series of layers stacked on top of each other with an object on each layer.

- Use the DRAWING TOOLS FORMAT tab's arrangement tools to change an object's stack order:

  - Bring to Front and Send to Back move the object all the way to the top or bottom of the stack, respectively.

  - Bring Forward and Send Backward move an object back or forward one layer at a time.

- To make it easy to select objects for arranging or other manipulation, use the Selection pane. Access it from the DRAWING TOOLS FORMAT tab.

- The Selection pane shows all objects currently displayed on the slide. To select any object, click it in the Selection pane. You can also click on the visibility symbol (the open eye) to hide an object.

  ✓ *You can click on an object name to open the default name for editing and supply your own names for objects. Meaningful names for objects can also help you when you are creating animations for slide objects.*

Try It! — Stacking Objects

1 Start PowerPoint, and open **P14Try** from the data files for this lesson.

2 Save the presentation as **P14Try_xx** in the location where your teacher instructs you to store the files for this lesson.

3 Click any of the shapes, and then click DRAWING TOOLS FORMAT > Selection Pane. The Selection pane opens.

4 In the Selection pane, click the eye symbol 👁 next to Oval 4. The circle disappears and the button changes to a blank. Click the blank button to make the circle reappear.

5 Click the circle to select it. Then hold down `SHIFT` and drag a corner selection handle on the circle to expand it so it is large enough to completely cover the star. Drag it to reposition it so it is directly over the star.

6 With the circle still selected, on the DRAWING TOOLS FORMAT tab, click the arrow to the right of the Send Backward button 🔲 and click Send to Back.

7 Adjust the size and position of the circle so that the tips of the star barely touch the edges of the circle.

8 Click the pentagon, either on the slide or in the Selection pane.

9 Click the arrow to the right of the Bring Forward button 🔲 and click Bring to Front.

10 Position the pentagon on top of the star, at its center.

11 Click DRAWING TOOLS FORMAT > Selection Pane to turn off the Selection pane. The design should look like that shown in the following figure.

12 Save the **P14Try_xx** file, and leave it open to use in the next Try It.

Select any object easily in this pane

Arrange and stack the pieces of the design

Grouping Objects

- You can **group** the objects within a drawing so that they can be treated as a single object. Grouping objects makes them easier to copy, move, or resize.

- You can ungroup objects when you want to work with the objects individually again.

- Some changes can be made to the individual elements of a grouped object without ungrouping it, such as changing the colors.

- To select the objects to be grouped, you can hold down `CTRL` as you click on each one, or you can drag a lasso around all the objects to be included. To lasso a group, drag the mouse pointer to draw an imaginary box around the items.

Try It!   Grouping Objects

1 In the **P14Try_xx** file, drag to lasso all the drawn shapes. Each one appears with its own selection handles.

2 Click DRAWING TOOLS FORMAT > Group ⊞ ▾ > Group. The group now has a single set of selection handles.

3 Hold down SHIFT and drag the bottom-right corner of the shape inward to shrink it in size by 1".

✓ *All shapes are resized together because they are all part of the group.*

4 Click to select the object if it is not already selected.

5 Click DRAWING TOOLS FORMAT > Group ⊞ ▾ > Ungroup. The shapes become ungrouped.

6 Save the **P14Try_xx** file, and leave it open to use in the next Try It.

Combining Shapes to Create a New Shape

■ PowerPoint 2013 lets you combine shapes to create a new shape, in the same way you can merge shapes in sophisticated graphics programs.

■ Merging differs from grouping in that the shapes used to create the combined object are transformed so that they cannot be separated back into their original shapes.

✓ *You can click Undo to reverse the joining process.*

■ Select two or more shapes to merge, and then choose a merge option (see Figure 14-1):

● Union joins all shapes into a single shape, with an outline that surrounds the entire merged shape.

● Combine groups the shapes into a single object. Regions that overlap are removed from the combined shape to create empty spaces.

● Fragment breaks the combined shapes into individual pieces that can be ungrouped and used separately.

● Intersect removes all parts of the shapes except the area where they overlap.

● Subtract removes one shape from the other shape where they overlap.

■ When you merge shapes, it makes a difference to the final result which shape you select first. The first shape you select controls the action. If the shapes are different colors, the combined shape will be the color of the shape you selected first, and in a subtract operation, the second shape you select will be subtracted from the first one.

Figure 14-1

Union   Combine   Fragment   Intersect   Subtract

Try It!   **Combining Shapes to Create a New Shape**

1 In the **P14Try_xx** file, on the HOME tab, click New Slide 📑.

2 On slide 2, click INSERT > Shapes ⬦ and select Heart from the Basic Shapes section.

3 Hold down ⌷SHIFT⌷ and drag to draw a heart about 5" high by 5" wide.

4 On the DRAWING TOOLS FORMAT tab, select a Rectangle shape from the Shapes gallery in the Insert Shapes group, hold down ⌷SHIFT⌷, and draw a square about 5" high. Move the square to overlap the bottom of the heart.

5 Right-click the square, click the Fill 🎨 shortcut button, and select the Gold, Accent 4 fill.

6 With the gold square still selected, hold down ⌷SHIFT⌷ and click the blue heart, and then, in the Insert Shapes group, click Merge Shapes ⊘ > Union. The two shapes are joined, and because the gold shape was selected first, the joined shape is gold.

7 Click Undo ↺, and then, with the shapes still selected, click Merge Shapes ⊘ > Subtract. The heart shape is removed, leaving the square with a chunk out of it that used to be the point of the heart.

8 Click Undo ↺, and then deselect the shapes.

9 Select the blue heart, then the gold square, and click Merge Shapes ⊘ > Fragment. Because you clicked the blue heart first, the new shape is blue.

10 Click outside the shape to deselect it, then click on the top of the heart and press ⬆ five times to nudge this part of the shape away from the other parts.

11 Nudge the square bottom downward to move it away from the point of the heart.

12 Save the **P14Try_xx** file, and leave it open to use in the next Try It.

Fragment creates separate objects from combined shapes

Rotating and Flipping Objects

■ When you **rotate** an object, you turn it on a central axis to a new orientation. You can rotate any PowerPoint object: shapes, pictures, text boxes, and placeholders.

■ Drag a selected object's rotation handle, at the top center of the object, to rotate the object.

   ✓ *Hold down* ⌷SHIFT⌷ *while dragging to rotate in 15 degree increments.*

■ You can also use a preset rotation such as Rotate Right 90° or Rotate Left 90° from the Rotate menu. Or click More Rotation Options to open the Format Shape task pane, where you can specify an exact degree of rotation.

■ If a shape or other object is not facing the way you want it to, you can use the flip options on the Rotate menu.

■ Flip Vertical switches the object from top to bottom, and Flip Horizontal switches the object from left to right.

Try It!   **Rotating and Flipping Objects**

① In the **P14Try_xx** file, display slide 1.

② Click the star graphic to select it and display the rotation handle 🔄.

③ Drag the rotation handle to the right so that the top star point is pointing to about 2 o'clock on the blue oval.

④ On the DRAWING TOOLS FORMAT tab, click the Rotate ◭▾ drop-down arrow, and then click Rotate Left 90°.

⑤ Click the Rotate ◭▾ drop-down arrow, and then click More Rotation Options to display the Format Shape task pane.

⑥ In the Rotation box, select the current value and type **0**.

⑦ Select the polygon, click the Rotate ◭▾ drop-down arrow, and then click Flip Vertical.

⑧ Hold down [SHIFT] and drag the polygon's rotation handle to the left until it has returned to its original orientation. The Rotation box in the Format Shape task pane should read 180°. Close the Format Shape task pane.

⑨ Select all three objects on slide 1, click DRAWING TOOLS FORMAT > Group ▦▾ , and click Regroup.

⑩ Save the **P14Try_xx** file, and leave it open to use in the next Try It.

Duplicating Objects

■ After drawing an object, you may want to duplicate it rather than drawing additional objects from scratch. For example, if you need three circles that are all exactly the same size, duplicating the first one twice ensures that they are identical.

■ You can duplicate either with drag-and-drop, or with copy-and-paste.

Try It!   **Duplicating Objects**

① In the **P14Try_xx** file, select the object on slide 1, and on the DRAWING TOOLS FORMAT tab, enter a Height and Width of 2" each.

  ✓ *This makes the shape small enough that multiple copies of it will fit on the slide.*

② Select the object and press [CTRL] + [C]. It is copied to the Clipboard.

③ Press [CTRL] + [V]. A copy is pasted on the slide.

④ Drag the copy to move it so it does not overlap the original.

⑤ Click the original object.

⑥ Hold down the [CTRL] key and drag the original to a different spot on the slide. It is copied there.

  ✓ *Now you have three copies of the shape, which you will use in the next Try It.*

⑦ Save the **P14Try_xx** file, and leave it open to use in the next Try It.

Aligning and Distributing Objects

- Sometimes it is important that the objects on a slide be precisely aligned, either with one another or with the slide itself.

- PowerPoint has several commands to help you accomplish this. You can use either commands from the DRAWING TOOLS FORMAT tab or use PowerPoint's new Smart Guides.

- The Align command aligns objects by their top, middle, bottom, right side, left side, or center. It can also be used to place one or more objects in relation to the slide itself. In Figure 14-2, the shapes are middle-aligned.

- On the Align button's menu is an Align to Slide command that is a toggle. When it is turned on, a check mark appears by it.

- When this command is on, the Align and Distribute commands apply to the object in relation to the slide, as well as in relation to the other selected objects.

- When this command is on, you can use Align or Distribute on a single object. When this command is off, the minimum number of selected objects to use Align is 2, and the minimum to use Distribute is 3.

- You can also use an Align menu command to distribute objects. Distributing equalizes space between objects. You can distribute objects either horizontally or vertically.

- PowerPoint 2013's new Smart Guides help you align and distribute objects by displaying onscreen guides that show you how objects are positioned relative to each other. (See Figure 14-2.)

- Smart Guides display as red dashed lines that appear when objects are moved near each other. A Smart Guide might display, for example, when the top of one object aligns with the top or bottom of another object, when objects align at their centers or middles, or when two objects align at their right or left sides.

- Smart Guides can also help you space objects evenly just by dragging. When you see the horizontal or vertical arrows between pairs of Smart Guides, the space between the objects is equal.

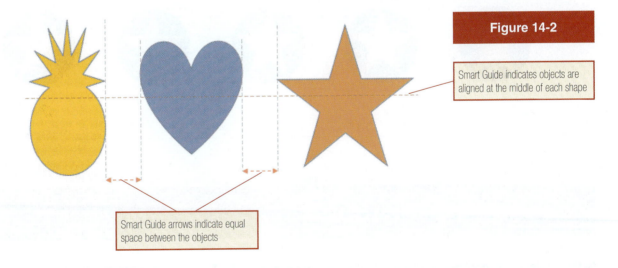

Figure 14-2

Smart Guide indicates objects are aligned at the middle of each shape

Smart Guide arrows indicate equal space between the objects

Try It! **Aligning and Distributing Objects**

1 In the **P14Try_xx** file, click the first object, click Align [icon], and then click Align Middle. The object moves to the vertical middle of the slide.

2 Drag the second object until the Smart Guides indicate that the bottom of this object aligns with the top of the first object.

3 Click the first object, hold down [SHIFT] and click the third object, and then click Align [icon] > Align Bottom. Click anywhere on the slide to deselect both objects.

4 Click the third object, hold down [CTRL], and drag a copy of the object to the right, using the Smart Guides to make sure the new object is aligned top and bottom with the third object.

5 Select all four objects, and then click Align [icon] > Distribute Horizontally.

6 Deselect all objects. Then, click the first object, hold down [CTRL], and drag a copy to the left, keeping it aligned at the bottom with the other objects.

7 After you drop the copy, drag it horizontally back and forth until you see the Smart Guide arrows that show the space between all objects is the same.

✓ *If you do not have room on the slide to distribute all of the objects, move them closer together using the Smart Guides to make sure the space stays the same between all objects.*

8 Close the **P14Try_xx** file, saving changes, and exit PowerPoint.

Smart Guides show that all objects are equally spaced

Lesson 14—Practice

In this project, you continue working with the presentation for Kelly Greenery. You practice working with shapes and objects by stacking, grouping, rotating, duplicating, aligning, and distributing. You also begin work on a combined shape.

DIRECTIONS

1. Start PowerPoint, if necessary, and open **P14Practice** from the data files for this lesson.

2. Save the presentation as **P14Practice_xx** in the location where your teacher instructs you to store the files for this lesson.

3. On slide 1, insert a text box and type your first and last name.

4. With slide 1 displayed, select the light-brown rectangle and then, on the DRAWING TOOLS FORMAT tab, click **Selection Pane** [icon] to display the Selection pane.

5. Click the **Send Backward** arrow ▾ in the Selection pane until the rectangle is behind the title text.

6. In the Selection pane, click **Picture 5** and click the **Send Backward** arrow ▾ in the Selection pane until the leaf is behind the title text.

7. In the Selection pane, click **Picture 13** and click the **Bring Forward** arrow ▲ in the Selection pane until the leaf is in front of the light brown rectangle and behind the title text.

8. Rotate the light brown leaf in the lower-left corner of the slide by dragging its rotation handle to give it a different orientation.

9. Select the light orange leaf near the upper-left corner of the light-brown rectangle and then click **PICTURE TOOLS FORMAT** > **Rotate** ⟁ ▾ > **Flip Vertical**. Close the Selection pane.

10. Display slide 3. Select the two clip art illustrations in the lower-left corner of the slide, and then click **PICTURE TOOLS FORMAT** > **Group** 〖▾ > **Group**.

11. With the group still selected, press CTRL + C, and then press CTRL + V four times to create four copies of the group.

12. Drag the last copied group to the right side of the slide, using the Smart Guides to make sure it is aligned at top and bottom with the original group.

13. Drag the other three groups to space them across the bottom of the slide, as shown in Figure 14-3.

14. Select all five objects, click **Align** ⯆ ▾ > **Align Bottom**, and then click **Align** ⯆ ▾ > **Distribute Horizontally**.

15. Click the group of two light gray triangles and drag them over the top of the pink oval, so that the group aligns with the oval at the top and the center.

16. With the group selected, click **DRAWING TOOLS FORMAT** > **Group** 〖▾ > **Ungroup**.

17. Select the pink oval and then select each gray triangle.

18. Click **DRAWING TOOLS FORMAT** > **Merge Shapes** ⦸ > **Fragment**. The three shapes are broken into components.

19. Click outside the pink oval to deselect the shapes, click each of the four pieces that originally made up the triangles, and press DEL to delete these partial shapes. You should be left with the pink oval that now has a jagged top to represent a tulip flower, as shown in Figure 14-3.

20. **With your teacher's permission**, print slides 1 and 3.

21. Close the presentation, saving changes, and exit PowerPoint.

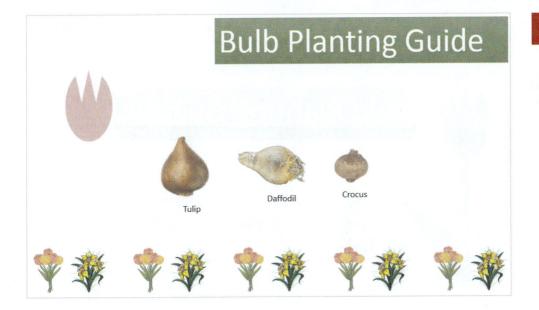

Bulk Planting Guide

Tulip

Daffodil

Crocus

Figure 14-3

Lesson 14—Apply

In this project, you complete the Kelly Greenery presentation by combining shapes to create a stylized tulip, and further modifying and adjusting shapes and objects in the presentation.

DIRECTIONS

1. Start PowerPoint, if necessary, and open **P14Apply** from the data files for this lesson.

2. Save the presentation as **P14Apply_xx** in the location where your teacher instructs you to store the files for this lesson.

3. On slide 1, insert a text box and type your first and last name.

4. Display slide 3. Select the green jagged-topped tulip flower and the vertical blue stem and align them at the center.

5. Select the blue tulip leaf shape and rotate it about half an inch to the right, and then move it until the bottom tip of the leaf overlaps the bottom of the stem.

6. Select the flower, the stem, and then the leaf in that order and merge the shapes, using the Union option.

7. With the combined shape selected, apply the Perspective Diagonal Upper Right shadow shape effect.

8. Drag the title placeholder near the tulip shape and use the Smart Guide to align the placeholder with the top of the shape. Then use Align Center to center the placeholder on the slide.

9. With the placeholder still selected, copy and then paste the placeholder shape. Remove the text from the pasted shape.

10. Use the Eyedropper to fill the blank shape with the same green as the combined tulip shape, and then send the blank shape behind the original placeholder to create a shadow effect.

11. Flip the daffodil bulb picture horizontally, and then middle align the three bulbs.

12. Use the Smart Guides to center align each bulb's label with the bulb picture, and then align the labels at the bottom.

13. Group each bulb with its label, and then distribute the groups horizontally. Your finished slide should look similar to Figure 14-4.

14. **With your teacher's permission**, print slides 1 and 3.

15. Close the presentation, saving changes, and exit PowerPoint.

Figure 14-4

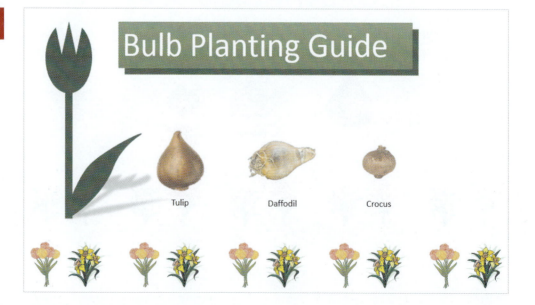

Lesson 15

Creating WordArt

➤ What You Will Learn

Understanding WordArt
Applying WordArt Styles to Existing Text
Inserting and Formatting WordArt

Software Skills WordArt enables you to apply special effects to text to make it appear more graphical. Using WordArt you can create logos and decorative text without a stand-alone graphics program.

WORDS TO KNOW

WordArt
Text that is formatted with graphical effects.

What You Can Do

Understanding WordArt

- Use **WordArt** to create a graphic from text. WordArt is useful whenever you want text to be both readable and decorative.
- WordArt is similar to drawn shapes in the ways you can format it. For example, you can apply a fill, an outline, and various formatting effects and styles to it. This formatting is the same as it is with shapes, which you learned about in the previous two lessons.
- The Transform command is unique to WordArt. It modifies the shape of the text to make it conform to a path. Figure 15-1 shows two Transform options applied to WordArt objects.

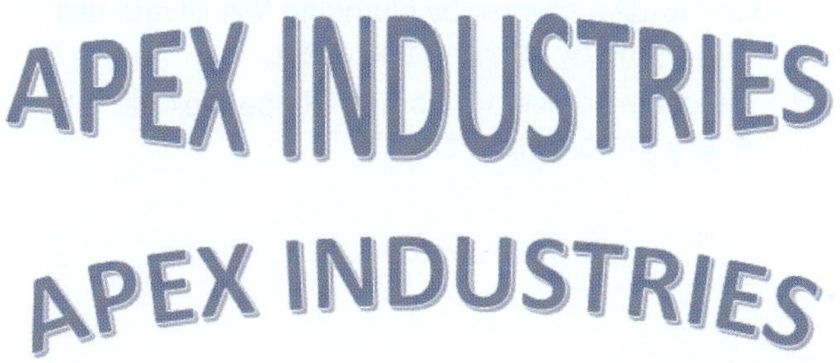
APEX INDUSTRIES
APEX INDUSTRIES

Figure 15-1

Applying WordArt Styles to Existing Text

■ Any text can be easily turned into WordArt. Select any existing text, and then on the DRAWING TOOLS FORMAT tab, use the WordArt Styles group's commands and lists to select the effects that you want.

<table>
<tr><td>**Try It!**</td><td colspan="2">**Applying WordArt Styles to Existing Text**</td></tr>
</table>

1 Start a new blank presentation, and save it as **P15Try_xx** in the location where your teacher instructs you to store the files for this lesson.

2 Click HOME > Layout 🔲 > Blank to change to a blank layout.

3 Click INSERT > Text Box 🅰.

4 Click on the slide, and type **Lowe Insurance**.

5 Press CTRL + A to select all the text.

6 Click the DRAWING TOOLS FORMAT tab.

7 Click the More button ▾ in the WordArt Styles group to open the WordArt Styles gallery.

8 Click the second style from the left in the second row from the top, Gradient Fill - Blue, Accent 1, Reflection.

9 Click the text box containing the WordArt.

10 Click the More button ▾ in the WordArt Styles group to open the WordArt Styles gallery.

11 Click Clear WordArt.

12 Save the **P15Try_xx** file, and leave it open to use in the next Try It.

Click this style   **Select a WordArt style**

Inserting and Formatting WordArt

■ You can also use the WordArt command to create a new WordArt object and then type the desired text in the object.

■ Styles and colors available in the WordArt gallery depend on the current theme. If you change the theme after inserting WordArt, the colors and formatting will change to reflect the styles for the new theme.

■ Use the tools in the WordArt Styles group to format the WordArt graphic by changing text fill and text outline and by applying text effects.

■ You can also use the Format Shape task pane to modify WordArt formats.

Try It!   **Inserting WordArt**

1 In the **P15Try_xx** file, click INSERT > WordArt ⓐ. A palette of WordArt samples appears.

  ✓ *These samples are the same as the ones that appeared in the WordArt Styles list you saw in the preceding steps.*

2 Click the third sample in the fourth row.

  ✓ *A WordArt object appears, with generic text. The text is highlighted, so if you type something, it will be replaced.*

3 Type **Apex Industries**. Your text replaces the generic text.

4 Save the **P15Try_xx** file, and leave it open to use in the next Try It.

Try It!   **Formatting WordArt**

1 In the **P15Try_xx** file, with the WordArt object selected, click DRAWING TOOLS FORMAT > Text Effects ⓐ > Transform. A gallery of transformation options appears.

2 In the Warp section, click the first sample in the second row (Chevron Up).

3 Drag the pink diamond at the left edge of the WordArt down as far as it will go.

  ✓ *The WordArt shape is further transformed.*

4 With the insertion point in the WordArt, press CTRL + A to select all the text.

  ✓ *If you do not select all the text, the formatting applies only to the word where the insertion point was.*

5 Click DRAWING TOOLS FORMAT > Text Fill ⓐ. A palette of colors appears.

6 Click the Light Blue square in the Standard Colors section.

7 Click DRAWING TOOLS FORMAT > Text Outline ⓐ. A palette of colors appears.

8 Click the Blue square in the Standard Colors section.

9 Click DRAWING TOOLS FORMAT > Text Outline ⓐ.

10 Point to the Weight command. A submenu appears.

11 Click the solid 1½ point line.

12 Right-click the text and click Format Text Effects to open the Format Shape task pane with text options selected.

13 Click the SHADOW heading to expand it.

14 Click the Presets button, and then click the first shadow in the Perspective section.

15 Click DRAWING TOOLS FORMAT > Text Effects ⓐ > Bevel.

16 Click the fourth sample in the third row of the Bevel section (Art Deco).

17 In the Format Shape task pane, click 3-D ROTATION, if necessary, to expand the options.

18 Click the Presets button, and then click the fourth sample in the second row of the Parallel section (Off Axis 2 Left). Close the Format Shape task pane.

19 Click away from the WordArt object to deselect it. It should look like the following figure.

20 Close the **P15Try_xx** file, saving changes, and exit PowerPoint.

The transformed WordArt object

The finished WordArt object

Lesson 15—Practice

In this project, you use WordArt to create a simple logo for Kelly Greenery.

DIRECTIONS

1. Start PowerPoint, if necessary, and open **P15Practice** from the data files for this lesson.

2. Save the presentation as **P15Practice_xx** in the location where your teacher instructs you to store the files for this lesson.

3. Click **INSERT** > **Text Box** . Click at the bottom of the slide and type your full name.

4. Click **INSERT** > **WordArt** and click the third sample in the second row.

5. Type **Kelly Greenery**.

6. Drag the WordArt so that the last letter overlaps the trunk of the tree graphic.

7. Press CTRL + A to select all the text.

8. Click **DRAWING TOOLS FORMAT** > **Text Fill** and click the Light Green square in the Standard Colors section.

9. Click **DRAWING TOOLS FORMAT** > **Text Outline** and click **No Outline**.

10. Click **DRAWING TOOLS FORMAT** > **Text Effects** > **Transform** and click the first sample in the fifth row of the Warp section (Wave 1).

11. Click the WordArt, hold down CTRL , and click the clip art.

12. Click **DRAWING TOOLS FORMAT** > **Group** > **Group**.Your slide should look like Figure 15-2.

13. **With your teacher's permission**, click **FILE** > **Print**. Select **Print All Slides**, and then click **Print** to print the presentation.

14. Close the presentation, saving changes, and exit PowerPoint.

Figure 15-2

Lesson 15—Apply

In this project, you use WordArt to create a different logo for Kelly Greenery.

DIRECTIONS

1. Start PowerPoint, if necessary, and open **P15Apply** from the data files for this lesson.

2. Save the presentation as **P15Apply_xx** in the location where your teacher instructs you to store the files for this lesson.

3. Insert a text box at the bottom of the slide, and type your full name in it.

4. Apply the Retrospect theme with the green variant.

5. Insert WordArt that uses the fourth sample in the third row of the WordArt gallery.

6. Replace the placeholder text with **Kelly Greenery**.

7. Move the WordArt graphic above the oval picture, using Smart Guides to center the WordArt with the picture and align the bottom of the WordArt with the top of the picture.

8. Apply the **Arch Up** transformation from the Follow Path section of the **Text Effects** Ⓐ > **Transform** menu.

9. Use the Text Fill Eyedropper to pick up a green from the grass.

10. Use the Text Outline Eyedropper to pick up a yellow color from the flowers in the picture.

11. With the insertion point in the WordArt text, right-click and then click Format Text Effects. Expand the SHADOW effects if necessary, click the Color button, and click Lime, Accent 1 from the theme colors to change the shadow color. Close the Format Shape task pane.

12. Change the font size of the WordArt text to **66**.

13. Increase the height of the WordArt frame to **3"** and the width to **5.5"** and then position the WordArt so it is arched over the clip art.

14. **With your teacher's permission**, print one copy of the slide. The finished logo is shown in Figure 15-3.

15. Close the presentation, saving changes, and exit PowerPoint.

Figure 15-3

Lesson 16

Creating SmartArt Diagrams

➤ What You Will Learn

Creating a SmartArt Diagram
Adding, Removing, and Resizing Shapes in a Diagram
Reordering Diagram Content
Changing the Diagram Type
Changing the Color and Style of a Diagram
Creating Picture-Based SmartArt

WORDS TO KNOW

SmartArt
Professionally designed graphics that organize and display information in various graphic types such as lists, processes, or hierarchical displays.

SmartArt style
The shading and texture effects on the shapes used in the diagram.

Software Skills   SmartArt enables you to combine graphics with text to present information in a much more interesting and attractive layout than a plain bulleted list provides.

What You Can Do

Creating a SmartArt Diagram

■   **SmartArt** is a tool that enables you to place text in graphical containers that make it more interesting to read. These container graphics are specially designed to arrange items in conceptually relevant ways, such as in an organization chart, cycle diagram, or pyramid.

■   You can insert a SmartArt graphic in a content slide layout, or you can add it without a placeholder using the SmartArt button on the INSERT tab. You can also, if desired, convert a list to a SmartArt graphic.

■   Each SmartArt diagram has a fly-out text pane where you can edit its content. Click the arrow button to the left of the diagram to open the text pane. You can also enter text by typing directly in the shapes. (See Figure 16-1 on the next page.) Click in a shape to position the insertion point, and then type the desired text. Move to the next text placeholder by clicking the mouse on the shape.

■   If you already have the text you need for the SmartArt diagram in another form, such as in a Word document, you can copy the text and paste it directly in a SmartArt shape.

■   The SmartArt layout determines how text appears and aligns in the shapes. You can, if desired, adjust alignment as you would any text.

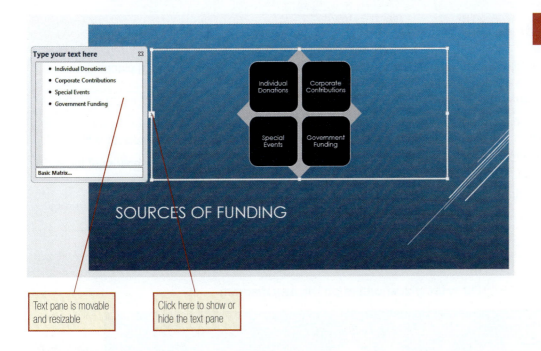

Figure 16-1

Text pane is movable and resizable

Click here to show or hide the text pane

Try It!   Converting a List to SmartArt

1 Start PowerPoint, and open **P16TryA** from the data files for this lesson.

2 Save the presentation as **P16TryA_xx** in the location where your teacher instructs you to store the files for this lesson.

3 Display slide 6. Click in the numbered list and press `CTRL` + `A` to select all the text.

4 Right-click the selected list and click Convert to SmartArt. A palette of samples appears.

5 Point to the Basic Timeline design (second design in the fourth row). The design is previewed behind the list.

6 Click the Continuous Block Process design (first design in the fourth row). The design is applied to the list.

7 Display slide 9. Click in the content area and press `CTRL` + `A` to select all the text.

8 Right-click the selected text and click Convert to SmartArt.

9 Click the Horizontal Bulleted List (the first sample in the second row). The design is applied to the list.

✓ *Because this slide contained a multilevel bulleted list, the subordinate levels appear as bulleted lists within the main shapes.*

10 Save the **P16TryA_xx** file, and leave it open to use in the next Try It.

Try It!   Inserting a New SmartArt Object

1 In the **P16TryA_xx** file, in the Thumbnail pane, click between slides 2 and 3 and press ENTER , inserting a new blank slide.

2 In the content area on the slide, click the Insert SmartArt Graphic icon. The Choose a SmartArt Graphic dialog box opens.

3 Click Matrix, and then click the Basic Matrix design (the first design).

4 Click OK. An empty diagram appears.

5 In the upper-left box, replace the [Text] placeholder with **Individual Donations**.

6 Replace the other three [Text] placeholders (going clockwise) with **Corporate Contributions**, **Government Funding**, and **Special Events**.

✓ *Notice that the text resizes automatically to fit.*

7 In the title placeholder at the bottom of the slide, type **SOURCES OF FUNDING**.

8 Save the **P16TryA_xx** file, and leave it open to use in the next Try It.

Fill in the placeholders on the new diagram

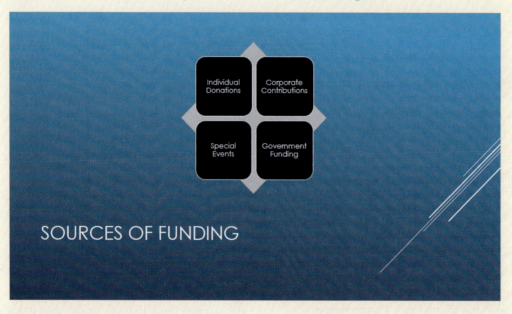

Adding, Removing, and Resizing Shapes in a Diagram

■ Each diagram begins with a default number of shapes, but you can add or remove them as needed. Use the commands on the SMARTART TOOLS DESIGN tab.

✓ *There are some exceptions; some diagram types require a certain number of shapes in them. For such diagrams the Add Shape command is unavailable.*

■ You can also resize each shape individually. Drag its selection handles to do so, just as you would any drawn shape. Instead of dragging, you can also use the Smaller or Larger buttons on the SMARTART TOOLS FORMAT tab.

Try It!   **Adding, Removing, and Resizing Shapes in a Diagram**

---

1 In the **P16TryA_xx** file, on slide 7, select the last shape ("Follow up to assess progress").

2 Press DEL. The shape is removed and the other shapes resize to fill the space.

3 With the rightmost shape selected on the diagram on slide 7, click SMARTART TOOLS DESIGN > Add Shape ⬚. A new shape appears.

> ✓ *The Add Shape button has a down arrow you can click to choose where the new shape will be added, but you don't need it in these steps because you want the new shape in the default position, to the right of the selected shape.*

4 Click in the new shape and type the text that appeared in the deleted shape before ("Follow up to assess progress").

5 On slide 7, click the first rounded rectangle in the diagram to select it.

6 Hold down CTRL and click on each of the other rounded rectangles.

7 Position the mouse pointer on a top selection handle on any of the selected shapes and drag upward 0.5". The height of each of the rectangles changes equally.

8 Click SMARTART TOOLS FORMAT > Smaller ⬚. Then, click it again to make the shapes one more step smaller.

9 Save the **P16TryA_xx** file, and leave it open to use in the next Try It.

Reordering Diagram Content

- Even though each shape in a SmartArt diagram is individually movable, you should not drag shapes to reorder them in a SmartArt diagram, because it interrupts the automatic flow of the layout. Instead, you should use the reordering commands on the SMARTART TOOLS DESIGN tab.

- The Promote and Demote commands change the level of the text within the diagram hierarchy. This is like promoting and demoting list levels on a text-based layout.

Try It!   **Reordering Diagram Content**

---

1 In the **P16TryA_xx** file, on slide 3, click the top left rounded rectangle to select it.

2 Click SMARTART TOOLS DESIGN > Move Down ⬇. The content of that shape is moved one position in the layout.

> ✓ *Notice that it moved to the right, and not literally down. In this case, down means to move it down in the flow one position, regardless of the direction of the flow. If the diagram's flow was top-to-bottom, moving "down" might even be up in the diagram.*

3 On slide 10, click in the *Get friends involved* bullet point in the second column.

4 Click SMARTART TOOLS DESIGN > Promote ⬅. That bullet point becomes a new shape.

5 Click SMARTART TOOLS DESIGN > Demote ➡. The text goes back to being a bullet point in the second shape.

6 Click SMARTART TOOLS DESIGN > Right to Left ⇄. The diagram changes its flow direction, so that the right and left columns switch places.

7 Save the **P16TryA_xx** file, and leave it open to use in the next Try It.

Changing the Diagram Type

- There are many diagram types to choose from. If you don't like the diagram type you started with, you can easily switch to another.

- The diagram types are arranged in categories, but there is some overlap; some designs appear in more than one category.

- On the SMARTART TOOLS DESIGN tab, you can open a gallery of layouts and choose the one you want to apply to the diagram.

Try It!　　**Changing the Diagram Type**

1. In the **P16TryA_xx** file, click the SmartArt diagram on slide 10, if necessary.

2. On the SMARTART TOOLS DESIGN tab, in the Layouts group, click the More button ⊽ to open the gallery of design samples.

3. Point at several different samples, and see previews of them on the slide, behind the open menu.

4. Click the Vertical Box List (last sample in the first row). The diagram changes to that layout.

5. Save the **P16TryA_xx** file, and leave it open to use in the next Try It.

Changing the Color and Style of a Diagram

- A SmartArt diagram's colors are determined by the color theme in use in the presentation. You can choose different combinations of those theme colors.

- **SmartArt style** refers to the shading and texture effects on the shapes used in the diagram. Some of the styles make the shapes look raised or shiny, for example.

Try It!　　**Changing the Color and Style of a Diagram**

1. In the **P16TryA_xx** file, click the SmartArt diagram on slide 10, if necessary.

2. On the SMARTART TOOLS DESIGN tab, click the More button ⊽ in the SmartArt Styles group to open a gallery of style choices.

3. Click Polished (the first sample in the first row of the 3D section). It is applied to the diagram.

4. On slide 10, with the diagram still selected, click SMARTART TOOLS DESIGN > Change Colors ⋮⋮. A palette of color presets appears.

5. Point to several of the presets, and see them previewed on the slide behind the open menu.

6. Click the fourth sample in the Colorful section. It is applied to the diagram.

   ✓ *The Colorful section's presets use a different color from the theme for each of the major shapes. Most of the other preset types stick to a single color.*

7. Save the **P16TryA_xx** file, and leave it open to use in the next Try It.

Creating Picture-Based SmartArt

- Some of the SmartArt layouts include picture placeholders. These are useful for providing small pieces of artwork, either to illustrate points being made in the text or as decoration.

- The main difference with this type of layout is that you have an extra step after inserting the SmartArt and typing the text—you must click each picture placeholder and select a picture to insert into it.

- In PowerPoint 2013, you can use the Picture Layout command on the PICTURE TOOLS FORMAT tab to convert any picture to a SmartArt graphic.

Try It! **Creating Picture-Based SmartArt**

1 In the **P16TryA_xx** file, on slide 5, select the picture and press DEL to remove the picture.

2 Select the bulleted list.

3 Right-click the bulleted list and click Convert to SmartArt > More SmartArt Graphics. The Choose a SmartArt Graphic dialog box opens.

4 Click the Picture category.

5 Click Picture Caption List (the third sample in the first row).

6 Click OK.

7 On the SmartArt diagram, double-click the Insert Picture from File icon in the leftmost picture placeholder. The Insert Pictures dialog box opens.

8 Click Browse and then navigate to the folder containing the files for this lesson.

9 Click **P16TryB_picture.jpg** and click Insert. The picture appears in the placeholder.

10 Using this same process, insert **P16TryC_picture.jpg** and **P16TryD_picture.jpg** in the other two placeholders on the slide.

11 Save the **P16TryA_xx** file, and leave it open to use in the next Try It.

Try It! **Creating SmartArt from a Picture**

1 In the **P16TryA_xx** file, display slide 11 and click the picture to select it.

2 Click the PICTURE TOOLS FORMAT tab, and then, in the Picture Styles group, click the Picture Layout button.

3 Click the Snapshot Picture List layout (the second from the right in the first row).

4 On the SMARTART TOOLS DESIGN tab, in the Create Graphic group, click the Text Pane button to display the Text pane.

5 Type **You Can Make a Difference**, and then press ENTER.

6 Click the Demote button →, and then type the following entries, pressing ENTER after the first two items:
People need help
Organizations need volunteers
Sign up today!

7 Close the Text pane.

8 On the SMARTART TOOLS FORMAT tab, click the Size button, click in the Height box and type **4.8"**; click in the Width box and type **9.5"**.

9 Close the **P16TryA_xx** file, saving changes, and exit PowerPoint.

Picture used to create a SmartArt graphic

Lesson 16—Practice

In the Wynnedale Medical Center presentation, most of the information is presented in bulleted lists. In this project, you will convert two of those lists to SmartArt for a more interesting and graphical presentation.

DIRECTIONS

1. Start PowerPoint, if necessary, and open **P16Practice** from the data files for this lesson.
2. Save the presentation as **P16Practice_xx** in the location where your teacher instructs you to store the files for this lesson.
3. Display slide 1, and click **INSERT** > **Text Box** 🗛. Click at the top of the slide and type your full name.
4. On slide 4, click in the content area and press CTRL + A to select all.
5. Right-click the selection and point to **Convert to SmartArt**.
6. Click **More SmartArt Graphics**, and in the Choose a SmartArt Graphic dialog box, click the **Relationship** category.
7. Click the **Opposing Ideas** diagram and click **OK**.
8. On the SMARTART TOOLS DESIGN tab, click the **More** button in the SmartArt Styles group to open the SmartArt Styles gallery.

9. Click **Intense Effect** (the last sample in the Best Match for Document section).
10. Display slide 6, right-click in the list, and point to **Convert to SmartArt**.
11. Click **More SmartArt Graphics**, and then click the **Picture** category.
12. Click the **Vertical Picture List** diagram and then click **OK**.
13. Click in each of the picture placeholders and insert clip art pictures that relate to money.
14. On the SMARTART TOOLS DESIGN tab, click the **Change Colors** button ⁙, and select **Colorful Range - Accent Colors 3 to 4**. Then apply the **Intense Effect** SmartArt Style.
15. Preview the presentation to see the new diagrams in place.
16. **With your teacher's permission**, print one copy of the presentation as handouts, 6 slides per page.
17. Close the presentation, saving changes, and exit PowerPoint.

Lesson 16—Apply

In this project, you continue to work with the Wynnedale presentation. You convert several more lists to SmartArt graphics and then format them to add eye-catching visual interest.

DIRECTIONS

1. Start PowerPoint, if necessary, and open **P16Apply** from the data files for this lesson.
2. Save the presentation as **P16Apply_xx** in the location where your teacher instructs you to store the files for this lesson.
3. Place a text box containing your full name at the top of slide 1.

4. On slide 4, convert the bulleted list to the Vertical Block List SmartArt design.
   - ✓ *You can determine a sample's name by hovering the mouse over it.*
5. Change the SmartArt Style to **Intense Effect**.
6. Change the colors to the first sample in the Colorful section of the color list. Figure 16-2 on the next page shows the finished slide.

7. On slide 5, change the colors for the SmartArt to the **Colored Fill** colors in the Accent 3 section of the color list.

8. On slide 9, convert the numbered list to the **Staggered Process** SmartArt.

   ✓ *You will need to open the Choose a SmartArt Graphic dialog box to find this design. After right-clicking the list, choose More SmartArt Graphics, and then look in the Process category.*

9. Change the colors for the diagram to the third sample in the Colorful section of the color list.

10. Change the SmartArt Style to **Polished** (the first sample in the 3D section of the SmartArt Styles gallery). Figure 16-3 shows the finished slide.

11. Preview the presentation, noticing how the SmartArt diagrams add more visual interest to the slides.

12. **With your teacher's permission**, print one copy of the presentation as handouts, 6 slides per page.

13. Close the presentation, saving changes, and exit PowerPoint.

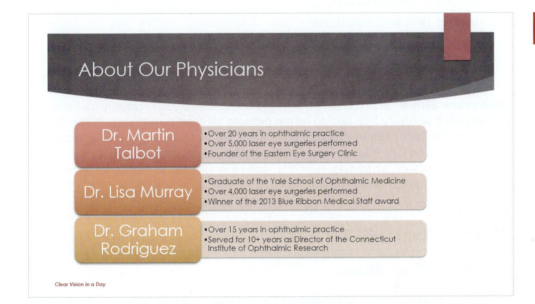

Figure 16-2

Figure 16-3

Lesson 17

Creating a Photo Album

➤ What You Will Learn

Creating a Photo Album
Editing a Photo Album
Adding Text and Captions
Compressing Pictures

WORDS TO KNOW

Photo album
A special type of presentation in which the main point is to display photos.

Resolution
The number of dots or pixels per linear unit of output. For example, a computer monitor's resolution is usually 72 pixels per inch.

Software Skills   A photo album presentation enables you to display multiple photographs with very little text, to let the pictures tell their own stories. PowerPoint has a special Photo Album feature that makes it easy to create and modify photo albums in PowerPoint. You can arrange the photos in a number of layouts and apply enhancements such as frames, captions, and other effects. To reduce the size of a presentation, you can also compress the pictures.

What You Can Do

Creating a Photo Album

- A **photo album** presentation doesn't have placeholders for bulleted lists or other text; it is designed to efficiently display and organize photos.

- Use the Photo Album dialog box to import and arrange the pictures for the photo album.

- The Photo Album dialog box is where you rearrange pictures in the album and select settings for the way the pictures will display.

- Selected picture file names display in the Pictures in album list in the center of the dialog box. The currently selected picture displays in the Preview area.

- Before you create the album, you can correct contrast and brightness and rotate images to change their orientation.

- You can also choose how to arrange pictures on your slides and apply frame styles.

Try It! — Creating a Photo Album

1. Start PowerPoint.

2. Click INSERT > Photo Album. The Photo Album dialog box opens.

3. Click the File/Disk button. The Insert New Pictures dialog box opens.

4. Navigate to the location where data files for this lesson are stored and click **P17TryA_picture.jpg**.

5. Hold down the CTRL key and click **P17TryB_picture**, **P17TryC_picture**, **P17TryD_picture**, and **P17TryE_picture**.

6. Click Insert. The file names appear on the Pictures in album list.

7. Click the check box for **P17TryB_picture** on the list, and then click the Decrease Brightness button.

8. Open the Picture layout drop-down list and click 2 pictures.

9. Open the Frame shape drop-down list and click Rounded Rectangle.

10. Click Create. The photo album is created in a new presentation file.

11. Save the presentation as **P17Try_xx** in the location where your teacher instructs you to store the files for this lesson, and leave it open to use in the next Try It.

Editing a Photo Album

- You can edit an existing photo album by displaying it in Normal view and then clicking the down arrow on the Photo Album button. Choosing Edit Photo Album opens the Photo Album dialog box.

- You can adjust the order of pictures, add a picture, or remove a selected picture.

- You can also change the appearance of your album by changing the theme and variant to provide a different background for the pictures.

- After you make changes, click the Update button to apply your changes to the album.

Try It! — Editing a Photo Album

1. In the **P17Try_xx** file, click INSERT > Photo Album down arrow.

2. Click Edit Photo Album.

3. Click the check box for the **P17TryE_picture** in the Pictures in album list.

4. Click the Move Up button four times to move it to the top of the list.

5. Clear the check mark from **P17TryE_picture**.

6. Click the check box for **P17TryA_picture** on the list, and click Remove to remove the item from the album.

7. Click the Frame shape down arrow and click Center Shadow Rectangle from the list.

8. Click the Browse button to the right of the Theme box. The Choose Theme dialog box displays.

9. Click Retrospect and click Select.

10. In the Edit Photo Album dialog box, click Update.

11. Save the **P17Try_xx** file, and leave it open to use in the next Try It.

(continued)

Try It!   Editing a Photo Album *(continued)*

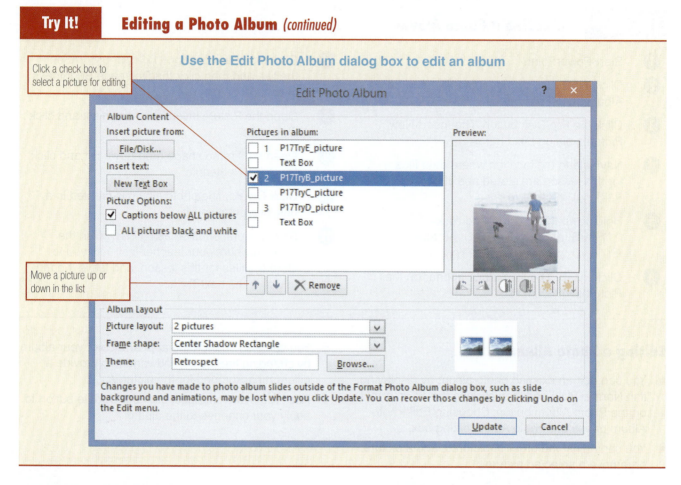

Use the Edit Photo Album dialog box to edit an album

Click a check box to select a picture for editing

Move a picture up or down in the list

Adding Text and Captions

- A PowerPoint photo album is just like a physical photo album in that it is designed primarily to showcase images, but you also can add text in the form of captions or text boxes.

- The Picture Options check boxes in the Photo Album dialog box allow you to add a caption to each picture or transform all pictures to black and white.

- By default, PowerPoint uses a picture's file name as its caption, but you can replace these captions with more descriptive ones on the slides.

- You can choose to add a text box to the list of pictures. Text boxes display according to the current picture layout, at the same size as the pictures.

- PowerPoint might insert a text box placeholder for you, if you choose a layout that requires more images on a slide than you've included in your album. You can remove this text box placeholder if you don't need it, just as you would remove any picture.

Try It!   Adding Text and Captions

1 In the **P17Try_xx** file, click the INSERT > Photo Album ▣ down arrow, and click Edit Photo Album.

2 In the Edit Photo Album dialog box, with the **P17TryE_picture** highlighted, click the New Text Box button in the Album Content area.

> ✓ *If the check box to the left of P17TryE_picture is selected, deselect it before you take the next step.*

3 Click the check boxes for Text Box and 4 Text Box, and then click Remove.

4 Select Captions below ALL Pictures.

5 Click Update and select slide 2.

6 Select the words *Text Box* on slide 2 and type **Friends for Life**.

7 Select the caption below the picture on slide 2.

8 Type **Chloe and friend share a treat**.

9 Save the **P17Try_xx** file, and leave it open to use in the next Try It.

Compressing Pictures

- A photo album—or any presentation that contains pictures, movies, or sounds—can turn into a large file that may be a challenge to store or take extra time to open.

- To streamline a presentation's file size, use the Compress Pictures option on the PICTURE TOOLS FORMAT tab to open the Compress Pictures dialog box.

- By default, PowerPoint will compress all pictures in the presentation. If you want to compress only a single picture, click the Apply only to this picture check box.

> ✓ *Note that by default PowerPoint compresses pictures automatically when the file is saved.*

- The Target output settings allow you to choose a **resolution** appropriate for the way the pictures will be viewed. Measurements for the resolution are given in ppi, pixels per inch.

- Document resolution is chosen by default, but you can change the setting for screen or e-mail output.

- If you have cropped pictures to hide areas you don't want to see, you can also choose to delete the cropped portions of the pictures. Keep in mind, of course, you cannot go back and uncrop a picture if you have deleted the cropped areas.

Try It!   Compressing Pictures

1 In the **P17Try_xx** file, click FILE > Info and note the size of the file in the Document Information pane on the right of the window.

2 Click the Back button ⬅ and select the picture on slide 2.

3 Click PICTURE TOOLS FORMAT > Compress Pictures 🖼.

4 Deselect Apply only to this picture in the Compression options area.

5 Select E-mail (96 ppi) in the Target output area.

6 Click OK.

7 Click FILE > Save and then click Info. Note that the file size in the Document Information pane on the right of the window has gone down significantly.

8 Close the **P17Try_xx** file, saving changes, and exit PowerPoint.

Compress Pictures dialog box

Lesson 17—Practice

Orchard School, a small private school in your area, has asked you to help create a photo album of pictures to market the school to local families. You will use the pictures you have been given so far to start the album.

DIRECTIONS

1. Start PowerPoint, if necessary.
2. Click **INSERT** > **Photo Album** 📷 . The Photo Album dialog box opens.
3. Click the **File/Disk** button. The Insert New Pictures dialog box opens.
4. Navigate to the location where data files for this lesson are stored and click **P17PracticeA_picture.jpg**.
5. Hold down the `CTRL` key and click **P17PracticeB_picture.jpg**.
6. Click **Insert**.
7. Open the **Picture layout** drop-down list and click **1 picture**.

8. Click the **Browse** button next to the Theme text box.
9. Click the **Organic** theme, and click **Select**.
10. Click **Create**. A new presentation is created.
11. On slide 1, change the subtitle to your full name, if necessary.
12. Save the presentation as **P17Practice_xx** in the location where your teacher instructs you to store the files for this lesson.
13. Preview your presentation to see the album pictures in place.
14. **With your teacher's permission**, print one copy of the presentation as handouts, 6 slides per page.
15. Close the presentation, saving changes, and exit PowerPoint.

Lesson 17—Apply

In this project, you complete the photo album for Orchard School by adding more slides, modifying album formats, and finally compressing pictures so you can e-mail the album to your client.

DIRECTIONS

1. Start PowerPoint, if necessary, and open **P17ApplyA** from the data files for this lesson.
2. Save the presentation as **P17ApplyA_xx** in the location where your teacher instructs you to store the files for this lesson.
3. At the bottom of slide 1, insert a text box and type your full name.
4. Open the Edit Photo Album dialog box, click **P17PracticeB_picture** in the Pictures in album list, navigate to the location where data files for this lesson are stored, and add **P17ApplyB_picture.jpg** through **P17ApplyG_picture.jpg** to the photo album.
5. Move the **P17PracticeA_picture** photo to the bottom of the list.

6. Remove **P17ApplyF_picture**.
7. Choose a picture layout of 2 pictures per slide.
8. Change the frame shape to Soft Edge Rectangle.
9. Insert a text box after the last picture in the list.
10. Change the theme to Ion.
11. Update the photo album.
12. Click in the text box on slide 5 and type **We Grow Greatness!**
13. Compress all pictures and select E-mail resolution.
14. Preview your presentation to see the pictures in the album.
15. **With your teacher's permission**, print one copy of the presentation as handouts, 6 slides per page.
16. Close the presentation, saving changes, and exit PowerPoint.

End-of-Chapter Activities

➤ PowerPoint Chapter 2—Critical Thinking

Using the Internet Wisely

Your company, Tech for All, is frequently asked to provide information to students and businesspeople about how to use the Internet safely and intelligently. You have been asked to put together a presentation on smart, safe Internet use that can be delivered to a broad audience.

In this project, working alone or in teams, you will research several issues related to smart Internet use and create the presentation. You will include a minimum of 8 slides covering the following topics:

Understanding Internet addresses; evaluating Web site security and integrity; understanding information privacy and the pros and cons of using social media; using information technology ethically; explaining the legal and illegal use of the Internet and Internet content; and describing netiquette and how it applies to the use of e-mail, social networking, blogs, texting, and chatting.

DIRECTIONS

Content for Slide 1

1. Start a new presentation, and save it as **PCT02_xx** in the location where your teacher instructs you to store the files for this chapter.

2. Apply a theme and variant of your choice.

3. Insert the title **Using the Internet Wisely**, and in the subtitle placeholder, type **A Presentation by** and then insert your first and last name.

4. Adjust the size of the title to fit on one line, if necessary, and then apply WordArt styles and formatting of your choice.

5. Insert somewhere on slide 1 an online picture that relates to the Internet.

6. Format the picture:
   a. Crop the picture if necessary, and position it using Smart Guides to align it attractively with the title.
   b. Recolor the picture, or remove its background.
   c. Apply an artistic effect, if appropriate, or any other picture style or effect.

7. Tech for All often uses images of a lightning bolt striking a cloud as a symbol of bringing the light of knowledge to uncertainty. Create a logo for Tech for All as follows:
   a. Use lightning bolt and cloud shapes from the Shapes gallery to create the graphic portion of the logo. Rotate shapes if necessary and adjust sizes and positions so the bolt is striking the cloud.
   b. Apply fill and outline formats as desired, and apply shape effects to customize the shapes.
   c. Insert a text box that contains the text **Tech for All**. Format the text box with a Quick Style, then position it under the cloud graphic. Group all logo shapes, and position the logo in the lower-right corner of the slide.

8. Add a slide to the presentation with the title Sources. Use this slide to record the Web addresses of sites where you find information for the research you will be doing in the next part of the project.

9. Insert a footer that displays today's date, slide numbers, and your name on all slides except the title slide.

Completing the Presentation

1. **With your teacher's permission**, use the Internet to research the topics listed above. Use valid and reputable sites for your research, and copy site information to your Sources slide.

2. When your research is complete, organize your material into topics and plan how to use it in your presentation. You may use a storyboard if desired. Select slide layouts suitable for the type of information you find. Use numbered lists as appropriate. Use SmartArt diagrams to present some of the information in a more visual way. Add illustrations as desired, using online pictures or other graphics.

3. Each topic should be represented by at least one slide. Use additional slides to expand the topic as necessary.

4. Apply transitions to enhance the presentation's effectiveness.

5. Check spelling.

6. Preview the presentation and then make any necessary corrections and adjustments.

7. Deliver the presentation to your class. Ask for comments on how the presentation could be improved.

8. After making changes, print the presentation as handouts with 6 slides per page.

9. Close the presentation, saving changes, and exit PowerPoint.

➤ PowerPoint Chapter 2—Portfolio Builder

White River Restoration Project

The White River Restoration Society is recruiting new members to help with the cleanup and reforestation of some land they recently received as a donation. They have a basic presentation with all the text in it, but they need some graphics to make it more interesting. You will help them out by adding online pictures, shapes, SmartArt, and WordArt.

DIRECTIONS

1. Start PowerPoint, if necessary, and open **PPB02** from the data files for this chapter.

2. Save the presentation as **PPB02_xx** in the location where your teacher instructs you to store the files for this chapter.

3. At the bottom of slide 1, create a new text box and type the following:

    Copyright 2014 Friends of the White River – Student Name.

4. Insert a copyright symbol © after the word *Copyright*. Replace *Student Name* with your first and last name.

5. Format the text box as follows:
    - Format the text in the text box as 14-point and italic.

    - Apply a background fill to the text box that uses the palest shade of the light green theme color (the third color in the theme).

    - Align the text box at the horizontal center of the slide.

6. On slide 1, create a piece of WordArt with the text **White River Restoration Project**:
    - Start with the Dark Red filled sample (second sample in the first row).

    - Press ENTER after the word *River*, so the text appears on two lines.

    - Apply the **Arch Up** transformation (the first sample in the Follow Path section).

    - Size the WordArt to exactly **3"** high and **9"** wide.

    - Apply bold to the text, and then use Align Center to center the graphic on the slide.

7. On slide 1, create the logo shown in Illustration 2A:
   - Both shapes were drawn with the Shapes feature.
   - The pentagon is orange, and the banner is olive green.
   - Both have the **Preset 2** shape effect applied.
   - Type the text directly into the banner shape.
   - Group the shapes, and then use Smart Guides to center the group horizontally on the slide.

8. On slide 2, convert the bulleted list to the **Vertical Bullet List** SmartArt layout.

9. Apply the **Moderate Effect** SmartArt style to the SmartArt.

10. Change the color of the SmartArt to Colorful Range - Accent Colors 3 to 4.

11. On slide 4, in the empty content placeholder, insert an online picture of people canoeing on a river. Use Smart Guides to align the picture with the top of the bulleted text, if necessary.

12. From the **PICTURE TOOLS FORMAT** tab's **Picture Effects** menu, apply the Preset 5 settings to the canoe image.

13. On slide 5, in the empty content placeholder, insert an online picture that you find with the keywords **river pollution**. Align the picture with the top of the bulleted list to the right, and apply the same picture effect you applied on slide 4.

14. On slide 6, convert the bulleted list to a **Vertical Box List** SmartArt diagram.

15. On slide 7, remove the bullet characters from both paragraphs.

16. Preview the presentation, making any necessary adjustments, and then deliver the presentation to your class.

17. **With your instructor's permission**, print the presentation (6 slides per page).

18. Close the presentation, saving changes, and exit PowerPoint.

Illustration 2A

Chapter 3

(Courtesy Blend Images/Shutterstock)

Enhancing a Presentation

Lesson 18

Modifying a Theme

➤ What You Will Learn

Changing Background Style
Changing Theme Colors
Changing Theme Fonts
Creating New Theme Fonts

WORDS TO KNOW

Font
A set of characters with
a specific size and style.

Software Skills   You can change slide background style and theme colors and
fonts to customize a presentation. You can also create new theme font combinations
to easily apply in later presentations.

What You Can Do

Changing Background Style

- Each theme has a specific background color, and some have background
  graphics or other effects such as gradients—gradations from one color to
  another. Theme variants usually have the same graphics and background
  designs, but the base color may differ.

- To customize a theme, you can change the background style to one of the
  choices offered by the current theme, such as those shown in the Background
  Styles gallery. You display the Background Styles gallery from the Variants
  gallery on the DESIGN tab.

- Background styles use the current theme colors. You can apply a new style to
  all slides or to selected slides.

- As you rest your pointer on different background styles, the current slide shows
  what that background style will look like.

- If you want to make a more radical change to the background, click Format
  Background on the DESIGN tab to open the Format Background task pane
  where you can create a new background using a solid color, a gradient, a texture,
  or even a picture file.

Try It!   **Changing Background Style**

1 Start PowerPoint, and open **P18Try** from the data files for this lesson.

2 Save the presentation as **P18Try_xx** in the location where your teacher instructs you to store the files for this lesson.

3 Select the words *Student Name* in the subtitle placeholder on slide 1 and type your name.

4 On the DESIGN tab, click the Variants More button ⊡ and then click Background Styles 🗔.

5 Click Style 9 to apply it to all the slides in the presentation.

6 With slide 1 displayed, click the Variants More button ⊡, click Background Styles 🗔, and then right-click Style 10 in the gallery.

7 Click Apply to Selected Slides.

8 Save the **P18Try_xx** file, and leave it open to use in the next Try It.

Changing Theme Colors

- Each PowerPoint theme uses a palette of colors selected to work well together. Theme variants offer a different palette of colors. These colors are automatically applied to various elements in the presentation, such as the slide background, text, shape fills, and hyperlink text.

- To see different palettes of colors you can apply, click Colors on the Variants gallery. Some color palettes have theme names, such as Median and Slipstream, but most are organized in color families, such as Blue Green, Orange Red, or Violet.

- PowerPoint offers several ways to adjust theme colors:
  - If you like the layout and fonts of a particular theme but not its colors, you can choose a different color palette from the Colors gallery.
  - You can change one or more colors in the current theme to customize the theme.

- You modify theme colors in the Create New Theme Colors dialog box.

- Change a color by clicking the down arrow for a particular color to display a palette. Select a different tint or hue of a theme color, choose one of ten standard colors, or click More Colors to open the Colors dialog box and pick from all available colors.

- As soon as you change a theme color, the preview in the Create New Theme Colors dialog box also changes to show how your new color coordinates with the others in the theme.

- You can name a new color scheme and save it. It then displays in the Custom area at the top of the Theme Colors gallery. Custom colors are available to use with any theme.

  ✓ *You can delete custom theme colors by right-clicking the color palette set and selecting Delete.*

Try It!   **Changing Theme Colors**

1 In the **P18Try_xx** file, select slide 2.

2 Click DESIGN > Variants ⊡ > Colors 🎨 to display the available color palettes.

3 Hover over several color themes. Live Preview shows you how the color theme will look on your slide.

4 Select the Slipstream theme.

5 Click DESIGN > Variants ⊡ > Colors 🎨 > Customize Colors.

6 In the Name box, type your name.

7 Click the down arrow for Accent 1.

8 Select Aqua, Followed Hyperlink, Darker 25% from the palette.

(continued)

Try It!   **Changing Theme Colors** *(continued)*

9   Click Save.

10   Save the **P18Try_xx** file, and leave it open to use in the next Try It.

Create a new theme color

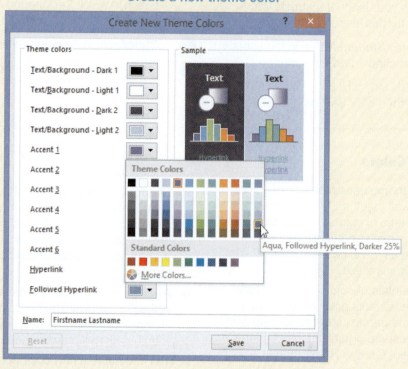

Changing Theme Fonts

- PowerPoint 2013 themes use a single **font** for all text on slides, including titles, lists, and text in text boxes.

- The Theme Fonts gallery lists other fonts you could use, organized by font name. Some choices on the Fonts gallery offer one font for headings and a different font for body text.

Try It!   **Changing Theme Fonts**

1   In the **P18Try_xx** file, select slide 2.

2   Click DESIGN > Variants 🔽 > Fonts Ⓐ.

3   Scroll through the available fonts.

4   Select Georgia.

5   Save the **P18Try_xx** file, and leave it open to use in the next Try It.

Creating New Theme Fonts

- If you do not find a font or set of fonts you like on the Fonts gallery, you can create your own theme fonts.

- Create new theme fonts in the Create New Theme Fonts dialog box. The Sample Preview window shows you the heading and body font as you select them.

- After you name your set of theme fonts, the set appears at the top of the Theme Fonts gallery in the Custom section.

  ✓ *You can delete custom theme fonts by right-clicking the font set and selecting Delete.*

Try It!   **Creating New Theme Fonts**

1 In the **P18Try_xx** file, click DESIGN > Variants ⬇ > Fonts Ⓐ.

2 Click Customize Fonts.

3 Click the Heading font down arrow and select Tahoma.

4 Click the Body font down arrow and select Bookman Old Style.

5 Type your first and last name in the Name box, and then click Save.

6 Close the **P18Try_xx** file, saving changes, and exit PowerPoint.

Lesson 18—Practice

In this project, you work on a presentation for Medi-Ready Urgent Care. You want to explore how changing theme elements might improve the appearance of a presentation you have prepared for use at a community health and wellness event.

DIRECTIONS

1. Start PowerPoint, if necessary, and open **P18Practice** from the data files for this lesson.

2. Save the presentation as **P18Practice_xx** in the location where your teacher instructs you to store the files for this lesson.

3. Click at the end of the subtitle text, press ENTER, type **Presented by**, and then add your name.

4. Click **DESIGN** > **Variants** ⬇ > **Fonts** Ⓐ > **Franklin Gothic**.

5. Click **DESIGN** > **Variants** ⬇ > **Background Styles** 🖼. The Background Styles gallery opens.

6. Select **Style 12** to apply the new background style to all slides.

7. Click **DESIGN** > **Variants** ⬇ > **Colors** and select the **Yellow** theme colors.

8. Click **DESIGN** > **Variants** ⬇ > **Colors** and click **Customize Colors**.

9. Click the **Accent 2** drop-down arrow and then click **Orange, Accent 2, Darker 25%**.

10. Type the name **Medi-Ready** in the Name box and click **Save**.

11. Scroll through all slides. If you discover the new colors have not been applied, click the Reset button 🖼 to update the slide colors.

    ✓ *If resetting resizes pictures, click Undo to reverse the picture size change.*

12. **With your teacher's permission**, print slide 1. Your printout should look similar to Figure 18-1 on the next page.

13. Close the presentation, saving changes, and exit PowerPoint.

Figure 18-1

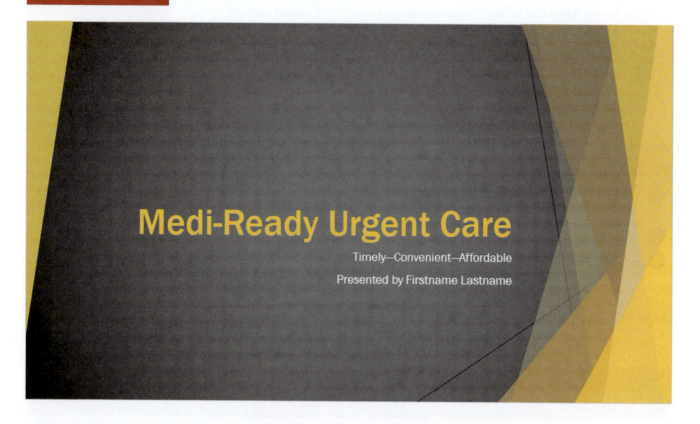

Lesson 18—Apply

In this project, you work with a different version of the Medi-Ready presentation. You customize theme fonts, adjust the background style, and apply new theme colors.

DIRECTIONS

1. Start PowerPoint, if necessary, and open **P18Apply** from the data files for this lesson.

2. Save the presentation as **P18Apply_xx** in the location where your teacher instructs you to store the files for this lesson.

3. Insert a text box on slide 1 that contains your first and last name, and format the text box with a shape style.

4. Apply the **Style 11** background style to all slides, and then apply **Style 9** to slide 1 only.

5. Change the theme colors to **Blue II**.

6. Customize the theme colors to change the Accent 2 color to **Dark Teal, Background 2, Lighter 60%**. Save the theme colors using your first and last name.

7. Create new theme fonts that use Calibri as the heading font and Bell MT as the body font. Save the theme fonts using your first and last name.

8. Preview the presentation to see the new theme formats in place.

9. **With your teacher's permission**, print all slides as handouts with 6 slides per page.

10. Delete any custom theme colors and fonts you created for this lesson.

11. Close the presentation, saving changes, and exit PowerPoint.

Lesson 19

Modifying a Background

➤ What You Will Learn

Creating Slides from an Outline
Hiding Background Graphics
Applying a Background Fill Color
Formatting a Slide Background with a Picture
Resetting the Slide Background

Software Skills   Word outlines can be readily imported to create slides. In some instances, you may want to hide the background graphics created as part of a theme. You can customize a slide background with a fill or a picture.

What You Can Do

Creating Slides from an Outline

- You can save time by reusing text created in other programs, such as Word, in your PowerPoint presentation.
- You can use Word to help you organize the contents of a presentation and then transfer that outline to PowerPoint.
- If you want to use a Word outline to create slides, you must format the text using Word styles that clearly indicate text levels.
    - ✓ *For instance, text formatted with the Word Heading 1 style become slide titles. Text styled as Heading 2 or Heading 3 becomes bulleted items.*
- You have two options for using a Word outline to create slides:
    - You can simply open the Word document in PowerPoint to create the slides. Use this option to create a new presentation directly from outline content.
    - You can use the Slides from Outline command on the New Slide drop-down list to add slides to an existing presentation.
        - ✓ *You cannot use this command unless a presentation is already open.*
- When a Word document is used to create a new presentation, the slides will display the same fonts and styles used in the document. These will not change even if a new theme or theme fonts are applied.
- If you want to change the fonts in a presentation created from an outline, you need to click the Reset button on the HOME tab.

✓ *You can also use this command to reverse changes made to slide layouts or themes.*

■ The Reset function will delete the Word styles and apply the theme defaults for colors, fonts, and effects.

■ Slides created from an outline may, in addition, be formatted with a layout called Title and Text. You can apply one of PowerPoint's default layouts such as Title and Content to make these slides more functional.

Figure 19-1

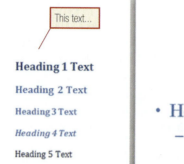

This text...

...Becomes slide content

Heading 1 Text

Heading 2 Text

Heading 3 Text

Heading 4 Text

Heading 5 Text

Heading 1 Text

• **Heading 2 Text**
  – **Heading 3 Text**
    • *Heading 4 Text*
     – Heading 5 Text

Try It!   **Creating Slides from an Outline**

1 Start PowerPoint, click Open Other Presentations, and navigate to the location where the data files for this lesson are stored.

2 In the Open dialog box, click All PowerPoint Presentations and select All Files.

3 Select the Word document **P19TryA** and click Open.

4 Scroll through the presentation to see how the Word styles are applied to the slides.

5 Save the presentation as **P19TryA_xx** in the location where your teacher instructs you to store the files for this lesson.

6 Close the file.

Try It!   **Adding Slides from an Outline to an Existing Presentation**

1 In PowerPoint, open **P19TryB** from the data files for this lesson.

2 Save the presentation as **P19TryB_xx** in the location where your teacher instructs you to store the files for this lesson.

3 Select slide 1 (the new slides will appear after this slide).

4 Click HOME > New Slide drop-down arrow 🗒.

5 Click Slides from Outline.

6 In the Insert Outline dialog box, navigate to the location where the data files for this lesson are stored and select **P19TryC**.

7 Click Insert.

8 Save the **P19TryB_xx** file, and leave it open to use in the next Try It.

Try It!   **Resetting a Slide**

1 In the **P19TryB_xx** file, select slides 2–4 in the Thumbnail pane.

2 Click HOME > Reset 🖹.

3 Click HOME > Layout 🖻 and click Title and Content.

4 Save the **P19TryB_xx** file, and leave it open to use in the next Try It.

Hiding Background Graphics

- Many themes include some type of graphics such as lines or shapes that form a part of the slide background.

- You can only select and modify theme background graphics in Slide Master view.

  ✓ *You will learn how to create and manipulate background graphics on slide masters in Lesson 24.*

- If you don't like these background graphics, you can hide them using the Format Background task pane.

- To open the Format Background task pane, click the Format Background button on the DESIGN tab.

- Remember that text colors are often chosen to contrast with the graphic background. If you hide the background graphic, the text colors might need to be changed so that they don't blend into the background.

Try It!   **Hiding Background Graphics**

1 In the **P19TryB_xx** file, select slide 1.

2 Click DESIGN > Format Background 🖻 to open the Format Background task pane.

3 Click the Hide background graphics check box in the FILL settings.

4 Save the **P19TryB_xx** file, and leave it open to use in the next Try It.

Applying a Background Fill Color

- Instead of changing the theme or variant in a presentation, you can change just the background color.

- You can apply a background fill color to one slide or to the entire presentation using the Format Background task pane.

Try It!   **Applying a Background Fill Color**

1 In the **P19TryB_xx** file, click DESIGN > Format Background 🖻 to display the Format Background task pane, if necessary.

2 With the Solid fill option selected, click the Color button.

3 Select Teal, Accent 6, Lighter 60%.

4 Click the Apply to All button at the bottom of the task pane.

5 Save the **P19TryB_xx** file, and leave it open to use in the next Try It.

(continued)

Try It!   **Applying a Background Fill Color** *(continued)*

The Format Background dialog box

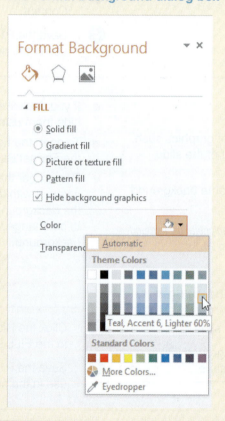

Formatting a Slide Background with a Picture

- Inserting a picture on your slide background adds interest and helps convey your message.

- You can format the background with a picture using the Format Background task pane.

- You can use online pictures or images stored on your system to add graphics to the slide background.

Try It!   **Formatting a Slide Background with a Picture**

❶ In the **P19TryB_xx** file, display slide 1, if necessary, and then click Format Background to display the Format Background task pane if it is not already open.

❷ In the Format Background task pane, click Picture or texture fill.

✓ *Note that the background of the slide automatically changes to the first texture option.*

❸ Click the Online button and type the keywords **helping hand** in the Clip Art box. Click the Search button 🔍 .

❹ Select the image of a man's reaching hand and click Insert.

❺ Save the **P19TryB_xx** file, and leave it open to use in the next Try It.

Resetting the Slide Background

- Only changes made to individual slide backgrounds can be reset. If you apply a change to all the slides in a presentation, you cannot reverse the change using the Reset Background option.

  ✓ *You can, however, use the Undo button to reverse global changes.*

Try It!   Resetting the Slide Background

1 In the **P19TryB_xx** file, with slide 1 displayed, click Format Background 🖼 to display the Format Background task pane if it is not already open.

2 Click the Reset Background button at the bottom of the task pane. Notice that the slide background changes immediately to the solid color fill you applied to all slides.

3 Close the Format Background task pane.

4 Close the **P19TryB_xx** file, saving changes, and exit PowerPoint.

Lesson 19—Practice

Your client, Voyager Travel Adventures, has supplied you with files they want you to use in the presentation you're creating for them. You'll also add information on each slide to help identify and organize the presentation.

DIRECTIONS

1. Start PowerPoint, click **FILE** > **Open**, and navigate to the location where the data files for this lesson are stored.

2. In the Open dialog box, click **All PowerPoint Presentations** and select **All Files**.

3. Select the Word document **P19Practice** and click **Open**.

4. Save the presentation as **P19Practice_xx** in the location where your teacher instructs you to store the files for this lesson.

5. Click slide 1 in the Thumbnail pane, and then click CTRL + A to select all the slides.

6. Click **HOME** > **Reset** 📄. Each slide will revert to the default formatting and placeholders.

7. Click slide 1, and then click **HOME** > **Layout** 📄 > **Title Slide**. Slide 1 changes to a Title Slide layout.

8. Click slides 2–4 in the Thumbnail pane, and then click **HOME** > **Layout** 📄 > **Title and Content**.

9. On the **DESIGN** tab, click the **More** button to display the Themes gallery, and then click **Parallax**. The entire presentation changes to reflect the new Parallax theme.

10. Click slide 1, and then click **DESIGN** > **Format Background** 🖼 > **Hide background graphics**. The graphics on the title slide disappear. Close the Format Background task pane.

11. Click **INSERT** > **Header & Footer** 📄. The Header and Footer dialog box opens.

12. Select **Footer** and type your name. Click **Apply** to apply the footer to the title slide only.

13. Preview the presentation.

14. **With your teacher's permission**, print slide 1.

15. Close the presentation, saving changes, and exit PowerPoint.

Lesson 19—Apply

In this project, you add slides to another version of the Voyager presentation. You will modify slide backgrounds for a custom look.

DIRECTIONS

1. Start PowerPoint, if necessary, and open **P19ApplyA** from the data files for this lesson.

2. Save the presentation as **P19ApplyA_xx** in the location where your teacher instructs you to store the files for this lesson.

3. Insert the slides from the Word outline **P19ApplyB** at the end of the presentation and reset the slides.

4. Move slide 4 to be the first slide and apply Title Slide layout.

5. Apply the Title and Content layout to slides 5 and 6.

6. Move slide 5 to be slide 3.

7. Display slide 1. Use the Format Background task pane to change the background styles as follows:

   a. Click the Color button under the Gradient stops color bar and change the color to **White, Text 1**. Apply the change to all the slides.

   b. Use the file **P19ApplyC_picture.jpg** located in the data files for this lesson as a picture fill on the title slide.

   c. Hide the background graphics on slide 1.

8. Insert a date that updates automatically, slide numbers, and a footer that includes your name. Do not show this information on the title slide, but apply it to all other slides. Your presentation should look like Figure 19-2.

9. Spell check and preview the presentation.

10. **With your teacher's permission,** print the presentation as a 6 slides per page handout.

11. Close the presentation, saving changes, and exit PowerPoint.

Figure 19-2

Lesson 20

Animating Slide Objects

➤ What You Will Learn

Applying Animation Effects
Setting Effect Options
Changing the Order of Animation Effects
Setting Animation Start and Timing Options
Applying Animation Effects with Animation Painter
Applying Animations to Objects, Charts, and Diagrams
Changing or Removing an Animation

Software Skills   PowerPoint allows you to add animations to make your slides more visually interesting during a presentation.

WORDS TO KNOW

Animate
To apply movement to text or an object to control its display during the presentation.

What You Can Do

Applying Animation Effects

- You can **animate** text and objects in a presentation to add interest or emphasize special points.

- Use the Animation gallery on the ANIMATIONS tab to apply animation effects organized in four categories: Entrance effects, Emphasis effects, Exit effects, and Motion Path effects.

Try It!   **Applying Animation Effects**

1. Start PowerPoint, and open **P20Try** from the data files for this lesson.

2. Save the presentation as **P20Try_xx** in the location where your teacher instructs you to store the files for this lesson.

3. On slide 1, click the title placeholder.

4. On the ANIMATIONS tab, click the Animation More button ▾ and scroll down to see the Motion Paths effects.

5. Click Lines.

6. On slide 2, click the content placeholder.

7. On the ANIMATIONS tab, click the Fly In animation from the gallery.

8. Click the title placeholder.

9. On the ANIMATIONS tab, click Float In.

10. Save the **P20Try_xx** file, and leave it open to use in the next Try It.

Setting Effect Options

- The Effect Options button on the ANIMATIONS tab offers options for controlling the direction and sequence of the selected animation.

- Options on this gallery depend on the selected animation effect. You may have up to eight choices for the direction the animation will take.

- You can also select how the animation will control multiple objects. List items, for example, can be animated as one object or by paragraph, with each list item animated separately.

Try It!   **Setting Effect Options**

1. In the **P20Try_xx** file, click the content placeholder on slide 2.

2. Click ANIMATIONS > Effect Options ⬆.

   ✓ *The direction of the arrow on the button shows the direction selected most recently.*

3. Click From Left.

4. Click ANIMATIONS > Effect Options ⬆.

5. Click By Paragraph if that option is not already selected.

6. Click the title placeholder on slide 2.

7. Click ANIMATIONS > Effect Options ⬆ > Float Down.

8. Save the **P20Try_xx** file, and leave it open to use in the next Try It.

The Effect Options drop-down list

Changing the Order of Animation Effects

- If you want more control over animation effects, use the Animation Pane. The Animation Pane allows you to control the order in which animations occur as well as preview specific animation effects.

- When you add an effect, the object name and an effect symbol display in the Animation Pane. This list represents the order in which the effects take place when the slide is viewed.

- Each type of animation effect has its own symbol, such as a green star for entrance effects and a red star for exit effects.

- You can adjust the order in which effects take place using the up and down arrows near the top of the task pane.

- If the object you are animating has more than one line or part, such as a text content placeholder or a chart or diagram, a bar displays below the effect with a Click to expand contents arrow. Clicking the arrow displays all the parts of the object.

- Displaying the parts of the object allows you to animate each part with a different effect, or adjust the timing for the separate parts.

- When you have finished animating the parts, use the Click to hide contents arrow to collapse the effect and save room in the animation list.

- The Play button in the Animation Pane allows you to preview a selected animation to make sure it displays as you want it to.

- You can use the Preview button on the ANIMATIONS tab to preview all animations on a slide.

Try It!   **Changing the Order of Animation Effects**

1 In the **P20Try_xx** file, on slide 2, click ANIMATIONS > Animation Pane 🕐◀.

2 In the Animation Pane, click Rectangle 1.

3 Click the up arrow ▲ near the top of the Animation Pane to move the title placeholder's animation effect above the content placeholder animation.

4 Click the content placeholder on the slide to select it, then click Effect Options ↑ and select From Bottom.

5 In the Animation Pane, click the Click to expand contents arrow ⌄ in the bar below the Rectangle 2 item.

6 Click item 2 in the Animation Pane ("Many of our …") and click the down arrow ▼ twice to move it to the bottom of the list.

7 Click item 3 and click the up arrow ▲ to move the item to the top of the list.

8 Click the Click to hide contents arrow ⌃ to hide the list.

9 Click the Play Selected button in the Animation Pane to preview the selected animation.

10 Click ANIMATIONS > Preview Animations ⭐ to preview all animations on the slide.

11 Save the **P20Try_xx** file, and leave it open to use in the next Try It.

Setting Animation Start and Timing Options

■ The ANIMATIONS tab contains Start, Duration, and Delay options for controlling the timing of your animations.

- The Start setting is On Click by default. You can adjust this setting to After Previous, to occur automatically after the previous event, or With Previous, to occur at the same time as the previous effect.

- Use the Duration setting to adjust the speed of the animation.

- Use the Delay setting to specify the amount of time that must elapse before the animation starts.

■ Some animations allow you to change the way they start and end. By default, PowerPoint applies a smooth start and smooth end timing to avoid jerkiness in the animation.

■ You can adjust start and end options in the effect options dialog box for the animation.

Try It!   **Setting Animation Start and Timing Options**

1 In the **P20Try_xx** file, on slide 2, select effect 1 in the Animations Pane.

2 Click the Start ▶ drop-down arrow and click With Previous.

3 Click effect 1 (Rectangle 2), click the Start ▶ drop-down arrow, and click After Previous.

4 With the Rectangle 2 effect still selected, click the Duration 🕐 up increment arrow until 02.00 displays.

5 With the Rectangle 2 effect still selected, click the Delay 🕘 up increment arrow until 01.00 displays.

6 With the Rectangle 2 effect still selected, click the down arrow at the right side of the effect, and then click Effect Options.

7 Drag the Bounce end slider to about 0.7 sec, and then click OK.

8 Click ANIMATIONS > Preview Animations ⭐ to preview changes to the animations on the slide.

9 Save the **P20Try_xx** file, and leave it open to use in the next Try It.

Applying Animation Effects with Animation Painter

- Creating just the right animation effect can be time-consuming. When you want to use the same animation effect on more than one slide, the best choice is to use the Animation Painter.

- Like the Format Painter, the Animation Painter duplicates the animation formatting from one placeholder to another.

- To copy the animation to another placeholder, select a placeholder that has the animation you want to use and click the Animation Painter button. Then, click the placeholder to which you want to apply it.

- To apply the animation to multiple placeholders, double-click the Animation Painter button after selecting your animation placeholder.

Try It!	**Applying Animation Effects with Animation Painter**

1. In the **P20Try_xx** file, select the text placeholder on slide 2.

2. Double-click ANIMATIONS > Animation Painter ✦.

3. Click slide 4 in the Thumbnail pane. Click the text placeholder.

4. Click slide 5 in the Thumbnail pane. Click the text placeholder.

5. Press ESC to turn off the Animation Painter.

6. Save the **P20Try_xx** file, and leave it open to use in the next Try It.

Applying Animations to Objects, Charts, and Diagrams

- Objects such as shapes and pictures, charts, and SmartArt diagrams can be animated using the same tools that you use to animate text. Animations can help you control the presentation of information in a chart or diagram to make it easier for your audience to understand each part of your data as you present it.

- Besides creating interesting entrance effects for objects, animations can be used to emphasize an object on a slide or to accompany an object's exit from a slide.

Try It!	**Applying Animations to Objects, Charts, and Diagrams**

1. In the **P20Try_xx** file, click the grouped graphic on slide 3.

2. In the Animations gallery, click the More button ▼ and click Teeter in the Emphasis effects.

3. On slide 6, click the chart to select it, and then click Fade in the Animation gallery.

4. Click the Effect Options button ↑ and click By Element in Series.

5. Click the Preview Animations button ✦ to see how each bar in the chart displays separately for each series.

6. On slide 7, click the picture to select it and then click the More button ▼ in the Animation gallery to display all effects.

7. Click Wipe in the Exit effects category.

8. Save the **P20Try_xx** file, and leave it open to use in the next Try It.

Changing or Removing an Animation

■ If you find that a particular animation option isn't giving you the effect you want, you can easily change the animation effect.

■ You can also delete the effect entirely by selecting the item in the Animation Pane to display the effect options down arrow and choosing Remove from the drop-down menu.

Try It!   **Changing or Removing an Animation**

1 In the **P20Try_xx** file, display slide 7 if necessary and click the picture to select it.

2 Click the Animation gallery More button ⟱ to display all effects and click Fade in the Exit effects category.

3 Display slide 3 and click the Group 9 effect in the Animation Pane to select the effect.

4 Click the drop-down arrow to the right of the effect name, and then click Remove.

5 Preview all slides in the presentation to see the animation effects you have applied.

6 Close the **P20Try_xx** file, saving changes, and exit PowerPoint.

Lesson 20—Practice

In this project, you work with the Medi-Ready presentation to improve the slides by adding animations to content placeholders and objects.

DIRECTIONS

1. Start PowerPoint, if necessary, and open **P20Practice** from the data files for this lesson.

2. Save the presentation as **P20Practice_xx** in the location where your teacher instructs you to store the files for this lesson.

3. Click following the word *Affordable* in the subtitle on slide 1. Press [ENTER], type **Presented by**, and then add your name.

4. Click the title placeholder on slide 1, click the **ANIMATIONS** tab, and click **Fade**.

5. Click **Start** ▶ and click **After Previous**.

6. Click the **Preview Animations** button ✷ to play the animations.

7. Click **Animation Pane** ⛟ to open the Animation Pane, and then make these adjustments to the animations on slide 1:

   a. With the Title 1 animation effect selected, click the move up button ▲ to move the effect to the top of the list.

   b. Select the Subtitle 2 effect, click the Animation More button ⟱, and then click **Fly In**.

   c. Click the **Effect Options** button ↑ and click **From Left**, and then click **All at Once** in the Sequence section of the gallery.

8. Display slide 2 and click the picture to select it.

9. Click **ANIMATIONS** > **Fly In**.

10. Select the content placeholder on slide 2 and click **ANIMATIONS** > **Fly In**.

11. With the content placeholder still selected, make the following adjustments:

    a. Click **Effect Options** ↑ and click **By Paragraph**, if necessary.

    b. Click **Start** ▶ and click **With Previous**.

    c. Click the **Duration** ⏱ up increment arrow to display **02.00**.

12. Click the Picture effect in the animation list, click **Start** ▶ and click **After Previous** and then click **Duration** ⏱ up increment arrow to display **02.00**. Your slide should look like Figure 20-1 on the next page.

13. Display slide 5 and click the picture to select it.

14. Click the Animation More button ⊡ to display the Animation gallery, and then click **Pulse** in the Emphasis category.

15. With the picture still selected, click **Start** ▶ and click **After Previous**.

16. With the picture still selected, click **ANIMATIONS** > **Animation Painter** ✸, and then click on the picture on slide 6.

17. Close the Animation Pane and then preview your presentation to see the animation effects.

18. Close the presentation, saving changes, and exit PowerPoint.

Figure 20-1

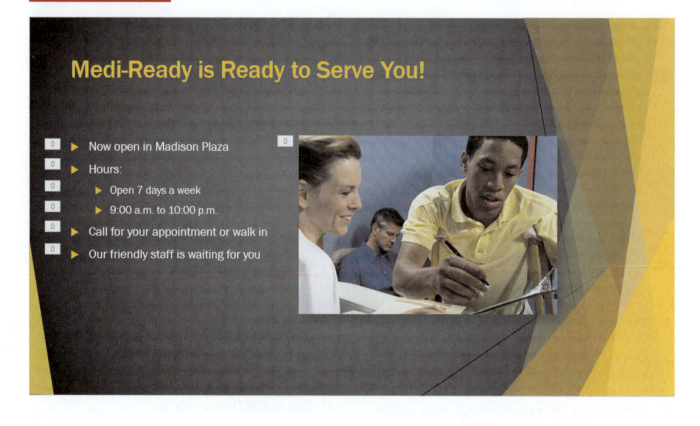

Lesson 20—Apply

In this project, you continue working with the Medi-Ready presentation. You will add more animations and modify existing ones to enhance the presentation's visual interest.

DIRECTIONS

1. Start PowerPoint, if necessary, and open **P20Apply** from the data files for this lesson.

2. Save the presentation as **P20Apply_xx** in the location where your teacher instructs you to store the files for this lesson.

3. Use the Animation Painter to copy the animation from the presentation title to the title placeholders on slides 2 through 6. Then adjust the order of animations if necessary so the title animation is first on all slides.

4. On slide 3, animate the SmartArt diagram with the **Wipe** animation effect, changing effect options to **From Left** and **One by One**. Change the Start to **After Previous** and the Duration to **02.00**.

5. Apply animations on slide 4 as follows:

   a. Animate the *Personal Injuries* placeholder to **Zoom** in **After Previous**.

   b. Animate the bullet list under *Personal Injuries* to **Fly In** from the left **After Previous**. Set a delay of **01.00**.

   c. Use the Animation Painter to copy the animation from *Personal Injuries* to *Illnesses*.

   d. Animate the bullet list under *Illnesses* in the same way as the left bullet list, changing the fly in direction for the bullets to **From Right**.

6. On slide 5, change the animation on the picture to **Fly In From Right**.

7. Animate the bulleted list on slide 5 to **Fly in** from left as one object.

8. On slide 5, adjust the order of animations so the picture animates at the same time as the bullet list. Make the same changes to the bullet list and the picture on slide 6.

9. On slide 7, apply the **Shapes** motion path effect to the WordArt graphic and have it start **After Previous**. Change the Smooth end setting for this effect to **0** sec.

10. Insert a text box on slide 1 with your name.

11. Watch the slideshow from start to finish, and then adjust any timings or effects to improve the presentation.

12. Close the presentation, saving changes, and exit PowerPoint.

Lesson 21

Creating Multimedia Presentations

➤ **What You Will Learn**

Analyzing the Effectiveness of Multimedia Presentations
Inserting a Video
Modifying Video Appearance and Length
Controlling a Video in a Presentation
Inserting Sounds and Music

Software Skills   A multimedia presentation can engage an audience with video and sound or music clips. You can modify the way the video displays on the slide and control playback options for both video and sound.

What You Can Do

Analyzing the Effectiveness of Multimedia Presentations

■ PowerPoint has many tools and features, but selecting the options that make your presentation effective depends on many factors, including the topic, the audience, and the purpose.

■ Always consider your audience when creating a presentation. Research the audience's needs and knowledge level, and tailor the presentation to it.

■ For example, a marketing presentation may be more effective if it uses lots of multimedia and animation effects, while a tutorial or training presentation may be more effective if it uses straightforward bullet text without distracting sounds and actions.

■ Also consider how the presentation will be delivered. Not all presentations are delivered by a live narrator to a live audience.

  ● Will it be printed? Select a light background and dark text for readability.

  ● Will it be standalone? Include navigation tools for the viewer.

  ● Will it run automatically in a loop? Keep it short so a viewer does not have to wait a long time for the presentation to begin anew.

  ● Will it be delivered over the Internet? Make sure the audio is high quality.

- Follow general design guidelines when preparing a presentation. For example:
  - Apply a consistent theme to all slides. That means using the same font and color scheme throughout, and repeating elements such as bullets and backgrounds.
  - Limit bullet points to no more than five per slide.
  - Limit the number of fonts to one or two per slide.
  - Use contrasting colors when necessary to make text stand out. For example, use a dark background color such as dark green or blue and a light contrasting text color, such as yellow.
  - Avoid the use of pastels, which can be hard to read.
  - Make sure text is large enough so that even someone at the back of the room can read it. Text should be no smaller than 18 points and no larger than 48 points.
  - Use graphics such as tables, charts, and pictures to convey key points.
  - Make sure graphics are sized to fill the slide.
  - Use consistent transitions, sounds, and animations that enhance the presentation and do not distract from the content.
- Be clear about the message you are trying to convey. For example, if you are creating a marketing presentation, be clear about what you are trying to sell. If you are creating a training presentation, be clear about what you are teaching.
- Know your time limit based on your audience. Younger people have a shorter attention span, but most people will lose interest if the presentation goes on too long.
- An effective presentation has a logical progression:
  - Introduction in which you tell your audience what you are going to present.
  - Body in which you present the information.
  - Summary in which you tell your audience what you presented.
- Do not use slang, incorrect grammar, jargon, or abbreviations that your audience might not understand.
- Your role in the delivery of a live presentation is key. Dress appropriately, speak loudly and clearly, and make eye contact with your audience.
- You can assess a presentation's effectiveness by testing it on a practice audience. Ask for constructive criticism to help you improve.

Inserting a Video

- Insert a video file using the Insert Video button in a content placeholder or the Video button on the INSERT tab.
- You have several options for adding a video to your presentation:
  - Insert a video file saved in a format such as AVI or MPEG.
  - Insert a video you find with a search tool such as Bing.
  - Insert a video stored on your SkyDrive.
  - Insert a video from the Web.
- By default, PowerPoint embeds the video file on the slide so it becomes part of the presentation. You can also choose to link the video to the presentation. Linking can reduce the size of the presentation.
- When you insert a video file or a video from the Web, the VIDEO TOOLS FORMAT and VIDEO TOOLS PLAYBACK tabs open. Use the tools on these tabs to modify the appearance of the video on the slide and to control playback options.

Try It! **Inserting a Video from a File**

1. Start PowerPoint, and open **P21TryA** from the data files for this lesson.

2. Save the presentation as **P21TryA_xx** in the location where your teacher instructs you to store the files for this lesson.

3. Select slide 4 and click the Insert Video icon in the content placeholder.

OR

Click INSERT > Video and then click Video on My PC.

(continued)

Try It!   **Inserting a Video from a File** *(continued)*

4 If necessary, click Browse. Navigate to the location where the data files for this lesson are stored and click **P21TryB_video**.

5 Click the down arrow on the Insert button and click Link to File. The video is now linked to the presentation.

6 Click Undo ↺ to remove the linked video.

7 Repeat steps 3 and 4 to navigate to the **P21TryB_video** file and select it.

8 Click Insert. The video is now embedded on the slide.

9 Save the **P21TryA_xx** file, and leave it open to use in the next Try It.

Insert a video from a file

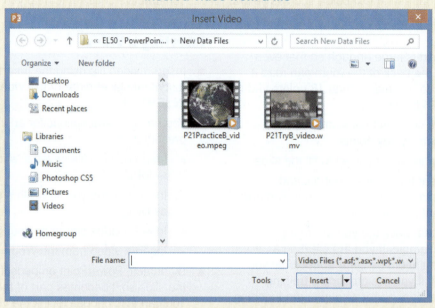

Modifying Video Appearance and Length

■ You have a number of options for changing the way a video object displays on the slide.

• You can crop the video to remove black margins at the left and right side of the object.

• You can apply a video style to give the object a more finished look. Fine-tune the style by changing the style's effects, changing the shape of the video object, or changing the color of a frame if one is applied.

• You can use the Color option to change the video's color. In addition to the most popular video color options—Black and White, Grayscale, Sepia, Washout—you can also choose to tint the video in 14 different variations, the same way you recolor a picture. Use More Variations to open a color palette for additional color options.

■ You find these formatting options on the VIDEO TOOLS FORMAT tab. You can also display the Format Video task pane to make formatting tools available.

■ You can use the Trim Video tool on the VIDEO TOOLS PLAYBACK tab to adjust the length of a video.

■ In the Trim Video dialog box, you can drag start and end point arrows to change where the video starts and ends. Or, set an exact start time in the Start Time box and an exact end time in the End Time box.

Try It!	**Modifying Video Appearance and Length**

1 In the **P21TryA_xx** file, select the video on slide 4.

2 On the VIDEO TOOLS FORMAT tab, click the Crop button.

3 Drag the left cropping handle to the right to remove the black.

4 Drag the right cropping handle to the left to remove the black.

5 On the VIDEO TOOLS FORMAT tab, click the Crop button again to complete the crop.

6 With the video object still selected, on the VIDEO TOOLS FORMAT tab, click the More button to open the Video Styles gallery.

7 Move your mouse over several styles to see the live preview and then choose Drop Shadow Rectangle, the last option in the Subtle category.

8 Right-click the video object, and click Format Video to display the Format Video task pane.

9 Click the Recolor button and choose Grayscale. Close the Format Video task pane.

10 On the VIDEO TOOLS PLAYBACK tab, click Trim Video.

11 Drag the end point arrow (the red arrow at the right end of the timeline) to the left until the End Time box shows about 18 seconds. Click OK.

12 Save the **P21TryA_xx** file, and leave it open to use in the next Try It.

Drag the left cropping handle to the right

Controlling a Video in a Presentation

■ Inserted video clips can be controlled using the standard play and pause controls on the bar beneath the video object.

■ In addition to these controls, PowerPoint allows you to hide the movie during the presentation, play it full screen, loop it continuously, rewind it, change its arrangement relative to other objects, or scale it.

Try It!	**Previewing a Movie in Normal View**

1 In the **P21TryA_xx** file, select the video on slide 4.

2 Click VIDEO TOOLS PLAYBACK > Play.

OR

Click the Play button below the video.

3 Watch for a few seconds and click VIDEO TOOLS PLAYBACK > Pause.

OR

Click the Pause button below the video.

4 Save the **P21TryA_xx** file, and leave it open to use in the next Try It.

Try It!   **Viewing a Video in a Slide Show**

1. In the **P21TryA_xx** file, select slide 4, if necessary.

2. Click Slide Show 🖳 on the status bar.

3. Hover your mouse over the video to display the Play button.

4. Click the Play button ▶.

5. Watch the video for a few seconds and then click the slide to progress to the next slide.

6. Press ESC .

7. Select the video on slide 4, if necessary, and click VIDEO TOOLS PLAYBACK > Start 🖳, and click Automatically.

8. Click Slide Show 🖳 on the status bar. Notice that the video starts immediately.

9. Press ESC .

10. Save the **P21TryA_xx** file, and leave it open to use in the next Try It.

Inserting Sounds and Music

- You can add sound and music clips to your presentation to make it more interesting or to emphasize a slide. Your computer must have speakers and a sound card to play music or sounds during a presentation.

- Use the Audio button on the INSERT tab to choose what kind of sound to insert: a sound file from your system, a sound from online audio files, or a sound that you record.

- As for video files, you can choose to link to a file on your system, rather than embed the audio file in the presentation.

- When you insert an audio clip, a sound icon displays on the slide. You can move this icon to a new location (or even off the slide) or resize it to make it less obtrusive.

  ✓ *The sound icon must appear on the slide if you intend to control a sound by clicking it during the presentation.*

- You can choose whether to play the sound automatically or when clicked. You can also choose to have the audio play across slides, so it continues as you progress through the presentation.

- Use the AUDIO TOOLS PLAYBACK tab to control sound options.

Try It!   **Inserting a Music File**

1. In the **P21TryA_xx** file, select slide 5.

2. Click INSERT > Audio 🔊 .

3. Click Audio on My PC.

4. In the Insert Audio dialog box, navigate to the location where the data files for this lesson are stored and select **P21TryC_audio.mid**.

5. Click Insert and drag the audio icon to the lower right of the slide.

6. On the AUDIO TOOLS PLAYBACK tab, click the Start down arrow 🖳, and click Automatically.

7. Save the **P21TryA_xx** file, and leave it open to use in the next Try It.

(continued)

Try It!	**Inserting a Music File** (continued)

PowerPoint gives you complete control over audio clips

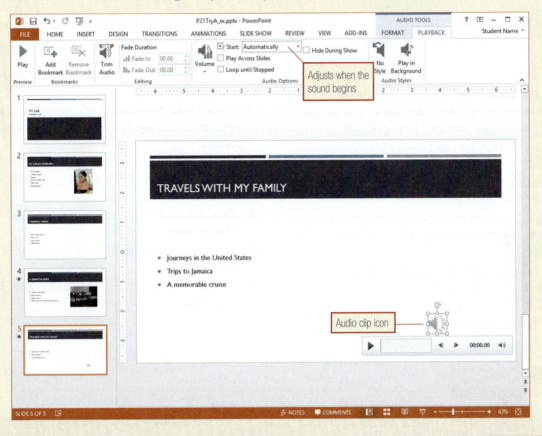

Try It!	**Inserting a Sound from Online Audio**

① In the **P21TryA_xx** file, select slide 1.

② Click INSERT > Audio ◀️.

③ Select Online Audio.

④ In the Insert Audio dialog box, click in the Clip Art box and type **music**. Click the Search button 🔍.

⑤ Click on several of the music clips returned by the search to hear a portion of the clip.

⑥ Double-click a music clip from the first row to insert the clip.

⑦ On the AUDIO TOOLS PLAYBACK tab, click the Start down arrow 🔽 and click Automatically.

⑧ Click SLIDE SHOW > From Beginning 🔲 and watch the presentation.

⑨ Close the **P21TryA_xx** file, saving changes, and exit PowerPoint.

Lesson 21—Practice

Planet Earth has asked you to continue work on their Earth Day presentation. In this project, you add a video and a picture to a new presentation design to create a multimedia presentation.

DIRECTIONS

1. Start PowerPoint, if necessary, and open **P21PracticeA** from the data files for this lesson.

2. Save the presentation as **P21PracticeA_xx** in the location where your teacher instructs you to store the files for this lesson.

3. Select slide 1, click inside the subtitle placeholder, and type your name.

4. Select slide 2 and then click the **Insert Video** icon in the right placeholder. The Insert Video dialog box opens.

5. Click **Browse** and then navigate to the location where the data files for this lesson are stored and select **P21PracticeB_video.mpeg**.

6. Click **Insert**. The video appears in the placeholder, as shown in Figure 21-1.

✓ PowerPoint will upgrade the video file for you to optimize it for playback.

7. Select slide 3 and in the placeholder, click the **Pictures** icon . The Insert Picture dialog box opens.

8. Navigate to the location where the data files for this lesson are stored and select **P21PracticeC_picture.jpg**.

9. Click **Insert**. The picture appears in the placeholder.

10. Preview the presentation, playing the video on slide 2.

11. Close the presentation, saving changes, and exit PowerPoint.

Figure 21-1

Lesson 21—Apply

In this project, you continue to work on the Planet Earth presentation. You format the video and add sound clips to improve the look and sound of the presentation.

DIRECTIONS

1. Start PowerPoint, if necessary, and open **P21Apply** from the data files for this lesson.

2. Save the presentation as **P21Apply_xx** in the location where your teacher instructs you to store the files for this lesson.

3. Replace the text *Student Name* on the title slide with your name.

4. Modify the video clip on slide 2 as follows:

   a. Drag the video down so that the top of it is more or less aligned with the top of the SAVING THE EARTH text in the placeholder to the left of the video.

   b. Apply the **Simple Frame, White** video style to the video. Your slide should look like Figure 21-2.

   c. Set the video to start automatically.

   d. Trim the video so it starts about 1 second later.

   e. Preview the video in Normal view.

5. Locate an appropriate online music file and insert it on slide 1. Set it to play automatically. Move the sound icon off the slide so it will not display when you show the slides. Set the audio to play across slides.

6. Locate an online audio clip of birds singing. Insert the sound on slide 3 and choose to have it play automatically. Move the sound icon off the slide so it will not display when you show the slides.

7. View the slides in Slide Show view to see the movie and hear the sounds.

8. **With your teacher's permission**, print slide 2.

9. Close the presentation, saving changes, and exit PowerPoint.

Figure 21-2

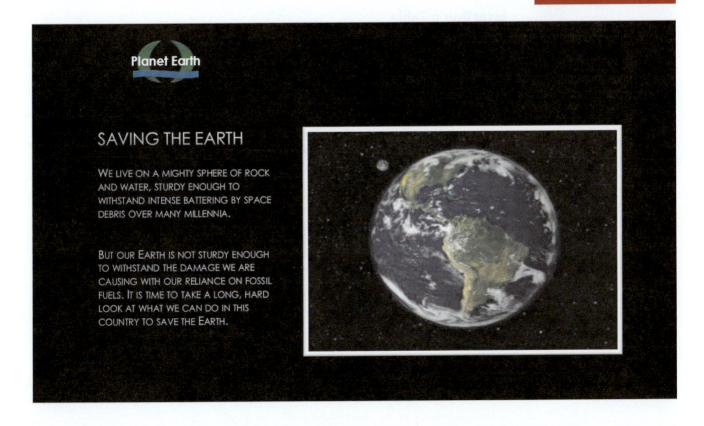

SAVING THE EARTH

WE LIVE ON A MIGHTY SPHERE OF ROCK AND WATER, STURDY ENOUGH TO WITHSTAND INTENSE BATTERING BY SPACE DEBRIS OVER MANY MILLENNIA.

BUT OUR EARTH IS NOT STURDY ENOUGH TO WITHSTAND THE DAMAGE WE ARE CAUSING WITH OUR RELIANCE ON FOSSIL FUELS. IT IS TIME TO TAKE A LONG, HARD LOOK AT WHAT WE CAN DO IN THIS COUNTRY TO SAVE THE EARTH.

Lesson 22

Working with Tables

> ## What You Will Learn

Inserting a Table
Formatting and Modifying a Table

Software Skills   Use tables to organize data in a format that is easy to read and understand. Table formats enhance visual interest and also contribute to readability.

What You Can Do

Inserting a Table

- Use a table on a slide to organize information into rows and columns so it is easy for your audience to read and understand.

- You have two options for inserting a table on a slide:
  - Click the Insert Table icon in any content placeholder to display the Insert Table dialog box. After you select the number of columns and rows, the table structure appears on the slide in the content placeholder.
  - Click the Table button on the INSERT tab to display a grid that you can use to select rows and columns. As you drag the pointer, the table columns and rows appear on the slide.

    ✓ *If you use this option on a slide that does not have a content layout, you may have to move the table to position it properly on the slide.*

- Note that the Table menu also allows you to access the Insert Table dialog box, draw a table using the Draw Table tool, or insert an Excel worksheet to organize data.

Try It! Inserting a Table

1 Start PowerPoint and open **P22Try** from the data files for this lesson.

2 Save the presentation as **P22Try_xx** in the location where your teacher instructs you to store the files for this lesson.

3 Select slide 2 and click the Insert Table icon in the content placeholder.

4 Type 2 in the Number of columns scroll box.

5 Type 5 in the Number of rows scroll box.

6 Click OK.

7 Select slide 4.

8 Click INSERT > Table.

9 Drag the pointer over the grid or use arrow keys to select 5 columns and 3 rows.

10 Click or press [ENTER] to insert the table on the slide.

11 Save the **P22Try_xx** file, and leave it open to use in the next Try It.

Using the Insert Table icon to insert a table

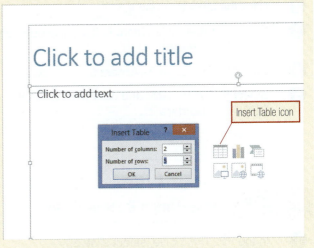

Using the Table Grid to insert a table

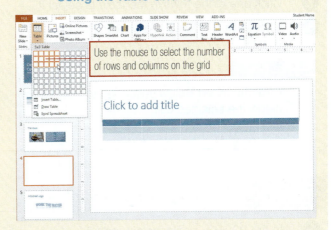

Formatting and Modifying a Table

- When a table appears on a slide, the TABLE TOOLS contextual tabs become active on the Ribbon.

- Use the TABLE TOOLS DESIGN tab to control formatting options, such as styles, shading, borders, and effects. You can also choose to emphasize specific parts of a table.

- Use the TABLE TOOLS LAYOUT tab to control the table structure, such as inserting or deleting rows and columns, merging or splitting cells, distributing rows or columns evenly, adjusting both horizontal and vertical alignment, changing text direction, and adjusting cell margins and table size.

- If you do not want to enter specific measurements for cells and table size, you can adjust rows, columns, or the table itself by dragging borders. You can also drag the entire table to reposition it on the slide if necessary.

Try It!   ## Applying Table Formats

1. In the **P22Try_xx** file, click slide 2.

2. Click the table to select it.

3. Click the Table Styles More button ▾ to open the Table Styles gallery.

4. Click Medium Style 2 - Accent 6.

5. Select the entire table and click TABLE TOOLS DESIGN > Borders ⊞.

6. Select All Borders.

   OR

   Click the Shading button 🎨 and select a color, picture, gradient, or texture to fill table cells.

7. Click the Effects button 🖵 and select from bevel, shadow, or reflection effects for the table.

8. Save the **P22Try_xx** file, and leave it open to use in the next Try It.

Try It!   ## Inserting a Row or Column

1. In the **P22Try_xx** file, select slide 2.

2. Click one of the rows in the table to select it.

3. Click TABLE TOOLS LAYOUT > Insert Above ⊞.

   OR

   Click the Insert Below button ⊞ to insert a row below the selected cell.

   OR

   Click the Insert Left button ⊞ to insert a column to the left of the selected cell.

   OR

   Click the Insert Right button ⊞ to insert a column to the right of the selected cell.

4. Save the **P22Try_xx** file, and leave it open to use in the next Try It.

Try It!   ## Deleting Part of the Table

1. In the **P22Try_xx** file, select slide 2.

2. Click one of the rows in the table to select it.

3. Click TABLE TOOLS LAYOUT > Delete 🗙.

4. Click Delete Rows.

   OR

   Click Delete Columns to delete the selected column instead.

5. Save the **P22Try_xx** file, and leave it open to use in the next Try It.

Try It! Merging Table Cells

1 In the **P22Try_xx** file, type **Table Heading** in the first row of the table on slide 2.

2 Select the heading row and click TABLE TOOLS LAYOUT > Merge Cells ▦ .

3 Click TABLE TOOLS LAYOUT > Center ≡ .

4 Save the **P22Try_xx** file, and leave it open to use in the next Try It.

Merging table cells

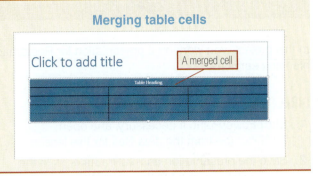

Try It! Distributing Rows Evenly

1 In the **P22Try_xx** file, select the third row in the table on slide 4.

2 Click TABLE TOOLS LAYOUT. In the Cell Size group, type **1** in the Height box 〖1"〗.

3 Select the entire table, and click TABLE TOOLS LAYOUT > Distribute Rows ⊞ .

4 Close the **P22Try_xx** file, saving changes, and exit PowerPoint.

Lesson 22—Practice

In this project, you work on a presentation for Restoration Architecture. You'll insert and format a table that lists planning services.

DIRECTIONS

1. Start PowerPoint, if necessary, and open **P22Practice** from the data files for this lesson.

2. Save the presentation as **P22Practice_xx** in the location where your teacher instructs you to store the files for this lesson.

3. Click the subtitle placeholder and move to the end of the text. Press ENTER three times and then type your name.

4. Click on slide 3 and then click **HOME** > **New Slide** > **Title Only**. A new slide appears at the end of the presentation.

5. Click the title placeholder and type **PLANNING SERVICES** as the slide title.

6. Click outside the placeholder and click **INSERT** > **Table** .

7. Drag to create a table that is five rows and five columns.

8. Fill in the table with the text shown in Figure 22-1.

9. On the **TABLE TOOLS LAYOUT** tab, in the Table Size group, type **3** in the **Height** 1" box. The table height is adjusted.

10. Click in the **Width** 1" box and type **8.5**. The table width is adjusted. Drag the table to position it as shown in Figure 22-1.

11. **With your teacher's permission**, print the presentation.

12. Close the presentation, saving changes, and exit PowerPoint.

Figure 22-1

PLANNING SERVICES

Price List				
Service	Zone 1	Zone 2	Zone 3	Zone 4
Site Study	$2,000	$2,500	$5,000	$3,000
Planning	$75/hour	$85/hour	$90/hour	$80/hour
Design	$150/hour	$250/hour	$400/hour	$200/hour

Lesson 22—Apply

In this project, you continue to work on the Restoration Architecture presentation. You edit the table you created in the last project to improve its appearance.

DIRECTIONS

1. Start PowerPoint, if necessary, and open **P22Apply** from the data files for this lesson.

2. Save the presentation as **P22Apply_xx** in the location where your teacher instructs you to store the files for this lesson.

3. You have decided to stop offering services for Zone 4. On slide 4, delete the *Zone 4* column in the table.

4. Use the TABLE TOOLS DESIGN tab to change the table style to **Themed Style 2 - Accent 5**. Apply All Borders to the table.

5. Center the entries in the last three columns, adjust column widths as desired, and position the table attractively on the slide.

6. Insert a row below the second row. Type the following:
   Permits $200 $350 $500

7. Merge the second, third, and fourth cell in the first row.

8. Select the first column and apply shading of Red, Accent 6, Darker 25%. Your slide should look like Figure 22-2.

9. Replace the text Student Name on the title slide with your name.

10. **With your teacher's permission**, print slide 4.

11. Close the presentation, saving changes, and exit PowerPoint.

Figure 22-2

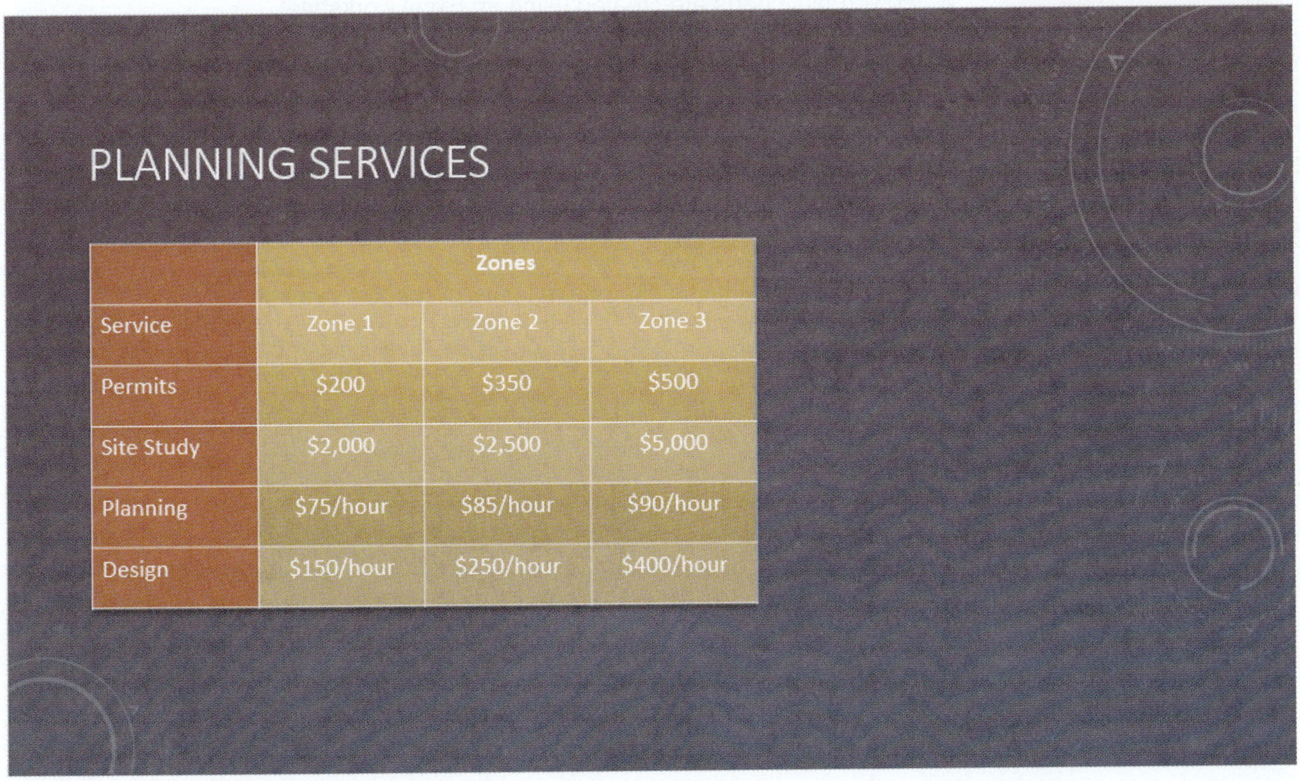

PLANNING SERVICES

Service	Zones		
	Zone 1	Zone 2	Zone 3
Permits	$200	$350	$500
Site Study	$2,000	$2,500	$5,000
Planning	$75/hour	$85/hour	$90/hour
Design	$150/hour	$250/hour	$400/hour

Lesson 23

Working with Charts

> ## ➤ What You Will Learn

> ### Inserting a Chart
> ### Formatting and Modifying a Chart

Software Skills   Add charts to a presentation to illustrate data and other concepts in a graphical way that is easy to understand. Charts can be formatted or modified as needed to improve the display.

What You Can Do

Inserting a Chart

- You can add a chart to your presentation to illustrate data in an easy-to-understand format or to compare and contrast sets of data.
- PowerPoint charts are created using an Excel worksheet.
- The chart you create from the Excel worksheet is embedded on the PowerPoint slide. To work with a chart, you use the same tools you would use when working with a chart in Excel.
- You can insert a chart into a content slide layout or add it without a placeholder using the Chart button on the INSERT tab.
- When you insert a new chart, Excel displays a worksheet containing sample data above a sample chart on the PowerPoint slide.
- You can type replacement data in the worksheet. As you change the data, the chart adjusts on the slide. You can save the Excel worksheet data for the chart and then close the worksheet to work further with the chart on the slide.

Try It!   **Inserting a Chart**

1. Start PowerPoint, and open **P23Try** from the data files for this lesson.

2. Save the presentation as **P23Try_xx** in the location where your teacher instructs you to store the files for this lesson.

3. Select slide 3 and click the Insert Chart icon ▮▮ in the content placeholder.

   OR

   Click INSERT > Insert Chart ▮▮ .

(continued)

Try It! **Inserting a Chart** *(continued)*

④ Select the Clustered Column chart type and click OK.

⑤ The chart is inserted on the slide and Excel displays a worksheet with sample data above the chart.

⑥ Close the Excel data file.

⑦ Save the **P23Try_xx** file, and leave it open to use in the next Try It.

Sample data used to create a PowerPoint chart

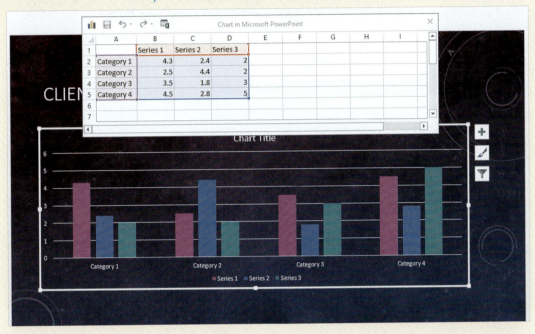

Formatting and Modifying a Chart

- When you click on a chart in PowerPoint, two content-specific tabs open on the Ribbon: CHART TOOLS DESIGN and CHART TOOLS LAYOUT.

- Use the tools on the CHART TOOLS DESIGN tab to modify the chart type and edit data. You can also select a new layout from the Quick Layout gallery, change the colors of the chart elements, or apply a chart style.

- You can choose from several chart types, including line, pie, bar, area, scatter, stock, surface, and radar.

- Use the tools on the CHART TOOLS FORMAT tab to apply special effects to the chart elements or insert a shape on the chart.

- A selected chart displays three buttons to the right of the chart selection border: the Chart Elements button, the Chart Styles button, and the Chart Filters button.

- Click the Chart Elements button to see a pop-out list of chart elements you can apply to the chart by clicking check boxes. When you point to an element in the list, a right-pointing arrow displays that you can click to show additional formatting options. This list makes it easy to show, hide, or change the position of chart elements such as legends and titles.

- Click the Chart Styles button to see a pop-out gallery of chart styles and color palettes to change the look of the chart.

- Click the Chart Filters button to see a pop-out list of the chart's series and categories. You can choose to display specific data by selecting only the series and categories you want to see.

- You can see options for modifying a particular chart element by right-clicking the element on the chart to display a Format task pane for that element.

- You can move, copy, size, and delete a chart just like any other slide object.

Try It! **Formatting and Modifying a Chart**

1 In the **P23Try_xx** file, click the chart to select it, if necessary.

2 Click CHART TOOLS DESIGN > Change Chart Type.

3 Click Clustered Bar and click OK.

4 Click the Chart Styles button to the right of the chart to display the pop-out gallery of styles to the left of the chart.

5 In the STYLE list, click Style 3.

6 Click COLOR in the pop-out gallery, and then click Color 2 in the Colorful section.

7 Click the Chart Styles button to close the gallery.

8 Save the **P23Try_xx** file, and leave it open to use in the next Try It.

The Change Chart Type dialog box

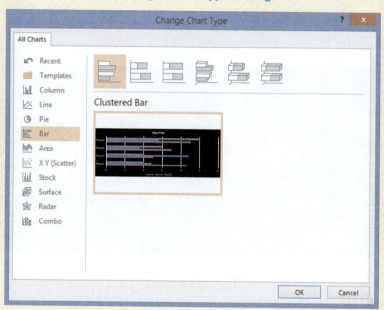

Try It! **Editing the Excel Data**

1 In the **P23Try_xx** file, click the chart to select it, if necessary.

2 Click CHART TOOLS DESIGN > Edit Data.

3 In the Excel data file, click cell A2.

4 Type **Project 1**, and press ENTER. Note that the change is immediately made in the chart as well.

5 Save the **P23Try_xx** file, and leave it open to use in the next Try It.

Try It! **Switching Rows and Columns**

1. Both the Excel worksheet and the **P23Try_xx** file should be open.

2. Click the chart to select it, and then, click CHART TOOLS DESIGN > Switch Row/ Column ▦ .

3. Close the Excel data file.

4. Save the **P23Try_xx** file, and leave it open to use in the next Try It.

Try It! **Filtering Data in the Chart**

1. In the **P23Try_xx** file, click the chart to select it, if necessary.

2. Click the Chart Filters button ▼ to the right of the chart to display the pop-out list of series and categories to the left of the chart.

3. Click in the Project 1 check box to clear the check mark.

4. Click Apply at the bottom of the pop-out list to remove the Project 1 entry.

5. Click the Chart Filters button ▼ again to close the pop-out list.

6. Save the **P23Try_xx** file, and leave it open to use in the next Try It.

Filtering data in the chart

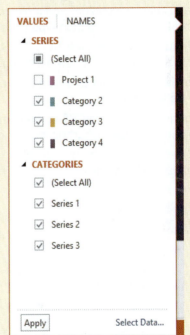

Try It! **Changing Chart Layout**

1. In the **P23Try_xx** file, click the chart to select it, if necessary.

2. Click the Chart Elements button ✚ to display the pop-out list of chart elements to the left of the chart.

3. Click the Chart Title check box to remove the check. The Chart Title is removed from the chart.

4. Click the Chart Elements button ✚ again to close the pop-out list.

5. Right-click the legend at the bottom of the chart and then click Format Legend on the shortcut menu to open the Format Legend task pane.

6. Select Right. Close the Format Legend task pane.

7. Close the **P23Try_xx** file, saving changes, and exit PowerPoint.

Lesson 23—Practice

In this project, you work on a presentation for the Campus Recreation Center. You insert a chart to show results of a usage survey.

DIRECTIONS

1. Start PowerPoint, if necessary, and open **P23Practice** from the data files for this lesson.

2. Save the presentation as **P23Practice_xx** in the location where your teacher instructs you to store the files for this lesson.

3. Click the subtitle placeholder and move to the end of the text. Press ENTER and then type your name.

4. Click on slide 3 and then click **HOME > New Slide** > **Title and Content**. A new slide appears.

5. Click the title placeholder and type **Survey Results** as the slide title.

6. Click the **Insert Chart** icon in the content placeholder. The Insert Chart dialog box opens.

7. Select **3-D Clustered Column** and click **OK**. An Excel data file appears.

8. Replace the sample data with the data shown in Figure 23-1. Then close the Excel data file.

9. Click the chart to select it, if necessary, click **CHART TOOLS DESIGN > Quick Layout** , and click **Layout 3**.

10. Click the **Chart Styles** button to the right of the chart, click **COLOR**, and click the first palette under Monochromatic (Color 5). Click the **Chart Styles** button again to close the gallery.

11. Select the chart title and type **Visits per Week**.

12. Preview the entire presentation.

13. **With your teacher's permission**, print slide 4. It should look like that shown in Figure 23-2 on the next page.

14. Close the presentation, saving changes, and exit PowerPoint.

Figure 23-1

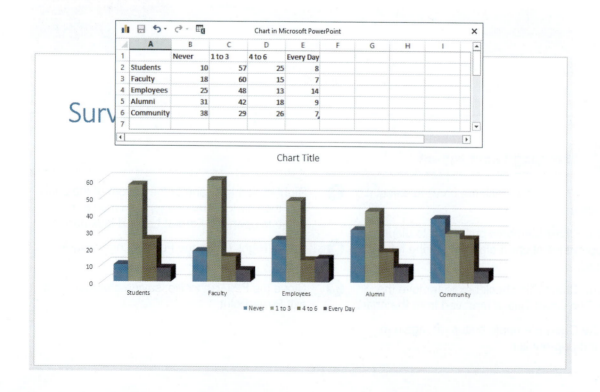

Figure 23-2

Lesson 23—Apply

In this project, you modify the chart you created in the last project. You change the chart type, adjust formats, and display new chart elements.

DIRECTIONS

1. Start PowerPoint, if necessary, and open **P23Apply** from the data files for this lesson.

2. Save the presentation as **P23Apply_xx** in the location where your teacher instructs you to store the files for this lesson.

3. On slide 4, change the appearance of the chart as follows:

   a. Change the chart type to **Clustered Column**.

   b. Click **Chart Elements** ➕, point to **Gridlines**, and click the right-pointing arrow. Click **Primary Major Vertical** in the list of additional Gridline options.

4. Edit the Excel data as follows:

   a. Change the Students value for 1 to 3 to **47**.

   b. Change the Every Day value for Students to **18**.

5. Switch the rows and columns, and then close the Excel data file.

6. Change the color of the chart bars to **Color 1** in the Colorful category.

7. Filter the data to hide the Community series.

8. Add a slide footer to the presentation that includes your name and an automatically updating date on all slides.

9. Preview the presentation to see how your chart looks.

10. **With your teacher's permission**, print slide 4.

11. Close the presentation, saving changes, and exit PowerPoint.

End-of-Chapter Activities

➤ PowerPoint Chapter 3—Critical Thinking

Creating an Effective Presentation

As the office manager at the Michigan Avenue Athletic Club, you have found that many staff members deliver ineffective presentations. You decide to research techniques to make presentations more effective, and create a presentation about it to deliver at the next staff meeting.

DIRECTIONS

1. Use the Internet to research the topic "Creating an effective presentation in PowerPoint."

2. Start PowerPoint, and create a new presentation.

3. Save the presentation as **PCT03_xx** in the location where your teacher instructs you to store the files for this chapter.

4. Apply the **View** theme to the presentation. Choose the variant with the orange vertical strip, and then hide background graphics on the title slide. Apply a different background style to the first slide only. Apply different theme colors and fonts if desired.

5. On slide 1, the title slide, enter the title **Effective Presentations** and the subtitle **Common Sense Rules for Delivering Your Message**.

6. Insert a footer that displays today's date and your name on all slides.

7. Add at least five slides to the presentation.
   a. Slide 2 should be an introduction.
   b. Slide 3 should be bullet points.
   c. Slide 4 should include a graphic.
   d. Slide 5 should be a conclusion or summary.
   e. Slide 6 should list your sources.
   f. You may choose to include additional slides between slide 4 and slide 5 to expand the topic, if necessary. Add graphics where they will enhance your message.

8. Apply transitions and animations to enhance the presentation's effectiveness.

9. If you have access to multimedia objects, insert them if they can enhance the presentation's effectiveness.

10. Save the presentation.

11. Preview the presentation to identify errors and problems, and assess how you might improve its effectiveness. For example, you might add slides so you can have fewer bullets per slide. You might adjust the font size or color to make it more readable. Save all changes.

12. Add notes to help you deliver the presentation.

13. Practice delivering the presentation, and then make changes to the presentation if necessary to improve its effectiveness. For example, you might want to make it longer or shorter, or change the timing for advancing between slides. Save changes.

14. Practice delivering the presentation again, until you are comfortable with it.

15. Deliver the presentation to your class.

16. **With your teacher's permission**, print the presentation.

17. Close the presentation, saving changes, and exit PowerPoint.

➤ PowerPoint Chapter 3—Portfolio Builder

Enhancing a Presentation

The Marketing Manager of Restoration Architecture has asked you to take a recent presentation and improve its appearance to help get it ready for an upcoming event. You'll take advantage of your new skills to change the background, theme, colors, and fonts. You'll also add animations to the slides and change the chart and table.

DIRECTIONS

1. Start PowerPoint, and open **PPB03** from the data files for this chapter.
2. Save the presentation as **PPB03_xx** in the location where your teacher instructs you to store the files for this chapter.
3. Change the theme colors to **Yellow**.
4. Change the background style for the title slide only to **Style 3**. Hide background graphics.
5. Change the font theme to **Gill Sans MT**.
6. Select the chart on slide 3 and change the chart type to **Pie**.
7. Change the chart style to **Style 7**.
8. Display the Chart Elements list and turn on Data Labels. Select **Outside End** for the data label position.
9. Change the colors in the chart to **Color 2**.
10. Right-click the dark gray chart area, click **Format Chart Area**, and then click No fill.
11. Select the table object on slide 5 and change its height to **3.5"** and the width to **8"**.

12. Center-align the table on the slide.
13. Change the table style to **Themed Style 2 - Accent 2**.
14. Select the WordArt graphic on slide 1 and change the WordArt style to **Fill - Orange, Accent 4, Soft Bevel**.
15. Insert an audio clip of music of your choice on slide 1. Format the clip to play automatically, and click **Play Across Slides** so the music will continue as you progress through the slides.
16. Add appropriate animations to text and objects.
17. Preview the presentation, and then make any necessary changes.
18. Deliver the presentation to your class.
19. Add a handout header and footer that includes a date that updates automatically and your name. Apply the footer to all.
20. **With your teacher's permission**, print a horizontal handouts page containing all the slides.
21. Close the presentation, saving changes, and exit PowerPoint.

Chapter 4

(Courtesy dotshock/Shutterstock)

Finalizing a Presentation

Lesson 24

Working with Masters

➤ What You Will Learn

Understanding the Slide Master
Customizing Slide Master Elements
Creating a Custom Layout
Working with Notes and Handout Masters

WORDS TO KNOW

Slide master
A slide that controls the appearance of all slides in a presentation. If you make a change to the master, all slides based on that master will display those changes.

Software Skills   A presentation's slide master controls the appearance and layout of all slides in the presentation. Use the master to easily adjust elements for an entire presentation. Create a new layout to further customize a presentation. The notes and handout masters allow you to change the layout of all notes pages or handouts.

What You Can Do

Understanding the Slide Master

- A **slide master** controls the appearance of slides in a presentation. PowerPoint supplies a slide master for each theme.
- The slide master stores information about background, fonts, colors, and the placement of placeholders on a slide.
- The easiest way to make global changes throughout a presentation—for example, specifying a new font for all titles or adding a logo to all slides—is to make the change once on the slide master.
- Each slide master includes layouts for each type of slide available for a theme.
- Switch to Slide Master view using the Slide Master button on the VIEW tab.
- The slide master displays at the top of the Thumbnail pane, and the available layouts display below the slide master.

Try It!   **Displaying the Slide Master**

1. Start PowerPoint, and open **P24Try** from the data files for this lesson.

2. Save the presentation as **P24Try_xx** in the location where your teacher instructs you to store the files for this lesson.

3. On the VIEW tab, in the Master Views group, click the Slide Master button 🖻.

4. Save the **P24Try_xx** file, and leave it open to use in the next Try It.

Slide master for the current theme

Slide elements

SLIDE MASTER tab

Slide master for the theme

Slide layouts for the theme

Click to edit Master title style

Customizing Slide Master Elements

- You can make changes to the slide master just as you would make changes in Normal view.

- The SLIDE MASTER tab offers basic options for making changes to the slide master, such as applying a new theme, colors, fonts, effects, or background.

- You can modify text formats, such as font, font style, font size, color, alignment, and so on, by clicking on the slide master in the Thumbnail pane and then applying the desired text formats.

- Modify the bullet symbols and colors by clicking in a bullet level and then selecting new formats in the Bullets and Numbering dialog box.

- Regardless of which theme or template you use, you can change the colors used in the presentation.

- You can also adjust the position of any placeholder or even delete any of the placeholders, including the title, content, date, footer, and slide number placeholders.

■ Some changes you make to the slide master will also appear on the other layouts. For example, if you change the title font on the slide master, the same change will be made to the title font on the Title and Content and Two Content layouts.

■ To adjust the elements of one of the other layouts, click it in the list below the slide master. Any changes you make to that layout will apply to all slides based on that layout.

Try It!   **Customizing Slide Master Elements**

① In the **P24Try_xx** file, click the slide master at the top of the Thumbnail pane, if necessary (it is labeled 1).

② Click SLIDE MASTER > Colors 🔲, scroll down the color list, and click Marquee. Colors change on all layouts below the slide master.

③ Click SLIDE MASTER > Fonts 🅰 and click Corbel. Fonts are changed on all layouts.

④ On the slide master, click the first-level bullet item in the content placeholder.

⑤ Click HOME > Bullets ≣ ▾ drop-down arrow, and select Hollow Square Bullets.

⑥ Click HOME > Bullets ≣ ▾ drop-down arrow, click Bullets and Numbering, click the Color button, and select Red, Accent 6. Click OK.

⑦ Click Title Slide Layout, just below the slide master. This layout controls the appearance of all slides formatted as title slides.

⑧ Click SLIDE MASTER > Hide Background Graphics.

⑨ On the Title Slide layout, click the light-gray rectangle at the left side of the slide to select it, and then click DRAWING TOOLS FORMAT > Shape Fill ⬧ > Gold, Accent 5, Darker 25%.

⑩ Click in the Click to edit Master title style paragraph and then click HOME > Center ≣ .

✓ *Notice that the changes you made to the Title Slide layout are not made on the slide master or other layouts.*

⑪ On the SLIDE MASTER tab, click Close Master View ❎ .

⑫ Scroll through the slides to see how the changes you made to the slide master appear on all slides and the changes you made to the Title Slide layout display on the first slide.

⑬ Save the **P24Try_xx** file, and leave it open to use in the next Try It.

Changes to the Title Slide Layout

Creating a Custom Layout

- You can create your own slide layout for a specific type of content.

- If you need several slides with this layout, creating a custom layout slide master can save time.

- Use the Insert Layout button to add a new slide master layout to the list in the Thumbnail pane.

- You can choose whether or not to display the title and footer information on the new layout.

- You can then use the Insert Placeholder list to add any of the typical placeholders to the slide: Content, Text, Picture, Chart, Table, SmartArt, Media, or Online Image.

- You draw and position the placeholders just as if they were shapes. If you insert a Text placeholder, you can format the text as desired so it will always display those formats on slides created from the layout.

- Once you've created your custom layout, click Rename and supply a new layout name to make it easy to find.

- Custom layouts display beneath the slide master in the Thumbnail pane along with the other default layouts.

Try It!   **Creating a Custom Layout**

1. In the **P24Try_xx** file, click VIEW > Slide Master and then click the slide master in the Thumbnail pane.

2. Click the Insert Layout button.

3. Choose to display master elements.

   - Click Title in the Master Layout group to show or hide the Title placeholder.

   - Click Footers in the Master Layout group to show or hide the footer placeholders.

   The Edit Master and Master Layout Groups

4. Click the Insert Placeholder button.

5. Click Picture, and then draw a 2" square.

6. Click in the Picture bullet item in the picture placeholder, and then click HOME > Bullets to turn off bullet formatting.

7. Click SLIDE MASTER > Insert Placeholder > Text.

8. Draw a placeholder to the right of the picture placeholder, 2" high and about 5.5" wide.

Add placeholders to complete the new layout

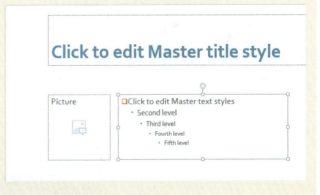

9. Click SLIDE MASTER > Rename.

10. In the Rename Layout dialog box, type **Specials** as the new name for the layout.

11. Click Rename.

12. Save the **P24Try_xx** file, and leave it open to use in the next Try It.

Working with Notes and Handout Masters

- The appearance of notes pages and handouts are controlled by their own masters, just as the appearance of slides is controlled by the slide master.

- You can use the notes master to adjust the size or position of the slide graphic or any of the text placeholders.

- You can also modify the text formats in any of the text placeholders.

- You can use the handout master to adjust the size, position, and text formats for any of the text placeholders on any of the handout options.

- You cannot move or resize the placeholders for the slides on the handout master.

Try It!   Working with Notes and Handout Masters

1. In the **P24Try_xx** file, click VIEW > Notes Master.

2. Click the notes placeholder below the slide image, and then click DRAWING TOOLS FORMAT > Shape Styles ⊟ > Subtle Effect - Blue, Accent 1.

3. Click VIEW > Normal to return to Normal view.

4. Click VIEW > Handout Master.

5. Click the Header placeholder, hold down SHIFT, and click the Date placeholder.

6. Click HOME > Font Size > 14, and then click HOME > Bold **B**.

7. Click VIEW > Normal to return to Normal view.

8. Close the **P24Try_xx** file, saving changes, and exit PowerPoint.

The notes master

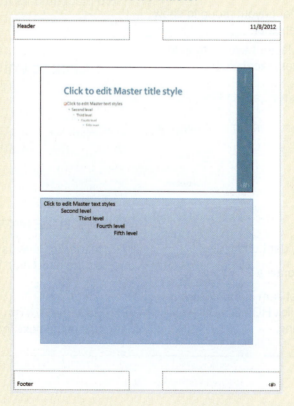

Lesson 24—Practice

Natural Light has asked you to fine-tune a presentation they are preparing for a home décor trade show. They have asked you to make some changes that will apply to a number of slides, so you will customize the slide master by changing colors and the background and adding a placeholder to the title slide.

DIRECTIONS

1. Start PowerPoint, and open **P24Practice** from the data files for this lesson.

2. Save the presentation as **P24Practice_xx** in the location where your teacher instructs you to store the files for this lesson.

3. Click **VIEW** > **Slide Master** and click the slide master in the Thumbnail pane.

4. Click **SLIDE MASTER** > **Background Styles** > **Style 6**.

5. Click **SLIDE MASTER** > **Colors** and select Blue.

6. In the content placeholder, select all five levels of bullet items, click the **Font Color** button on the Mini toolbar, and click **Dark Blue, Text 2**.

7. Select the master title style text, click **HOME** > **Font Color** > **Dark Blue, Text 2**.

8. Click the Footer placeholder, hold down SHIFT, click the slide number placeholder, and then click the date placeholder.

9. Click **HOME** and click the **Font Color** button to apply the same font color as for the other text on the slide master.

10. Click the Title Slide layout in the Thumbnail pane. Make changes to the title slide as follows:

    a. Select the subtitle text and change the font color to **Turquoise, Accent 2, Darker 25%**.

    b. Select the title placeholder and then click **DRAWING TOOLS FORMAT** > **Shape Height** and click the down increment arrow to change the height to **1.8"**.

    c. Change the height of the subtitle placeholder to **0.6"** and drag the subtitle straight up close to the title placeholder.

    d. Click **SLIDE MASTER** > **Insert Placeholder** > **Online Image** and draw the placeholder in the space beneath the subtitle, as shown in Figure 24-1.

    e. Remove the bullet from the Online Image text.

11. Close Slide Master view and display slide 1. Click **HOME** > **Reset** if necessary to display the changed title layout.

12. Preview your slides in Slide Show view to see the new master formats.

13. On slide 1, click the Online Image placeholder, type the keyword **kitchen**, and select an online image. Click **Insert**.

14. **With your teacher's permission,** print the title slide of your presentation.

15. Close the presentation, saving changes, and exit PowerPoint.

Figure 24-1

Lesson 24—Apply

In this project, you continue to work with the Natural Light presentation masters. You will adjust bullet formats, add a custom layout, and format the notes master.

DIRECTIONS

1. Start PowerPoint, and open **P24Apply** from the data files for this lesson.

2. Save the presentation as **P24Apply_xx** in the location where your teacher instructs you to store the files for this lesson.

3. Display the slide master and change colors to Orange Red.

4. Modify the bullet symbols and colors as shown in Figure 24-2 on the next page.

   a. Change the first-level bullet as marked. (Choose Customize in the Bullets and Numbering dialog box to locate the star in the Wingdings font.)

   b. Change the second-level bullet as marked.

5. Create a custom layout to display featured products as shown in Figure 24-3 on the next page.

   a. Change the title placeholder as marked.

   b. Create an Online Image placeholder as marked. Remove the bullet formatting from the placeholder label.

   c. Create a Text placeholder as marked.

   d. Rename the custom layout as **Featured Item**.

6. Add a new slide at the end of the presentation with the new Featured Item layout. Add content as follows:

   a. Insert the title **Featured Item**.

   b. Insert an online image of a chandelier.

   c. Type the following text in the text box: **Chandeliers are in! We have an amazing variety, from rustic wrought iron to brass to glittering crystal.**

   d. Add the following note text: **Pictured chandelier is item #JT265 for $2,500.**

7. Modify the notes master as follows:

   a. Change the size of the text in the notes placeholder to 20 point and center the text.

   b. Decrease the size of the text placeholder.

8. In the Header and Footer dialog box, create a header for the Notes and Handouts pages as follows:

   a. Add an automatically updating date.

   b. Add your name to the header.

9. Preview the notes page for slide 5 to see your changes to the masters.

10. Preview the presentation. If your slide master changes do not display, reset each slide.

11. Close the presentation, saving changes, and exit PowerPoint.

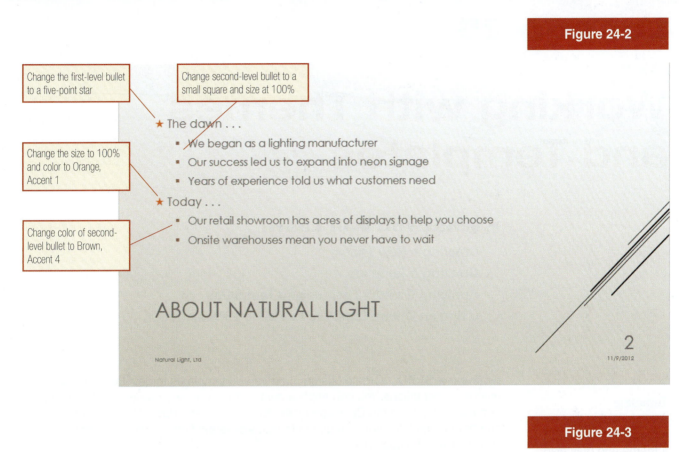

Figure 24-2

Change the first-level bullet to a five-point star

Change second-level bullet to a small square and size at 100%

Change the size to 100% and color to Orange, Accent 1

Change color of second-level bullet to Brown, Accent 4

★ The dawn . . .
  ▪ We began as a lighting manufacturer
  ▪ Our success led us to expand into neon signage
  ▪ Years of experience told us what customers need
★ Today . . .
  ▪ Our retail showroom has acres of displays to help you choose
  ▪ Onsite warehouses mean you never have to wait

ABOUT NATURAL LIGHT

Natural Light, Ltd

2
11/9/2012

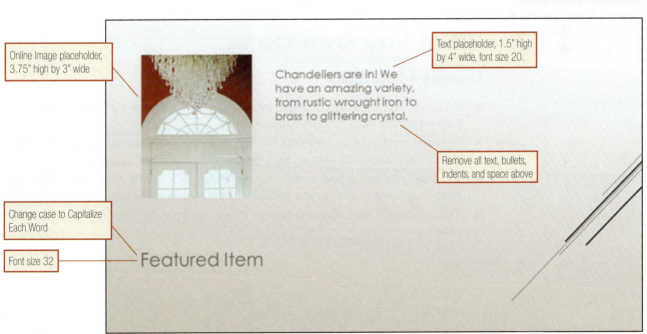

Figure 24-3

Online Image placeholder, 3.75" high by 3" wide

Text placeholder, 1.5" high by 4" wide, font size 20.

Chandeliers are in! We have an amazing variety, from rustic wrought iron to brass to glittering crystal.

Remove all text, bullets, indents, and space above

Change case to Capitalize Each Word

Font size 32

Featured Item

Pictured chandelier is item #JT265 for $2,500.

Lesson 25

Working with Themes and Templates

➤ **What You Will Learn**

Creating a New Theme
Creating a Template
Applying Custom Themes and Templates
Using an Online Template to Create a Presentation

WORDS TO KNOW

Template
A presentation that is already formatted with a theme and may also include sample text to guide you in completing the presentation.

Software Skills   Create custom themes and templates to develop your own unique presentations. You can apply a custom theme to any presentation. Custom templates display in the Backstage view for easy access. PowerPoint provides a number of templates you can use to format a presentation or help you create a specific kind of presentation.

What You Can Do

Creating a New Theme

- In Lesson 18, you learned how to modify an existing theme by changing the theme's colors, fonts, and background style.

- You can create your own custom theme by saving your changes to colors, fonts, layouts, and background in an existing theme.

- You can apply colors and fonts in Normal view, but to make adjustments that you want to apply to all slides, you should work in Slide Master view.

- If you no longer want to use a custom theme, you can delete it from the Themes gallery.

Try It!   Creating a New Theme

① Start PowerPoint, if necessary, and click Blank Presentation.

② Click VIEW > Slide Master 🖵, and then click the slide master at the top of the Thumbnail pane.

③ Click SLIDE MASTER > Colors 🔲 and select Aspect.

④ Click SLIDE MASTER > Colors 🔲 > Customize Colors to display the Create New Theme Colors dialog box.

⑤ Click Accent 3, and then click Blue in the Standard Colors palette. Click Save to save the new theme colors as Custom 1.

⑥ Click SLIDE MASTER > Fonts 🅰 and select Arial-Times New Roman.

⑦ Click in the first-level bullet item, click HOME > Bullets ≔ ▾ drop-down arrow, and select Arrow bullets in the gallery.

⑧ Click HOME > Bullets ≔ ▾ drop-down arrow > Bullets and Numbering, and then click Color and select Dark Blue, Accent 3.

⑨ Click the Title Slide layout beneath the slide master and make the following changes:

   a. Click in the master title text, and then click HOME > Align Left ≡ .

   b. Click in the subtitle text and click HOME > Align Left ≡ .

   c. Click SLIDE MASTER > Background Styles 🔲 > Format Background to open the Format Background task pane.

   d. Click Gradient fill, and then click Preset gradients and select Top Spotlight – Accent 3 from the gallery. Close the Format Background task pane.

⑩ Close Slide Master view.

⑪ Save the presentation as **P25TryA_xx**.

⑫ Click DESIGN > Themes ▾, and then click Save Current Theme on the Themes gallery.

   ✓ *PowerPoint automatically takes you to the folder where document themes are stored.*

⑬ Type **P25TryA_xx_theme** in the File name box, and then click Save.

⑭ Click the Themes gallery's More button ▾ to see that the new theme has been added to the Custom section of the Themes gallery.

⑮ Save the **P25TryA_xx** file, and leave it open to use in the next Try It.

Creating a Template

■ Like themes, PowerPoint **templates** contain a unique combination of formatting elements, such as colors, fonts, images, and effects, to create a predefined coordinated set.

■ You can save a presentation that you have customized as a template. Then, you can use the template to create new presentations.

■ To create a template, you can customize an existing theme or template and then save your version with a new name.

■ You can also create a template from scratch. Use Slide Master view to format the background, fonts, colors, and layouts as desired.

Try It! Creating a Template

1 In the **P25TryA_xx** file, click FILE > Save As.

2 Type **P25TryA_xx_template** in the File name box.

3 Click the Save as type drop-down arrow and click PowerPoint Template.

4 Save the template in the location where your teacher instructs you to save the files for this lesson.

✓ *Because you are not saving your template to the default location, you will not see the template among the other templates on the New tab in the Backstage view.*

5 Press `CTRL` + `W` to close the file, leaving PowerPoint open.

Applying Custom Themes and Templates

■ When you save a custom theme, PowerPoint will display it under the CUSTOM heading on the New tab. You can click the theme to start a new presentation formatted with that theme.

■ You can also apply a custom theme from the Custom section of the Themes gallery. A custom theme will change the formats of any other theme to those of the custom theme.

■ You can begin a new presentation from a custom template by displaying the template file in File Explorer, right-clicking it, and selecting New.

■ By default, templates are stored in the Custom Office Templates folder in the My Documents folder in the Documents library.

Try It! Starting a New Presentation from a Custom Template

1 Use File Explorer to display the folder where your teacher has instructed you to store files for this lesson.

2 Right-click **P25TryA_xx_template** and click New. A new presentation opens based on the template you created.

3 Close the file without saving changes.

Try It! Applying a Custom Theme to an Existing Presentation

1 In PowerPoint, click FILE > New.

2 Click Blank Presentation.

3 Click DESIGN > Themes ⤓ to display the Themes gallery.

4 Click the **P25TryA_xx_theme** in the Custom section of the gallery.

5 Close the file without saving changes, and leave PowerPoint open.

Apply a custom theme to a presentation

Using an Online Template to Create a Presentation

- Besides providing you with a number of interesting themes from which you can create new presentations, PowerPoint offers a wide variety of templates from many categories you can use to create a presentation.

- Online templates usually provide a number of slides with sample text and graphics as well as slide layouts specifically designed for the template.

- You can find PowerPoint templates by searching on the New tab in the Backstage view.

- Click one of the suggested search links, such as Business, Education, or Photo Albums, or type keywords in the search box to find templates that match the keywords.

- A Category list opens to the right after you do a search so that you can refine your search. Click any of the categories to filter the results so you can find exactly what you need.

- Once you choose your template, click Create. PowerPoint opens the template with a default title such as Presentation1.

- You may need to modify a presentation you create from an online template to adjust slide size. You may also want to make changes in the slide master to adjust colors, fonts, position of placeholders, and so on to suit the template for your use.

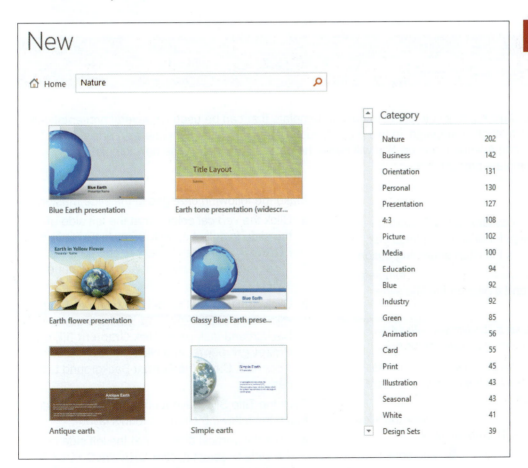

Figure 25-1

Try It!   **Using an Online Template to Create a Presentation**

1 Click FILE > New to display templates in the Backstage view.

2 In the Suggested searches list, click Nature to see presentation templates relating to nature.

3 In the Category list, click Green to further filter the nature templates.

4 Click Earth tone presentation (widescreen). The title slide displays in a window.

5 Click the More Images right arrow to scroll through the slide layouts provided with this template.

6 Click Create to create a new presentation based on the template.

7 On the title slide, type **Planet Earth** in the title placeholder.

8 Replace the subtitle with your full name.

9 Press F5 to start a slide show and preview each slide in the presentation.

10 Save the presentation as **P25TryB_xx** in the location where your teacher instructs you to store files for this lesson, and then close the file and exit PowerPoint.

Lesson 25—Practice

Michigan Avenue Athletic Club wants you to create a custom template that can be used for several presentations as part of a special public relations campaign. In this project, you will use an online template as a basis for creating the new Michigan Avenue template. You will begin the process of creating the new template by customizing the online template presentation.

DIRECTIONS

1. Start PowerPoint, if necessary. In the Backstage view, click in the Search for online templates box, type **exercise**, and click the Start searching button.

2. Click the **Class presentation with video** template, which shows a man and a bike on the title slide. Click **Create**.

   ✓ Note that this presentation is Standard size, with a 4:3 orientation. You will leave the presentation at this size.

3. Save the presentation as **P25Practice_xx** in the location where your teacher instructs you to store the files for this lesson.

4. Click **VIEW** > **Slide Master** and select the slide master at the top of the Thumbnail pane.

5. Click **SLIDE MASTER** > **Colors** and select the **Median** color palette.

6. Make the following changes to the slide master:

   a. Click the vertical color bar at the left side of the slide to select it, click **DRAWING TOOLS FORMAT** > **Shape Styles**, and click the **Moderate Effect – Green, Accent 5** shape style.

   b. Click **SLIDE MASTER** > **Background Styles** > **Format Background**. On the Format Background task pane, click **Gradient fill**, click **Preset gradients**, and click **Light Gradient – Accent 5**. Close the Format Background task pane.

7. Click the Title Slide layout under the slide master. Make the following changes to this layout:

   a. Click the vertical color bar at the left side of the slide to select it, click **DRAWING TOOLS FORMAT** > **Shape Styles**, and click the **Moderate Effect – Green, Accent 5** shape style.

b. Click **SLIDE MASTER** > **Background Styles** , right-click **Style 1**, and click **Apply to Selected Layouts**.

c. Click the picture of the man with the bike and press DEL to remove it from the slide.

d. Click **INSERT** > **Pictures**, navigate to the data files for this lesson, and click **P25Practice_picture.jpg**. Click **Insert**.

e. Resize the picture to be **5.4"** high and position it as shown in Figure 25-2.

f. Change the font size of the master title text to **66** points. Then close Slide Master view.

8. Replace the subtitle with your full name, and type **Michigan Avenue Athletic Club** in the title placeholder.

9. Press F5 to start a slide show and preview each slide in the presentation to see the formats supplied by the template.

10. Close the presentation, saving changes, and exit PowerPoint.

Figure 25-2

Lesson 25—Apply

In this presentation, you finalize the Michigan Avenue Athletic Club's new template. You will make some additional adjustments to slide master layouts, save the presentation as a theme and a template, and apply the theme to a new presentation to which you will add some sample text.

DIRECTIONS

1. Start PowerPoint, if necessary, and open the file **P25Apply**.

2. Save the presentation as **P25ApplyA_xx** in the location where your teacher instructs you to store files for this lesson.

3. Switch to Slide Master view.

4. Change the fonts to **Tw Cen MT**.

5. Select the picture on the Title Slide layout, click **PICTURE TOOLS FORMAT** > **Color** 🖼 , and select **Green, Accent color 5 Light**.

6. Scroll down to locate the Two Content layout and select it. Notice that the title placeholder overlays the two content placeholders.

   a. Click the first content placeholder, hold down ⌗SHIFT , and click the second content placeholder. Click one of the top center sizing handles and drag downward to just below the title placeholder to reduce the height of both placeholders.

   b. Click the title placeholder, click the right center sizing handle, and drag to the right until the placeholder aligns at the right with the right content placeholder.

7. Close Slide Master view and save your changes.

8. Save the presentation as a theme with the name **P25ApplyA_xx_theme**.

9. Save the presentation as a template with the name **P25ApplyA_xx_template** in the location where your teacher instructs you to store the files for this lesson. Close the file, leaving PowerPoint open.

10. Start a new presentation and apply the **P25ApplyA_xx_theme**. Change the slide size to **Standard**, maximizing content.

11. Save the presentation as **P25ApplyB_xx**.

12. Insert your full name in the subtitle placeholder and type **Michigan Avenue Athletic Club** in the title placeholder.

13. Insert a new Title and Content slide and insert the content shown in Figure 25-3 on the next page.

14. Insert a new Two Content slide and insert the content shown in Figure 25-4 on the next page. Locate an online picture of your choice for the left content placeholder.

15. Add the current date and slide numbers to all slides except the title slide.

16. Preview all slides to check text and the position of objects.

17. **With your teacher's permission**, print the presentation as handouts with 4 slides per page.

18. Remove all custom colors and themes you created in this lesson.

19. Close the presentation, saving changes, and exit PowerPoint.

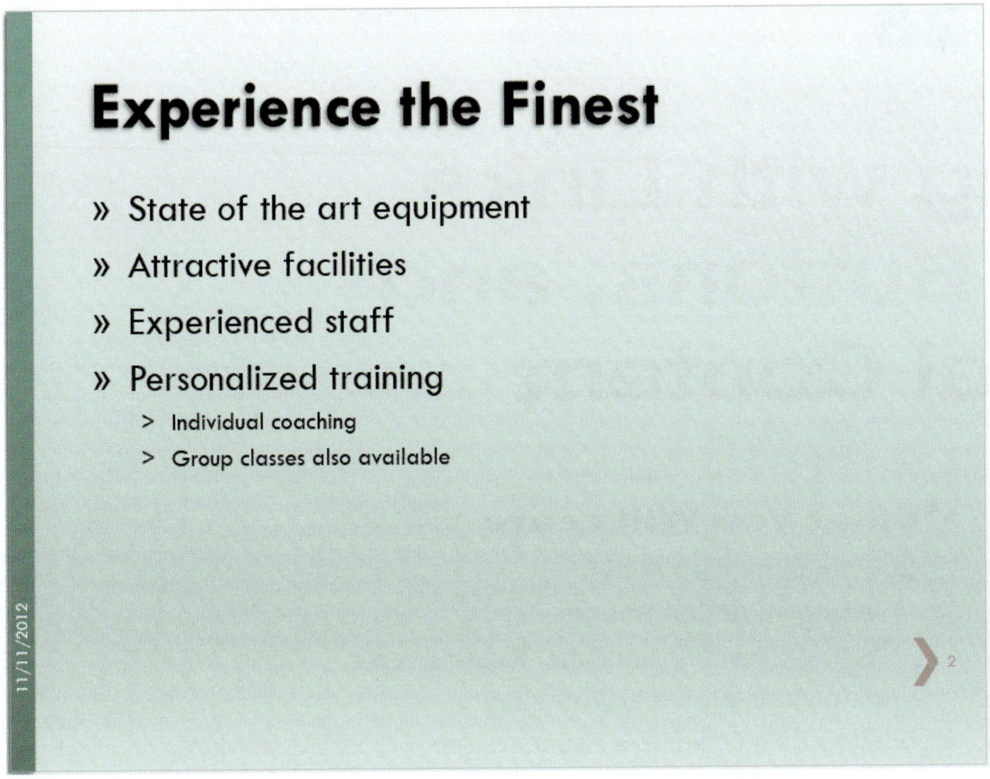

Figure 25-3

Experience the Finest

» State of the art equipment

» Attractive facilities

» Experienced staff

» Personalized training
  > Individual coaching
  > Group classes also available

11/11/2012

> 2

Figure 25-4

Find Your Center at Michigan

» New at Michigan Avenue Athletic Club:
  > Yoga for all skill levels
  > Barre classes
  > Pilates

11/11/2012

 3

Lesson 26

Working with Links, Action Buttons, and External Content

➤ What You Will Learn

Inserting Links on Slides

Inserting an Action Button

Inserting Objects from Other Applications

Working with an Excel Worksheet

Linking Excel Data to a Presentation

WORD TO KNOW

Action button
A shape that is programmed to perform a specific action, such as running an application or jumping to a specific slide.

Embed
Insert data in a destination application from a source application so that you can edit it using the source application's tools.

Link
Insert data in a destination application from a source application so that a link exists between the source and the destination data.

Software Skills   Links and action buttons allow you to move quickly from one slide to a distant one, connect to the Internet, or open other documents or applications.

What You Will Learn

Inserting Links on Slides

- Use the Hyperlink button in the Links group on the INSERT tab to set up links from a slide to another slide, to a different presentation or document, to a Web site, or to an e-mail address.

- The Insert Hyperlink dialog box allows you to select the target of the link—the slide that will display or the page that will open when the link is clicked.

- Links are displayed in a different color with an underline, as on a Web page. Links are active only in Slide Show view.

- You can also use an object such as a shape, picture, or other graphic as the link object.

Try It! | Inserting Links on Slides

1 Start PowerPoint, and open **P26TryA** from the data files for this lesson.

2 Save the presentation as **P26TryA_xx** in the location where your teacher instructs you to store the files for this lesson.

3 Display slide 2 and select the text *Contact Information.*

4 On the INSERT tab, click the Hyperlink button 🔗.

5 Click Place in This Document from the Link to pane.

6 Select slide 8 from the list.

7 Click OK.

8 Display slide 8 and click at the end of the E-mail bullet item.

9 Press ENTER and then press TAB.

10 Click INSERT > Hyperlink 🔗, and then select E-mail Address in the Link to pane.

11 In the E-mail address box, type **contact@voyagertraveladventures.net**.

✓ *PowerPoint automatically adds the text* mailto *at the beginning of the e-mail address.*

12 In the Text to display box, delete the word *mailto.* Click OK.

13 Click at the end of the Web site bullet item.

14 Press ENTER and then press TAB.

15 Click INSERT > Hyperlink 🔗, and then select Existing File or Web Page in the Link to pane.

16 In the Address box, type the following:

www.voyagertraveladventures.net

and then click OK.

17 Save the **P26TryA_xx** file, and leave it open to use in the next Try It.

Links to an e-mail address and Web site on a slide

Contact Information

- Address
  - 450 Ormond Street – Clifton, OH – 45220
- Phone
  - (513) 555-5678
- E-mail
  - contact@voyagertraveladventures.net
- Web site
  - http://www.voyagertraveladventures.net/

Inserting an Action Button

- You can use **action buttons** to jump quickly from one slide to another.

- Action buttons are programmed to perform specific tasks, such as jump to the previous slide, play a sound, or run a program or a macro.

- Action buttons appear at the bottom of the Shapes gallery. Select the action button and then draw the button on the slide to open the Action Settings dialog box.

- Use the Action Settings dialog box to specify the button's action.

- By default, the action will occur when you click the mouse button; however, you can use the Action Settings dialog box to modify when the action occurs.

- Action buttons can be formatted like any other shapes. You can apply fills, outlines, and effects. They can also be resized or moved anywhere on the slide.

- You can turn any object, such as a picture or placeholder, into an action button by using the Action button on the INSERT tab to give it an action to perform.

Try It!   Inserting an Action Button

1. In the **P26TryA_xx** file, click slide 8 if necessary.

2. On the HOME tab, click the Shapes More button ▾.

3. Select the Action Button: Back or Previous ◁ from the Action Buttons group at the bottom of the gallery.

4. Draw the button shape (about 1" wide and 0.5" high) on the lower-right side of the slide.

5. In the Action Settings dialog box, click the Hyperlink to drop-down arrow.

6. Select Slide… to specify a slide.

7. In the Hyperlink to Slide dialog box, select slide 2.

8. Click OK and then click OK again.

9. Press F5 to start the slide show from the beginning. On slide 2, click the Contact Information link to go to slide 8.

10. On slide 8, click the Web site link. This is a dummy link that does not connect to a live Web site. Close the browser and then click the action button to return to slide 2.

11. Save the **P26TryA_xx** file, and leave it open to use in the next Try It.

Inserting Objects from Other Applications

- You can add content from other applications to a PowerPoint presentation, such as a Word table, an Excel chart, or an Excel worksheet.

- You have several options for adding external content to a slide.

  - You can use Copy and Paste to insert the content on the slide. When you use these commands, the content becomes part of the PowerPoint presentation. A Word table would become a PowerPoint table, and an Excel chart would become a PowerPoint chart.

  - You can use the Paste Special dialog box to **embed** the object. An embedded object maintains its identity as an object from another application, so you can use that application's tools to edit the object.

- Objects that have been copied or embedded can be resized like other PowerPoint objects.

Try It! Inserting Objects from Other Applications

1 In the **P26TryA_xx** file, display slide 7.

2 In Excel, open the **P26TryB** file from the data files for this lesson.

3 Click the worksheet chart to select it, then click HOME > Copy.

4 Switch to the presentation and click HOME > Paste. Notice that the columns in the chart change color to those that would appear if the chart had been created in PowerPoint and the chart tools are those from PowerPoint.

5 Click Undo to remove the chart from the slide.

6 Click the Paste button's drop-down arrow and click Paste Special.

7 In the Paste Special dialog box, make sure the Paste option is selected and the As list has Microsoft Excel Chart Object selected.

8 Click OK. Notice that the chart colors are the same as those in the worksheet.

9 Double-click the chart and notice the diagonal-line border around the object and the Excel tools in the Ribbon.

10 Click outside the chart to deselect it, and then drag the lower-right corner to enlarge the object on the slide.

11 Save the **P26TryA_xx** file, and leave it open to use in the next Try It. Leave the Excel file open to use in a later Try It.

Paste Special dialog box

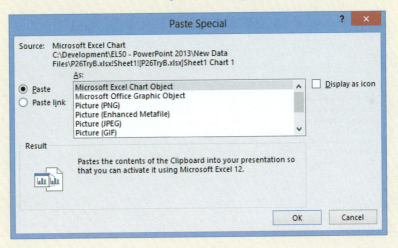

Working with an Excel Worksheet

- If you need to show data that may need to be recalculated or otherwise manipulated, you can insert an Excel worksheet directly on a slide.

- The Excel Spreadsheet option in the Tables group of the INSERT tab displays a blank Excel worksheet that you can resize as necessary. You can enter text, values, and formulas in the worksheet just as you would in Excel.

- If the data you want to add to the slide already exists in an Excel worksheet, you can embed the worksheet data on the slide by copying and pasting or by using the Insert Object command.

- To enter or modify data in a worksheet, you must open it for editing by double-clicking it. A worksheet ready for editing has a diagonal line border.

- You may need to adjust the size of embedded worksheet data (and increase or decrease the size of text in the object) by dragging a corner of the object container.

- To eliminate blank columns and rows from the view, you crop the worksheet using the bottom or right handle while in editing mode.

Try It!   Inserting an Excel Worksheet on a Slide

1. In the **P26TryA_xx** file, display slide 5.

2. Click INSERT > Table ▦ > Excel Spreadsheet. A default-sized worksheet appears on the slide as soon as you click the command.

3. Click the right corner of the spreadsheet object and drag to add columns and rows as necessary.

4. Click outside the worksheet to deselect it.

5. Display slide 4.

6. On the INSERT tab, click the Object button ▭.

7. In the Insert Object dialog box, click Create from file and then click Browse.

8. Navigate to the location of the data files for this lesson and select **P26TryC.xlsx**.

9. Click Open and then click OK.

10. Click on the lower-right corner and drag to resize the entire object without distorting text in the worksheet.

11. Save the **P26TryA_xx** file, and leave it open to use in the next Try It.

Excel worksheet on a slide

Cruise Deals for Spring

Cruise	Port of Call	Disembark Port	Number of Days	Cost	Special Rate
Alaskan Whale Adventure	Juneau, AK	Juneau, AK	10	3995	3499
New England Exploration	Boston, MA	Montreal, Quebec, CA	7	4999	3999
Orient Cruise Express	Seatle, WA	Singapore	25	5499	4999
Panama Canal	Vancouver, B.C. CA	Tampa, FL	21	2199	1999
Mexican Coast	Los Angeles, CA	Cabo San Lucas, Mexico	7	999	499
Greek Isles	Venice, Italy	Corfu, Greece	7	919	799
Cruise to Nowhere	New York, NY	New York, NY	2	379	299

Try It!   Editing Worksheet Data

1. In the **P26TryA_xx** file, with slide 4 displayed, double-click the worksheet object to open it for editing.

2. Select the range D2:D8, the values under the Number of Days heading.

3. On the HOME tab, click Center ≡.

4. Click outside the worksheet to close it.

5. Display slide 5 and double-click the worksheet object to open it for editing.

6. Click in cell A1 and type **This is an Excel worksheet**.

7. Click the sizing handle at the bottom center of the diagonal line border and drag up to display only rows 1 through 7. Click the right center sizing handle in the diagonal line border and drag to the left to display only columns A through E.

8. Click outside the worksheet object to close it.

9. Save the **P26TryA_xx** file, and leave it open to use in the next Try It.

Linking Excel Data to a Presentation

- If the data you need to show might change over time, the best option is to maintain a **link** between worksheet data in Excel and the data displayed on a slide.

- To insert linked data on a slide, copy it in Excel and then use the Paste Special option on PowerPoint's Paste button.

- When you modify the worksheet in Excel, the slide data updates to show the same modifications.

- You can modify linked data by double-clicking the object to open it in its original application.

Try It!　**Linking Excel Data to a Presentation**

1. Switch to Excel, and save the **P26TryB.xlsx** file as **P26TryB_xx** in the location where your teacher instructs you to store the files for this lesson.

2. Select cells A4:E10, which contain the data to link.

3. Click HOME > Copy 📋 .

4. In the **P26TryA_xx** presentation, select slide 6.

5. Click HOME > Paste drop-down arrow, and then click Paste Special.

6. In the Paste Special dialog box, click Paste link and then click OK.

7. Close the workbook without saving changes, and exit Excel.

8. Save the **P26TryA_xx** file, and leave it open to use in the next Try It.

Try It!　**Editing Data in a Linked Worksheet**

1. In the **P26TryA_xx** file, display slide 6 if necessary.

2. Click the linked worksheet object to select it, click on the lower-right corner, and drag diagonally to the lower-right to enlarge the object.

3. Double-click the worksheet object to open the linked file in Excel.

4. In cell C4, type **Travel** before the word *Guide*, save the file, and close Excel.

5. In the **P26TryA_xx** presentation, check that the change you made to the Excel data is reflected in the worksheet object on slide 6.

6. Close the **P26TryA_xx** file, saving changes, and exit PowerPoint.

Linked data updates automatically on the slide

Adventure Travel Packages

Destination	Number of Days	Travel Guide	Price	Date
Magical Madagascar	18	Jino Malotoniro	$5,495	May 1 - 19
Exploring Patagonia	14	Juan Ismareldo	$3,999	June 14 - 28
Climbing Kilimanjaro	18	Samia Asindamu	$7,999	July 1 - 19
Himalayan Mountain Kingdoms	14	Hashmat Sing	$6,799	August 1 - 15
Walking Across the Serengeti	10	Steve Raymond	$6,999	Sept 10 - 20
Passage to India	9	Aarmann Acharya	$1,499	Nov 1 - 9

Lesson 26—Practice

The manager of the Campus Recreation Center has asked you to create a presentation outlining the membership costs and the swim lesson schedule. You will create an Excel worksheet on a slide and insert data in the worksheet. You will also insert a table object from Word, and add a link to connect slides.

DIRECTIONS

1. Start PowerPoint, if necessary, and open **P26PracticeA** from the data files for this lesson.

2. Save the presentation as **P26PracticeA_xx** in the location where your teacher instructs you to store the files for this lesson.

3. Display slide 3 and then click **HOME** > **New Slide** > **Title Only**.

4. Click in the title placeholder and type **Proposed Programs**.

5. Click **INSERT** > **Table** > **Excel Spreadsheet**.

6. Insert text in the worksheet as shown in Figure 26-1. Adjust the column widths as needed to create an attractive table. You may also apply the same theme in Excel as in the presentation (Metropolitan) and apply shading as shown in the figure.

7. Click **HOME** > **New Slide** > **Title Only**.

8. Click in the title placeholder and type **Program Details**.

9. In Word, open **P26PracticeB** from the data files for this lesson.

10. Select the table data, click **HOME** > **Copy** , and then close the Word file.

11. With slide 5 displayed, click **HOME** > **Paste** .

12. Hold down SHIFT and drag the lower-right corner to enlarge the object on the slide. Then move the object to position it attractively on the slide.

13. Click **TABLE TOOLS DESIGN** > **Table Styles** > **Medium Style 2 – Accent 1**, if necessary.

14. Display slide 3 and select the text *survey results* near the bottom of the slide.

15. Click **INSERT** > **Hyperlink** .

16. Click **Place in This Document** and then click **7. Survey Results**. Click **OK**.

17. Replace the text *Student Name* with your first and last name in the slide footers.

18. Preview the presentation, testing the link on slide 3 and viewing the Excel worksheet on slide 4 and the Word table on slide 5.

19. **With your teacher's permission**, print handouts of the entire presentation using a format with four slides to a page.

20. Close the presentation, saving changes, and exit PowerPoint.

Figure 26-1

Proposed Programs

	Will Likely Appeal To . . .		
	Students	Faculty/Staff	Community
Youth swim lessons		X	X
Adult swim lessons	X	X	X
Youth stroke clinic		X	X
Lifeguarding course	X		X
Masters swim team			X
Aquacize	X	X	X

11/11/2012
FIRSTNAME LASTNAME

4

Lesson 26—Apply

In this project, you continue to work on the Campus Recreation Center presentation. You edit worksheet data, insert worksheet data that you will link to the original Excel file, and you add an action button to the presentation.

DIRECTIONS

1. Start PowerPoint, if necessary, and open **P26ApplyA**.

2. Save the presentation as **P26ApplyA_xx** in the location where your teacher instructs you to store the files for this lesson.

3. On slide 4, open the worksheet object for editing and adjust the size of the object to display an additional row at the bottom.

4. In cell B9, type the following formula: **=COUNTA(B3:B8)**. Copy the formula to cells C9 and D9. Center the values in cells B9:D9 and boldface them. Apply shading or Total cell style formatting as desired.

5. Create a new Title Only slide following slide 5, and change the title to **Fee Structure**.

6. Open the Excel data file **P26ApplyB.xlsx** and save the file as **P26ApplyB_xx** in the location where your teacher instructs you to store the files for this lesson.

7. Copy the data in the range **A1:F6**, and link this data to slide 6 in the presentation.

8. Move the linked object on the slide to align it at left with the slide title, and, using the **DRAWING TOOLS FORMAT** > **Shape Width** box, change the width of the object to **10"**.

9. Double-click the linked data to add the following parking fees data to the Excel worksheet.

Part-time/Graduate Students   10
Faculty/Employees   15
Alumni   18
Community   24

10. Save and close the Excel workbook. Your slide should look like the one in Figure 26-2 on the next page.

11. Display slide 8 and insert an action button that will return the viewer to slide 3.

12. Change the shape style to one that suits the presentation and place text next to the box that says **Return to slide 3**, as shown in Figure 26-3 on the next page.

13. Replace *Student Name* in the footer with your first and last name.

14. Run the slide show and work your way through each of the links and action buttons to ensure that everything moves as it should.

15. **With your teacher's permission**, print handouts of the entire presentation using a format with six slides to a page.

16. Close the presentation, saving changes, and exit PowerPoint.

Figure 26-2

Fee Structure

	Membership		Parking/ Month	Monthly Total	Yearly Total
	Monthly	Yearly			
Part-time/Graduate Students	$20	$200	$10	$30	$320
Faculty/Employees	$40	$440	$15	$55	$620
Alumni	$50	$560	$18	$68	$776
Community	$60	$680	$24	$84	$968

11/11/2012
FIRSTNAME LASTNAME

Figure 26-3

Survey Results

11/11/2012
FIRSTNAME LASTNAME

Lesson 27

Organizing and Rehearsing a Slide Show

➤ What You Will Learn

Inserting Sections
Creating a Custom Show
Hiding Slides
Rehearsing Timings

Software Skills   Use sections and custom shows to organize parts of a presentation so that you can easily manage them during a presentation. Hide slides that you don't want to show during a particular presentation. You can rehearse the show to make sure you have allowed enough time for the audience to view slide content.

WORDS TO KNOW

Custom show
A show in which you specify the slides and the order in which the slides appear during the presentation.

What You Can Do

Inserting Sections

- Sections are used to organize large presentations into more manageable groups.
- You can also use presentation sections to assist in collaborating on projects. For example, each colleague can be responsible for preparing slides for a separate section.
- You can apply unique names and effects to different sections.
- You can also choose to print by section.

Try It!   Inserting Sections

1   Start PowerPoint, and open **P27Try** from the data files for this lesson.

2   Save presentation file as **P27Try_xx** in the location where your teacher instructs you to store the files for this lesson.

3   Click slide 5 in the Thumbnail pane.

4   Click HOME > Section 📋 and then click Add Section on the drop-down list.

5   Right-click between slides 10 and 11 and click Add Section.

6   Save the **P27Try_xx** file, and leave it open to use in the next Try It.

Try It!   Renaming Presentation Sections

1   In the **P27Try_xx** file, right-click the Untitled Section heading between slides 4 and 5.

2   Select Rename Section from the content menu.

    OR

    Click HOME > Section 📋 > Rename Section.

3   In the Rename Section dialog box, type **Company Graphics.**

4   Click Rename.

5   Right-click the Untitled Section heading between slides 10 and 11, click Rename Section, and type the new section name **Gallery**. Click Rename.

6   Save the **P27Try_xx** file, and leave it open to use in the next Try It.

Rename Section dialog box

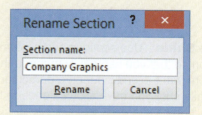

Try It!   Working with Presentation Sections

1   In the **P27Try_xx** file, click the downward pointing arrow to the left of the Company Graphics section to collapse this section.

2   Click HOME > Section 📋 > Collapse All.

3   Right-click the Gallery section name and select Move Section Up.

4   Click the Company Graphics section name and drag it above the Gallery section.

5   Right-click the Gallery section name and select Remove Section.

6   Click HOME > Section 📋 > Expand All.

7   Save the **P27Try_xx** file, and leave it open to use in the next Try It.

Collapsed presentation sections

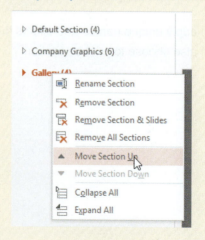

Creating a Custom Show

- You can create **custom shows** to organize groups of slides that you want to be able to show separately from the other slides in the presentation.

- Creating custom shows allows you to show only a portion of the slides to a specific audience. For example, although you would show the board of directors a presentation containing all the information about the status of a project, you might want to show the sales staff only the slides that contain sales data.

- Use the Custom Slide Show command on the SLIDE SHOW tab to define a new custom show. Use the Define Custom Show dialog box to name the show and select the slides that will be part of the custom show

- Once you have created a custom show, you can specify it when running a presentation unattended, link to it, or jump to it during the presentation. You can also choose to print only the slides from the custom show.

- When you create a link to a custom show, you can use the Show and return option to display the slides in the custom show and then resume the slide show where you left off.

Try It!   **Creating a Custom Show**

1. In the **P27Try_xx** file, on the SLIDE SHOW tab, click Custom Slide Show 🖥 and then click Custom Shows.

2. In the Custom Shows dialog box, click New.

3. In the Define Custom Show dialog box, type **Gallery** in the Slide show name box.

4. Click in the check box for slide 11 in the Slides in presentation pane.

5. Click Add to add the slide to the custom show.

6. Add slides 12, 13, and 14.

7. Click OK and then click Close.

8. Display slide 3 and select the text *Expertise with many architectural styles*.

9. Click INSERT > Hyperlink 🔗.

10. In the Insert Hyperlink dialog box, click Place in This Document, and then click Custom Shows in the Select a place in this document pane to expand the Custom Shows section.

11. Click Gallery under Custom Shows, then click Show and return. Click OK.

12. Save the **P27TryA_xx** file, and leave it open to use in the next Try It.

Select the slides for a custom show

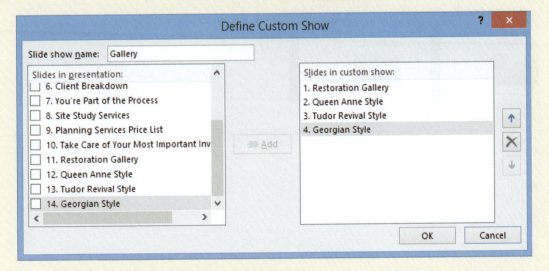

Hiding Slides

- You can hide slides in your presentation so they do not show when you run the slide show. For example, you might hide certain slides to shorten the presentation, or hide slides that don't apply to a specific audience.

- Hidden slides remain in the file and appear in all views except Slide Show view.

- PowerPoint indicates a slide is hidden by positioning a diagonal line across the slide number in the Thumbnail pane or Slide Sorter view and graying out the slide.

- You can print hidden slides if desired.

- You can go to a hidden slide while in Slide Show view by using the See All Slides command on the slide show shortcut menu to display the Slide Navigator. Click the hidden slide to display it.

Try It!   **Hiding Slides**

1 In the **P27Try_xx** file, select slide 10 in the Thumbnail pane.

2 On the SLIDE SHOW tab, click the Hide Slide button.

    ✓ *Click the Hide Slide button again to unhide a slide.*

3 Save the **P27Try_xx** file, and leave it open to use in the next Try It.

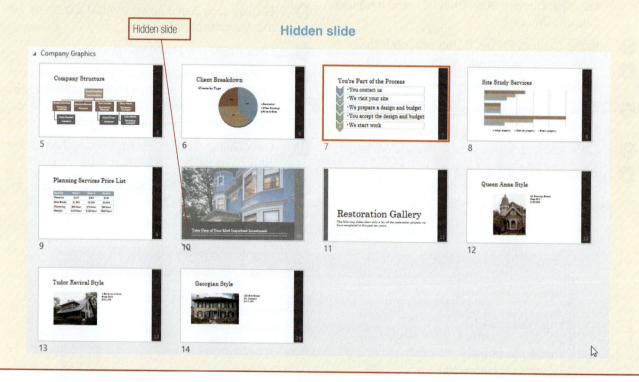

Hidden slide

Hidden slide

Rehearsing Timings

- To make sure you have allowed enough time for your audience to view your slides, you can rehearse the presentation.

- Use the Rehearse Timings command on the SLIDE SHOW tab to start the presentation and display the Recording toolbar. As you view each slide, the timers show how much time you have spent on that slide as well as the total time elapsed for the show.

- You can use buttons on the Recording toolbar to pause and restart the show, and you can also repeat a slide if you find you need to start again.

- After you have finished viewing all slides, PowerPoint asks if you want to keep the slide timings. If you click Yes, these timings replace any other advance timings you have set.

Try It!   Rehearsing Timings

① In the **P27Try_xx** file, click Slide Show, and then click the Rehearse Timings button.

② Advance to slide 3, reading slide contents and any comments you intend to make in the presentation.

③ On slide 3, click the link to the custom show and view those slides. You should return at the end of the custom show to slide 3.

④ Continue with the remaining slides until you reach slide 11. Notice that you will not see the hidden slide 10.

⑤ At the end of the show, click Yes to keep slide timings.

OR

Click No to discard slide timings.

⑥ Close the **P27Try_xx** file, saving changes, and exit PowerPoint.

The Recording toolbar

Lesson 27—Practice

In this project, you work with the Campus Recreation Center presentation. You will create a custom show, insert sections, hide a slide, and rehearse slide timings.

DIRECTIONS

1. Start PowerPoint, if necessary, and open **P27Practice** from the data files for this lesson.

2. Save the presentation as **P27Practice_xx** in the location where your teacher instructs you to store the files for this lesson.

3. Click **SLIDE SHOW** > **Custom Slide Show** > **Custom Shows**.

4. Click **New**, and then type the slide show name **Family**.

5. In the Slides in presentation pane, click the check boxes for slides **10**, **11**, **12**, and **13**.

6. Click **Add**, click **OK**, and then click **Close**.

7. Right-click between slides 3 and 4, and click **Add Section**.

8. Right-click the new section label, click **Rename Section**, and type **Proposals**.

9. Click **Rename**.

10. Right-click between slides 9 and 10 and click **Add Section**.

11. Right-click the new section label, click **Rename Section**, and type **Family Programs**.

12. Click **Rename**.

13. Click the downward pointing arrow to the left of the **Family Programs** section name to collapse the section.

14. Click slide 8, and then click **SLIDE SHOW** > **Hide Slide** .

15. Click **SLIDE SHOW** > **Rehearse Timings** , and progress through the show from the first to the last slide. Click **Yes** to save slide timings at the end of the show.

16. Click **INSERT** > **Header & Footer** to open the Header and Footer dialog box.

17. On the Notes and Handouts tab, click **Footer**, type your name and click Apply to All.

18. **With your teacher's permission,** print the slides as handouts with 9 slides per page.

19. Close the presentation, saving changes, and exit PowerPoint.

Lesson 27—Apply

In this project, you continue to work on the Campus Recreation Center presentation. You will adjust sections, create a custom show and set up a link to the show, and rehearse timings.

DIRECTIONS

1. Start PowerPoint, if necessary, and open **P27Apply** from the data files for this lesson.

2. Save the presentation as **P27Apply_xx** in the location where your teacher instructs you to store the files for this lesson.

3. Click **INSERT** > **Header & Footer** to open the Header and Footer dialog box.

4. On the Slides tab, click **Footer,** type your name and click **Apply to All**.

5. Remove the Family Programs section.

6. Unhide slide 9.

7. Switch to Slide Sorter view and move slide 14 to follow slide 9.

8. Create a custom show named **Memberships** that includes slides 9 and 10.

9. Move the Survey Results slide to be the last slide in the Default Section.

10. Create a new section named **Membership** to contain slides 10 and 11.

11. Create a new section named **Family** to include the remaining slides.

12. In Normal view, collapse all sections.

13. Move the Membership section to be the last one in the Thumbnail pane.

14. Expand all sections, and then display slide 4.

15. Create a link from the Family programs text to the Family custom show. Select Show and return.

16. Create a link from the Memberships text to the Memberships custom show. Select Show and return.

17. Rehearse slide timings as follows:

    a. View slides 1 and 2, and then, on slide 3, click the *survey results* link.

    b. Use the action button to return to slide 3.

    c. On slide 4, click each link to view the custom shows.

    d. Stop the slide show when you reach slide 10, Family Programs.

    e. Save slide timings.

18. Close the presentation, saving changes, and exit PowerPoint.

Lesson 28

Setting Up and Running a Slide Show

➤ What You Will Learn

Setting Slide Show Options
Controlling Slides During a Presentation
Annotating Slides During a Presentation
Using Presenter View

Software Skills   You can specify how a slide show runs for different kinds of presentations. When presenting slides, you have a number of options for controlling slide display. You can annotate slides during the presentation and save annotations if desired. PowerPoint's Presenter view gives you a great deal more control over the process of presenting a slide show.

What You Can Do

Setting Slide Show Options

- Before finalizing a presentation, you must decide how it will be presented and set the slide show options accordingly.
- Use the Set Up Show dialog box to specify options for the slide show, such as the following:
  - Specify how the slides will be shown—presented by a speaker, browsed by an individual reviewing the presentation onscreen, or viewed at a kiosk.
  - Specify how to show the presentation—looping continuously until ESC is pressed, without recorded narration, or without animation, and the color of the pen or laser pointer used.

    ✓ *You can use a built-in laser pointer during your presentation by pressing* CTRL *while pressing the left mouse button.*

  - You can also choose to disable hardware graphics acceleration if your system does not have the hardware required to display dynamic content smoothly.
  - Choose a range of slides to present or choose a custom show if the presentation has one.
  - Specify how to advance slides—manually or using timings.
  - Specify whether to display the presentation on multiple monitors.

✓ *Remember, not every projection system can handle multiple monitors.*

● By default, PowerPoint will use your monitor's current resolution to display the slides.

● Hidden text is not displayed on-screen or printed unless you select to display it.

■ Using Presenter view, you can use a second monitor to show your presentation notes and other computer resources that can help with your presentation while your audience views the main presentation.

■ If you plan to run the presentation unattended, without a speaker to control the slides, you need to set up the show to loop continuously.

■ For example, you might use a looping presentation at a trade show booth where the audience can view but not interact with the slides.

■ Use the Set Up Show dialog box to create a looping presentation, by specifying the following options:

● In the Show type area, specify Browsed at a kiosk so that it will run unattended.

● In the Show options area, specify Loop continuously until 'Esc'.

✓ *This option will be selected automatically if you choose Browsed at a kiosk.*

● In the Advance slides area, select Using timings, if present.

✓ *Remember that you will need to create timings for the presentation in order for it to advance appropriately.*

Try It!   Setting Slide Show Options

① Start PowerPoint, and open **P28Try** from the data files for this lesson.

② Save the presentation as **P28Try_xx** in the location where your teacher instructs you to store the files for this lesson.

③ On the SLIDE SHOW tab, click Set Up Slide Show 🖳 to open the Set Up Show dialog box.

④ Click Presented by a speaker (full screen) if necessary.

⑤ Click Pen color and select Orange, Accent 2.

⑥ In the Advance slides area, click Manually.

⑦ Click OK.

⑧ Save the **P28Try_xx** file, and leave it open to use in the next Try It.

Set Up Show dialog box

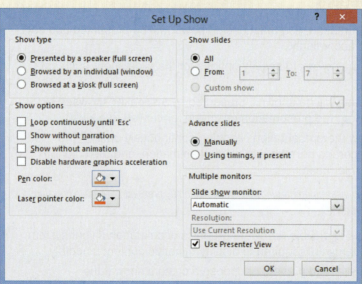

Controlling Slides During a Presentation

- There are a number of other ways to control slide advance using keys or onscreen prompts.

- The Slide Show view shortcut menu also provides a number of ways to control slides.

- You can use this shortcut menu to navigate from slide to slide, go to the last-viewed slide or a specific slide (even a hidden slide), or go to a custom show.

- The See All Slides option on the shortcut menu displays the Slide Navigator, similar to Slide Sorter view. Slides are arranged as thumbnails you can click to select. Sections are listed at the left side of the screen for easy selection.

- If you are using slide timings, you can use the Pause command to stop the automatic advance and then Resume to continue.

Try It!   **Controlling Slides During a Presentation**

1. In the **P28Try_xx** file, click SLIDE SHOW > From Beginning 💻.

2. Right-click the screen and click Next.

   OR

   Use any of the following keyboard shortcuts to move through the slide show.
   - Press [N]
   - Press [→]
   - Press [↓]
   - Press [PG DN]
   - Press [ENTER]
   - Press [SPACE]

   OR

   Click the Right Presentation Arrow [▶] at lower-left corner of screen.

3. After you reach the end of the presentation, click SLIDE SHOW > From Beginning 💻 to begin again.

4. Click the screen once to advance to slide 2.

5. Right-click the screen and click Previous or Last Viewed.

   OR

   Use any of the following keyboard shortcuts to move backward through slides.
   - Press [P]
   - Press [←]
   - Press [↑]
   - Press [PG UP]
   - Press [BACKSPACE]

   OR

   Click the Left Presentation Arrow [◀] at lower-left corner of screen.

6. Click SLIDE SHOW > From Beginning 💻.

7. Right-click the screen and click See All Slides. Slide Navigator opens to allow you to see the presentation's slides.

8. Click slide 3.

9. Right-click the screen and click End Show.

10. Save the **P28Try_xx** file, and leave it open to use in the next Try It.

Annotating Slides During a Presentation

- You can add annotations, such as writing or drawing, to a slide during a slide show to emphasize a specific point on a slide or add a comment to the slide.

- When you use the annotation feature, the mouse pointer becomes a pen.

- You can choose how you want the annotations to appear by selecting different pen colors and pen styles, such as pen or highlighter.

- You can also switch to a Laser Pointer to make it easy to point out items on your slides.

- PowerPoint suspends automatic timings while you use the annotation feature.

■ You can use an eraser to remove annotations.

■ When you have finished annotating a slide, press ESC to change the pen pointer back to the mouse pointer.

■ PowerPoint offers you the option of saving your annotations or discarding them. If you save them, you will see them in Normal view and they can be printed.

Try It!   Annotating Slides During a Presentation

① In the **P28Try_xx** file, click SLIDE SHOW > From Beginning 🖳.

② Right-click the screen and click Pointer Options.

③ Select Pen.

④ Hold down the mouse button and drag to circle the name *Michigan* on the first slide.

⑤ Press ESC to restore the mouse pointer.

⑥ Advance to slide 2.

⑦ Right-click the screen, click Pointer Options, and click Highlighter.

⑧ Drag over the text *Individual coaching* to highlight it.

⑨ Right-click the screen, click Pointer Options, and click Eraser.

⑩ Move the eraser over an annotation to erase.

OR

Press E to erase all annotations on the slide.

⑪ End the slide show. Click Keep to save your annotations.

OR

Click Discard to remove the annotations.

⑫ Save the **P28Try_xx** file, and leave it open to use in the next Try It.

Select Pointer Options for annotating slides

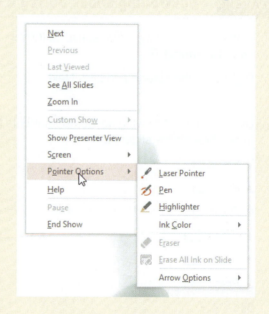

Using Presenter View

■ Presenter view is new in PowerPoint 2013. It allows you to see on one screen not only what your audience is seeing but also notes and tools for working with the presentation.

■ In previous versions, you could run Presenter view if you had multiple monitors attached to your system. In PowerPoint 2013, you do not need multiple monitors—you can use Presenter view with a single monitor.

■ Along with tools such as the pointer options, Presenter view offers a Zoom feature to allow you to enlarge content in one area of a slide, a timer to show you how long a slide has been displayed, and a preview of the next slide. You can also choose to enlarge or reduce the size of notes text to make it easier for you to read.

■ You can choose to show or hide the taskbar, adjust display settings, or end the slide show without having to right-click and select a command.

■ PowerPoint will determine if your system setup supports Presenter view and display it automatically when you select Use Presenter View in the Set Up Show dialog box. If you have only one monitor, you can display Presenter view by pressing ALT + F5 .

Preview of current slide

Preview of the next slide

Figure 28-1

Slide show tools

Adjust size of notes text

Notes pane

Try It!   **Using Presenter View**

1 In the **P28Try_xx** file, press ALT + F5 to start the presentation with Presenter view active.

2 Click the Advance to the next slide arrow at the bottom center of the screen to move to slide 2. Notice the note in the Notes pane below the Next slide preview.

3 Click the Pen and laser pointer tools button , select the Highlighter, and highlight the text *Experienced staff*.

4 Click the Black or unblack slide show button to black out the current slide.

   ✓ *You might want to do this to hide the slide while discussion is going on.*

5 Click the Black or unblack slide show button again to restore the current slide.

6 Click the See all slides button to display the Slide Navigator. Click slide 7.

7 Click the Zoom into the slide button and drag the highlight rectangle over the picture on the slide. Click to zoom in.

8 Press ESC to zoom back out.

9 Click END SLIDE SHOW at the top of the screen, and then click Discard to throw out annotations.

10 Close the **P28Try_xx** file, saving changes, and exit PowerPoint.

Lesson 28—Practice

In this project, you return to the Restoration Architecture presentation and set up the slide show for presentation. Then, you will run the slide show, practicing ways to display the presentation content. You will also annotate slides as you present them.

DIRECTIONS

1. Start PowerPoint, if necessary, and open **P28Practice**.

2. Save the presentation as **P28Practice_xx** in the location where your teacher instructs you to store the files for this lesson.

3. Click **SLIDE SHOW > Set Up Slide Show** to open the Set Up Show dialog box.

4. In the Advance slides area, click **Manually**, and then click **OK**.

5. Click **SLIDE SHOW > From Beginning**.

6. Use any option to advance to slide 2.

7. Right-click on the slide to display the shortcut menu, click **See All Slides**, and then click slide 5, the first in the Company Graphics section.

8. Proceed to slide 9, then right-click, click **See All Slides**, and click slide 10, which is currently hidden.

9. Right-click and click **Last Viewed** to return to slide 9.

10. Right-click, click **See All Slides**, and click slide 2.

11. Point to the lower-left corner of the screen to display the presentation tools, and then click the Pen tool to display a pop-up menu of pointer options.

12. Click Pen and underline the word *Superior* with a double underline.

13. Press ESC and move to the next slide.

14. Click the Pen tool to display the pop-up menu, select Highlighter, and then click Light Blue from the color palette.

15. Highlight the text *Reasonable fees*, as shown in Figure 28-2.

16. Right-click, point to **Custom Show**, and then click **Gallery**. View the final four slides in the presentation and end the show. Choose to keep the annotations.

17. Insert your name in the footer for notes and handouts.

18. **With your teacher's permission**, print the presentation as handouts with 6 slides per page.

19. Close the presentation, saving changes, and exit PowerPoint.

Figure 28-2

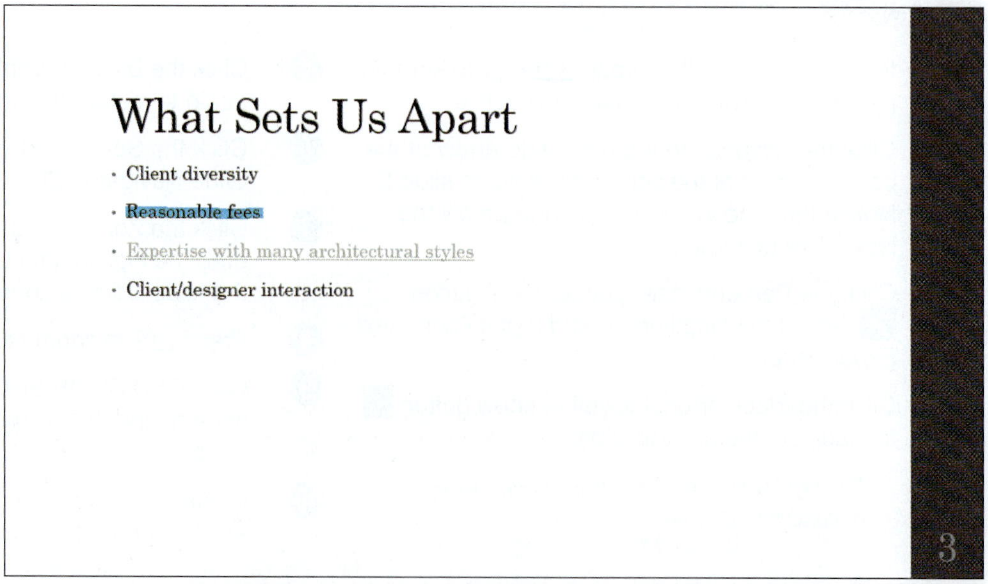

What Sets Us Apart

- Client diversity
- Reasonable fees
- Expertise with many architectural styles
- Client/designer interaction

3

Lesson 28—Apply

In this project, you will review the Restoration Architecture presentation in Presenter view. Then, you will set up the show to run automatically so your client can present it at a kiosk at a trade show.

DIRECTIONS

1. Start PowerPoint, if necessary, and open **P28Apply**.

2. Save the presentation as **P28Apply_xx**.

3. Insert your first and last name in the footer for all slides and display the date on all slides.

4. Press ⌐ALT⌐ + ⌐F5⌐ to start the presentation in Presenter view.

5. Proceed through the slides up to slide 9, reading the notes when available.

6. Display the hidden slide 10, then black out the screen.

7. Show all slides and click slide 12. Zoom in on the house.

8. Show all slides and click slide 6. Use the Pen pointer with a color of your choice to draw an arrow pointing to the Residential section of the pie chart.

9. Move to slide 7 and use the highlighter to highlight *You* in the title placeholder.

10. Go to slide 1 and then proceed through all slides to the end of the presentation.

11. Display the Set Up Show dialog box, and set up the show to be browsed at a kiosk using available timings.

12. End the show, saving the annotations.

13. **With your teacher's permission**, print slides 6 and 7 as handouts with 2 slides per page.

14. Close the presentation, saving changes, and exit PowerPoint.

Lesson 29

Reviewing a Presentation

➤ What You Will Learn

Using the Thesaurus
Working with Comments
Sending a Presentation for Review
Comparing Presentations
Reviewing Changes

WORDS TO KNOW

Antonyms
Words with opposite meanings.

Comment
A note you add to a slide to provide corrections or input to the slide content.

Synonyms
Words with the same meaning.

Thesaurus
A listing of words with synonyms and antonyms.

Software Skills   Use PowerPoint's built-in thesaurus to recommend alternative words to improve your writing. Use comments to suggest changes to a presentation. Use PowerPoint's Share feature to send a presentation for review. Compare presentations to identify changes made to different versions or by different people. You can accept or reject changes to incorporate revisions.

What You Can Do

Using the Thesaurus

■ A **thesaurus** can improve your writing by helping you to eliminate repetitive use of common words and to choose more descriptive words.

■ You can use a shortcut menu to quickly find a **synonym** for any word in a presentation.

■ You can use the thesaurus to look up synonyms, definitions, and **antonyms** for any word. PowerPoint displays a list of results in the Thesaurus task pane.

  • Click a right-pointing arrow to expand the list to show additional words.

  • Click a downward-pointing arrow to collapse the list to hide some words.

■ Use the available drop-down list to insert a word at the current insertion point location, or copy it to a different location.

■ Use the Back button in the Thesaurus task pane to return to the content you previously viewed in the pane.

■ By default, PowerPoint searches an English thesaurus, but you can select to search a thesaurus in a different language.

1. Start PowerPoint, and open **P29TryA**.

2. Save the presentation as **P29TryA_xx** in the location where your teacher instructs you to store the files for this lesson.

3. On slide 2, right-click the word *Excellent* in the first bullet.

4. On the shortcut menu, click *Synonyms*.

5. On the submenu, click *Outstanding*.

6. Save the **P29TryA_xx** file, and leave it open to use in the next Try It.

Select a synonym from a shortcut menu

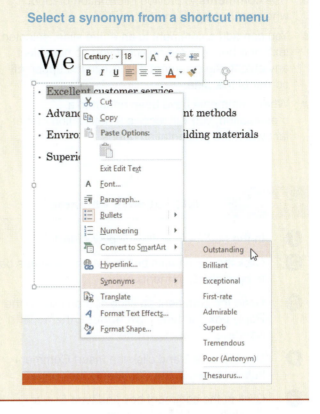

1. In the **P29TryA_xx** file, click in the word *Superior* on slide 2.

2. Click REVIEW > Thesaurus 📖.

   ✓ *A list of synonyms and antonyms for the word* Superior *displays in the Thesaurus task pane. Antonyms display at the bottom of the list for each category of synonyms.*

3. Click the downward-pointing arrow for Larger to collapse the list.

4. In the Excellent category, click Exceptional to see a list of synonyms and antonyms for this word.

5. Click the Back button ⬅ to return to the Superior synonyms.

6. Rest the mouse pointer on the word *Exceptional*, click the down arrow that displays, and then click Insert.

7. Close the Thesaurus task pane.

8. Save the **P29TryA_xx** file, and leave it open to use in the next Try It.

The Thesaurus task pane

Working with Comments

- Use **comments** to provide information or input when editing a presentation.

- You can add a comment to an entire slide, selected text, or other selected object. If you do not select any object, the comment displays in the upper-left corner of the slide.

- When comments have been added to a presentation, you will receive a notification of that fact when the presentation opens.

- Click the Comments button on the status bar to open the Comments task pane. The name that displays on each comment is that of the user who created the comment. Comments also display the day or time the comment was created.

- Use the tools in the Comments task pane to work with comments. You can add new comments or move to the next or previous comment. You can also find these tools in the Comments group on the REVIEW tab.

- As you view a comment, you can insert a reply to the comment or delete it.

Try It!   **Working with Comments**

1. In the **P29TryA_xx** file, display slide 1.

2. Click the Comments button 🗨 on the status bar to open the Comments pane.

3. Read the comment on slide 1, then click in the Reply box and type **How about a theme with a darker slide background?**

4. Display slide 2 and click the Insert Comment button ⬚New in the Comments task pane.

5. Click in the comment box and type **See text changes in the content area.**

6. In the Comments task pane, click the Next button ⬚ to move to the comment on slide 8.

7. Click in the Reply box and type **Okay**.

8. Click the Next button ⬚ twice to move to the comment on slide 9.

9. Click the Delete Comment button ⬚ on the REVIEW tab to remove the comment.

10. Click REVIEW > Next Comment ⬚, review the comment, and then click REVIEW > Delete Comment ⬚.

11. Click REVIEW > Next Comment ⬚, review the comment, and then click the delete button ✕ within the comment.

12. Close the Comments task pane.

13. Save the **P29TryA_xx** file, and leave it open to use in the next Try It.

Type a new comment in the comment box

Sending a Presentation for Review

- When you are ready to share a presentation with colleagues, PowerPoint makes it easy to send the presentation for review and feedback, which is particularly useful in collaborative environments such as companies and organizations.

- Options for sharing a presentation using e-mail can be found on the Share tab in the Backstage view. You can choose among the following:

- Send as Attachment. You can e-mail individual copies of the presentation.

- Send a Link. You can e-mail a link to a presentation that is stored on the same server as the e-mail recipient's. This allows everyone to work on the same copy of the presentation.

- Send as PDF. This option saves the presentation as a PDF image and attaches it to an e-mail message. PDFs preserve the fonts and formatting on every computer, but recipients can't add comments or make changes.

- Send as XPS. This option saves the presentation in a format that can be viewed on most computers and attaches it to an e-mail message. XPS files maintain the fonts and formatting on most computers, but the recipients can't make changes.

- Send as Internet Fax. If you have a fax service provider, you can send a printed version of the presentation to a recipient's fax machine.

✓ *You must have an e-mail account to send a presentation as an e-mail attachment. You must have an active Internet connection to e-mail the file.*

Try It! **Sending a Presentation for Review**

1 In the **P29TryA_xx** file, click FILE > Share.

2 Click Email and then click Send as Attachment.

3 When the e-mail message window opens, type the e-mail address of the person to whom you are sending the presentation.

✓ *Notice that the subject is filled in with the name of the presentation.*

4 In the message window, type **Here is a copy of the Restoration Architecture presentation.**

5 Press ENTER and then type **Student Name**.

6 Click Send.

7 Save the **P29TryA_xx** file, and leave it open to use in the next Try It.

Share tab

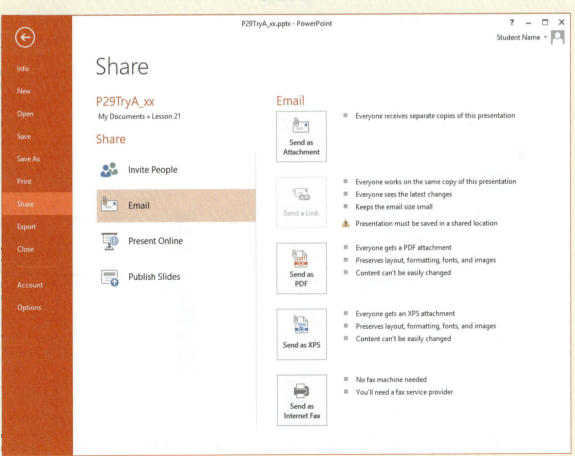

Comparing Presentations

- After a presentation has been reviewed, it can be helpful to compare the reviewed version with the original version.

- To compare presentations, you open the original document and then select the presentation to compare.

- PowerPoint merges the two and marks the differences with markup icons and in the Revisions task pane.

- To view a description of the change, click the markup icon, or select the change in the Revisions task pane.

- The Revisions task pane has two tabs. Select the SLIDES tab to view changes for the current slide only. This tab will also tell you the next slide that has changes marked. Select the DETAILS tab to see all markup on a slide, including comments, and also display a list of changes made to the presentation as a whole.

- Click the Show Comments drop-down arrow and select Show Markup to toggle the markup icons off or on.

- Click the Reviewing Pane button in the Compare group on the Ribbon to toggle the Revisions task pane off or on.

Try It!   **Comparing Presentations**

1. In the **P29TryA_xx** file, click the REVIEW tab, and then click the Compare button 📋.

2. Navigate to the location where the data files for this lesson are stored, select **P29TryB**, and then click Merge.

3. Save **P29TryA_xx** as **P29TryC_xx**, and leave it open to use in the next Try It.

Markup icon for presentation changes

Markups display in a merged presentation

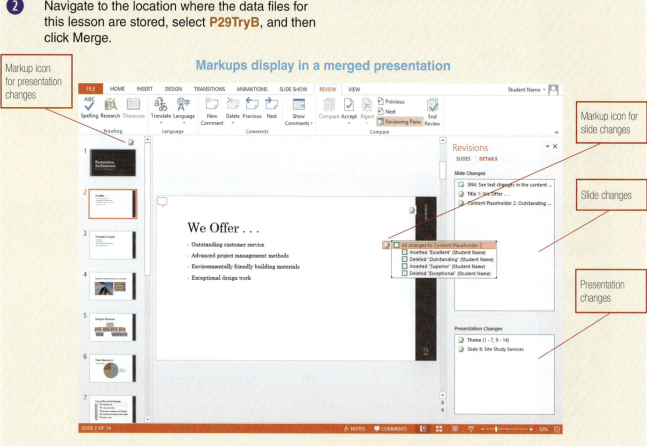

Markup icon for slide changes

Slide changes

Presentation changes

Reviewing Changes

- When you compare presentations, PowerPoint inserts a markup icon at the location where differences occur.

- Markup icons representing changes that affect the entire presentation, such as a new theme or deleted slide, display in the Thumbnail pane, as well as on the DETAILS tab of the Revisions pane.

- Markup icons representing changes that affect a single slide, such as edited text or a new graphic, display on the slide.

- Use the buttons in the Compare group on the REVIEW tab of the Ribbon to review the differences between compared presentations.

- Click the Next Change button to select and display the next change.

- Click the Previous Change button to select and display the previous change.

- To mark a change for acceptance, click to select the check box in the markup icon.

- To reject a change, leave the check box blank.

- When you have finished reviewing changes, click the End Review button. Changes marked for acceptance will be incorporated into the presentation, and changes marked for rejection will be removed.

- You can also use the Accept button and Reject button drop-down arrows to display options for accepting or rejecting the current change, all changes on the current slide, or all changes in the entire presentation.

Try It!   **Reviewing Changes**

1. In the **P29TryC_xx** file, display slide 1 if necessary.

2. In the Revisions task pane under Presentation Changes, click Theme (1 - 7, 9 - 14).

3. Click the Accept button ☑ in the Compare group on the Ribbon. The change is accepted and a new theme is applied to the presentation. Note the check marks indicating changes marked for acceptance in the Presentation Changes section and in the markup icon at the top of the Thumbnails pane.

4. Click the SLIDES tab in the Revisions task pane and then click the Next button 🔁 . The next change to the presentation is shown with a markup icon in the Thumbnails pane next to slide 8.

5. Click the check box next to Deleted "Site Study Services". The slide is immediately deleted from the presentation.

6. Click the markup icon on the new slide 8 to accept changes to the table.

7. Click Next 🔁 to display changes on slide 9.

8. On slide 9, click the Accept button ☑ drop-down arrow and click Accept All Changes to This Slide.

9. Click Next 🔁 to display changes on slide 10. Leave the markup check box open to reject changes to this slide.

10. Click Next 🔁 and then click Continue to return to the beginning of the presentation.

11. Make slide 2 active.

12. Click the first markup icon to display the change made in the title placeholder.

13. Click the Accept button ☑ drop-down arrow and then click Accept All Changes to This Slide.

14. Click Next 🔁 and accept the change on slide 3.

15. Click Next 🔁 to display slide 5.

16. Click in the markup icon check box that indicates a change to diagram contents to accept the change.

17. Accept the change to the chart on slide 6.

18. Click the End Review button 📝 in the Compare group.

19. Click Yes to accept all changes marked for acceptance and delete the changes that are not marked.

20. Delete comments remaining in the presentation.

21. Close the **P29TryC_xx** file, saving changes, and exit PowerPoint.

Lesson 29—Practice

You have been collaborating on a presentation for Whole Grains Bread with co-workers. In this project, you will compare versions of the presentation, work with comments, and use PowerPoint's thesaurus to replace selected words. You will then send the presentation for final review.

DIRECTIONS

1. Start PowerPoint, if necessary, and open **P29PracticeA** from the data files for this lesson.

2. Save the presentation as **P29PracticeA_xx** in the location where your teacher instructs you to store the files for this lesson.

3. Click the **REVIEW** tab, and then click the **Compare** button.

4. Navigate to the location where the data files for this lesson are stored, select **P29PracticeB**, and then click Merge.

5. Click to select the check box in the Theme markup icon.

6. Click on the comment on slide 1 to open the Comments pane.

7. Click in the reply box and type **I'm not sure about this particular theme. What do you think?**

8. Click the **Next** button in the Compare group on the Ribbon.

9. Click the **Accept** button drop-down arrow and then click **Accept All Changes to This Slide**. Then delete the comment on the slide.

10. Click the **Next** button in the Compare group on the Ribbon until you see the changes on slide 4.

11. Click the **Accept** button drop-down arrow and then click **Accept All Changes to This Slide**.

12. Click the **Next** button in the Compare group on the Ribbon.

13. Accept all changes on slide 5.

14. Click the **Next** button until you see the change on slide 6.

15. Click in the markup icon check box to insert the picture, and then delete the comment on the slide.

16. Click the **End Review** button in the Compare group on the Ribbon, and then click **Yes**. Close the Comments task pane.

17. Make slide 1 active.

18. Right-click the word **EVERY** in the subtitle.

19. Click **Synonyms** on the shortcut menu, and then click **EACH**.

20. Make slide 6 active.

21. Click on the word **incorporate**.

22. On the **REVIEW** tab, click the **Thesaurus** button.

23. In the Thesaurus list, click the word **combine**.

24. In the Thesaurus list, scroll down to display the mix synonyms, rest the mouse pointer on the word **blend**, click the down arrow that displays, and then click **Insert**.

25. Close the Thesaurus task pane.

26. Insert a footer with your name and today's date fixed on every slide.

27. Save the changes to the presentation.

28. Preview the presentation.

29. **With your teacher's permission**, click FILE > Share > Email, and send the presentation as an attachment to your teacher or to another student in your class.

30. Close the presentation, saving changes, and exit PowerPoint.

Lesson 29—Apply

In this project, you continue to work with the Whole Grains Bread presentation. You compare presentations and review markup, revise text with the thesaurus, and send the presentation for review.

DIRECTIONS

1. Start PowerPoint, if necessary, and open **P29ApplyA** from the data files for this lesson.

2. Save the presentation as **P29ApplyA_xx** in the location where your teacher instructs you to store the files for this lesson.

3. Compare the open presentation with **P29ApplyB**, which is stored with the data files for this lesson.

4. Accept the change to the new theme, and then delete both comments on slide 1.

5. Accept the inserted pictures on slides 1 through 4.

6. On slide 6, do not accept the change to the content placeholder.

7. Remove any remaining comments.

8. End the review and incorporate the changes you marked for acceptance.

9. On slide 2, use the thesaurus to look up synonyms for the word **Selection**.

10. Replace the word **Selection** with the word **Variety**.

11. On slide 3, use the thesaurus to look up synonyms for the word **range**.

12. Replace the word **range** with the word **assortment**.

13. Insert a footer with your name and today's date fixed on every slide.

14. Apply the **Push** transition to all slides in the presentation, set to advance on a mouse click.

15. Save the changes to the presentation.

16. Preview the presentation. If necessary, adjust the size and position of pictures so they look good on the slides, and then save the changes.

17. **With your teacher's permission**, print all slides in the presentation, using the **6 Slides Horizontal Handout** layout. The page should look similar to Figure 29-1.

18. Send the final presentation to your teacher.

19. Close the presentation, saving changes, and exit PowerPoint.

Figure 29-1

Lesson 30

Inspecting and Protecting a Presentation

➤ ## What You Will Learn

Inspecting a Presentation
Checking Compatibility and Accessibility
Setting Passwords and Permissions
Marking a Presentation As Final
Adding a Digital Signature to a Presentation

WORDS TO KNOW

Digital signature
An electronic signature that is stored with the presentation to let others know the file is authentic or meets a standard that is important to the group.

Software Skills   Use the Document Inspector to remove personal or confidential information from your presentations. Check compatibility to identify features that might not be compatible with earlier versions of PowerPoint and accessibility to make sure your presentation can be understood by those with visual impairments. Apply passwords, set permissions, and mark a presentation as final to protect the presentation from unauthorized changes. A digital signature can let people with whom you share presentations know that the presentation has not been changed since you saved it.

What You Can Do

Inspecting a Presentation

- Run the Document Inspector to identify information you might not want to share with other people working with your presentation files.
- The Document Inspector will check for the following types of information in the presentation:
  - Comments and Annotations
  - Document Properties and Personal Information
  - Task Pane Apps
  - Custom XML Data
  - Invisible On-Slide Content
  - Off-Slide Content
  - Presentation Notes
- The Document Inspector prepares a report that shows which of these types of information are present. You can then remove the content if you wish.

Try It!   Inspecting a Presentation

1 Start PowerPoint, and open **P30Try** from the data files for this lesson.

2 Save the presentation as **P30Try_xx** in the location where your teacher instructs you to store the files for this lesson.

3 On the Info tab in the Backstage view, click the Check for Issues button, and then click Inspect Document.

4 In the Document Inspector dialog box, click to clear the Custom XML Data check box, and then click Inspect.

5 To the right of Comments and Annotations, click Remove All.

6 To the right of Document Properties and Personal Information, click Remove All.

7 Click Close. Note on the Info tab in the Backstage that the author name and other document properties have been removed.

8 Save the **P30Try_xx** file, and leave it open to use in the next Try It.

The Document Inspector dialog box after inspecting

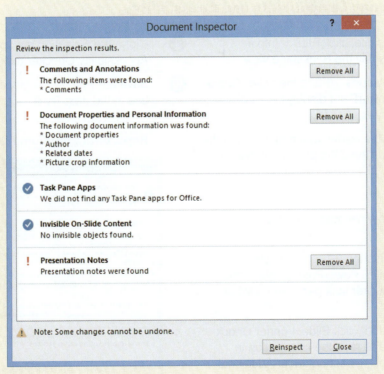

Checking Compatibility and Accessibility

■ If you know you will be saving presentations for use on systems that have earlier versions of PowerPoint installed, it can be helpful to check how compatible your current presentation is with those earlier versions.

■ Checking compatibility allows you to adjust any features that may not display correctly in another version.

■ By default, the Compatibility Checker runs automatically when you use the Save As command to save a presentation in PowerPoint 97-2003 format.

■ After checking the presentation, PowerPoint displays a summary list of incompatible features.

■ The summary list includes the number of times the feature is used and what steps PowerPoint will take to resolve the incompatibility issue when the presentation is saved in an earlier format.

- You can run the Compatibility Checker at any time from the Check for Issues drop-down menu on the Info tab in the Backstage view.

- You can also find the Accessibility Checker in the Backstage view.

- The Accessibility Checker looks for places in your presentation that could potentially make it difficult for someone with disabilities to view the entire presentation.

- When the Accessibility Checker finds problems, it will open a task pane listing each issue and classifying them as Errors, Warnings, or Tips.

  - Errors are listed for content that will be extremely difficult, if not impossible, for someone with disabilities to understand.

  - Warnings are places where the content might be difficult for people with disabilities to understand.

  - Tips are suggestions about places that can be modified to make it easier for someone with disabilities to understand.

- When the Accessibility Checker finds problems, it will provide you with instructions that you can use to eliminate the problems.

- You can choose whether you want to resolve the issues found or leave the presentation as is.

Try It!   Checking Compatibility and Accessibility

1 In the **P30Try_xx** file, click FILE > Info if necessary to display the Backstage view.

2 Click Check for Issues and then click Check Compatibility. PowerPoint displays a list of compatibility issues.

3 Review each of the issues that might need to be addressed if you saved the presentation in an earlier version.

4 Click OK.

5 Click FILE > Info if necessary to display the Backstage view.

6 Click Check for Issues and then click Check Accessibility. PowerPoint displays the Accessibility Checker task pane with a list of errors and tips.

7 In the TIPS section, click Slide 4 under Check Reading Order and read the information in the Why Fix scrolling section under Additional Information.

8 Fix the reading order on slide 4 as follows: Click HOME > Select > Selection Pane. In the Selection task pane, click TextBox 5 and then click the Send Backward arrow to move this object below Picture 6.

9 Close the Selection task pane and the Accessibility Checker task pane.

10 Save the **P30Try_xx** file, and leave it open to use in the next Try It.

Report from the Compatibility Checker

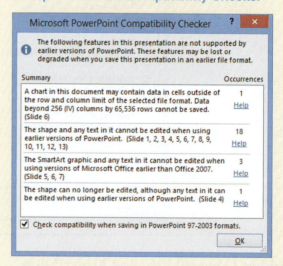

Setting Passwords and Permissions

- Adding a password to a presentation is one of the simplest ways to protect your content.
- Commands for adding a password are found on the FILE tab in the Backstage view.
- Once a password is set, the Info tab displays a Permissions setting in the Backstage view indicating that a password is required to open the presentation.
- When others open your presentation, the Password dialog box appears first, prompting users for the necessary password before the file will open.
- Be sure to write your password in a safe location, because PowerPoint does not save the password in a place you can access it if you forget it later.
- For a stronger level of security, you can restrict permission to work with a presentation using Office's Information Rights Management (IRM). IRM is particularly useful when a presentation may contain sensitive information that you don't want a general audience to have access to.
- To set permissions for a presentation, click Protect Presentation in the Info tab of the Backstage view, and then click Restrict Access.

- If your system is set up for Information Rights Management, a pop-out menu appears with options for setting restrictions.
- Clicking Restricted Access opens the Permission dialog box where you can enter the e-mail addresses of persons who are allowed to read or change the presentation.
  - By default, those you designate to read the presentation cannot edit it, print it, or copy it.
  - Those you designate to change the presentation can read, edit, copy, and save changes, but cannot print the presentation.
- A More Options button opens another dialog box in which you can apply additional permissions, such as permission to print or copy, and provide an e-mail address for requesting additional permissions.
- You can also set a date on which the permission will expire.
- A presentation with restricted access displays a warning bar across the top of the screen. You can click Change Permission to modify permissions.

Try It! — Setting a Password

1. In the **P30Try_xx** file, click FILE > Info.
2. Click Protect Presentation 🔒.
3. Click Encrypt with Password.
4. In the Encrypt Document dialog box, type the password **P30Try!**.
5. Click OK.
6. In the Confirm Password dialog box, type **P30Try!** and click OK.
7. Save changes and close the presentation.
8. Click FILE and, in the Recent Presentations section, click **P30Try_xx**.
9. Type **P30Try!** and click OK to open the presentation.
10. Leave the presentation open to use in the next Try It.

Marking a Presentation As Final

- When you mark your presentation as final, PowerPoint changes it to read-only mode. Others viewing the presentation see that it is marked as read-only so no further changes can be made.
- A read-only file cannot be edited; however, it is possible to save the presentation with a different name and then edit it.

- If you need true presentation security, add a password or restrict others' editing privileges before sharing the file.
- When a file is marked as final, the Marked as Final icon displays in the status bar.
- The Information bar at the top of the PowerPoint window indicates that the file is marked as final.
- Click the Edit Anyway button to remove the editing restrictions and work in the file.

Try It!   Marking a Presentation As Final

1 In the **P30Try_xx** file, click FILE > Protect Presentation 🔒.

2 Click Mark as Final.

3 Click OK twice.

4 Click the HOME tab if necessary. Note the words Read-Only in the title bar, the Marked as Final icon in the status bar, and the Marked as Final message in the Information bar.

5 Leave the file open to use in the next Try It.

Adding a Digital Signature to a Presentation

- A **digital signature** helps others receiving your presentation know that the file is authentically from you.

- You can assign a digital signature to your PowerPoint presentation using the Add a Digital Signature option from the Protect Presentation menu in the Backstage view.

✓ *Be sure to follow your instructor's direction on how—or whether—to use digital signatures with PowerPoint.*

- The digital signature remains valid as long as the presentation is not changed. If you change the presentation at a later time, you will need to sign the presentation again to make the signature valid.

Try It!   Adding a Digital Signature to a Presentation

1 In the **P30Try_xx** file, click FILE > Protect Presentation 🔒, and then click Add a Digital Signature.

2 If necessary, follow instructions to create a new digital ID.

3 In the Sign dialog box, click the Commitment Type down arrow and click Created and approved this document.

4 In the Purpose for signing this document box, type **Validate authenticity of presentation**.

5 Click Sign and then click OK.

6 On the Info tab, click View Signatures to display the Signatures task pane, where you can view, edit, or remove the signature in your document.

7 Close the **P30Try_xx** file, and exit PowerPoint.

Presentation signed with a digital signature

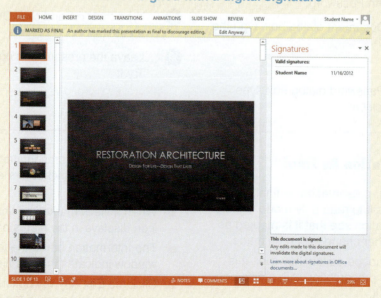

Lesson 30—Practice

In this project, you will finalize the Whole Grains Bread presentation. You will inspect the presentation, add a password, and mark the presentation as final.

DIRECTIONS

1. Start PowerPoint, if necessary, and open **P30Practice**.
2. Save the presentation as **P30Practice_xx** in the location where your teacher instructs you to store the files for this lesson.
3. Click **FILE** > **Info** > **Check for Issues** 🕮, and then click **Inspect Document**.
4. Deselect **Custom XML Data**, and then click **Inspect**.
5. Click **Remove All** next to Comments and Annotations and Document Properties and Personal Information.
6. Click **Close**.

7. Click **Protect Presentation** 🔒 and then click Encrypt with Password.
8. In the Encrypt Document dialog box, type **P30Practice!** and then click **OK**.
9. In the Confirm Password dialog box, type **P30Practice!** and then click **OK**.
10. Click **INSERT** > **Header & Footer** 📄 and insert today's date in Fixed format and your full name as the footer on all slides.
11. Click **FILE** > **Info** > **Protect Presentation** 🔒 and then click **Mark as Final**.
12. Click **OK** and then click **OK** again.
13. Close the presentation, and exit PowerPoint.

Lesson 30—Apply

In this project, you will do some additional finalizing on the Whole Grains Bread presentation. You will inspect the document, check compatibility and accessibility, and add a digital signature.

DIRECTIONS

1. Start PowerPoint, if necessary, and open **P30Apply**.
2. Save the presentation as **P30Apply_xx** in the location where your teacher instructs you to store the files for this lesson.
3. Inspect the document and remove all properties and personal information.
4. Check compatibility with previous versions of PowerPoint.

5. Check accessibility and read about the changes you might need to make to be sure the presentation is accessible to all viewers.
6. Add a digital signature, choosing a Commitment Type and entering a purpose for signing the presentation.
7. Close the presentation, and exit PowerPoint.

Lesson 31

Sharing a Presentation

➤ **What You Will Learn**

Packaging a Presentation for CD
Presenting a Slide Show Online
Creating a Video of a Presentation
Publishing Slides

Software Skills   You have a number of options for sharing a presentation with others. You can package the presentation materials on a CD. You can also create a video or use other output options, such as storing the presentation on your SkyDrive or saving the presentation as a PowerPoint Show.

What You Can Do

Packaging for CD

- Use the Package Presentation for CD feature when you want to run a slide show on another computer.

- When you package a presentation show, it automatically includes a link to download the PowerPoint Viewer, which allows the presentation to be viewed on a PC even if PowerPoint is not installed.

    ✓ *The recipient must be able to connect to the Internet to download the PowerPoint Viewer.*

- The Package Presentation for CD dialog box lets you control the process of packaging the presentation files and copying them to a folder or a CD.

- If you choose the folder option, you can store the presentation on removable media such as a flash drive that can be easier to transport than a CD.

- To see options for packaging the presentation's files, click the Options button in the Package Presentation for CD dialog box. By default, PowerPoint links all files used in the presentation, such as videos and images.

- PowerPoint will also embed the TrueType fonts used to create the text, so that even if the computer on which you will present the slides does not have the fonts, they will display correctly during the presentation.

- If your presentation includes images or media files such as videos or sounds, you should optimize and compress the media objects before you package the presentation. You can find these options on the Info tab.

Try It! — Packaging for CD

1. Start PowerPoint, and open **P31TryA** from the data files for this lesson.

2. Save the presentation as **P31TryA_xx** in the location where your teacher instructs you to store the files for this lesson.

3. Click FILE > Info > Optimize Compatibility. When the optimization is complete, click Close.

4. Click Compress Media and then select Presentation Quality. When compression is complete, click Close.

5. Insert a recordable CD in the appropriate drive in the computer.

6. Click FILE > Export > Package Presentation for CD.

7. Click Package for CD.

8. In the Package for CD dialog box, type **P31TryA_xx** in the Name the CD box.

9. Click Options to see the items that will be included with the presentation, and then click OK.

10. Click Copy to CD.

11. When asked if you want to use linked files, click Yes.

12. Click No if asked if you want to copy the same files to another CD.

13. Click Close.

Try It! — Copying to a Folder

1. In the **P31TryA_xx** presentation, click FILE > Export > Package Presentation for CD > Package for CD.

2. Type **P31TryA_xx** in the Name the CD box.

3. Click Copy to Folder.

4. Type **P31TryA_xx** in the folder name box.

5. Navigate to the folder where your teacher instructs you to store the files for this lesson and click Select.

6. Click OK and click Yes when prompted to copy linked files to the folder.

7. Close the File Explorer window that shows the files in the **P31TryA_xx** folder.

8. Click Close.

Presenting a Slide Show Online

- The Present Online feature allows you to share a presentation with others via the Internet.

- Use the Present Online option on the Share tab in the Backstage view or on the SLIDE SHOW tab.

  ✓ You will need a Windows Live ID to present your slide show online. If you do not already have one, you can sign up for one for free.

- Anyone who can access the Internet will be able to follow the provided link and view the presentation, even if they don't have PowerPoint 2013 installed on their PC.

- The Office Presentation Service will provide you with a URL that you can give to up to 50 people so they can watch the presentation.

- You will still control the presentation by starting and pausing the presentation as desired.

Try It!   **Presenting a Slide Show Online**

1 In the **P31TryA_xx** file, click SLIDE SHOW > Present Online 🖥 .

OR

Click FILE > Share > Present Online 🖥 .

2 Click in the Enable remote viewers to download the presentation check box and then click CONNECT or Present Online.

The Present Online dialog box

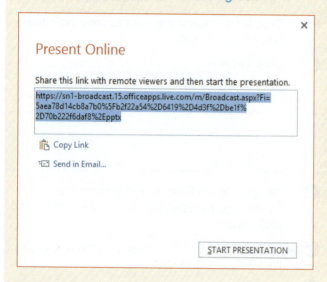

3 Click Send in Email, if you want to send the provided URL to your attendees using Outlook.

OR

Click Copy Link to send the URL to your attendees in a memo or any other format.

When you open the document you plan to send to the attendees, press CTRL + V to paste the link.

4 Click START PRESENTATION when you and your attendees are ready to begin the presentation.

5 Advance through the presentation as you normally would. Your attendees will view the slide show through their browser window.

6 Click End Online Presentation on the PRESENT ONLINE tab.

7 Click End Online Presentation when warned that the remote viewers will be disconnected.

8 Leave the presentation open for the next Try It.

Creating a Video of a Presentation

- You can save your PowerPoint presentations as video that can be shared with others to be viewed on a PC or uploaded to the Internet.

- PowerPoint will save the presentation as an MP4 file, which can be uploaded to YouTube, Facebook, or other Web sites.

- When you save your presentation as a video, it can be played on any computer or DVD player that can handle the MP4 format.

- Your presentation video can include unique timings and narration, or you can set a specific number of seconds that each slide will be paused.

Try It! **Creating a Video of a Presentation**

1 In the **P31TryA_xx** file, click FILE > Export > Create a Video.

2 In the Create a Video pane, click Computer & HD Displays and then select the resolution you want to use.

3 Change the number of seconds that you want to spend on each slide to 6:00.

  ✓ *If you're unsure about the number of seconds to use, you can set the number of seconds and then click the second button (Don't Use Recorded Timings and Narrations) to see what it will look like.*

  OR

  Click Don't Use Recorded Timings and Narrations to see the options available.

  ✓ *This second button says Don't Use Recording Timings and Narrations because these items haven't been set yet. If you had already recording timings and narrations the button would say Use Recorded Timings and Narrations.*

4 Select Record Timings and Narration.

5 In the Record Slide Show dialog box, select one or both of the following:

  ■ Slide and animation timings
  ■ Narrations and laser pointer

6 Click Start Recording.

  ✓ *At this point, you would begin the process of recording your presentation. For more information review the Rehearsing Timings section in Lesson 27.*

7 Click Create Video.

8 Navigate to the location where your teacher instructs you to store the files for this lesson.

  ✓ *The file name box will have the same name that your PowerPoint presentation has. If you want to use a different name, select the name in the box and type a new name.*

9 Type the file name **P31TryB_xx**, and then click Save.

10 Save the **P31TryA_xx** file, and leave it open to use in the next Try It.

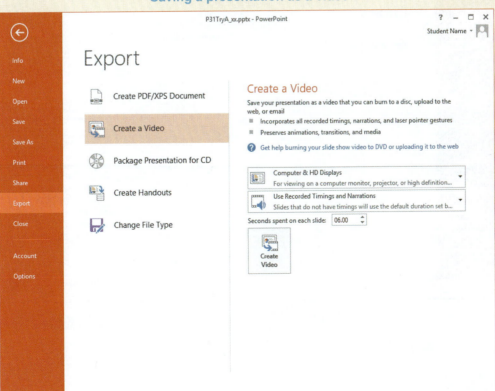

Saving a presentation as a video

Publishing Slides

- You have other output options for a PowerPoint presentation.

- You can publish it to your Windows SkyDrive site, where it can be viewed or edited online.

- You can save the presentation as a PowerPoint Show, which will open automatically in Slide Show view to save time.

- You can save the presentation to SharePoint, so that it is ready for collaboration.

- You can also set up a presentation to print on overhead transparencies, nonstandard paper sizes, or 35mm slides.

Try It!   **Saving a Presentation on the SkyDrive**

1 In the **P31TryA_xx** file, click FILE > Save As, and click the SkyDrive option for your login name.

2 Click the Documents folder in the right pane to open the Save As dialog box.

3 Change the file name to **P31TryC_xx**, and then click Save.

4 Close the **P31TryC_xx** file, and leave PowerPoint open.

Saving a presentation to the SkyDrive

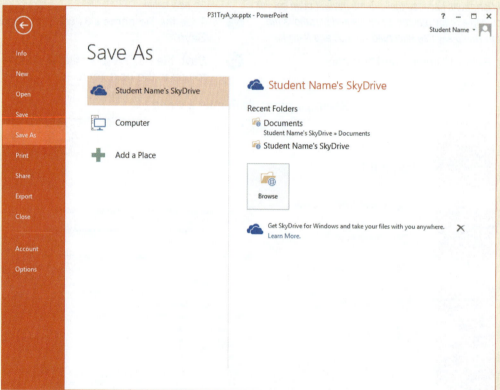

Try It! **Viewing a Presentation on the SkyDrive**

1. Start Internet Explorer and type **https://skydrive.live.com** in the address bar. Press ENTER .

2. In the Microsoft account box, type your Microsoft login e-mail address.

3. Press TAB and type your Microsoft account password.

4. Click Sign In. SkyDrive opens in your browser.

5. Click the Documents folder to display the presentation you saved to the SkyDrive.

6. Click the presentation name to open it in the PowerPoint Web App.

7. Navigate through the slides using the next and previous arrows at the bottom of the window.

8. When you reach the end of the presentation, sign out of your SkyDrive and close the browser.

Try It! **Saving a Presentation As a Show**

1. In PowerPoint, click FILE > Open.

2. In the Recent Presentations list, click **P31TryA_xx**.

3. Navigate to the location where your teacher instructs you to store the files for this lesson.

4. Click the Save as type arrow, and click PowerPoint Show.

5. Type **P31TryD_xx**.

6. Click Save.

7. Close the file, and exit PowerPoint.

Lesson 31—Practice

The Campus Recreation Center is ready to start getting information out and wants to publish its presentation for several outlets. In this project, you create a video from the presentation slides.

DIRECTIONS

1. Start PowerPoint, if necessary, and open the **P31Practice** presentation from the data files for this lesson.

2. Click **FILE** > **Export** > **Create a Video**.

3. Click **Computers & HD Displays** and then click **Internet & DVD**. The presentation video will have good clarity, but keep the file size small.

4. Click **Don't Use Recorded Timings and Narrations** and then click **Preview Timings & Narration** to see how the presentation will look with the default 5:00 seconds spent on each slide.

5. Click the screen at the end of the slide show to return to the Create a Video options.

6. Type **6:00** in the Seconds to spend on each slide box.

7. Click **Create Video**. The Save As dialog box opens.

8. Navigate to the location where your teacher instructs you to store the files for this lesson. Type **P31Practice_xx** in the File name text box, and then click **Save**, as shown in Figure 31-1 on the next page.

   ✓ Keep in mind that it will take several minutes for the video file to be completed.

9. Close the presentation, and exit PowerPoint.

10. In File Explorer, navigate to the location where you stored the video and double-click it. Choose to play it with Windows Media Player, if you have that option.

11. View the video, and, when it ends, close Media Player.

Figure 31-1

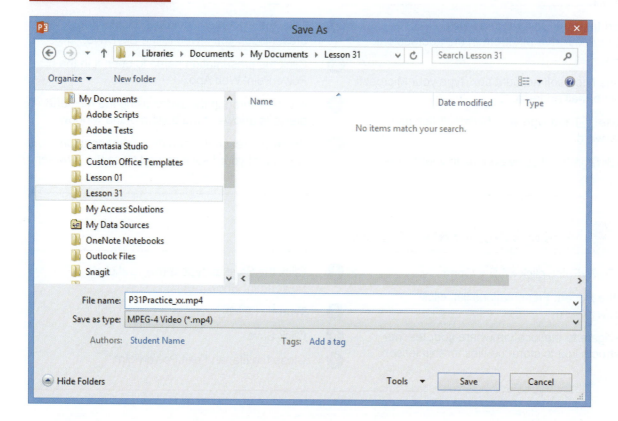

Lesson 31—Apply

You continue working with the Campus Recreation Center presentation. In this project, you will package the presentation on a CD or in a folder so that it can be transported to other locations.

DIRECTIONS

1. Start PowerPoint, if necessary, and open the **P31Apply** presentation from the data files for this lesson.

2. Save the presentation as **P31ApplyA_xx** in the location where your teacher instructs you to store the files for this lesson.

3. Package the presentation as follows:

   a. Name the CD folder in which to store the files **P31ApplyA_xx**.

   b. Display Options and choose to embed TrueType fonts, if necessary.

   c. If you have the ability to copy to a CD, do so.

   d. If you cannot create a CD, then use Copy to Folder to save the folder where your teacher instructs you to store the files for this lesson.

4. Save the presentation as a PowerPoint Show with the name **P31ApplyB_xx**.

5. Navigate to the location where you stored the PowerPoint Show, double-click the file, and choose to view the show.

6. Close the file, saving changes, and exit PowerPoint.

End-of-Chapter Activities

➤ PowerPoint Chapter 4—Critical Thinking

Job-Readiness Skills

As a manager at the Michigan Avenue Athletic Club, you have noticed that some of the part-time employees hired to help out in summer and other busy times lack some basic employability skills. You have decided to prepare a presentation that new part-time employees can view to refresh their understanding of how to be a good employee.

In this project, working alone or in teams, you will research job-readiness skills. You will include a minimum of 8 slides covering two major components of employability skills: positive work practices (such as appropriate dress for the workplace, personal grooming, punctuality, time management, and organization) and positive interpersonal skills (such as communication, respect, and teamwork).

DIRECTIONS

1. Start a new presentation. You may start from a blank presentation or use a PowerPoint template.

2. Save the presentation as **PCT04_xx** in the location where your teacher instructs you to store the files for this chapter.

3. Customize the slide master and layouts as desired. You may:

   a. Change theme colors to a different set or customize theme colors.

   b. Change theme fonts.

   c. Change bullet formats.

   d. Change the background for one layout or all layouts.

   e. Adjust the position of placeholders on the slide master or supporting layouts.

   f. Create a new layout for a specific type of content.

4. Insert the title **Employability Skills**, and in the subtitle placeholder, type **A Presentation by** and then insert your first and last name.

5. Add a slide to the presentation with the title **Sources**. Use this slide to record the Web addresses of sites where you find information for the research you will be doing in the next part of the project.

6. With your teacher's permission, use the Internet to research the topics listed above. Use valid and reputable sites for your research, and copy site information to your Sources slide.

7. When your research is complete, organize your material into topics and plan how to use it in your presentation. You may use a storyboard if desired. Select slide layouts suitable for the type of information you find. Add illustrations as desired, using online pictures or other graphics.

8. Each topic should be represented by at least one slide. Use additional slides to expand the topic as necessary.

9. Organize the material into sections, renaming the sections as appropriate.

10. Create custom shows to make it possible to show only the positive work practices material or only the positive interpersonal skills material.

11. Create a Contents slide on which you insert links to the custom shows and to other important slides in the presentation. Insert action buttons to return to the contents slide, or set the custom show links to Show and return.

12. Use the thesaurus to fine-tune vocabulary in the presentation, and then check spelling.

13. Insert a footer that displays today's date, slide numbers, and your name on all slides except the title slide.

14. Rehearse the presentation, checking your links and action buttons, but do not save slide timings.

15. Deliver the presentation to your class using Presenter view. Annotate at least one slide during the presentation, and save the markup. Ask for comments on how the presentation could be improved.

16. After making changes, inspect the presentation and remove any comments or document properties.

17. Mark the presentation as final, or apply a digital signature, and then send the presentation as an attachment to your teacher.

18. Close the presentation, saving changes, and exit PowerPoint.

➤ PowerPoint Chapter 4—Portfolio Builder

Finalize and Package Bakery Presentations

Whole Grains Bread has asked you to finalize a slide show that can run unattended in a kiosk or as a video on their Web site as well as a custom show that can be presented to prospective catering clients. In this project, you will add the finishing touches, including transitions, animations, links, and custom shows, and then output the presentation in several ways.

DIRECTIONS

1. Start PowerPoint, if necessary, and open **PPB04A** from the data files for this chapter.

2. Save the presentation as **PPB04A_xx** in the location where your teacher instructs you to store the files for this chapter.

3. In Slide Master view, add a bullet character to the first-level list, and change the bullet character for the second-level list. Adjust colors, sizes, and indents as desired.

4. Apply a different background to the Title Slide layout only, and then modify the font and color of the title text on the Title Slide layout.

5. Add a title-only slide between slides 8 and 9 and enter the title **Catering Bread Pricing**.

6. Embed the table from the **PPB04B** Word document located in the data files for this chapter. Format the table so that it blends in with the rest of the presentation, as shown in Illustration 4A on the next page.

7. Apply transitions of your choice to all slides.

8. Display slide 5 and adjust the timing on the animation of the stars so that each one appears at the same time you begin to read that item.

   ✓ *Use the Delay setting in the Timing group.*

9. Display slide 7 and animate the text box below the picture using an entrance effect of your choice.

10. Insert the following comment on slide 4: **Link these items to custom shows**.

11. Create a custom show with the name **Catering** for slides 8 through 10. Create a second custom show with the name **Rental** for slides 11 through 12.

12. On slide 7, insert an action button or link that will take the viewer back to slide 1. Format the action button as desired.

13. Link the bullet items on slide 4 to the custom shows you created. Specify Show and return for these custom shows.

14. Delete the comment on slide 4.

15. Rehearse the slide show as it will be presented: on slide 4, jump to the first custom show; then, after the custom show ends and slide 4 appears again, jump to the second custom show. After the second show ends, proceed from slide 4 to slide 7 and then use the action button to return to slide 1.

16. Save slide timings, and then save your changes so far.

17. Package this version of the presentation in a folder named **PPB04C_xx**. Include TrueType fonts with the package.

18. Remove the action button from slide 7. Then save the current version as a video named **PPB04D_xx** that will be played on their Web site.

19. Save the current file as a PowerPoint presentation named **PPB04E_xx**.

20. Hide slide 4. Set up the show to be browsed at a kiosk using the current slide timings. (Check to make sure all slides have slide timings.)

21. Run the show to make sure it loops properly. Stop after you have seen slide 2 the second time.

22. **With your teacher's permission,** print slide 9.

23. Close the presentation, saving changes, and exit PowerPoint.

Illustration 4A

Catering Bread Pricing

Item	Per Item	Dozen/Per Item	Two Dozen/Per Item
Bread	$3.50	$2.99	$1.99
Croissants	$2.00	$1.75	$1.25
Bagels	$0.90	$0.60	$0.45
Baguettes	$2.50	$2.00	$1.75
Muffins	$1.50	$1.25	$1.00

(Courtesy Monkey Business Images/Shutterstock)

Working with Masters, Handouts, and Text

Lesson 32

Working with Advanced Slide Master Features

➤ **What You Will Learn**

Adding Graphics to Slide Master Layouts
Customizing a Slide Master Background
Customizing Placeholders on Slide Layouts

WORDS TO KNOW

Gradient
A fill option that uses gradations of one or more colors.

Gradient stop
Point at which a gradient changes from one color to another color.

Transparency
Amount of light that can pass through an object.

Software Skills   You can customize slide masters by adding a shape or picture, by creating a custom background, or by modifying the placeholder arrangement.

What You Can Do

Adding Graphics to Slide Master Layouts

■ Graphics such as shapes, lines, and pictures can be added to slide master layouts. These graphics appear on every slide to which that layout is applied.

■ Use the shapes on the HOME tab or INSERT tab to draw basic objects, such as lines, rectangles, and circles, as well as more complex shapes such as stars, banners, and block arrows, on a slide master layout.

   ✓ *You can also create your own custom objects by merging shapes.*

■ Use the Pictures or Online Pictures command on the INSERT tab to locate a picture to display on a slide master layout.

Try It!   Adding Graphics to Slide Master Layouts

1 Start PowerPoint, and open **P32Try** from the data files for this lesson.

2 Save the presentation as **P32Try_xx** in the location where your teacher instructs you to store the files for this lesson.

3 Click VIEW > Slide Master 🖿.

4 Display the Title Slide layout if necessary.

5 Click INSERT > Shapes ⬦.

6 Select the Rectangle shape.

7 Draw a shape 0.5" high by 2.5" wide and position it at the bottom center of the gray rectangle at the right side of the slide.

8 Right-click the shape, select Edit Text, and type **Helping Hands**.

9 Click INSERT > Pictures 🖾.

10 Navigate to the data files for this lesson, select the **P32Try_picture.tif** image, and click Insert.

11 Adjust the width of the picture to 2.5" and position it on top of the shape, as shown in the figure.

12 Click the Close Master View button ❌ .

13 Save the **P32Try_xx** file, and leave it open to use in the next Try It.

Picture and shape placed on a slide master

Customizing a Slide Master Background

■ As you know, backgrounds on slide masters are controlled by the applied theme. You can, however, customize one or more slide master layouts by applying a **gradient**, a texture, or a picture as a background.

■ PowerPoint includes preset gradients you can apply at the click of a button, but you can also create your own custom gradient using options on the Format Background task pane. You can use the same process to create a gradient for any object, such as a placeholder, text box, shape, or even text.

■ Create a gradient by selecting **gradient stops** and then choosing a color for each stop. You can also choose the direction and the angle for the gradient to control how color flows.

- Add gradient stops to add additional colors to the gradient. Drag gradient stops along the gradient color bar to change where the color starts. Remove gradient stops to simplify the gradient.

- PowerPoint includes a gallery of textures you can choose among to give a slide layout an interesting background appearance.

- When you apply a texture, you may want to adjust the **transparency** setting so that text can easily be read against the texture. The same holds true if you insert a picture as a slide background.

- You can adjust the transparency of textures and pictures in the Format Background task pane.

Try It!   Customizing a Slide Master Background

1. In the **P32Try_xx** file, click VIEW > Slide Master ▭.

2. In Slide Master view, click the Blank layout that is currently used by slide 2.

3. Click SLIDE MASTER > Background Styles ▨ > Format Background.

4. In the Format Background task pane, click Gradient fill. A default gradient is applied to the slide master.

Apply a color to a gradient stop

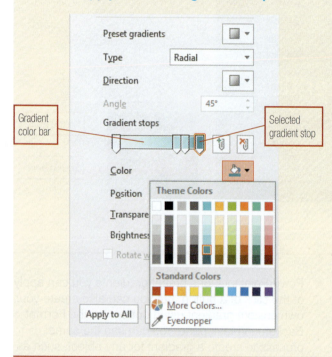

Gradient color bar

Selected gradient stop

5. Click the Type drop-down arrow and select Radial.

6. Click the Direction drop-down arrow and select From Top Left Corner.

7. Click the far-right gradient stop on the gradient color bar, click the Color button below, and select Turquoise, Accent 1, Darker 25%.

8. In the Thumbnail pane, click the Content with Caption layout that is currently used by slide 8.

9. In the Format Background task pane, click Picture or texture fill. A default texture is applied to the slide.

10. In the Format Background task pane, click the Texture drop-down arrow to display a gallery of textures.

11. Click the Woven mat texture, the second from the right in the top row of the gallery.

12. In the Format Background task pane, drag the Transparency slider to the right until the transparency setting is 65%.

13. Close the Format Background task pane, and close Slide Master view to see the texture on the slide in Normal view. Scroll up to see the custom gradient on slide 2.

14. Save the **P32Try_xx** file, and leave it open to use in the next Try It.

Customizing Placeholders on Slide Layouts

■ When a slide layout is selected (rather than the slide master), the Title and Footers check boxes are active in the Master Layout group on the SLIDE MASTER tab.

■ Deselect the Title check box to remove the title placeholder from the layout. Deselect the Footers check box to remove the date, footer, and slide number placeholders from the layout. Display these placeholders again by selecting the appropriate check box.

■ You can also select and delete any default placeholder on a layout.

■ You can restore deleted placeholders using the Master Layout dialog box. This command is active when the slide master is selected.

■ The dialog box shows all placeholders with check boxes selected to show which are active on the slide. To restore a placeholder you have deleted, simply click the appropriate check box.

| **Try It!** | **Customizing Placeholders on Slide Layouts** |

1 In the **P32Try_xx** file, click VIEW > Slide Master ⊞.

2 Scroll down in the Thumbnail pane and select the Two Content layout, currently used by no slides.

3 In the Master Layout group, click the Title check box to remove the title placeholder.

4 Click the Title check box to restore the placeholder.

5 Select the slide master at the top of the Thumbnail pane.

6 Click the border of the slide number placeholder.

7 Press DEL .

8 Click SLIDE MASTER > Master Layout ⊞.

9 Select the Slide number check box to restore the placeholder.

10 Click OK.

11 Close Slide Master view.

12 In Normal view, click INSERT > Header & Footer ⊡, select Slide number, and click Apply to All to display the slide number on all slides.

13 Close the **P32Try_xx** file, saving changes, and exit PowerPoint.

The Master Layout dialog box

Master Layout   ?   ×

Placeholders
☑ Title
☑ Text
☑ Date
☐ Slide number
☑ Footer

OK   Cancel

Lesson 32—Practice

In this project, you work on a presentation for Yesterday's Playthings. You customize and add graphic elements to the slide master.

DIRECTIONS

1. Start PowerPoint, if necessary, and open **P32Practice** from the data files for this lesson.

2. Save the presentation as **P32Practice_xx** in the location where your teacher instructs you to store the files for this lesson.

3. Click **VIEW** > **Slide Master** 🗔.

4. Click the **Title Slide** layout.

5. Click the aqua rectangle and press [DEL] to remove it.

6. Click **SLIDE MASTER** > **Background Styles** 🖾 > **Format Background**.

7. On the Format Background task pane, click **Picture or texture fill**.

8. Click the **Texture** drop-down arrow and click the **Recycled paper** texture. Then drag the Transparency slider until the transparency is **30%**. Close the Format Background task pane.

9. Scroll up to click the slide master.

10. On the slide master, draw a Rectangle shape that is **1.1"** wide and **7.5"** high.

11. Remove the shape outline and fill the shape with **Aqua, Accent 2, Darker 25%**.

12. Move the shape to the far right side of the slide, as shown in Figure 32-1.

13. Draw a Right Triangle shape that is **2"** wide and **7.5"** high.

14. Click **DRAWING TOOLS FORMAT** > **Rotate** 🔺▾ > **Flip Horizontal**.

15. Remove the shape outline and use the same fill as for the rectangle.

16. Move the triangle shape to align at the right side with the rectangle shape, as shown in Figure 32-1. (Both shapes should align at the right with the right edge of the slide.)

17. Select both shapes and then click **DRAWING TOOLS FORMAT** > **Send Backward** 🖾 > **Send to Back** to move the shapes behind the footer and the slide number placeholders.

18. Select the slide number placeholder and press [DEL] to remove it.

19. Click **SLIDE MASTER** > **Close Master View** ✖.

20. Preview the slides to see the new formats in place.

21. Close the presentation, saving changes, and exit PowerPoint.

Figure 32-1

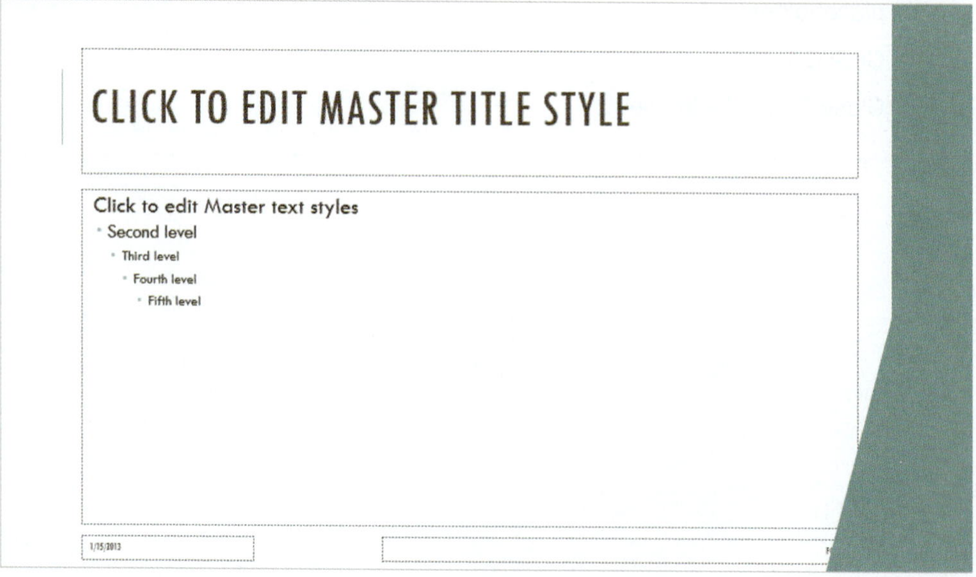

Lesson 32—Apply

You continue to work on the presentation for Yesterday's Playthings. In this project, you return to the slide master to adjust the appearance of the shapes you added in the practice exercise, create a gradient background, and insert a picture to appear on all slides.

DIRECTIONS

1. Start PowerPoint, if necessary, and open **P32Apply** from the data files for this lesson.

2. Save the presentation as **P32Apply_xx** in the location where your teacher instructs you to store the files for this lesson.

3. Switch to Slide Master view and display the slide master.

4. Display the Format Background task pane, select the rectangle shape, and change the transparency to **40%**.

5. Select the triangle shape and change the transparency to **35%**.

6. Create a gradient on the slide master as follows:

   a. With the Format Background task pane displayed and no shape selected, choose to create a gradient fill.

   b. Select the **Light Gradient – Accent 2** preset gradient.

   c. Change the direction of the gradient to **Linear Diagonal – Bottom Left to Top Right**.

   d. With the first gradient stop selected, click the **Color** button and select **White, Background 1**. Then drag the gradient stop to the right until the Position box reads **25%**.

   e. Click the gradient stop at the far right of the gradient color bar and then click the **Remove gradient stop** button ⬛ to remove the color from the gradient.

   f. Click the right-most gradient stop, and change its color to **Aqua, Accent 2, Lighter 40%**.

   g. Click the center gradient stop, change its color to **Gold, Accent 3, Lighter 80%**, and drag it to the left until its position is **55%**. Close the Format Background task pane.

7. Remove the Date placeholder from the slide master.

8. Search for an online picture using the keyword **toys** and then insert a picture of a toy such as the wooden top shown in Figure 32-2.

9. Crop the picture to remove as much of the background as possible. Then resize the image to be **1.8"** wide.

10. Reposition the image in the lower-left corner of the slide, as shown in Figure 32-2 on the next page.

11. Close Slide Master view.

12. Insert a footer with your full name on all slides.

13. Preview the presentation to see the new formats in place.

14. **With your teacher's permission,** print slide 2. It should look similar to Figure 32-2.

15. Close the presentation, saving changes, and exit PowerPoint.

Figure 32-2

Lesson 33

Customizing Themes and Effects

➤ **What You Will Learn**

Applying a Theme to Selected Slides
Customizing Effects

Software Skills   To add visual interest to a presentation using themes, you can apply a theme to selected slides. Choose the slides to which you want to apply the theme, or apply a theme to an entire section. Choose a different set of effects to customize the appearance of graphics in a presentation.

What You Can Do

Applying a Theme to Selected Slides

- One way to add visual interest to a presentation is to add a second slide master so that you have a number of different layouts to choose among when formatting slides.

- If you want to apply a different theme to only a few slides, however, you can do so in Normal view using one of these options:

  - Select the slides you want to format with a different theme and then use the Apply to Selected Slides command to apply the new theme only to those slides.

  - Select a section in the presentation and then apply a theme. The theme will automatically apply only to the slides in the section.

- When applying a different theme to selected slides in a presentation, try to make sure that the new theme coordinates with the existing theme, and do not apply more than two or three themes to avoid a loss of consistency among the presentation's slides.

Try It!   **Applying a Theme to Selected Slides**

1. Start PowerPoint, and open **P33Try** from the data files for this lesson.

2. Save the presentation as **P33Try_xx** in the location where your teacher instructs you to store the files for this lesson.

3. Click slide 2.

4. Click DESIGN > Themes More button ⊡ and right-click the Basis theme.

5. Click Apply to Selected Slides.

6. Click the second variant from the right, the variant with the orange border.

7. Click the Who Needs Help section name to select the three slides in this section.

8. Click DESIGN > Themes More button ⊡ and click the Metropolitan theme. The theme is applied only to the slides in the selected section.

9. Save the **P33Try_xx** file, and leave it open to use in the next Try It.

Customizing Effects

- When you customize a theme for a particular presentation, you can change colors, fonts, and background styles, either in Normal view or on the slide master.

- You can also choose a different scheme of effects. Effects control the appearance of objects to which you have applied Quick Styles, such as placeholders, text boxes, or shapes.

- Each theme supplies a set of effects that you can see applied to sample shapes in the Shape Styles gallery.

- To further customize a theme, you can select a different effects scheme by clicking Effects on the Variants drop-down menu. Choosing a different scheme applies that scheme to the current presentation.

- You can also apply a different group of effects in Slide Master view to customize a shape or placeholder on the slide master.

Try It!   **Customizing Effects**

1. In the **P33Try_xx** file, display slide 1.

2. Click DESIGN > Variants More button ⊡ > Effects to display the Effects gallery. The default effects scheme for the current theme is Subtle Solids.

3. Watch the two shapes on the slide as you move the pointer over some of the different effects schemes.

4. Click the Top Shadow effects scheme.

5. Click VIEW > Slide Master 🖽 and select the slide master at the top of the Thumbnail pane.

6. Click the turquoise rectangle behind the Master title style placeholder to select it.

7. Click DRAWING TOOLS FORMAT > Shape Styles More button ⊡ and then select the Moderate Effect – Turquoise, Accent 1 style.

8. Click SLIDE MASTER > Effects ◎ and then click the Inset effect.

9. Click SLIDE MASTER > Close Master View ❌ .

10. Display slide 6 to see the change in effects to the placeholder rectangle as well as the shapes on the slide.

   ✓ *Because you applied the Inset effects scheme in Slide Master view, the effects are applied globally throughout the presentation.*

11. Close the **P33Try_xx** file, saving changes, and exit PowerPoint.

(continued)

Try It! **Customizing Effects** (*continued*)

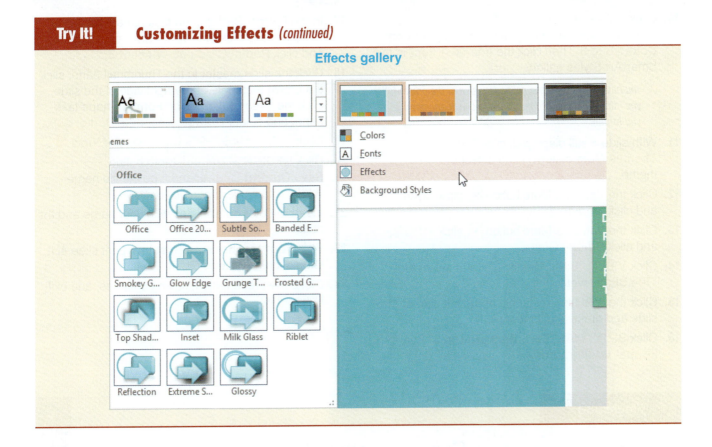

Lesson 33—Practice

Restoration Architecture wants you to customize the appearance of a presentation to give it a bit more visual interest. You begin that task in this project by creating a simplified version of the presentation from a Word outline. You apply and modify a theme by changing colors, background styles, and effects. You then save the theme so that you can apply it to Restoration Architecture's presentation in the next exercise.

DIRECTIONS

1. Start PowerPoint, and click **Open Other Presentations** to display the Open tab in Backstage view.

2. Navigate to the location where the data files for this lesson are stored, and choose to display All Files.

3. Select **P33Practice.docx** and click **Open**.

4. Save the presentation as **P33Practice_xx** in the location where your teacher instructs you to store the files for this lesson.

5. Click **VIEW** > **Outline View** 🔲 to display the Outline pane.

6. Right-click *Design for Life—Design That Lasts* and click **Demote** to move this slide title back to slide 1 as a subtitle.

7. Click **VIEW** > **Normal** 🔲 to return to Normal view.

8. Display each slide and click **HOME** > **Reset** 📄 to reset the slide formats. Apply the **Title Slide** layout to slide 1 and **Title and Content** to the remaining slides.

9. On slide 4, click the **Insert a SmartArt Graphic** icon 🔲 in the content placeholder, click **Hierarchy**, and click the **Organization Chart** layout. Click **OK**.

10. Click **SMARTART TOOLS DESIGN** > **Change Colors** ⁙ and select **Colorful Range – Accent Colors 5 to 6**. Then click the **Intense Effect** in the SmartArt Styles gallery.

    ✓ *You have now set up a simplified version of the presentation you intend to modify so that you can check appearance as you format.*

11. With slide 4 still displayed, click **DESIGN** > **Themes** More button ⏷ and select the **View** theme.

12. Click the **Variants** More button ⏷, click **Colors**, and click **Median**.

13. Click the **Variants** More button ⏷, click **Effects**, and click **Smoky Glass**.

14. Click **VIEW** > **Slide Master** ▭, and select the **Title Slide** layout.

15. Click the light blue rectangle at the left side of the slide and press DEL to remove it.

16. Click **SLIDE MASTER** > **Background Styles** ▨ > **Format Background**.

17. In the Format Background task pane, click **Gradient fill**, click the **Preset gradients** button, and click **Radial Gradient – Accent 2**.

18. Click the slide master in the Thumbnail pane, click the brown rectangle at the right side of the slide, click the **Color** button in the Format Shape task pane, and select **Orange, Accent 2, Darker 25%**.

19. Click **SLIDE MASTER** > **Close Master View** ⊠ .

20. Click **DESIGN** > **Themes** More button ⏷ > **Save Current Theme**, and type the file name **P33Practice_xx_theme**. Click **Save**.

21. Insert a footer on all slides with your name and the date.

22. **With your teacher's permission**, print slide 4. It should look similar to Figure 33-1.

23. Close the presentation, saving changes, and exit PowerPoint.

Figure 33-1

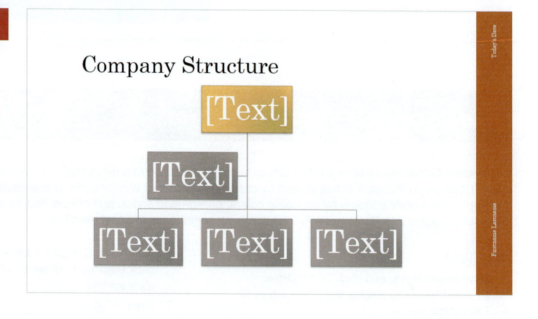

Lesson 33—Apply

In this project, you apply the theme you created in the practice exercise to selected portions of the existing Restoration Architecture presentation.

DIRECTIONS

1. Start PowerPoint, if necessary, and open **P33Apply** from the data files for this lesson.

2. Save the presentation as **P33Apply_xx** in the location where your teacher instructs you to store the files for this lesson.

3. With slide 1 displayed, on the DESIGN tab, right-click the custom theme you created in the practice exercise, **P33Practice_xx_theme**, and apply the theme to the selected slide.

4. Click the Company Graphics section name and apply **P33Practice_xx_theme** to the slides in that section. Note the change in colors and effects for the SmartArt diagrams and the charts.

5. Display slide 4 and click the text box to the right of the picture.

6. Apply the **Smoky Glass** effects scheme so this object will match the effect appearance of the other objects in the presentation.

7. Preview the entire presentation to see the changes you have made.

8. Insert a footer with your name and the date on all slides.

9. **With your teacher's permission,** print slide 5. It should look similar to Figure 33-2.

10. Save changes, close the file, and exit PowerPoint.

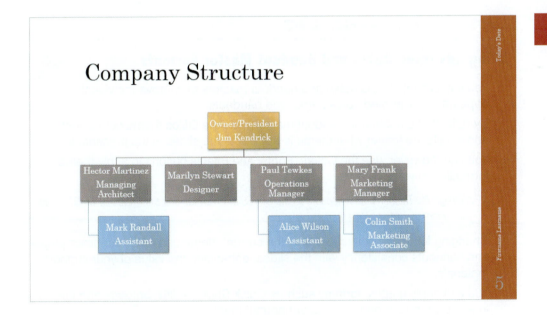

Figure 33-2

Lesson 34

Working with Notes and Handouts

➤ **What You Will Learn**

Using Advanced Notes and Handout Master Formats
Working with Linked Notes (OneNote 2013)

Software Skills   You can customize your notes and handouts by making changes to the notes and handout masters. You can also use the Linked Notes feature to take notes on a presentation and share your notes with others.

What You Can Do

Using Advanced Notes and Handout Master Formats

- You can customize the notes and handout masters to improve the visual appearance of printed notes pages and handouts.

- By default, the notes and handout masters use the Office theme colors, fonts, and effects, no matter what theme is applied to the slides in the presentation.

- You can, however, use the Colors, Fonts, and Effects buttons to apply theme formatting to your masters.

  ✓ *Although the Themes button appears on the NOTES MASTER tab and the HANDOUT MASTER tab, you cannot use it to apply a theme.*

- Changing fonts and colors to match the current theme can give your notes pages and handouts consistency with the slides, enhancing the value of your support materials.

- You can apply graphic formats such as Quick Styles or fills, borders, and effects to any placeholder on the notes or handout master.

- Use the Background Styles option in the Background group to apply a background that fills the entire notes page or handout. Background colors are controlled by the theme colors you have applied to the master.

- You can also add content, such as a new text box or a graphic, to the handout master. The content will appear on all pages.

- When adding content such as a text box to the handout master, be sure to position the content so it doesn't interfere with slide image placeholders for other layouts.

- If you insert a text box above the slide image on the one-slide-per-page layout, for example, it will obscure the slide images for other handout layouts.

Try It!   **Applying Notes Master Formats**

1 Start PowerPoint, and open **P34Try** from the data files for this lesson.

2 Save the presentation as **P34Try_xx** in the location where your teacher instructs you to store the files for this lesson.

3 Click slide 10.

4 Click VIEW > Notes Master ▣.

5 Click NOTES MASTER > Fonts A and select the Corbel font scheme to match the fonts used on the slides.

6 Click the Notes placeholder, then click DRAWING TOOLS FORMAT > Shape Styles > Colored Outline – Blue, Accent 1.

7 Click NOTES MASTER > Background Styles ▧ and select Style 6.

8 Click NOTES MASTER > Close Master View ▣ .

9 Click VIEW > Notes Page ▤ to display the presentation in Notes Page view. Scroll through the pages to see the formats you added to the master.

10 Click VIEW > Normal ▤ to return to Normal view.

11 Save the **P34Try_xx** file, and leave it open to use in the next Try It.

Applying custom formats to the notes master

Try It!   **Applying Handout Master Formats**

① In the **P34Try_xx** file, click VIEW > Handout Master 🔳.

② Click HANDOUT MASTER > Theme Colors 🔳.

③ Select the Blue Green theme colors.

④ Click HANDOUT MASTER > Background Styles 🔳 and select Style 9.

⑤ Click INSERT > Shapes 🔲 > Rectangle.

⑥ Draw a rectangle that covers the top of the page, as shown in the figure.

⑦ Right-click the shape, click the Outline shortcut button 🖊, and click No Outline.

⑧ Right-click the shape and select Send to Back.

⑨ Select the Header and Date placeholders, then click HOME > Font Color 🅰 ▾ and select White.

⑩ Click HANDOUT MASTER > Close Master View ❌.

⑪ Click INSERT > Header & Footer 📄. On the Notes and Handouts tab, choose to display the date and time and the page number. In the Header box, type your full name. In the Footer box, type **The Power of Giving**. Click Apply to All.

⑫ Click FILE > Print, click Full Page Slides and select 1 Slide Handout to see how the new handout will look. Then return to Normal view without printing.

⑬ Save the **P34Try_xx** file, and leave it open to use in the next Try It.

A formatted handout

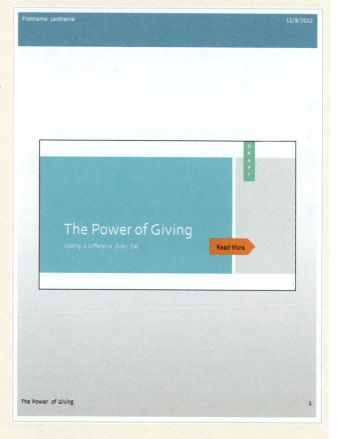

Working with Linked Notes (OneNote 2013)

■ Linked notes enable you to keep a set of notes on a presentation that retain the context of the original slides.

■ You can create linked notes using the Linked Notes button on the REVIEW tab.

■ If you have OneNote installed, but don't see the Linked Notes button on your REVIEW tab, you can add it using the PowerPoint Options dialog box.

   ✓ *You will need to start OneNote to set up the application before you can begin working with it. You may also need to dock a OneNote window to your desktop before the Linked Notes button can be added to the REVIEW tab.*

■ OneNote attaches a note-taking dock to the desktop beside the PowerPoint window.

■ When you take linked notes in the dock, a PowerPoint icon appears next to the note to show what application the note is linked to.

■ To see the subject of the note, hover over the icon. To review the original presentation, just click the icon.

■ You can tag a note as a To Do item using the keyboard shortcut CTRL + 1.

■ When you use shared OneNote notebooks to store your Linked Notes, team members can see and respond to each other's notes.

Try It!   Adding the Linked Notes Button to the Ribbon

1   In the **P34Try_xx** file, click FILE > Options > Customize Ribbon.

> ✓ *Remember that OneNote 2013 must be installed on your computer in order to use this feature.*

2   On the Customize Ribbon page, select All Tabs in the Choose commands from drop-down menu.

3   Click the button next to Review in the Main Tabs list on the left to expand the Review tab options and select OneNote.

> ✓ *If you do not see the OneNote option on the Review tab, start OneNote, choose Dock to Desktop on the VIEW tab, close OneNote, and close PowerPoint. After you restart PowerPoint, you should then see the OneNote option on the Review tab.*

4   Select the Review tab in the Main Tabs list on the right as the location for the button.

5   Click the Add button and click OK.

6   Save the **P34Try_xx** file, and leave it open to use in the next Try It.

Try It!   Working with Linked Notes (OneNote 2013)

1   In the **P34Try_xx** file, select slide 8.

2   Click REVIEW > Linked Notes.

3   Select any section or page, such as Quick Notes under your notebook, in the All Notebooks area and click OK.

> ✓ *Click the three dots at the top of the docked OneNote pane, if necessary, to display the Ribbon, and click New Page on the PAGES tab.*

4   In the header area above the date, type your name and press ENTER .

5   In the note area, type **Find out when the MS Walk and AIDS Awareness Week will take place.**

> ✓ *If you receive a message about the linked note, click OK.*

6   Display slide 10.

7   In the docked OneNote panel, click on the note box to select it. Hover your mouse over the PowerPoint icon next to the note box to see the original slide.

8   Close the OneNote dock. Close the **P34Try_xx** file, saving changes, and exit PowerPoint.

Select Location in OneNote dialog box

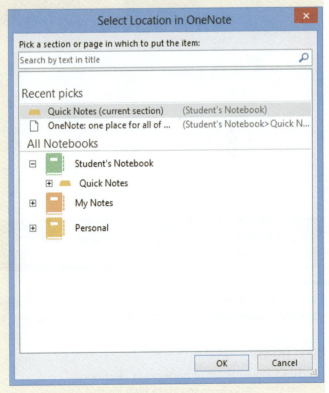

(continued)

Try It!   **Working with Linked Notes (OneNote 2013)** *(continued)*

A linked note

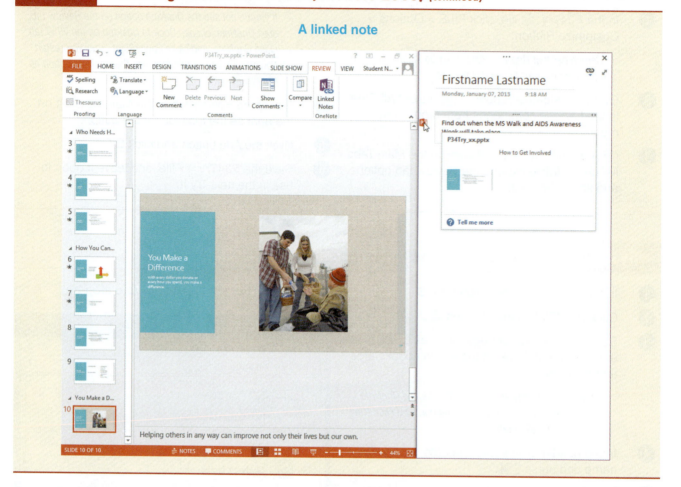

Lesson 34—Practice

Planet Earth, a local environmental action group, has asked you to prepare a presentation that can be shown at your civic garden center to inspire residents to go green. In this project, you customize the notes master.

DIRECTIONS

1. Start PowerPoint, if necessary, and open **P34Practice** from the data files for this lesson.

2. Save the presentation as **P34Practice_xx** in the location where your teacher instructs you to store the files for this lesson.

3. Click **VIEW** > **Notes Master** 🖼.

4. Click **NOTES MASTER** > **Colors** 🎨 and select **Green**.

5. Click **NOTES MASTER** > **Background Styles** 🎨 > **Format Background** to open the Format Background task pane.

6. In the Format Background task pane, click **Gradient fill**.

7. Click the **Preset gradients** button and click **Top Spotlight – Accent 2**. Close the Format Background task pane.

8. Click **NOTES MASTER** > **Close Master View** ❌ .

9. Click **INSERT** > **Header & Footer** 📄 and insert a header on the Notes and Handouts tab that includes your full name and today's date.

10. Click **VIEW** > **Notes Page** 🗐 to see the formats you added to the notes master. Your notes page should look similar to Figure 34-1.

11. Close the presentation, saving changes, and exit PowerPoint.

Figure 34-1

Firstname Lastname   Today's Date

COMPOSTING HELPS!

A compost pile can be used to recycle kitchen wastes, grass clippings, outside leaves, and other plant materials.

Click to add text

5

Lesson 34—Apply

In this project, you continue to work on the Planet Earth presentation. You complete the formatting of the notes pages and apply custom formatting to the handout master.

DIRECTIONS

1. Start PowerPoint, if necessary, and open **P34Apply** from the data files for this lesson.

2. Save the presentation as **P34Apply_xx** in the location where your teacher instructs you to store the files for this lesson.

3. Display the presentation in Notes Master view.

4. Draw a rectangle that covers the top of the page; make the rectangle the same height as the header and date placeholders.

5. Use the Shape Styles gallery to apply **Intense Effect – Green, Accent 1** to the rectangle, and send the rectangle to the back.

6. Change the size of the header and date text to 14 point, apply bold, and change the color if desired to contrast better with the shape behind the text.

7. Select the notes placeholder and apply the **Colored Outline – Lime, Accent 3** shape style.

8. Change the fonts to the **Gill Sans MT** scheme.

9. Close the Notes Master view and switch to the Notes Page view. Display slide 1.

10. In the notes placeholder, type **Going green can help save the planet, but it is also a great way to save you real green in your wallet!**

11. Insert your full name in the header, today's date, and an appropriate footer.

12. Display the handout master, choose to format the background, and choose to insert an online image as the page background.

13. Search for an image using the keyword **Earth**, and select an appropriate image.

14. Adjust the transparency to make the picture light enough that the slides will be easy to see on the handout.

15. Preview the handout pages to make sure your inserted picture is formatted correctly. Figure 34-2 on the next page shows one way that your page might look.

16. Preview the notes page for slide 1. It should look similar to Figure 34-3.

17. **With your teacher's permission**, print the notes page for slide 1.

18. Close the presentation, saving changes, and exit PowerPoint.

Figure 34-2

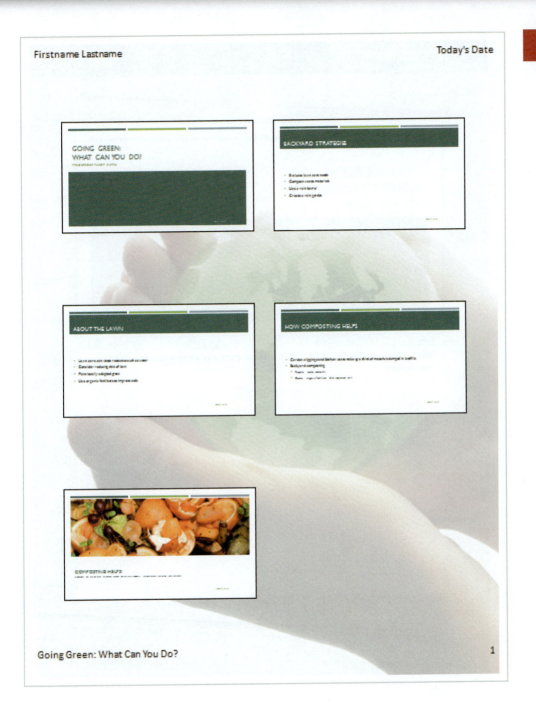

Figure 34-3

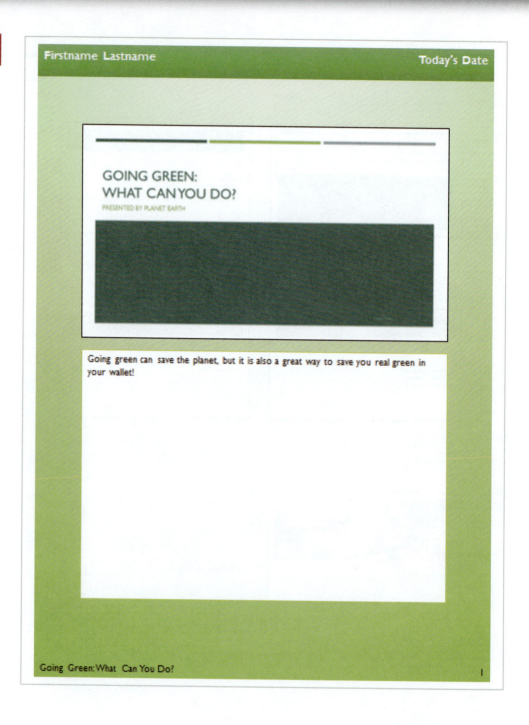

Lesson 35

Integrating PowerPoint with Word

➤ **What You Will Learn**

Exporting Handouts to Word
Linking Presentations to Word
Communicating with Others

Software Skills   Send presentation materials to Microsoft Word to take advantage of Word's formatting options. You can also choose to link the presentation materials to a Word document. Handouts linked to a presentation will change automatically when the presentation is updated.

What You Can Do

Exporting Handouts to Word

- When you are preparing a presentation, one aspect you should consider carefully is identifying and creating supporting materials that will enhance the presentation for your audience.

- Having handouts that include thumbnails of each slide will help your audience stay focused on and engaged with your presentation.

- Besides simply printing handouts from PowerPoint, you can send presentation data to Microsoft Word to create handouts or an outline. Exporting a presentation to Microsoft Word gives you the option of using Word's tools to format the handouts.

- You can modify the size of the slide images, format text, and add new text as desired to customize your handouts.

- Use the Create Handouts command on the Export tab in Backstage view to begin the process of sending materials to Word.

- The Send to Microsoft Word dialog box opens to allow you to select an export option.

- You have two options for positioning slide notes relative to the slide pictures and two options for placing blank lines that your audience can use to take their own notes.

WORDS TO KNOW

Active listening
Paying attention to a message, hearing it, and interpreting it correctly.

Communication
The exchange of information between a sender and a receiver.

Nonverbal communication
The exchange of information without using words.

Verbal communication
The exchange of information by speaking or writing.

- Slide thumbnails in the Word document usually display a border on three sides. You can delete this partial border, if desired, using the Borders tab in the Borders dialog box.

- You can also choose to send only the outline. The exported outline retains the font used in the presentation and displays at a large point size. You can then, if desired, apply Word heading styles to create a more useful document.

Try It!   Exporting Handouts to Word

1 Start PowerPoint, and open **P35Try** from the data files for this lesson.

2 Save the presentation as **P35TryA_xx** in the location where your teacher instructs you to store the files for this lesson.

3 Click FILE > Export.

4 Click Create Handouts in the Export list, and click Create Handouts in the right pane.

5 Select Blank lines next to slides and Paste under Add slides to Microsoft Word document.

6 Click OK.

7 Click the Word icon on the taskbar to display the newly created Word document to see how the handouts look. Close Microsoft Word without saving changes.

8 Save the **P35TryA_xx** file, and leave it open to use in the next Try It.

The Send to Microsoft Word dialog box

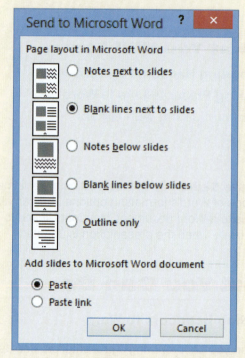

Linking Presentations to Word

- If the presentation might change over time, the best option is to maintain a link between the handouts in Word and the material displayed on a slide.

- When you choose the Paste link option in the Send to Microsoft Word dialog box, you create a link between the Word document and the PowerPoint presentation. Any changes you save to the slides in PowerPoint will appear in the Word document.

   ✓ *You do not have the paste/paste link options when exporting an outline.*

Try It! **Linking Presentations to Word**

1 In the **P35TryA_xx** file, click FILE > Export.

2 Click Create Handouts under Export, and click Create Handouts in the right pane.

3 Select Notes next to slides, if necessary, and Paste link under Add slides to Microsoft Word document.

4 Click OK.

5 View the newly created Microsoft Word document to see how the handouts look.

6 Return to **P35TryA_xx**, click DESIGN, and change the variant to the second variant from the right.

7 Save the changes, close **P35TryA_xx**, and exit PowerPoint.

8 Return to the Microsoft Word document and note that the slide thumbnails show the new variant you applied in PowerPoint.

9 Save the file as **P35TryB_xx** in the location where your teacher instructs you to store the files for this lesson.

10 Close the document, and exit Microsoft Word.

Updated linked handouts

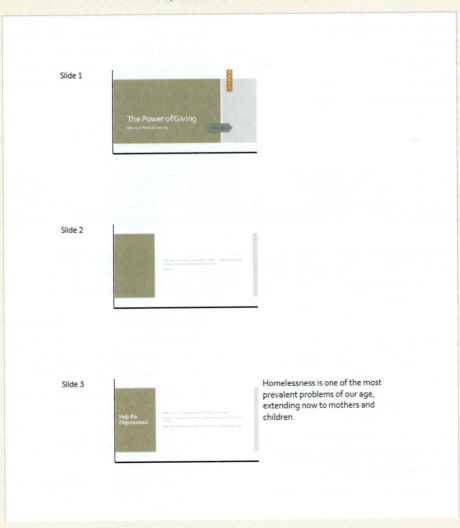

Communicating with Others

- When you prepare a presentation, you should always remember that the presentation is a form of **communication** and you should strive to make it as effective as possible.

- You communicate effectively when your audience interprets the information in the presentation in the way you intended it to be interpreted.

- As you prepare the presentation and its supporting materials, choose options that contribute to effective communication:
  - Make sure the slides are visually interesting.
  - Make sure text is easy to read and understand.
  - Use charts and tables to organize information for improved comprehension.

- A presentation's effectiveness also depends on how it is delivered.

- If you are presenting the slides yourself or using narration on slides, use good **verbal communication** skills:
  - Speak slowly and clearly, allowing plenty of time for your audience to view each slide.
  - Avoid speaking in a monotone or reading the slide text verbatim.

- Ask the audience if they have questions or encourage them to participate in the discussion, if appropriate, to foster communication between audience members and the speaker.

- Remember that you also deliver a message using **nonverbal communication** cues. Being at ease on the podium, smiling, and making eye contact with your audience are nonverbal ways to foster effective communication with others.

- You can ensure effective communication with your audience even if you are setting up a presentation to be browsed by an individual. Make sure the slides are displayed long enough that the content can be viewed and absorbed by people with all levels of reading skills.

- If the presentation does not loop automatically, make sure a viewer can easily navigate the presentation by including action buttons, links, and other prompts.

- As a presenter, you want to do everything you can to encourage active listening. **Active listening** is a sign of respect from your audience. It shows that they are engaged in the presentation, willing to communicate with you, and interested in you and your message.

Lesson 35—Practice

Surgeons from Wynnedale Medical Center want you to prepare handouts to accompany a presentation they will be making at a health fair. In this project, you send the presentation data to Microsoft Word to create handouts. You use some Word table formatting options to improve the appearance of the handouts.

DIRECTIONS

1. Start PowerPoint, if necessary, and open **P35Practice** from the data files for this lesson.

2. Click **FILE** > **Export**.

3. Click **Create Handouts** under Export and click **Create Handouts** in the right pane.

4. Select **Notes next to slides**, if necessary.

5. Make sure **Paste** is selected under Add slides to Microsoft Word document and click **OK**.

6. Close **P35Practice** without saving any changes.

7. View the newly created Microsoft Word document, and save it as **P35Practice_xx**.

8. Make the following changes to the table in which the slide information is stored:

   a. Select the table and apply the **Grid Table 1 Light – Accent 1** table style.

   b. In the Table Style Options group, click **First Column** to apply bold to the first column of the table.

   c. Select the center and right columns and click **TABLE TOOLS LAYOUT** > **Align Center Left**.

9. Insert a header with your name and today's date.

10. **With your teacher's permission,** print the document. It should look similar to Figure 35-1.

11. Close the document, saving changes, and exit Word.

Figure 35-1

Lesson 35—Apply

The surgeons at Wynnedale Medical Center plan to make changes to their presentation to suit particular audiences. They have asked you to link the slides to handouts so that they can easily print handouts that will reflect changed content in the presentation. In this project, you link the presentation to a Word document.

DIRECTIONS

1. Start PowerPoint, if necessary, and open **P35Apply** from the data files for this lesson.

2. Save the presentation as **P35ApplyA_xx** in the location where your teacher instructs you to store the files for this lesson.

3. Export the presentation as handouts. Select the Paste link option and Notes below slides.

4. Save the Word document as **P35ApplyB_xx**.

5. In PowerPoint, apply the **Slice** theme to the presentation. Adjust the positions of pictures as necessary. Save your changes and close the presentation.

6. Return to the Word document. If necessary, right-click each slide thumbnail and click **Update Link**.

7. Right-click each slide thumbnail and click **Borders and Shading**. In the Borders dialog box, click **None** to remove the border from the slide thumbnail.

8. Click **INSERT** > **Header** and choose **Slice 2** from the list of built-in header styles.

9. Click **INSERT** > **Footer** and choose **Slice**. Your name should be inserted automatically in the footer.

10. **With your teacher's permission,** print the document. Page 1 should look similar to Figure 35-2 on the next page.

11. Close the document, saving changes, and exit Word.

Figure 35-2

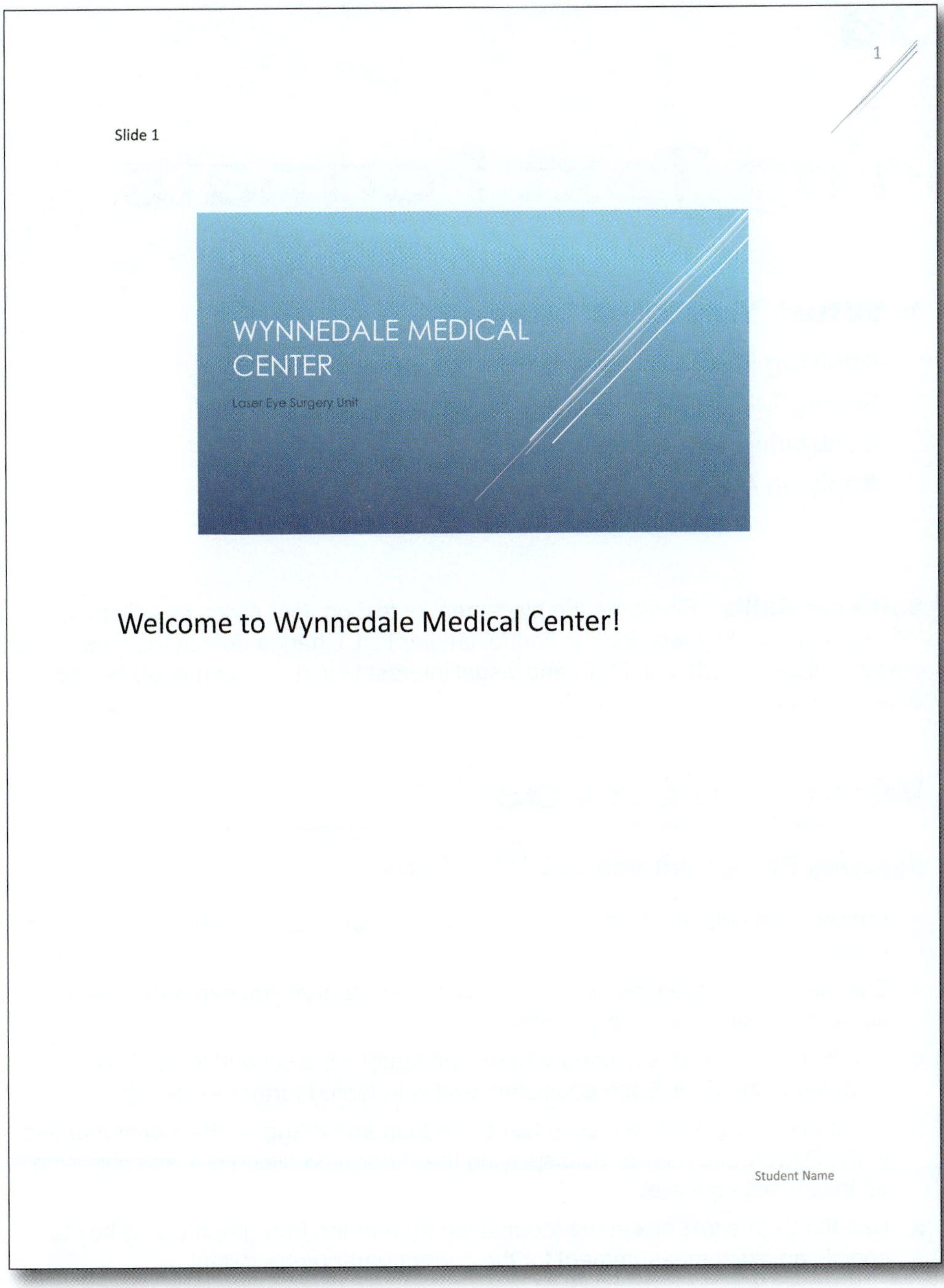
1
Slide 1
WYNNEDALE MEDICAL CENTER
Laser Eye Surgery Unit
Welcome to Wynnedale Medical Center!
Student Name

Lesson 36

Fine-Tuning Text Formats

➤ What You Will Learn

Applying Paragraph and Special Indents
Setting Tab Stops
Controlling Text Box Margins
Applying Advanced Text Formats

WORDS TO KNOW

First-line indent
The first line of a paragraph moves to the right so there is a space between the margin and the first word.

Hanging indent
The first line of the paragraph aligns at the left margin, and all other lines of the paragraph are indented.

Indents
Indents enable you to control the amount of space between the text and the edges of the text box or placeholder.

Tab stops
Tab stops, also called tabs, enable you to align text according to settings you specify. You can choose to create left, center, right, or decimal tabs.

Software Skills   Fine-tune the placement of text on your slides by adjusting indents and inserting tab stops to control tabular text. Change default margins in text boxes to allow more text to fit. To add visual interest to text, you can apply fill and outline formats.

What You Can Do

Applying Paragraph and Special Indents

- **Indents** can help you format your text so that your audience will be able to read it easily.
- Each level of bulleted text has a different indent, so that you can easily see how some items are subordinate to others.
- The first level of text is aligned with the left margin; the second level of text is indented to the right. Each additional level is indented further to the right.
- You can easily indent your slide text by clicking and dragging the indent markers in the PowerPoint ruler or by displaying the Paragraph dialog box and choosing an indent setting there.
- Use the Before text box in the Indentation area of the Paragraph dialog box to specify an exact measurement for the current paragraph's indent.
- Use the Special settings to apply a first-line or hanging indent.
  - A **first-line indent** moves the first line of a paragraph to the right; remaining lines of the paragraph align at the left margin.
  - A **hanging indent** aligns the first line of a paragraph with the left margin; remaining lines of the paragraph are indented.

Try It!   Adjusting an Indent on the Ruler

1 Start PowerPoint, and open **P36Try** from the data files for this lesson.

2 Save the presentation as **P36Try_xx** in the location where your teacher instructs you to store the files for this lesson.

3 If the rulers are not currently displayed, click VIEW > Ruler to display them.

4 Display slide 2.

5 Click in the second paragraph in the text box and then drag the first-line indent marker to the 0.5" mark on the ruler. The text indents.

6 Display slide 5 and click in the second paragraph in the content area.

7 Drag the left indent marker to the 1" mark on the ruler.

8 Save the **P36Try_xx** file, and leave it open for the next Try It.

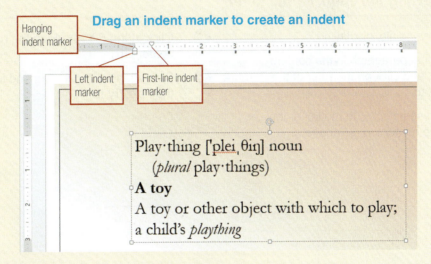

Drag an indent marker to create an indent

Hanging indent marker

Left indent marker

First-line indent marker

Play·thing ['pleɪˌθɪŋ] noun
(*plural* play·things)
A toy
A toy or other object with which to play;
a child's *plaything*

Try It!   Setting Indents in the Paragraph Dialog Box

1 In the **P36Try_xx** file, click in the third paragraph on slide 5.

2 On the HOME tab, click the Paragraph dialog box launcher ⌐ to open the Paragraph dialog box.

3 In the Indentation section, click in the Before text box and type **2**.

4 Click OK. The third paragraph is indented 2 inches.

5 Display slide 2.

6 Click in the last paragraph in the text box (*A toy or other object . . .*).

7 Click HOME > Paragraph dialog box launcher.

8 In the Special area of the Indentation section, click the drop-down arrow to the right of (none) and click First line.

9 Click OK. A first-line indent is applied to the paragraph.

10 Click the Paragraph dialog box launcher.

11 In the Before text box in the Indentation section, click the up arrow until 0.5" appears. In the Special section, click the drop-down arrow to the right of First line and click Hanging.

12 Click OK. The first-line indent changes to a hanging indent.

13 Save the **P36Try_xx** file, and leave it open for the next Try It.

Setting Tab Stops

- **Tab stops** enable you to create tabular text on your PowerPoint slides. You can choose to insert four different types of tabs: Left, Right, Center, and Decimal.

- You can set tabs by selecting the tab stop style you want to create and clicking the PowerPoint ruler, or you can display the Paragraph dialog box, click the Tabs button, and enter the settings for the tab in the Tabs dialog box.

- Adjust a tab by dragging it on the ruler. Removing a tab is equally simple—just drag it off the ruler.

- You can also clear all tabs at once by clicking the Clear All button in the Tabs dialog box.

Try It!   **Setting Tab Stops on the Ruler**

1 In the **P36Try_xx** file, display slide 7.

2 Click in the first paragraph in the content placeholder, and click on the ruler at the 3" mark to set a left tab.

3 Click the tab selector ⌐ to the left of the ruler until the center tab ⊥ appears.

4 Click at the 5.5" mark on the ruler to set a center tab.

5 Save the **P36Try_xx** file, and leave it open for the next Try It.

Click on the ruler to set a tab

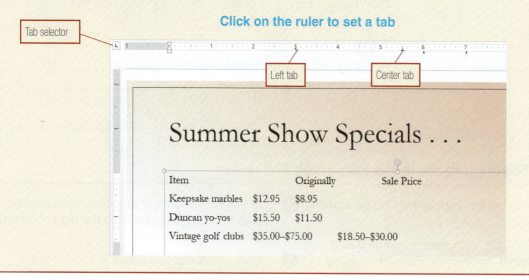

Tab selector

Left tab

Center tab

Summer Show Specials . . .

Item	Originally		Sale Price
Keepsake marbles	$12.95	$8.95	
Duncan yo-yos	$15.50	$11.50	
Vintage golf clubs	$35.00–$75.00		$18.50–$30.00

Try It! Setting Tab Stops in the Tabs Dialog Box

1 In the **P36Try_xx** file, with slide 7 displayed, select the second, third, and fourth paragraphs in the content placeholder.

2 Click HOME > Paragraph dialog box launcher ⌐.

3 Click the Tabs button.

4 In the Tabs dialog box, click in the Tab stop position box, type **3**, click the Decimal option button, and click Set.

5 In the Tab stop position box, type **5.5**, click the Center option button, and click Set.

6 Click OK, and then click OK again to close the Paragraph dialog box.

7 Save the **P36Try_xx** file, and leave it open for the next Try It.

Try It! Adjusting a Tab Stop on the Ruler

1 In the **P36Try_xx** file, with slide 7 displayed, note that the original prices for marbles and yo-yos are not lined up correctly under the column heading.

2 Select the second and third paragraphs in the content placeholder.

3 Drag the decimal tab on the ruler to the 3.4" mark.

4 Save the **P36Try_xx** file, and leave it open for the next Try It.

Controlling Text Box Margins

- Text boxes are designed to fit closely around text, with default margins of 0.1" at the left and right sides and 0.05" at the top and bottom.

- If you need to enter several sentences in a text box that you have formatted with a fill, these default margins can make the text look crowded in the box.

- You can use the Textbox settings in the Format Shape task pane to adjust text box margins. You can also choose options for wrapping and fitting text in the text box.

Try It! Controlling Text Box Margins

1 In the **P36Try_xx** file, display slide 6.

2 Click INSERT > Text Box ▤ and draw a text box 3" wide on the slide near the bottom of the slide between the two content placeholders.

3 Type the following text: **We are always adding events to our calendar. To find out when we are coming to a location near you, visit our Web site.**

4 Click DRAWING TOOLS FORMAT > Shape Styles More button ▾ and apply the Moderate Effect – Ice Blue, Accent 1 shape style.

5 Right-click the text box and click Format Shape on the shortcut menu.

6 In the Format Shape task pane, click TEXT OPTIONS and then click Textbox ▤.

7 In the Left margin box, click the up increment arrow to change the margin to 0.2".

8 In the Top margin box, click the up increment arrow to change the margin to 0.1".

9 In the Bottom margin box, click the up increment arrow to change the margin to 0.1".

10 Close the Format Shape task pane.

11 Save the **P36Try_xx** file, and leave it open for the next Try It.

Applying Advanced Text Formats

- One way to add visual interest to text is to create a WordArt graphic or apply WordArt styles directly to selected text.

- If you do not find a WordArt style that complements your presentation, however, you can use the Text Fill, Text Outline, and Text Effects options on the DRAWING TOOLS FORMAT tab or Format Shape task pane to apply custom formats to any text on a slide.

- When you are applying text fill and outline formats, your formats will have more impact if you use a heavy, wide font at a large point size to display the fill and outlines clearly. Applying these formats to smaller text can make the text harder to read.

Try It!   **Applying Advanced Text Formats**

1. In the **P36Try_xx** file, display slide 1.

2. Select the title text *Yesterday's Playthings*.

3. Click DRAWING TOOLS FORMAT > Text Fill ⬛ and then click Orange, Accent 2.

4. Click DRAWING TOOLS FORMAT > Text Fill ⬛ and then click Gradient.

5. Under Dark Variations, click the Linear Down gradient.

6. With the text still selected, click DRAWING TOOLS FORMAT > Text Outline ⬛ and then click Eyedropper.

7. Use the Eyedropper to sample a dark brown color from the baseball glove to the left or above the baseball in the picture.

✓ *To sample the color, click with the eyedropper on the location where you want to pick up the color.*

8. With the text still selected, right-click and select Format Text Effects. The Format Shape task pane opens with Text Effects active.

9. Click SHADOW to expand the shadow options.

10. Click the Presets button and select Offset Bottom in the Outer section.

11. Close the Format Shape task pane.

12. Close the **P36Try_xx** file, saving changes, and exit PowerPoint.

Whole Grains Bread is branching out into a new market: donuts that are made fresh several times a day in select mall locations. As part of this venture, the company plans to offer delivery of fresh donuts to corporate clients. In this project, you create a new presentation that incorporates existing slides from another presentation and then adjust indents, tabs, and text formats.

DIRECTIONS

1. Start PowerPoint, if necessary, and open **P36PracticeA** from the data files for this lesson.

2. Save the presentation as **P36PracticeA_xx** in the location where your teacher instructs you to store the files for this lesson.

3. Click **HOME** > **New Slide** 📄 down arrow, and click **Reuse Slides**.

4. In the Reuse Slides task pane, click **Browse** and then click **Browse File**.

5. Navigate to the location where data files are stored, select **P36PracticeB**, and click **Open**.

6. Insert slides from the Reuse Slides task pane as follows:

    a. Click the first slide in the task pane to insert it in the presentation. In the Thumbnail pane, move the new slide so that it is the first slide in the presentation.

    b. Insert the fourth slide from the task pane.

    c. Click slide 5 in the Thumbnail pane, then insert the last slide from the task pane.

    d. Close the Reuse Slides task pane.

7. Display slide 3.

8. Click in the second *Donuts* paragraph and then drag the left indent marker on the ruler to the **3"** mark.

9. Click in the third *Donuts* paragraph and then drag the left indent marker on the ruler to the **7"** mark.

10. Make the following changes in the text box on slide 3:

    a. Click in the text, click the Paragraph dialog box launcher, and change the Special indent to **(none)**. Click **OK**.

    b. Right-click anywhere in the text, click **Format Text Effects**, and click the **Textbox** icon 📇 in the Format Shape task pane.

    c. Change the text box margins to **0.2"** on all sides and then close the task pane.

    d. Click **HOME** > **Justify** ≡ to justify the text in the text box.

11. Display slide 4.

12. Click in the first paragraph and set tabs as follows:

    a. Set center tabs at the **4.5"** and the **6"** marks on the ruler.

    b. Set a left tab at the **7"** mark on the ruler.

13. Select the remaining four paragraphs in the content placeholder, click the Paragraph dialog box launcher, and click **Tabs**.

14. In the Tabs dialog box, set tabs as follows:

    a. Type **3.4** in the Tab stop position box, click **Right**, and click **Set**.

    b. Type **4.5** in the Tab stop position box, click **Center**, and click **Set**.

    c. Type **6** in the Tab stop position box, click **Decimal**, and click **Set**.

    d. Type **7** in the Tab stop position box, click **Left**, and click **Set**.

    e. Click **OK** twice.

15. Insert a footer with your name and today's date on all slides.

16. **With your teacher's permission,** print slide 4. It should look similar to Figure 36-1 on the next page.

17. Close the presentation, saving changes, and exit PowerPoint.

Figure 36-1

Lesson 36—Apply

In this project, you continue to work on the Whole Grains Bread presentation. You adjust tabs and indents, apply more interesting text formats for the presentation title, and finally replace several of the figures to customize the presentation for the new donut venture.

DIRECTIONS

1. Start PowerPoint, if necessary, and open **P36Apply** from the data files for this lesson.

2. Save the presentation as **P36Apply_xx** in the location where your teacher instructs you to store the files for this lesson.

3. On slide 1, select the slide title and change the font to **Bauhaus 93**. Reduce the font size until the title fits on one line in the placeholder.

   ✓ *If you do not have Bauhaus, choose another heavy, wide font.*

4. Apply a gradient fill to the text and then adjust the gradient as desired. Apply an outline and a text effect such as a shadow, glow, or reflection.

5. On slide 4, insert a center tab to center the heading *Package* over the packages in the table below. Then click to the left of the word *Package* and press TAB to tab the heading to the new tab stop.

6. On slide 6, select all paragraphs and insert a left tab stop on the ruler at the **1.5"** mark. Press TAB after the boldfaced word at the beginning of each paragraph to move the explanatory text to the tab. Then apply a hanging indent of **1.5"** to all paragraphs to align the second lines of text with the first word following the tab.

7. On slide 5, draw a text box to the right of the bulleted text and type the text shown in Figure 36-2 on the next page. (Use Wingding star symbols for the ratings.) Use indents and tabs to align the text as shown.

8. Apply a shape style to the text box and then adjust the text box margins as desired to improve appearance.

9. Display slide 1, right-click the picture, and click **Change Picture**. In the Insert Pictures dialog box, type **donuts** in the Office.com Clip Art box and press ENTER . Choose an appropriate donut picture.

10. Repeat step 9 to replace the picture on slide 7 with a different donut picture.

11. Insert a footer with your full name and the current date on all slides.

12. Preview the presentation. Make any adjustments necessary.

13. **With your teacher's permission,** print the slides as handouts with 4 slides per page.

14. Close the presentation, saving changes, and exit PowerPoint.

Figure 36-2

Lesson 37

Using Research Tools

➤ What You Will Learn

Using the Research Task Pane
Translating Text

Software Skills If you want to add to the content of your presentation—including the latest information on a particular subject—you can use the research tools built right into PowerPoint to find what you need. These tools include options for searching the Web and translating text into different languages.

What You Can Do

Using the Research Task Pane

- You can research more about your topic from within PowerPoint.
- Display the REVIEW tab and click Research in the Proofing group.
- You can choose the reference books or sites you want to use from the Research task pane.
- Click the result in the Research list to find out more about the selection.
- You can update the research services that are set up to work with PowerPoint or purchase additional services online.
- By default, PowerPoint offers research options that include the Bing search tool, several thesauruses, the Encarta dictionary, and translation options you will use later in this lesson.

Try It!   Using the Research Task Pane

1 Start PowerPoint, and open **P37Try** from the data files for this lesson.

2 Save the presentation as **P37Try_xx** in the location where your teacher instructs you to store the files for this lesson.

3 Display slide 5.

4 Click REVIEW > Research 🔍 to open the Research task pane.

5 In the Search for box, type **rain gardens**.

6 Click the All Reference Books down arrow, if necessary, and click Bing.

7 Click the Wikipedia entry to open your browser to this Web site.

8 Read the article to find out what a rain garden is and how it can be useful in an urban landscape.

9 Select the first sentence of text in the Wikipedia article, right-click, and click Copy.

10 On slide 5, type **according to Wikipedia:** at the end of the first bulleted item and then press ENTER and TAB.

11 Press CTRL + V to paste the text you copied.

12 Return to the Web page, click in the address bar, click CTRL + C to copy the URL, and then paste it at the end of the Wikipedia text on the slide.

13 Save the **P37Try_xx** file, and leave it open to use in the next Try It.

Use the Research task pane to find information

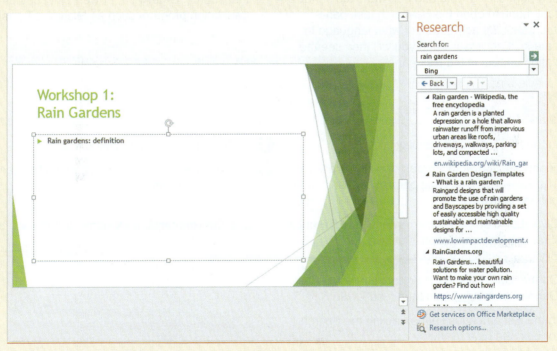

Try It! **Using a Dictionary in the Research Task Pane**

① In the **P37Try_xx** file, display slide 6.

② In the Search for box, type **compost**.

③ Click the down arrow of the box that lists Bing as the current reference tool and click Encarta Dictionary. Definitions from the Encarta Dictionary appear in the Research task pane.

④ In the Research task pane, under the heading *1. decayed plant matter*, drag the pointer over the definition, right-click, and click Copy.

⑤ On the slide, click at the end of the bulleted item, press ENTER , and then press TAB.

⑥ Type **According to the Encarta Dictionary, compost is** and then press CTRL + V to paste the definition.

⑦ Insert quotation marks before and after the definition you pasted.

⑧ Save the **P37Try_xx** file, and leave it open to use in the next Try It.

Translating Text

- PowerPoint offers you the option of translating slide text without your having to leave the program to open a translator.

- You can right-click a word and use Translate on the shortcut menu to open the Research task pane with the translator active. Select what language to translate to, if necessary, and you will then see the translation appear in the task pane.

- You can also click the Translate button on the REVIEW tab to open the Research task pane and then type the word or phrase you want translated.

- If PowerPoint can find the word in an installed bilingual dictionary, it displays the translation from that source. Otherwise, PowerPoint uses an online translation program such as Microsoft Translator.

Try It! **Translating Text**

① In the **P37Try_xx** file, display slide 7.

② Right-click the word *Garden* and click Translate. The Research task pane opens with translation options active.

③ Click the To box's down arrow and select French (France). The translation is shown from the Bilingual Dictionary, *jardin*.

④ On the slide, click to the right of the word *Garden*, press TAB, and then type **jardin**.

⑤ In the Research task pane, click in the Search for box and type **truck**.

⑥ Click the To box's down arrow and select Spanish (Spain). The translation is shown from the Bilingual Dictionary, *camión*.

⑦ On the slide, position the insertion point in the Spanish column for the *Truck* paragraph and type **camión**.

   ✓ Use the Symbol dialog box to find the letter o with the correct accent.

⑧ Close the Research task pane.

⑨ Close the **P37Try_xx** file, saving changes, and exit PowerPoint.

Use the Research task pane to translate text

Research   ▼ ✕

Search for:

truck   ➡

Translation   ▼

← Back ▼ → ▼

▲ Translation

Translate a word or sentence.

From

English (United States)   ▼

To   Spanish (Spain)   ▼

Translation options...

▲ Bilingual Dictionary

  ▲ truck

    camión *masculino*

Lesson 37—Practice

The Clifton Community Center (CCC) runs a presentation on a screen in the lobby to keep community members up to date with the latest events in the community and at the center for a given month. The CCC is committed to serving a diverse population with information for and about different cultures. In this project, you begin work on the November presentation. You use the Translator and the Research task pane to locate information about a November event and define a word.

DIRECTIONS

1. Start PowerPoint, if necessary, and open **P37Practice** from the data files for this lesson.

2. Save the presentation as **P37Practice_xx** in the location where your teacher instructs you to store the files for this lesson.

3. Display slide 2.

4. Click at the end of the bullet item, press ⏎ENTER , and type **The Encarta Dictionary defines mincemeat as follows:**

5. Double-click the word *mincemeat* that you just typed, and then click **REVIEW** > **Research** 📖 to open the Research task pane with the word *mincemeat* already shown in the Search for box.

6. Click the drop-down arrow for the reference tools list and select **Encarta Dictionary**. Definitions display in the task pane.

7. Under the heading *1. fruit and spice mixture*, drag over the definition (*a mixture of spiced . . .*), right-click, and click **Copy**.

8. On the slide, press ⏎ENTER at the end of the second bullet item, press TAB, and then press CTRL + V to paste the definition.

9. Remove the bullet formatting from the definition, change the first letter to a capital *A*, and then drag the left indent marker on the ruler to create a **1"** left indent. Your slide should look similar to Figure 37-1.

Figure 37-1

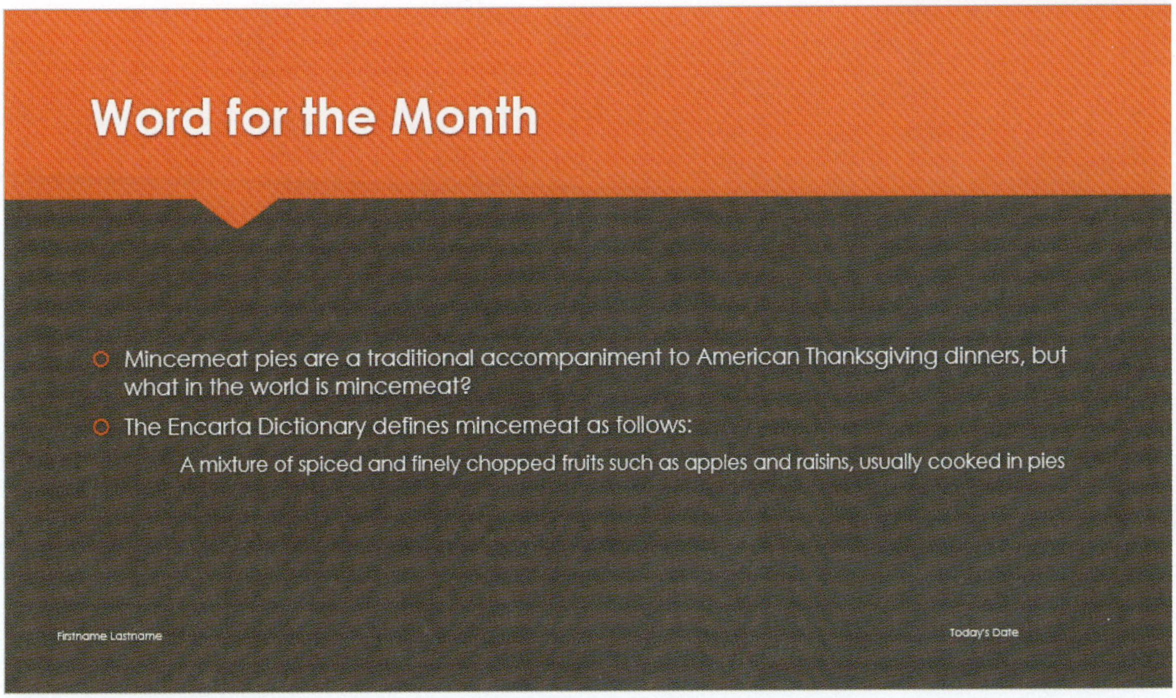

Word for the Month

- Mincemeat pies are a traditional accompaniment to American Thanksgiving dinners, but what in the world is mincemeat?
- The Encarta Dictionary defines mincemeat as follows:
    A mixture of spiced and finely chopped fruits such as apples and raisins, usually cooked in pies

Firstname Lastname   Today's Date

10. Create a new Two Content slide at the end of the presentation and insert the title **CCC Explores the World**.

11. Click the **Online Pictures** icon 🖼 in the right content placeholder and search for a map of Mexico. Adjust size as desired, and apply a picture style of your choice.

12. In the left content placeholder, type the following text:

    Our focus this month is on Mexican holidays

    One of the most important is the day of the dead

13. Select the phrase *day of the dead*, and click **REVIEW** > **Translate** aあ > **Translate Selected Text**.

14. In the Research task pane, change the Translation settings to translate from English to Spanish, if necessary.

15. Under Microsoft Translator, note the translation, and then click **Insert** to replace the selected phrase with its proper Spanish wording.

16. With *day of the dead* still displayed in the Search for box in the Research task pane, click the Translation down arrow and select Bing for research on this phrase. Click the Wikipedia article for more information on this holiday.

17. Notice in the article that *Día* and *Muertos* should be capitalized. Make this change on slide 3.

18. Select the phrase *Día de los Muertos*, and press CTRL + C to copy it.

19. Insert a new Two Content slide, and press CTRL + V to paste the copied phrase in the title placeholder.

20. In the left content placeholder, insert several bullet items to explain the holiday, using the information you find from one of the references in the Research task pane.

21. Use Online Pictures in the right content placeholder to locate a picture that relates to the information you inserted on the slide. Adjust the size of the text placeholder, as necessary, to contain all text.

22. Preview the presentation and make any necessary adjustments.

23. Insert a footer with your name and today's date on all slides.

24. **With your teacher's permission,** print the presentation as handouts with 4 slides per page.

25. Close the presentation, saving changes, and exit PowerPoint.

Lesson 37—Apply

In this project, you continue working for the Clifton Community Center to create the December presentation. You research a topic, translate a word, and use a dictionary to find a definition.

DIRECTIONS

1. Start PowerPoint, if necessary, and open **P37Apply** from the data files for this lesson.

2. Save the presentation as **P37Apply_xx** in the location where your teacher instructs you to store the files for this lesson.

3. Change the theme colors to a scheme more appropriate for winter.

4. On slide 2, use any research tool to look up Boxing Day, and paste the definition in a new text box below the last bullet. Format the text box attractively. Figure 37-2 shows one option.

   ✓ *You may want to align the text in the content placeholder at the top of the placeholder, as shown in Figure 37-2.*

5. On slide 3, add the following text:

   Have you ever heard the Christmas carol *O Tannenbaum*?

   ***Tannenbaum* is German for**

6. Use the translator to translate *tannenbaum* from German to English, and then add the translation to the end of the second bullet.

7. On the slide, insert a picture that has to do with Germany, such as a map or flag.

8. Insert a new slide and add the slide title **O Christmas Tree**.

9. Use the Research task pane to research the custom of decorating a tree at Christmas. Insert the most important points you learn on slide 4, and then add an appropriate picture.

10. Preview the presentation and make any necessary adjustments.

11. Insert a footer with your name and today's date on all slides.

12. **With your teacher's permission,** print the presentation as handouts with 4 slides per page.

13. Close the presentation, saving changes, and exit PowerPoint.

Figure 37-2

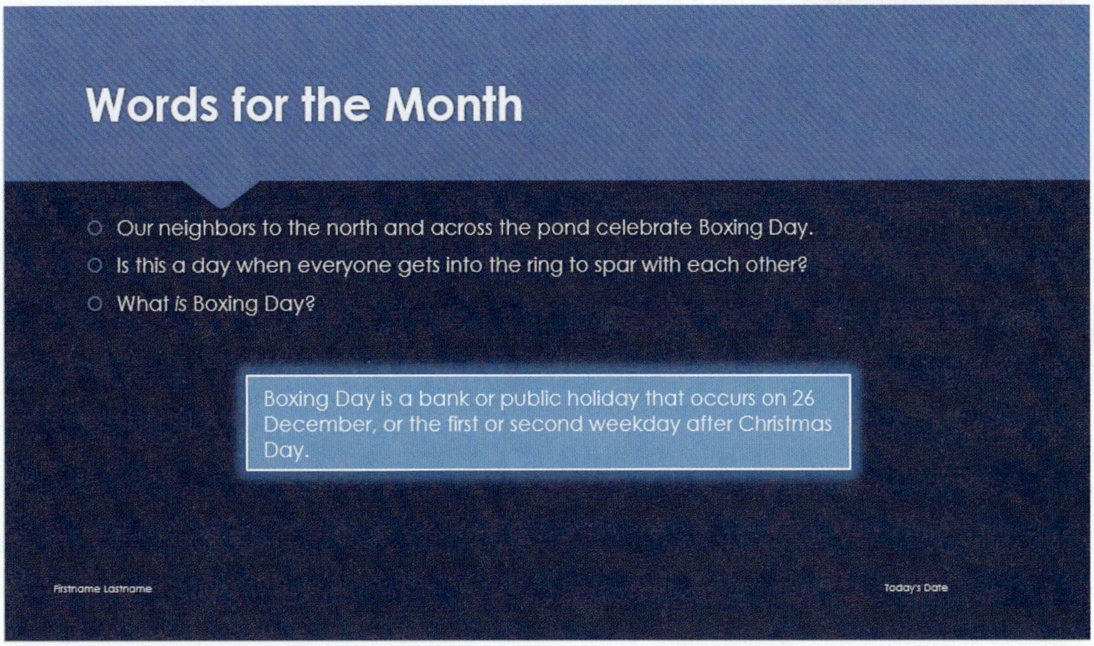

End-of-Chapter Activities

➤ PowerPoint Chapter 5—Critical Thinking

Communicating with Coworkers and Clients

You and your colleagues at Restoration Architecture work with clients every day. Some recent misunderstandings and miscommunications have convinced you that the staff could benefit from a presentation that reviews how to communicate effectively not only with clients but also with coworkers.

In this project, working alone or in teams, you will research effective workplace communication. Your research should cover the following topics:

- Communicating effectively with colleagues and clients.
- Recognizing the difference between verbal and nonverbal forms of communication.
- Understanding how both verbal and nonverbal behaviors help you communicate with coworkers and clients.
- Employing active listening to help you understand issues.
- Employing strategies that will help you communicate with clients and colleagues from diverse backgrounds.
- Understanding how to resolve conflicts that might arise within a diverse workforce and client base.

As part of this project, you should prepare support materials that will enhance the presentation.

DIRECTIONS

1. Start a new presentation, and save it as **PCT05A_xx** in the location where your teacher instructs you to store the files for this chapter.

2. Insert the title **Effective Workplace Communication**. In the subtitle placeholder, type **A Presentation by** and then insert your first and last name.

3. Apply a theme and variant of your choice. In Slide Master view, customize the background of at least one slide layout with a gradient, picture, or texture.

4. Change the font on the title slide to a heavy, bold font and apply advanced text formatting such as a fill, outline, and effect.

5. Add a slide to the presentation with the title **Sources**. Use this slide to record the Web addresses of sites you use to find information for this presentation.

6. **With your teacher's permission,** use the Research task pane to research the topics listed above. Use valid and reputable sites for your research, and copy site information to your Sources slide.

7. When your research is complete, organize your material into topics and plan how to use the material in your presentation. You may use a storyboard, if desired. Select slide layouts suitable for the type of information you find. Add illustrations as desired, using online pictures or other graphics.

8. Use at least one slide for each topic. Use additional slides to expand the topic as necessary.

9. On one slide, define the word *communication* using a source from the Research pane. Adjust indents as desired to present the definition clearly.

10. Check spelling.

11. Apply transitions to enhance the presentation's effectiveness.

12. Preview the presentation and then make any necessary corrections and adjustments.

13. Deliver the presentation to your class. Ask for comments on how the presentation could be improved.

14. Export the presentation to Word as handouts with blank lines beneath slides. Apply the same theme to the handouts that you applied to the slides.

15. Insert a Motion (Odd Page) header to the Word document with your name as the title. Save the Word document as **PCT05B_xx**.

16. **With your teacher's permission**, print the handout document.

17. Close the document, saving changes, and exit Word. Close the presentation, saving changes, and exit PowerPoint.

➤ PowerPoint Chapter 5—Portfolio Builder

Creating a Kiosk Presentation

Peterson Home Health Care has asked you to create a presentation that can be used at local health fairs to give viewers information about the company's home health care options. You will start work on that presentation in this project.

DIRECTIONS

1. Start PowerPoint, if necessary, and open **PPB05** from the data files for this chapter.

2. Save the presentation as **PPB05_xx** in the location where your teacher instructs you to store the files for this project.

3. Click **VIEW** > **Slide Master** 🖻.

4. On the slide master, make the following changes.

   a. Select the Date placeholder and use **DRAWING TOOLS FORMAT** > **Align** ⯈ > **Align Center** to move it to the horizontal center of the slide.

   b. Use **INSERT** > **Online Pictures** 🖼 to insert a medical symbol. Recolor the symbol if necessary using **PICTURE TOOLS FORMAT** > **Color** 🖼 to match the current theme.

5. On the Two Content layout, insert a narrow rectangle shape along the bottom edge of the right-hand content placeholder. Apply a Quick Style of your choice to the rectangle shape.

6. Select an Effects scheme of your choice.

7. Close Slide Master view and insert your name, slide numbers, and the current date on all slides. Slide 4 should look similar to Illustration 5A.

Illustration 5A

4

After-Surgery Care

► Daily visits as needed
► Wound care
► Bathing
► Nutrition and diet consultation
► Home helper as needed

Firstname Lastname   Today's Date

8. Display slide 7, and adjust the tabs in the content placeholder to organize the information into a table.

9. On slide 7, apply a new shape style to the text box and then adjust margins to improve appearance. Move the text box as necessary on the slide to avoid crowding the table.

10. On slide 2, indent the second paragraph **1"** from the left margin, and then indent the third paragraph an additional **1"**.

11. Display the notes master and make the following changes to the master.

  a. Apply theme fonts that are the same as those used on the slides.

  b. Apply theme colors that complement those in the slides.

  c. Insert a picture background that uses the same symbol you used on the slide master, and adjust transparency as necessary so notes text can easily be read.

  d. Change the size of the text in the notes placeholder to 14 point.

12. On notes pages and handouts, insert a header with your full name and the date. Your notes pages should look similar to the one shown in Illustration 5B.

13. Preview the presentation and then make any necessary corrections and adjustments.

14. Deliver the presentation to your class. Ask for comments on how the presentation could be improved.

15. **With your teacher's permission,** print the presentation.

16. Close the presentation, saving changes, and exit PowerPoint.

Illustration 5B

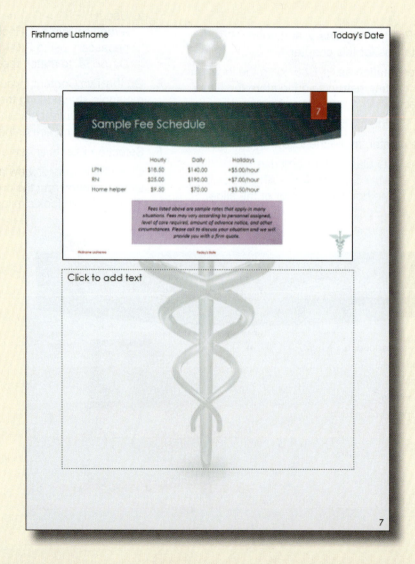

Chapter 6

(Courtesy Yuri Arcurs/Shutterstock)

Working with Graphic Objects and Media

Lesson 38

Applying Advanced Picture Formatting

➤ What You Will Learn

Understanding Picture Formats
Formatting Different Types of Pictures
Using a Picture As a Fill
Using Advanced Cropping Techniques

WORDS TO KNOW

Bitmap image
Graphic created from arrangements of small squares called *pixels.* Also called raster images.

Lossless compression
Compression accomplished without loss of data.

Lossy compression
Compression in which part of a file's data is discarded to reduce file size.

Pixel
Term that stands for picture element, a single point on a computer monitor screen.

Vector image
Drawing made up of lines and curves defined by vectors, which describe an object mathematically according to its geometric characteristics.

Software Skills   Understanding picture formats helps you select an appropriate file type for your presentation. Different types of pictures can be formatted in different ways. Use a picture to fill any shape for a more sophisticated presentation. Advanced cropping options enable you to crop to a shape or a specific aspect ratio and choose how a picture will fill an area.

What You Can Do

Understanding Picture Formats

- PowerPoint 2013 accepts a number of picture formats, including **bitmap** and **vector images**.

- Understanding the advantages and disadvantages of these common graphic file formats can help you choose pictures for your presentations.

- Table 38-1 on the next page lists some of the more common formats that PowerPoint supports, with their file extensions.

- When selecting pictures, consider the following:
  - If you plan on displaying the picture only on a screen, GIF and JPEG files will provide a good-quality appearance.
  - If you plan to print your slide materials, you may want to use TIFF images for a better-quality printed appearance.
  - For small graphics with a limited number of colors, a picture in GIF or PNG format will be perfectly adequate.
  - Photographs, on the other hand, should be saved in JPEG or TIFF format.
  - Remember that the higher the picture quality, the larger the presentation's file size.
  - You can decrease the file size by compressing pictures you have inserted in the presentation.

Table 38-1	Supported File Types for PowerPoint	
Format	**Extension**	**Characteristics**
WMF	.wmf	Windows Metafile. Contains both bitmap and vector information and is optimized for use in Windows applications.
PNG	.png	Portable Network Graphics. A bitmap format that supports **lossless compression** and allows transparency; no color limitations.
BMP	.bmp	Windows Bitmap. Does not support file compression so files may be large; widely compatible with Windows programs.
GIF	.gif	Graphics Interchange Format. A widely supported bitmap format that uses lossless compression; maximum of 256 colors; allows transparency.
JPEG	.jpg	Joint Photographic Experts Group. A bitmap format that allows a tradeoff of **lossy compression** and quality; best option for photographs and used by most digital cameras.
TIFF	.tif	Tagged Image File Format. Can be compressed or uncompressed; uncompressed file sizes may be very large. Most widely used format for print publishing; not supported by Web browsers.

Formatting Different Types of Pictures

- The PICTURE TOOLS FORMAT tab offers a number of options for working with pictures of various formats.

- For any type of picture, use the tools in the Adjust group to remove the picture background, correct brightness and contrast, sharpen or soften an image, adjust color saturation and tone, recolor an image using the current theme colors or any other color, apply artistic effects, or compress the image.

- Use the tools in the Picture Styles group to apply a picture style, a border, or an effect such as Shadow, Reflection, Glow, or 3-D Rotation.

- If you have inserted a PNG or GIF image, both of which support transparency, you can use Set Transparent Color on the Color menu to remove any color in the image to make that area transparent.

- Use the Format Picture task pane to make more detailed adjustments to images.

Try It!   Formatting Different Types of Pictures

1. Start PowerPoint, and open **P38TryA** from the data files for this lesson.

2. Save the presentation as **P38TryA_xx** in the location where your teacher instructs you to store the files for this lesson.

3. With slide 1 displayed, click INSERT > Pictures and navigate to the data files for this lesson.

4. Click **P38TryB_picture.png** and then click Insert.

5. With the picture selected, click PICTURE TOOLS FORMAT > Color > Set Transparent Color, and then click the black area surrounding the picture of Earth to make that area transparent.

6. With the picture still selected, click PICTURE TOOLS FORMAT > Color and then click the Dark Teal, Accent color 1 Light option in the bottom row of the Recolor options.

7. Move the image to the right side of the teal color bar on slide 1.

(continued)

Try It!   **Formatting Different Types of Pictures** *(continued)*

8 Display slide 2.

9 Click INSERT > Pictures and navigate to the data files for this lesson.

10 Click **P38TryC_picture.jpg** and then click Insert.

   ✓ *Don't worry about the size of the picture; you will adjust the size in a later exercise.*

11 With the picture selected, click PICTURE TOOLS FORMAT > Corrections and then click Sharpen: 25% in the Sharpen/Soften gallery.

12 With the picture still selected, click PICTURE TOOLS FORMAT > Corrections . In the Brightness/Contrast area, click Brightness: +20% Contrast: -20%.

13 With the picture still selected, click PICTURE TOOLS FORMAT > Color > Temperature: 8800 K in the Color Tone gallery.

14 Display slide 4 and select the picture.

15 Click PICTURE TOOLS FORMAT > Picture Border > Eyedropper. Use the Eyedropper to sample a dark red color from the object in the lower-right corner of the picture.

16 With the picture still selected, click PICTURE TOOLS FORMAT > Picture Border > Weight > 4½ pt.

17 Save the **P38TryA_xx** file, and leave it open to use in the next Try It.

Reformatted PNG image

Using a Picture As a Fill

- You can use a picture to provide a fill for any object such as a shape or placeholder.

- Use the Picture option on the Shape Fill gallery to insert a picture fill. In the Insert Picture dialog box, you can choose to browse to a file, search for clip art, do an image search with Bing, or find a picture on your SkyDrive.

- The picture you select will completely fill the selected shape, like any solid color or gradient fill, but you can still format the picture using tools on the PICTURE TOOLS FORMAT tab.

Try It!   **Using a Picture As a Fill**

1 In the **P38TryA_xx** file, display slide 3.

2 Select the shape at the right side of the slide, right-click, and click the Fill shortcut button ◇.

3 Click Picture on the Shape Fill gallery.

4 Click in the Office.com Clip Art box, type **garden**, and click the Search button 🔍.

5 Click a picture in landscape format (such as the one shown in the illustration with the ScreenTip *Path to a gate in a garden of flowers*) and then click Insert.

6 With the shape still selected, click DRAWING TOOLS FORMAT > Shape Outline ✎ > No Outline.

7 With the shape still selected, click PICTURE TOOLS FORMAT > Artistic Effects 🖾 > Paint Brush.

8 With the shape still selected, click PICTURE TOOLS FORMAT > Picture Effects ◉ > Shadow > Perspective Diagonal Upper Left.

9 Save the **P38TryA_xx** file, and leave it open to use in the next Try It.

Picture used as a fill for a shape

Using Advanced Cropping Techniques

■ Clicking the Crop button on the PICTURE TOOLS FORMAT tab displays crop handles at the outside edges of a picture. You can drag a handle to remove a portion of the image on that side.

 ✓ *Hold down* CTRL *while you drag a side to crop the opposite side at the same time.*

■ Clicking the Crop button's down arrow displays a gallery of other options you can use to achieve a specific effect with the crop.

● Use Crop to Shape to crop an image to any shape in the Shapes gallery.

● Select an option from the Aspect Ratio menu to crop the image in a square or in a portrait or landscape aspect ratio.

■ When you crop to a shape, the shape will be as wide and as high as the original image, and the image fills the shape. Areas outside the shape border are cropped but not removed entirely.

 ✓ *When you compress an image, the cropped areas are removed.*

- If you resize the shape to which you have cropped, you can select whether the image will fill the shape at its original aspect ratio or fit the entire image into the shape.

- If the image is larger than the shape, you can move the image to display the desired part of it in the shape.

Try It!   Using Advanced Cropping Techniques

1. In the **P38TryA_xx** file, display slide 2 and select the picture.

2. On the PICTURE TOOLS FORMAT tab, click the Crop button 🖼 down arrow, point to Aspect Ratio, and click 1:1 in the Square section. The crop handles appear to show how the image would be cropped into a shape that is as wide as it is high.

3. Click Undo ↺ on the Quick Access Toolbar to undo the crop.

4. Click the Crop button's down arrow and point to Crop to Shape.

5. In the Shapes gallery that pops out, click Oval in the Basic Shapes section. The image is cropped to an oval shape as wide and high as the original image.

6. Drag the left center sizing handle on the oval to the right until the shape fits into the right side of the slide area. It should be about 5.4" wide.

7. Drag the top center sizing handle downward until the shape is about 4" high. Note that resizing the shape has distorted the image within the shape.

8. Click the Crop button's down arrow and click Fit to fit the entire image in the resized shape. Note that the image does not completely fill the shape.

9. Click the Crop button's down arrow and click Fill to completely fill the resized shape.

10. Click on the image in the center of the shape and drag it to the left until the right edge of the image aligns with the right side of the shape.

11. Click the Crop button to complete the crop.

12. With the image still selected, click the Beveled Oval, Black picture style on the PICTURE TOOLS FORMAT tab.

13. Close the **P38TryA_xx** file, saving changes, and exit PowerPoint.

Drag the image to reposition it within the shape

Lesson 38—Practice

Thorn Hill Gardens wants to run a presentation on a kiosk at the main entrance to advertise the annual Butterfly Show. In this project, you add several pictures to a presentation, apply various formatting options, and use image correction options to improve the appearance of the pictures.

DIRECTIONS

1. Start PowerPoint, if necessary, and open **P38PracticeA** from the data files for this lesson.

2. Save the presentation as **P38PracticeA_xx** in the location where your teacher instructs you to store the files for this lesson.

3. On slide 1, click **INSERT** > **Pictures** 🖼 and navigate to the data files.

4. Select **P38PracticeB_picture.jpg** and click **Insert**.

5. With the picture still selected, click **PICTURE TOOLS FORMAT** > **Crop** 🖾 > **Crop to Shape** and select **Oval** from the Shapes gallery.

6. Click **PICTURE TOOLS FORMAT** > **Crop** 🖾 > **Aspect Ratio** and select **1:1** from the Square section.

7. Click on the image in the center of the shape and drag to the left until the right edge of the image aligns with the right side of the circle. Then click **Crop** 🖾 to complete the crop.

8. Resize the picture to be **4"** square and move the picture to the lower-right side of the slide.

9. With the picture still selected, click **PICTURE TOOLS FORMAT** > **Picture Border** ✎ , and select **Lime, Accent 1** from the Theme Colors palette. Click **Picture Border** again, point to **Weight**, and click **4½ pt**.

10. Display slide 2 and click the butterfly shape to select it.

11. Click **DRAWING TOOLS FORMAT** > **Shape Fill** 🖌 > **Picture**.

12. In the Insert Pictures dialog box, click in the Office.com Clip Art search box, type **flowers**, and click **Search** 🔍 .

13. Scroll down the search results to find a red-orange flower such as the one shown in Figure 38-1 on the next page, select it, and click **Insert**.

14. With the shape still selected, click **PICTURE TOOLS FORMAT** > **Picture Effects** 🗨 > **Reflection** > **Half Reflection, 4 pt offset**.

15. Display slide 5 and click the **Pictures** icon in the content placeholder.

16. Navigate to the data files, if necessary, click **P38PracticeC_picture.jpg**, and click **Insert**.

17. With the picture still selected, click **PICTURE TOOLS FORMAT** > **Corrections** ☀ and click **Sharpen 50%** in the Sharpen/Soften gallery.

18. With the picture still selected, click **PICTURE TOOLS FORMAT** > **Artistic Effects** 🖼 and click **Paint Brush** in the effects gallery.

19. Preview the slides to see the images in place. Then insert your full name and the date on all slides.

20. **With your teacher's permission**, print the presentation as handouts.

21. Close the presentation, saving changes, and exit PowerPoint.

Figure 38-1

Lesson 38—Apply

In this project, you continue to work on the presentation for Thorn Hill Gardens. You insert and format a GIF image, add another picture, and do some corrections on existing images. You also crop a picture to a shape for a final touch.

DIRECTIONS

1. Start PowerPoint, if necessary, and open **P38ApplyA** from the data files for this lesson.

2. Save the presentation as **P38ApplyA_xx** in the location where your teacher instructs you to store the files for this lesson.

3. On slide 1, select the picture and adjust its color by selecting **Color** on the **PICTURE TOOLS FORMAT** tab and then choosing **Saturation: 200%** from the Color Saturation gallery.

4. Display slide 3 and then insert **P38ApplyB_ picture.gif** from the data files. Modify the picture as follows:

   a. Make the yellow background color around the butterfly transparent.

   b. Display the Color gallery, click **More Variations** at the bottom of the gallery, and then click **Light Green** from the Standard Colors palette.

   c. Resize the image to be about **4.3"** wide and rotate it to the left. Position the image attractively at the right side of the slide.

   d. Apply the **Plastic Wrap** artistic effect.

5. On slide 4, insert **P38ApplyC_picture.jpg** in the content placeholder. Adjust the image as follows:

   a. Right-click the image and select **Format Picture** to display the Format Picture task pane.

   b. Click the **Picture** icon , expand **PICTURE CORRECTIONS**, and then adjust Brightness to **20%** and Contrast to **25%**. Close the task pane.

   c. Apply the **Drop Shadow Rectangle** picture style.

6. On slide 6, insert **P38ApplyD_picture.jpg** and format the image as follows:

   a. Crop the image to the **Oval Callout** shape.

   b. Resize the shape by dragging handles to be about **4"** high by **5.5"** wide.

   c. Select the **Fit** cropping option to make sure the entire image width is included, and then adjust the crop oval so that there are no blank areas at the top of the oval or at the point of the callout arrow. The final image should be about 3.6" high. Complete the crop.

   d. Select the image, if necessary, and move it to the right side of the slide. Drag the yellow adjustment handle on the callout arrow to point to the text in the left placeholder.

   e. Apply a picture border using the Eyedropper to sample a color from the image. Change the border weight as desired.

   f. Apply a picture effect such as a reflection or shadow. Figure 38-2 shows one way the image could be formatted.

7. Preview the presentation to see the formatted images. Then insert your full name and the date on all slides.

8. **With your teacher's permission,** print the presentation as handouts.

9. Close the presentation, saving changes, and exit PowerPoint.

Figure 38-2

Lesson 39

Working with Advanced Multimedia Features

➤ What You Will Learn

Understanding Multimedia Presentations
Inserting a Web Video in a Presentation
Setting Advanced Video Options
Setting Advanced Audio Options

Software Skills   Media clips can add considerable impact to a presentation as well as convey information in ways that other graphic objects cannot. You can insert video from a Web source or a file and use formatting options to fine-tune the video appearance and playback. Use audio options to customize sounds in a presentation.

What You Can Do

Understanding Multimedia Presentations

- Multimedia presentations display information in a variety of media, including text, pictures, videos, animations, and sounds.

- Multimedia content not only adds visual and audible interest to slides but also presents information in ways that plain text cannot.

- A simple picture can convey an image that would take many words to describe; likewise, a video can show a process or sequence of events that might take many pictures to convey.

- You can choose how much or how little multimedia content to include in a presentation.

- When deciding on multimedia options for a presentation, you must consider the tradeoff between multimedia impact and the presentation's file size. Multimedia files such as videos and sounds can be quite large.

- You also need appropriate computer resources, such as speakers and video or sound cards, to play media files successfully.

- Use good research standards when locating multimedia content. Always request permission to use materials you find on the Internet, or follow directives for crediting persons or agencies.

- When creating a presentation for personal use, you can use CD music tracks for background sound, but do not use such copyrighted materials if you plan to sell your presentation or post it to a location such as a public SkyDrive folder.

- If you decide to include multimedia content in a presentation, PowerPoint offers a number of options for playing both videos and sounds.

Inserting a Web Video in a Presentation

- PowerPoint 2013 makes it easy to insert a video from the Web in a presentation.

- Online videos can include files you locate on a site such as YouTube, files you locate using a search tool such as Bing, or files from your SkyDrive.

- Use the Insert Video dialog box to control the insertion of a video from within PowerPoint.

- You can also use an embed code to insert a video on a slide. On YouTube, for example, use the Share option below the video to display the embed code. You can copy this code and then paste it in the Insert Video dialog box to place the video on the slide.

- After you insert a video you downloaded from the Web, the next time you open the presentation you will see a security warning bar below the Ribbon. The warning indicates that access to external media objects has been blocked.

- To allow the video to be played, click Enable Content in the warning bar.

Try It!   **Inserting a Web Video in a Presentation**

1. Start PowerPoint, and open **P39Try** from the data files for this lesson.

2. Save the presentation as **P39Try_xx** in the location where your teacher instructs you to store the files for this lesson.

3. Display slide 4.

4. Click INSERT > Video ▣ > Online Video.

5. Click in the Bing Video Search box and type **turning Earth**, and then click the Search button 🔍 .

6. Select any video in the search results and click Insert.

7. Click the video on the slide to select it, if necessary, and use the Video Height arrow on the VIDEO TOOLS FORMAT tab to change the height to 3.5".

8. Click VIDEO TOOLS FORMAT > Align ▤ ▾ > Align Center.

9. Click VIDEO TOOLS FORMAT > Play ▶ and then click the play button on the video to preview the video on the slide.

10. Save the **P39Try_xx** file, and leave it open to use in the next Try It.

Setting Advanced Video Options

- You need to understand video formats to determine the quality of video clips you intend to insert.

- A file in MPEG-1 format, for example, is not likely to display with the same quality as an MPEG-2 file, but it will be smaller in size. An MPEG-4 file will have the best appearance and allows for more efficient compression than MPEG-2.

- Table 39-1 on the next page shows the video formats that PowerPoint supports. Note that PowerPoint does not support some popular video formats, such as QuickTime and RealMedia files.

- Use the tools on the VIDEO TOOLS PLAYBACK tab to work with a video.

- Insert a bookmark so you can jump to a specific point in the video.

- Trim a video to remove portions of it that you don't need.

- Apply Fade settings to fade a video in or out.

- Choose options such as Play Full Screen or Hide While Not Playing to control the appearance of the video on the slide during the presentation.

- You can also choose to loop a video until you stop it, or return the movie to its first frame after it has finished playing.

- Use the Volume button to control the sound of the individual video clip within the overall presentation.

Table 39-1	**Supported Video Formats for PowerPoint**	
Format	**Extension**	**Characteristics**
ASF	.asf	Advanced Systems Format. Microsoft's streaming format that can contain video, audio, slide shows, and other synchronized content.
AVI	.avi	Audio Video Interleave. A file format that stores alternating (interleaved) sections of audio and video content; widely used for playing video with sound on Windows systems; AVI is a container (a format that stores different types of data), not a form of compression.
MPEG	.mpg, .mpeg, .mp4, .m4v, .mov	Moving Picture Experts Group. A standard format for lossy audio and visual compression that comes in several formats, such as MPEG-1 (CD quality), MPEG-2 (DVD quality), and MPEG-4 (broadcast quality).
SWF	.swf	Adobe Flash Media. Flash uses vector and bitmap objects to create animations that can include text, graphics, and audio.
WMV	.wmv	Windows Media Video. Microsoft's lossy compression format for motion video; it results in files that take up little room on a system.

Try It!	**Setting Advanced Video Options**

1. In the **P39Try_xx** file, display slide 3 and click the video to select it.

2. Add a timed fade to the beginning of the video: on the VIDEO TOOLS PLAYBACK tab, click the up arrow to increase the Fade In time to 00.50.

3. Click the Play button below the video and let it run for about 10 seconds, then stop it.

4. Click VIDEO TOOLS PLAYBACK > Add Bookmark 🔖 to add a bookmark at the current location on the video timeline.

Bookmark in a video

5. Click VIDEO TOOLS PLAYBACK > Trim Video 🎬.

6. In the Trim Video dialog box, drag the red End Time indicator to the left until the End Time box shows about 00:20:00.

7. Click OK.

8. Click VIDEO TOOLS PLAYBACK > Rewind after Playing.

9. Click Slide Show 🖳 on the status bar and click the video to play it, noting the fade-in and the rewind when finished.

10. Move the pointer over the video after it has finished and click the bookmark to jump to that location. Click the play button to play the remainder of the video.

11. Press ESC to end the presentation.

12. Save the **P39Try_xx** file, and leave it open for the next Try It.

Setting Advanced Audio Options

- Options on the AUDIO TOOLS PLAYBACK tab are very similar to those on the VIDEO TOOLS PLAYBACK tab.

- As for a video, you can add a bookmark to an audio file, trim it, and fade it in or out.

- You can adjust the volume and choose to play the sound across slides or loop it.

- Use the Hide During Show option to prevent the audio file icon from appearing during the presentation.

- Selecting the Play in Background option sets the audio file to start automatically, play across slides, and loop until stopped.

Try It! — Setting Advanced Audio Options

1. In the **P39Try_xx** file, display slide 1 and click the audio object in the lower-right corner of the slide.

2. Click AUDIO TOOLS PLAYBACK and click the Fade In up arrow until 01.00 appears.

3. Click Volume and click Medium.

4. Click Hide During Show.

5. Click Play in Background.

6. Click Slide Show on the status bar to play the presentation. Notice that the audio object is hidden; the music plays automatically and continues to play as you view each slide.

7. Close the **P39Try_xx** file, saving changes, and exit PowerPoint.

Lesson 39—Practice

Voyager Adventure Travel is beginning the task of adding a new hiking package to its list of adventures. The decision-making process requires consideration of both pros and cons for each suggested venue, and you have been asked to prepare a slide show to present the information. In this project, you begin work on the presentation with pros and cons for Glacier National Park.

DIRECTIONS

1. Start PowerPoint, if necessary, and open **P39PracticeA** from the data files for this lesson.

2. Save the presentation as **P39PracticeA_xx** in the location where your teacher instructs you to store the files for this lesson.

3. Display slide 5 and click **INSERT** > **Video** > **Video on My PC**. The Insert Video dialog box opens.

4. Navigate to the data files for this lesson and select **P39PracticeB_video.mpg**.

5. Click **Insert**. The video will be upgraded before being inserted.

6. Center the video in the content area.

7. Point to the timeline beneath the video to display a counter that moves as you move the pointer, and click when the counter reaches **00:02.30**.

8. Click **VIDEO TOOLS PLAYBACK** > **Add Bookmark** to bookmark this location in the video.

9. Click the **Fade In** up arrow to set the beginning fade to **01.00**.

10. Click the **Start** down arrow and select **Automatically**.

11. Display slide 6 and click **INSERT** > **Audio** > **Online Audio**.

12. In the Office.com Clip Art box, type **helicopter** and click Search.

13. Locate a clip that sounds like a helicopter flyover and insert it.

14. With the audio clip selected on slide 6, on the AUDIO TOOLS PLAYBACK tab, change the **Fade In** setting to **00.50**, the **Fade Out** setting to **00.50**, and the Volume to **Medium**.

15. On the AUDIO TOOLS PLAYBACK tab, click **Play Across Slides**, and then click the **Start** down arrow and select **Automatically**.

16. On the AUDIO TOOLS PLAYBACK tab, click **Hide During Show**.

17. Preview the presentation from the beginning. On slide 5, play the entire video, then select the bookmark and play the video from that location.

18. Play the remaining slides, noting how the sound fades in and out and plays through the remaining slides.

19. Close the presentation, saving changes, and exit PowerPoint.

Lesson 39—Apply

In this project, you continue working with the Voyager Adventure Travel presentation. You adjust video and audio settings, add another video from the Web, and insert a picture to add a final touch to this multimedia presentation.

DIRECTIONS

1. Start PowerPoint, if necessary, and open **P39ApplyA** from the data files for this lesson.

2. Save the file as **P39ApplyA_xx** in the location where your teacher instructs you to store the files for this lesson.

3. Display slide 5 and select the video.

4. Remove the Fade In setting and then trim the video so it starts at approximately **00:01.00**.

5. On the VIDEO TOOLS FORMAT tab, select the **Drop Shadow Rectangle** video style.

6. Display slide 6 and choose to insert an online video.

7. In the Bing Video Search box, type **Red Eagle forest fire** and click **Search** 🔎.

8. Click the first search result and insert it on the slide.

9. Adjust the video size to **3.4"** high and position the video on the right side of the slide, aligned with the top of the left content area.

10. Apply the **Drop Shadow Rectangle** video style.

11. On slide 7, insert the **P39ApplyB_picture.jpg** file in the right content placeholder and then apply the **Drop Shadow Rectangle** picture style. Your slide should look like Figure 39-1 on the next page.

12. Display slide 1. Insert an online audio music file and format it with the Play in Background style so it will start automatically and play across slides.

13. View the slide show to play the new sound and the new video and view changes to other objects.

14. Insert your name and the date on all slides.

15. **With your teacher's permission,** print the presentation as handouts with 4 slides per page.

16. Close the presentation, saving changes, and exit PowerPoint.

Figure 39-1

Smoke Hazards

Prevailing winds distribute smoke over a wide region

Even if active fires are distant, smoke may be present in other parts of the park

Smoke obscures the gorgeous views and may constitute an air quality hazard

The picture above was taken many miles from an active fire, but as can be seen, the smoke is dense enough to darken the sky.

Today's Date
FIRSTNAME LASTNAME

Lesson 40

Applying Advanced Animations

➤ What You Will Learn

Applying More Than One Animation to an Object
Adjusting a Motion Path Animation
Applying Advanced Effect Options
Controlling an Animation with a Trigger
Working with the Animation Timeline

WORDS TO KNOW

Trigger
An object you click to start the animation of another object.

Software Skills Using custom animation options, you can fine-tune the way objects enter, exit, and move on slides. Use advanced features to trigger animations, and use the timeline to control when animations start and how long they last.

What You Can Do

Applying More Than One Animation to an Object

- You can apply more than one animation effect to any object on a slide.
- For example, apply an entrance effect to display an object and then an exit effect to remove the object from the slide.
- Use the Add Animation button on the ANIMATIONS tab to add another animation to an object.

Try It!   **Applying More Than One Animation to an Object**

1. Start PowerPoint, and open **P40Try** from the data files for this lesson.

2. Save the presentation as **P40Try_xx** in the location where your teacher instructs you to store the files for this lesson.

3. Display slide 7 and click the Profit text box to select it.

4. Click ANIMATIONS > Preview to see the animations already applied on this slide.

5. With the Profit text box still selected, click ANIMATIONS > Add Animation to display a gallery of animation effects.

6. In the Emphasis section of the gallery, click Pulse.

7. Click ANIMATIONS > Preview to view the added animation on the Profit text box.

8. Display slide 8 and click the pointing arrow shape to select it.

9. Click ANIMATIONS > Add Animation and select Wipe.

10. Click ANIMATIONS > Effect Options ↑ > From Right.

11. Click ANIMATIONS > Add Animation and select Shrink & Turn from the Exit gallery.

12. Click ANIMATIONS > Preview to view the animations on the arrow.

13. Save the **P40Try_xx** file, and leave it open to use in the next Try It.

Choose an Exit effect for an object

Adjusting a Motion Path Animation

- PowerPoint offers many options for setting objects in motion on your slides. You can choose among lines, turns, arcs, and special shapes.

- If you cannot find a default motion path that suits your needs, you can adjust any motion path to specify exactly where you want an object to be at the beginning and the end of the animation.

- A green handle or pointer marks the beginning of a motion path, and a red handle or pointer marks the end of the path. You can drag these handles as desired to reposition the path.

- You will see a shaded version of the object at the end of the motion path to help you position it correctly at the end of the path.

- You may also want to edit curve points along the path or use the Effect Options gallery to change the direction of the motion.

Try It!   **Adjusting a Motion Path Animation**

1 In the **P40Try_xx** file, display slide 1 and click the Planet Earth object in the upper-right corner. (Click the outside border to select the entire group.)

2 Click ANIMATIONS > Add Animation ⭐ and scroll down to display the Motion Paths effects.

3 Click Lines to apply a straight-line motion path to the object.

4 Click the red handle in the center of the shaded object as shown in the illustration and drag to the lower-left of the slide to position the end of the path below the words *Planet Earth*.

5 Release the mouse button when you are satisfied with the position of the object.

6 Click the Start down arrow and select After Previous. Set the Duration to 3:00.

7 Click ANIMATIONS > Preview 🌟 to view the adjusted motion path.

8 Save the **P40Try_xx** file, and leave it open to use in the next Try It.

Drag the handle at the end of the path to adjust the path

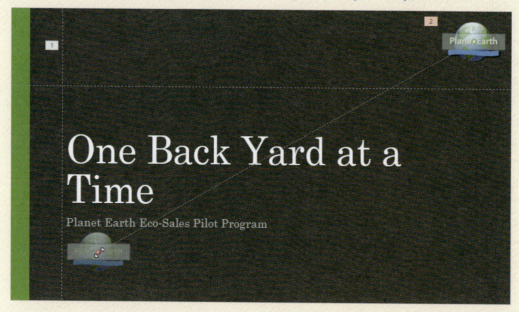

Applying Advanced Effect Options

- When you select an animation in the Animation Pane, a down arrow appears containing a number of options that you can use to modify an effect.

- Selecting Effect Options from the content list opens a dialog box for the currently selected effect. The Effect tab offers a number of special effects that you can apply to an object, depending on the type of object being animated.

- You can adjust the direction of the animation and choose Smooth start and Smooth end to control how the object starts and stops during the animation.

- All animation types enable you to select a sound effect from the Sound list to accompany the effect.

  ✓ *Use sound effects sparingly; it can be distracting to hear the same sound effect over and over when multiple parts of an object are animated.*

- The After animation menu gives you a number of options for emphasizing or deemphasizing an object after the animation ends. You can hide the object after the animation, hide it the next time you click the mouse, or change its color.

- If the animated object contains text, the Animate text settings become active, enabling you to animate the text all at once, by word, or by letter, and set the delay between words or letters.

Try It!   Applying Advanced Effect Options

(1) In the **P40Try_xx** file, display slide 9.

(2) Click ANIMATIONS > Animation Pane 🔊 to display the Animation Pane.

(3) Select the Title 1 animation and then click Fade in the Animation gallery to change the animation effect from Split to Fade.

(4) Select the Title 1 animation again in the Animation Pane, if necessary, and click the down arrow to the right of the animation title.

(5) Click Effect Options to open the Fade options dialog box.

(6) Click the Animate text down arrow and click By word.

(7) Click the Timing tab in the Fade dialog box, click the Start down arrow and select With Previous. Click the Duration down arrow and select 5 seconds (Very Slow).

(8) Click OK to apply the animation effects.

(9) Click the subtitle on the slide, and apply the Fly In animation.

(10) With the subtitle animation selected in the Animation Pane, click the animation's down arrow and click Effect Options.

(11) Click the Direction down arrow and select From Right; click the Bounce end up arrow to apply a 0.5 sec bounce; click the After animation down arrow and select Hide After Animation.

(12) Click the Timing tab, set the Start to After Previous and the Duration to 5 seconds (Very Slow).

(13) Click OK to apply the animation effects.

(14) Preview the effects on the slide.

(15) Save the **P40Try_xx** file, and leave it open to use in the next Try It.

Advanced effect options for the Fly In animation

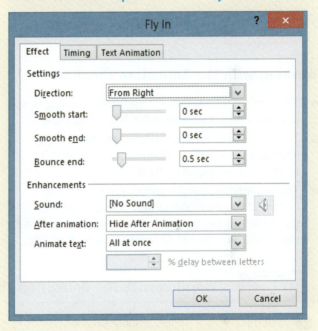

Controlling an Animation with a Trigger

■ You can specify that an animation will begin when you click an object called a **trigger**.

■ Using triggers is one way to make a slide show interactive. A presenter can click one object during the presentation to start the animation of another object.

■ Use the Trigger button in the Advanced Animation group to set the trigger that will start an animation sequence. You can also set a trigger from within an effect's options dialog box.

Try It!   **Controlling an Animation with a Trigger**

1 In the **P40Try_xx** file, display slide 7.

2 Select the chart and the three text boxes at the bottom of slide 7.

✓ *Hint: Press* CTRL *to enable you to select multiple objects.*

3 Click ANIMATIONS > Float In.

4 Click ANIMATIONS > Trigger ⚡ > On Click of > TextBox 7.

5 Click Slide Show 🖵 on the status bar to display the current slide in Slide Show view. The first two text boxes animate automatically. Click the slide to display the Profit box. Click to display the Pulse animation effect.

6 Point to the Profit box, which is the trigger for the next animation. Click the Profit box to display the chart and the remaining text boxes.

7 Click ESC to end the slide show.

8 Save the **P40Try_xx** file, and leave it open to use in the next Try It.

Working with the Animation Timeline

- The easiest way to fine-tune animation timing is to use the timeline feature in the Animation Pane.

- The bar next to an effect in the Animation Pane indicates the duration of the effect and when it starts relative to other effects.

- The timeline includes a seconds gauge at the bottom of the Animation Pane. You can use this gauge to see the duration of each effect as well as the overall duration of all animations on the slide.

- You can use the timeline to set a delay or adjust the length of an effect.

- You can double-click a timeline bar to open the Timing dialog box for further adjustments.

- Before you use the timeline to adjust animations, you may need to change the order in which the animations play. You can drag animations in the Animation Pane to change their order or use the Reorder Animation buttons Move Earlier and Move Later to change animation order.

Try It!   **Working with the Animation Timeline**

1 In the **P40Try_xx** file, display slide 6.

2 Click ANIMATIONS > Preview 🌟 to see how the objects are currently animated.

3 In the Animation Pane, click the Title 2 animation, which has a green star indicating an entrance effect.

4 In the Timing group, click the Move Earlier button ▲ to move the animation to the top of the Animation Pane.

5 Click the Group 8 animation, which has a red star indicating an exit effect, and then click the Move Later button ▼ twice to move the animation to the bottom of the list.

6 Click the Seconds down arrow at the bottom of the Animation Pane and select Zoom Out.

7 Click the Picture 11 animation in the Animation Pane, and position the pointer on the right edge of the green timeline box until the pointer changes to a double-headed arrow pointer. A ScreenTip indicates the start time and end time.

8 Drag the right edge of the timeline box to the right until the ScreenTip indicates 2.5s.

✓ *To make it easier to adjust the timeline, you can increase the width of the Animation Pane by dragging its left border to the left.*

9 Click the expand contents arrow ⌄ below the Content Placeholder effect in the Animation Pane to see both list items.

10 Use the left and right edges of the first effect's timeline box to adjust the timing on the first paragraph to Start 2s, End 3s.

(continued)

Try It! **Working with the Animation Timeline** *(continued)*

Using the timeline to change the duration of an effect

Setting a delay by dragging a timeline box

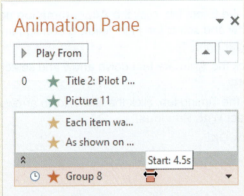

⑪ Adjust the timing of the second paragraph to Start 3s, End 4s.

⑫ Click the Seconds down arrow and click Zoom In.

⑬ Position the pointer on the Group 8 exit effect's timeline so that it becomes a horizontal two-headed arrow. Click and drag the entire timeline box to the right until the ScreenTip shows Start: 4.5s.

⑭ Preview the animations on the slide to see how timeline adjustments have changed duration and delay.

⑮ Close the **P40Try_xx** file, saving changes, and exit PowerPoint.

Lesson 40—Practice

Natural Light has asked you to add animations to a presentation that will be available in the showroom for visitors to browse. In this project, you work with a number of custom animation options.

DIRECTIONS

1. Start PowerPoint, if necessary, and open **P40Practice** from the data files for this lesson.

2. Save the file as **P40Practice_xx** in the location where your teacher instructs you to store the files for this lesson.

3. On slide 1, select the Star object.

4. Click **ANIMATIONS** > **Add Animation** ⭐ > **Color Pulse** in the Emphasis section of the gallery.

5. Click **ANIMATIONS** > **Effect Options** and select the last color on the top row.

6. Click **ANIMATIONS** > **Start** > **After Previous**.

7. Click **ANIMATIONS** > **Animation Pane** ⏱◀ .

8. In the Animation Pane, click the Star animation's down arrow and select **Timing** from the menu.

9. In the dialog box, click the **Repeat** down arrow and select **Until Next Click**. Click **OK**.

10. Select the title and subtitle placeholders on slide 1 and click **ANIMATIONS** > **Add Animation** ⭐ > **More Entrance Effects**.

11. Select **Dissolve In** and click **OK**.

12. Select the subtitle placeholder and click **ANIMATIONS** > **Start** > **After Previous**.

13. In the Animation Pane, click the title animation down arrow and select **Effect Options**.

14. On the Effect tab, click the **After animation** down arrow and select the pale yellow-green square at the far right.

15. Click the **Animate text** down arrow and select **By word**.

16. On the Timing tab, click the **Start** down arrow and select **With Previous**.

17. Click **OK**.

18. Select the timeline box for the title animation and drag the right edge to the right until the ScreenTip reads **By Word: 4.0s**.

19. Drag the right edge of the subtitle animation to end the animation at **7.0s**.

20. Close the Animation Pane and click the **Slide Show** button 🖵 on the status bar to view your animations in Slide Show view. Click ⌷ESC⌷ to end the slide show.

21. Insert a footer with your name and the date on all slides except the first slide.

22. Close the presentation, saving changes, and exit PowerPoint.

Lesson 40—Apply

In this project, you continue to work on the Natural Light presentation. You add and adjust animations to complete the presentation.

DIRECTIONS

1. Start PowerPoint, if necessary, and open **P40Apply** from the data files for this lesson.

2. Save the presentation as **P40Apply_xx** in the location where your teacher instructs you to store the files for this lesson.

3. Display slide 4 and apply animation effects as follows:

   a. Set the **Sales** placeholder to **Fade**, **After Previous**, **Fast**.

   b. Select the content placeholder below the Sales object and fade the text into view **After Previous**.

   c. Select the **Sales** placeholder and then click **ANIMATIONS** > **Animation Painter** ✨ .

   d. Click the **Service** placeholder to apply the same settings to the Service placeholder that you applied to the Sales placeholder.

   e. Delay the start of the Service placeholder by 1.5 seconds.

   f. Use the Animation Painter to apply the settings from the left content placeholder to the right one under Service. (You may need to reapply After Previous timing to the second bullet in this placeholder.)

4. Display slide 5 and apply a **Fly In** entrance animation to the SmartArt graphic, **After Previous**, **Fast From Left**. Then modify the animation effects as follows:

   a. Change the SmartArt Animation option in the Effect Options dialog box to **One by one**, then expand the effect to see all the shapes that make up the diagram. (You may need to apply After Previous timing to shapes after the first one.)

   b. Using the timeline, adjust the duration and delay of each shape so that a viewer has time to read the Step 1 shape before the first list shape appears, read the text in this shape before the Step 2 shape appears, and so on.

   c. Use the **Play From** button in the Animation Pane and the **Slide Show** button to test your delays until you are satisfied with the results.

5. On slide 6, set a trigger to animate the picture with a **Wipe** entrance effect, **From Top**, **Fast**, when the slide title is clicked. Then animate the picture description with a **Fade** effect so it appears after the picture.

   ✓ *Hint: You might need to reorder the effects to get the animation right.*

6. On slide 7, apply to the WordArt object the **Fade** entrance effect, the **Grow/Shrink** emphasis effect, and the **Fade** exit effect. Apply the following settings:

   a. Apply **After Previous** to all of the effects.

   b. Change the timing of the entrance effect to **Slow**.

   c. Make sure the timing of the emphasis effect is **Medium**.

   d. Change the timing of the exit effect to **Slow**.

7. On slide 7, add a motion path to the Star object so that it moves to the center of the slide after the WordArt object exits. Then apply a **Grow/Shrink** emphasis effect and use the Effect Options dialog box to increase the size of the object **200%**. Apply **After Previous** to both effects. The motion path should look similar to Figure 40-1.

8. View the slide show to see the effects. Make any adjustments necessary.

9. Insert your name and the date in a footer on all slides except the first slide.

10. Close the presentation, saving changes, and exit PowerPoint.

Figure 40-1

Lesson 41

Drawing and Adjusting Tables

➤ What You Will Learn

Drawing a Table
Using the Eraser to Merge Cells
Adjusting Column Width and Row Height
Adjusting Cell and Table Size
Changing Text Alignment and Direction

Software Skills   Tables can help you present information clearly and succinctly by displaying information in a column-and-row format. You can customize tables by drawing the structure and adjusting the size of rows and columns, cells, and the table itself. Change the text direction and alignment for a final, expert touch.

What You Can Do

Drawing a Table

- You can create a new table using the Insert Table dialog box to specify the number of columns or rows. Or, you can click the Table button on the INSERT tab and then drag the pointer over the table grid to select rows and columns.

- To create a table that may not consist of a regular column-and-row grid, you can use the Draw Table option on the Table menu.

- After you click Draw Table, the pointer changes to a pencil, indicating that you can draw the table you want on the screen.

- Click and drag the outline of the table. Then select Draw Table in the Draw Borders group on the TABLE TOOLS DESIGN tab to activate the Draw Table pointer so you can create the table's columns and rows.

- You can change the color, style, and thickness of the lines you draw by using the Pen Style, Pen Weight, and Pen Color tools, also in the Draw Borders group.

- You can also use the Draw Table tool to change border formats on existing tables. Just choose the desired formats (pen style, pen weight, and pen color) and then drag the Draw Table pointer over existing borders to apply the new formats.

Try It!   Drawing a Table

1 Start PowerPoint, and begin a new presentation using the Retrospect design.

2 Save the presentation as **P41Try_xx** in the location where your teacher instructs you to store the files for this lesson.

3 Click HOME > Layout and select Title Only.

4 Click INSERT > Table.

5 Click Draw Table.

6 Drag the pencil to draw the table outline in the content area of the slide. Release the mouse button when the outline is as large as you want it.

7 Save the **P41Try_xx** file, and leave it open to use in the next Try It.

Drag the pencil to draw the outline of the table

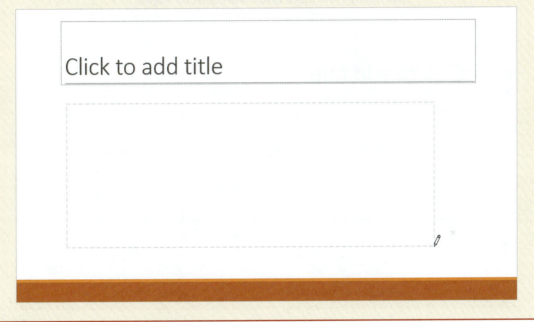

Click to add title

Try It!   Adding Rows and Columns

1 In the **P41Try_xx** file, click TABLE TOOLS DESIGN > Draw Table.

2 Click on the left side of the new table about one-quarter of the way down from the top border and drag the pencil to the right border.

  ✓ *Click slightly inside the border of the table to begin drawing; otherwise, PowerPoint may create a table within a table. If you accidentally insert a new table by clicking in the wrong place, simply press CTRL + Z to undo the error and try again.*

3 Repeat until you have created four rows.

4 Click just inside the top border about halfway across the table and drag the pencil down to the bottom border.

5 Repeat to create a third column.

6 Save the **P41Try_xx** file, and leave it open to use in the next Try It.

Try It!   **Changing Border Formats As You Draw**

1 In the **P41Try_xx** file, click TABLE TOOLS DESIGN > Pen Style down arrow. Select one of the dotted line styles.

2 Click TABLE TOOLS DESIGN > Pen Weight down arrow and select 3 pt.

3 Click TABLE TOOLS DESIGN > Pen Color and select Blue from the Standard Colors palette.

4 Click just inside the top table border to the right of the existing column lines, and draw a new line in the new style, weight, and color that extends to the bottom table border.

5 Choose a new Pen Style, Weight, and Color and draw a fourth line, similar to the third.

6 Save the **P41Try_xx** file, and leave it open to use in the next Try It.

Drawing new table lines with various styles

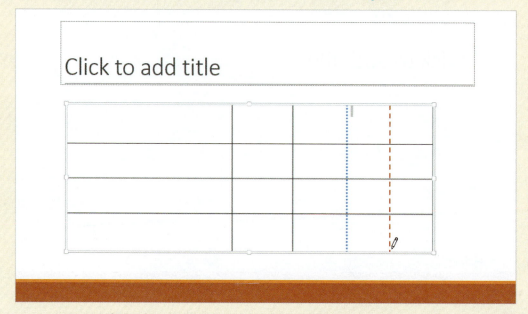

Using the Eraser to Merge Cells

- In some cases, you may want to merge cells to create a larger area.

- You might do this, for example, when you want to create a table heading that spans the width of the table, or when you want to create one cell for a column header that spans two subheads.

- One way to combine cells is to use the Merge Cells button on the TABLE TOOLS LAYOUT tab. Another way is to use the Eraser tool to remove cell borders.

- The Eraser tool is available in the Draw Borders group of the TABLE TOOLS DESIGN tab.

- To erase a line, select the Eraser tool and then click the line segment you want to erase. You can also drag the eraser over the line to erase several segments.

- When you erase a row or column line, the cells in the affected row or column merge to make a larger cell.

- The Eraser tool remains selected until you click Eraser again or click a different tool.

Using the Eraser to Merge Cells

1 In the **P41Try_xx** file, click the table, if necessary, to select it.

2 Click TABLE TOOLS DESIGN > Eraser ▨.

3 Click the first vertical segment in row 1 of your table.

4 Click the remaining vertical segments in row 1.

5 Click TABLE TOOLS DESIGN > Eraser ▨ again to turn off the tool.

6 Click in the merged row 1 and type **New Courses**.

7 Click outside the table to deselect it.

8 Save the **P41Try_xx** file, and leave it open to use in the next Try It.

Adjusting Column Width and Row Height

- PowerPoint makes it simple for you to adjust the column widths in your table.

- Simply position the mouse pointer over the column border you want to adjust. When the pointer changes to double vertical lines with right- and left-pointing arrows, click and drag the column border to increase or decrease the column width.

- Similarly, to adjust the row height, hover the mouse pointer over the row you want to change.

- The mouse pointer changes to double horizontal lines with up- and down-pointing arrows. Click and drag the row border to increase or reduce the height.

Adjusting Column Width and Row Height

1 In the **P41Try_xx** file, position the mouse pointer over the leftmost column divider.

2 When the pointer changes, click and drag the column divider to the left, enlarging the second column.

3 Release the mouse button to complete the move.

4 Adjust the three columns on the right by dragging the column dividers until the columns appear to be of equal width.

Drag column and row dividers to adjust the table layout

Click to add title

New Courses

(continued)

Try It!   **Adjusting Column Width and Row Height** *(continued)*

5 Position the mouse pointer over the row divider above the bottom row of the table.

6 When the pointer changes, drag the row divider downward, enlarging the height of the middle row and making the table a little taller.

7 Release the mouse button to complete the operation.

8 Save the **P41Try_xx** file, and leave it open to use in the next Try It.

Adjusting Cell and Table Size

- The tools in the TABLE TOOLS LAYOUT tab enable you to adjust cell and table size.

- Use the Table Column Width and Table Row Height boxes in the Cell Size group to set specific column widths or row heights.

- To space the rows or columns evenly throughout the table, use the Distribute Rows or Distribute Columns tool.

- In the Table Size group, you can enter size values for the Height and Width of the table.

- You can also drag a table handle or border to change the size of the table on the slide.

- Click the Lock Aspect Ratio check box if you want to preserve the shape of the current table no matter how you may resize it.

Try It!   **Changing Cell Size**

1 In the **P41Try_xx** file, click in the second row in the table.

2 Click TABLE TOOLS LAYOUT, click in the Row Height box, and type **0.75**.

3 Click TABLE TOOLS LAYOUT, click in the Column Width box, and type **1.5**. Press ENTER .

✓ *Notice that the new column or row value is applied only to the current selection. To apply the new value to more than one column or row, select the additional columns or rows you want to change before entering the new value.*

4 Save the **P41Try_xx** file, and leave it open to use in the next Try It.

Try It!   **Distributing Rows and Columns**

1 In the **P41Try_xx** file, click in column 2 in the table.

2 Click TABLE TOOLS LAYOUT > Distribute Rows ⊞ . All rows in the table are now the same height.

3 Click TABLE TOOLS LAYOUT > Distribute Columns ⊞ . All columns in the table are now the same width.

4 Save the **P41Try_xx** file, and leave it open to use in the next Try It.

Try It!   Resizing the Table

1 In the **P41Try_xx** file, select the table.

2 Click the Lock Aspect Ratio check box on the TABLE TOOLS LAYOUT tab.

3 Click in the Height box and type **4**.

4 Click the lower-right corner of the table and enlarge the size of the table by dragging to the right until the Width shows **8.5**.

5 Release the mouse button. Because aspect ratio is locked, the height may also change as you adjust the width.

6 Save the **P41Try_xx** file, and leave it open to use in the next Try It.

Resize the table with Lock Aspect Ratio selected

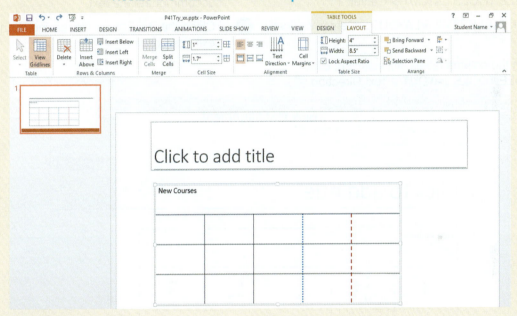

Changing Text Alignment and Direction

- The way you align your text can help readers make sense of the information you're presenting.

- You can align text horizontally at the left, center, or right, or vertically at the top, middle, or bottom of a table cell.

- You can also change text direction so that text appears vertically in a cell. This is sometimes helpful when you have long column titles but don't want to use wide columns.

- When changing text direction, you can choose Horizontal, Rotate all text 90°, Rotate all text 270°, or Stacked.

- You can also choose More Options in the Text Direction list to further control cell margins, alignment, and spacing options.

Try It!   **Changing Text Alignment and Direction**

1 In the **P41Try_xx** file, click in the second row of the table, and type the following in each of the cells:

No.
Course Title
Instructor
Days Offered
Features

2 Select the row of text you just entered and click TABLE TOOLS LAYOUT > Center ☰.

3 Click TABLE TOOLS LAYOUT > Center Vertically ▤.

4 With the column labels still selected, click TABLE TOOLS LAYOUT > Text Direction ⅢA.

5 Click Rotate all text 270°.

6 Click TABLE TOOLS LAYOUT > Text Direction ⅢA, then click More Options. The Format Shape task pane appears.

7 Click the Vertical alignment down arrow and select Center Middle.

8 Close the task pane.

9 Adjust the row height as needed to accommodate the text.

10 Close the **P41Try_xx** file, saving changes, and exit PowerPoint.

New text alignment

Click to add title

New Courses					
No.	Course Title	Instructor	Days Offered	Features	

Lesson 41—Practice

Your local community college is offering a series of summer classes that give students a range of experiences in different fields. One of the professors has asked you to create a PowerPoint presentation that tells a bit about each class. At the end of the presentation, you want to include a table that shows the features in each class so that students can easily decide among the course offerings. In this project, you begin by drawing the table and aligning text.

DIRECTIONS

1. Start PowerPoint, if necessary, and open **P41Practice** from the data files for this lesson.

2. Save the presentation as **P41Practice_xx** in the location where your teacher instructs you to store the files for this lesson.

3. Display slide 2 and click in the title placeholder. Type **Course Offerings**.

4. Click **INSERT** > **Table** ⊞ > **Draw Table**, and move the pointer to the content area.

5. Click and drag the pencil to draw a table about **4"** high by **10"** wide.

   ✓ *Don't worry if the table border uses the same formats you applied earlier in the Try It exercise.*

6. On the TABLE TOOLS DESIGN tab, click the **Pen Style** down arrow and choose the solid line, if necessary.

7. Click the **Pen Weight** down arrow and click **2¼ pt**.

8. Click **Pen Color** 🖉 and choose a dark orange color.

9. Click just below the top border of the table and drag the mouse down to the bottom to create a column divider.

10. Repeat the previous step three times so that you create five columns.

11. Click at the left side of the table and draw a line to the right side of the table to create a new row.

12. Repeat the previous step four times so that you have a total of six rows in your table.

13. Click **TABLE TOOLS DESIGN** > **Eraser** 🔲 and erase all the column segments in row 1. Click the Eraser button a second time to turn off the tool.

14. Merge the last two columns by highlighting all cells in the last two columns of the table and then clicking **TABLE TOOLS LAYOUT** > **Merge Cells** ⊞.

15. Resize the column on the right to about **3"** by dragging the rightmost column divider to the right.

16. Add the table title and column labels as shown in Figure 41-1 on the next page.

17. Select the column labels and click **TABLE TOOLS LAYOUT** > **Center** ≡.

18. With the labels still selected, click **TABLE TOOLS LAYOUT** > **Center Vertically** 🗐.

19. Insert your name and the date on all slides.

20. **With your teacher's permission,** print slide 2. It should look similar to Figure 41-1.

21. Close the presentation, saving changes, and exit PowerPoint.

Figure 41-1

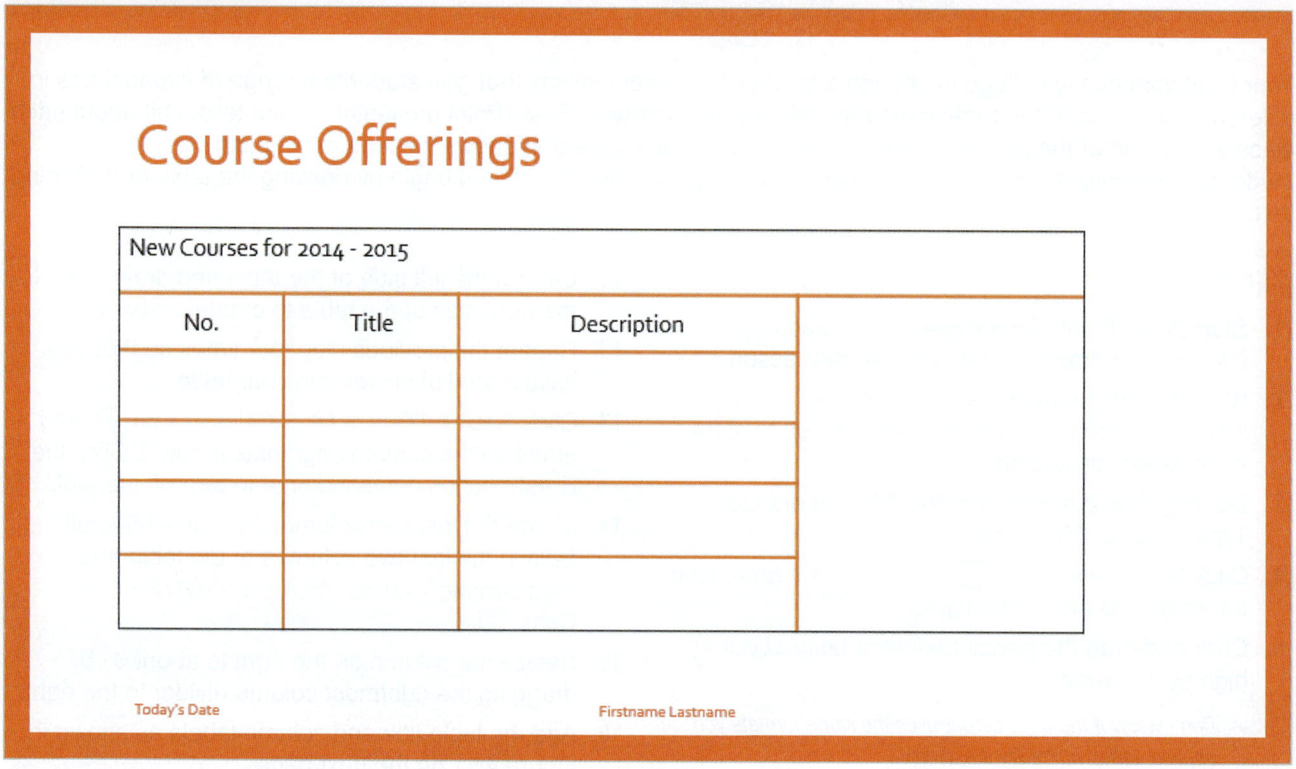

Course Offerings

New Courses for 2014 - 2015			
No.	Title	Description	

Today's Date   Firstname Lastname

Lesson 41—Apply

In this project, you continue working with the Sinclair College presentation. You adjust cell sizes, change alignments and text direction, and use the Draw Table tool and Eraser to change the table layout.

DIRECTIONS

1. Start PowerPoint, if necessary, and open **P41Apply** from the data files for this lesson.

2. Save the presentation as **P41Apply_xx** in the location where your teacher instructs you to store the files for this lesson.

3. Display slide 2 and use **Distribute Rows** to make all rows the same height.

4. Use **Distribute Columns** to make all columns the same width.

5. Use the **Draw Table** tool to draw a diagonal line in the last, empty column, as shown in Figure 41-2 on the next page.

6. Click at the top of the divided column and type **300 and above for**, press ENTER , and type **Full-Time students**.

7. Press ENTER eight times and then change to right alignment. Type **299 and below for**, press ENTER , and type **Part-Time students**.

8. Insert a new column at the far left of the table, and use the Eraser tool to erase all row borders in the new column.

9. Change the column width to **1"** and type **2014 - 2015**.

10. Change the text direction to rotate all text 270°, and then center the text vertically and horizontally. Change the font size to **36 points**.

11. Delete the text *for 2014 - 2015* from the first row of the table.

12. Change the width of the No. column to **1.5"**, the Description column to **3"**, and the divided column to **2.6"**.

13. Insert your name and the date on all slides.

14. **With your teacher's permission,** print slide 2. It should look similar to Figure 41-2.

15. Close the presentation, saving changes, and exit PowerPoint.

Figure 41-2

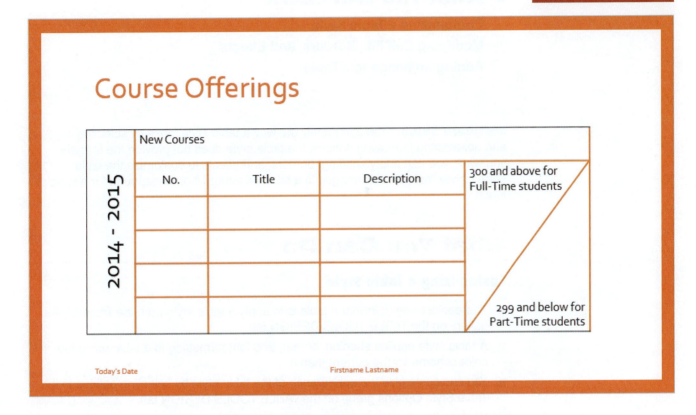

Lesson 42

Formatting Tables

➤ **What You Will Learn**

Customizing a Table Style
Modifying Cell Fill, Borders, and Effects
Adding an Image to a Table

Software Skills   You can modify the way a table style looks by selecting and deselecting formatting options. If a table style does not provide the formats you want, you can apply shading, borders, and effects to customize the table appearance. You can add images to a table as either fill or background for a special touch.

What You Can Do

Customizing a Table Style

- The easiest way to format a table is to apply a table style from the Table Styles gallery on the TABLE TOOLS DESIGN tab.

- A table style applies shading, border, and font formatting to a table using the color scheme for the current theme.

- You can customize the appearance of the table style by selecting options in the Table Style Options group on the TABLE TOOLS DESIGN tab.

- Click on the check boxes in the Table Style Options group to add specific elements to your table, such as emphasis on the header row or first column, or banded rows or columns.

- These options control how shading and borders are used in your table style.

- As you select or deselect these options, the table styles shown in the Table Styles gallery change to reflect your choices.

Try It! Customizing a Table Style

1 Start PowerPoint, and open **P42TryA** from the data files for this lesson.

2 Save the presentation as **P42TryA_xx** in the location where your teacher instructs you to store the files for this lesson.

3 Click in the table to select it and display the TABLE TOOLS DESIGN tab.

4 In the Table Styles gallery, click the More button ▾ and then select the Medium Style 1 – Accent 1 table style to apply it.

5 In the Table Style Options group, click Total Row to add formatting for a total row—a double-line border above the last row in the table.

6 Deselect Total Row and select First Column. Bold formatting is added to the entries in the first column.

7 Select Banded Rows to apply shading on alternate rows of the table.

8 Save the **P42TryA_xx** file, and leave it open for the next Try It.

Customize a table style

Modifying Cell Fill, Borders, and Effects

- After you apply a table style to your table, you can fine-tune the look by changing the appearance of selected cells, rows, or columns using shading, borders, or effects available on the TABLE TOOLS DESIGN tab.

- For example, you can make a section of a table stand out by changing the shading of the section.

- Shading options include solid colors, pictures, gradients, and textures.

- You can also use borders to give a section of cells a special look.

- Adjust Pen Style, Pen Weight, and Pen Color options and then apply those formats to cell or table borders.

- You can apply the Cell Bevel effect to emphasize cells, or apply shadow or reflection effects to the table as a whole.

- You can also use the Format Shape task pane to apply formatting to the table or its cells.

Try It!   Modifying Cell Fill, Borders, and Effects

1 In the **P42TryA_xx** file, select the cells under the column header *Workshop Name*.

2 Click TABLE TOOLS DESIGN > Shading 🖌 ▾ .

3 Click Gold, Accent 2 in the Theme Colors palette.

4 With the cells still selected, click TABLE TOOLS DESIGN > Shading 🖌 ▾ > Gradient > More Gradients. The Format Shape task pane appears.

5 In the Format Shape task pane, click the Gradient fill option button. The cells fill with a default gradient. Close the Format Shape task pane.

6 Select the cells under *Ages*.

7 On the TABLE TOOLS DESIGN tab, click Pen Style and select the dashed line style. Click Pen Weight and click 2¼ pt. Click Pen Color 🖊 and click Red, Accent 6.

8 Click TABLE TOOLS DESIGN > Borders ▦ ▾ .

9 Click All Borders.

10 Select all the cells in the row containing the column labels.

11 Click TABLE TOOLS DESIGN > Effects 🔲 ▾ .

12 Click Cell Bevel and click the Cool Slant bevel style.

13 Click outside the table to see the effect of the beveling.

14 Save the **P42TryA_xx** file, and leave it open for the next Try It.

Add a border to cells

Adding an Image to a Table

- You can add a special touch to your tables by including pictures or textures.

- You might add pictures of products you're introducing, company logos, or images that represent particular programs or people.

- You cannot insert a pictures as an object in a table cell; you must instead insert the picture as a fill by using the Picture option on the Shading palette.

- After you select the Picture option, you can browse to a file on your computer, search the Web for an image, or search for an online picture from Office.com.

- If you choose an image that is not large enough to fill the selected area, PowerPoint will tile the image so the amount of space you selected is covered.

- Pictures may be distorted when they are inserted in table cells that have a height and width different from the picture. The cell will not automatically resize to fit the picture. You may need to adjust row height and column width to display the picture correctly.

- You can add an image to an individual cell or apply the image to the entire table background.

- An image added to the table background may be obscured by table style formatting you have already applied to the table. To see a table background, you may need to remove shading or other fills from the table cells.

- If you add an image to the table background, be sure to preview your slides to ensure that the text shows up against the image you have added.

Try It!   **Adding an Image to a Cell**

① In the **P42TryA_xx** file, click the first cell in column 3 beneath the column label.

② Click TABLE TOOLS DESIGN > Shading 🎨 > Picture.

③ Click Browse in the From a file area, navigate to the data files for this lesson, click **P42TryB_picture.jpg**, and click Insert.

④ Resize the row height and column width to display the photo without distortion.

⑤ In the rows below, insert two additional photos in the data files folder, **P42TryC_picture.jpg** and **P42TryD_picture.jpg**. Adjust row height as necessary.

⑥ Remove the unused table rows by right-clicking each row and choosing Delete Rows on the Mini toolbar.

⑦ Save the **P42Try_xx** file, and leave it open for the next Try It.

Add pictures to cells

Try It!   **Adding an Image to the Table Background**

1 In the **P42TryA_xx** file, click TABLE TOOLS DESIGN > Shading 🪣 ▾ > Table Background > Picture.

2 Click Browse, navigate to the data files for this lesson, and choose **P42TryE_picture.jpg**.

3 Click Insert. You will not see the background because of the table style shading.

4 Select all cells and click TABLE TOOLS DESIGN > Shading 🪣 ▾ > No Fill. The background image appears.

5 Close the **P42TryA_xx** file, saving changes, and exit PowerPoint.

Lesson 42—Practice

Thorn Hill Gardens wants you to work on several tables in a new presentation on the organization's events and workshops. In this project, you customize formats and add pictures to one of the tables.

DIRECTIONS

1. Start PowerPoint, if necessary, and open **P42PracticeA** from the data files for this lesson.

2. Save the presentation as **P42PracticeA_xx** in the location where your teacher instructs you to store the files for this lesson.

3. Display slide 2 and select the table.

4. On the TABLE TOOLS DESIGN tab, in the Table Style Options group, select **Header Row**, if necessary, and then select **First Column**.

5. In the Table Styles gallery, click the **Medium Style 1 – Accent 1** table style.

6. Adjust the table style by applying **Banded Columns**.

7. Click in the first cell under the Snapshot column heading.

8. Click **TABLE TOOLS DESIGN** > **Shading** 🪣 ▾ > **Picture**.

9. In the Insert Pictures dialog box, click in the Office.com Clip Art box and type **poinsettia**. Click **Search** 🔍 .

10. Choose a picture or photo in the search results and click **Insert**.

11. Click in the second cell under the Snapshot heading, and click **TABLE TOOLS DESIGN** > **Shading** 🪣 ▾ > **Picture**.

12. Click **Browse**, navigate to the location of the data files, click **P42PracticeB_picture.jpg**, and click **Insert**.

13. Repeat steps 11 and 12 to insert the **P42PracticeC_picture.jpg** file in the third cell under the Snapshot heading.

14. Adjust the height of the rows that contain pictures to **1.3"**.

15. Adjust the height of the column header row to **0.6"** and apply Center Vertically alignment.

16. With the column header row selected, click **TABLE TOOLS DESIGN** > **Effects** 🔲 ▾ > **Cell Bevel**. Click the **Angle** bevel option.

17. On the TABLE TOOLS DESIGN tab, in the Draw Borders group, click **Pen Style** and select the single line, click **Pen Weight** and select ¾ **pt**, and click **Pen Color** and select **Lime, Accent 1**. The Draw Table pointer becomes active.

18. Draw along the column borders from the header row to the bottom of the table to apply green border formatting to the columns, as shown in Figure 42-1 on the next page.

19. Preview the slide in Slide Show view, and then insert a footer with your name and the date on all slides.

20. **With your teacher's permission,** print slide 2. It should look similar to Figure 42-1.

21. Close the presentation, saving changes, and exit PowerPoint.

Figure 42-1

Thorn Hill Events

Event Name	When	Cost	Snapshot
Holidays at Thorn Hill	November 20 – January 1	$5 donation	
Spring Forward	February 2 – March 30	Free	
Butterfly Show	May 1 – July 31	$10/person	

Today's Date   FIRSTNAME LASTNAME

Lesson 42—Apply

In this project, you continue to work with the Thorn Hill presentation. You concentrate on the workshop table and improve its appearance by adding a picture background and customizing shading and border options.

DIRECTIONS

1. Start PowerPoint, if necessary, and open **P42ApplyA** from the data files for this lesson.

2. Save the presentation as **P42ApplyA_xx** in the location where your teacher instructs you to store the files for this lesson.

3. Display slide 3, select the table, and insert **P42ApplyB_picture.jpg** as the table background.

4. Select row 1 and apply shading of **Lime, Accent 1**. Then apply the **Linear Left** gradient from the Dark Variations gallery.

5. Select the cells in the first column below the *Program* heading.

6. Right-click the selected cells and click **Format Shape**.

7. In the Format Shape task pane, expand the **FILL** settings and click **Picture or texture fill**. Click the **Texture** down arrow and select the **Stationery** texture. Adjust transparency to **30%**.

8. To make it easier to read the text in the rest of the table, select the remaining unformatted cells, apply a **Solid fill** of **White, Background 1**, and adjust transparency to **30%**.

9. Change all borders in the table to a dotted or dashed line format with a weight and color of your choice.

10. Apply a Shadow effect of your choice to the table.

11. Insert your name and the date on all slides.

12. **With your teacher's permission,** print slide 3. It should look similar to Figure 42-2.

13. Close the presentation, saving changes, and exit PowerPoint.

Figure 42-2

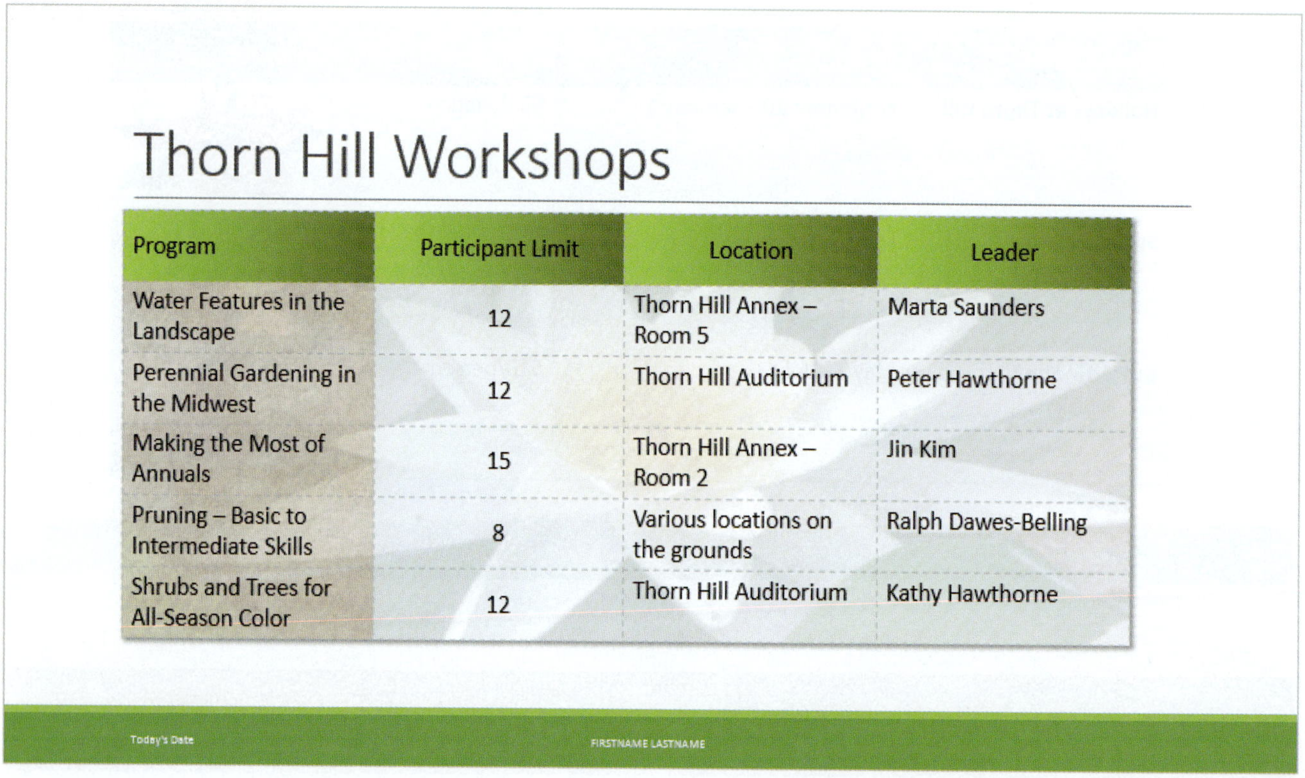

Thorn Hill Workshops

Program	Participant Limit	Location	Leader
Water Features in the Landscape	12	Thorn Hill Annex – Room 5	Marta Saunders
Perennial Gardening in the Midwest	12	Thorn Hill Auditorium	Peter Hawthorne
Making the Most of Annuals	15	Thorn Hill Annex – Room 2	Jin Kim
Pruning – Basic to Intermediate Skills	8	Various locations on the grounds	Ralph Dawes-Belling
Shrubs and Trees for All-Season Color	12	Thorn Hill Auditorium	Kathy Hawthorne

Today's Date   FIRSTNAME LASTNAME

Lesson 43

Formatting Charts

➤ What You Will Learn

Adding Trendlines and Error Bars

Formatting Chart Text

Fine-Tuning Chart Appearance

Software Skills   You can customize a chart by changing a wide variety of formatting options. Insert trendlines and error bars to make chart analysis easier. Apply font formatting to emphasize the chart text. Format any part of the chart to make it stand out on the slide.

What You Can Do

Adding Trendlines and Error Bars

■ PowerPoint includes a number of features you can use to add advanced formatting to your chart elements. You will explore some of those features in this lesson. Not all advanced formatting options are available for all types of charts.

■ Two advanced tools that can help you analyze and present your data are **trendlines** and **error bars**.

■ Trendlines show the progression of your data over time, and error bars show the amount of uncertainty that may be possible for the given data item.

■ You cannot add trendlines to 3-D, radar, pie, doughnut, or surface charts.

■ You can customize trendlines and error bars by changing the line color, style, regression type, and format.

WORDS TO KNOW

Error bars

A chart feature available for some chart types that enables you to display the amount of error that may be present in a graphed quantity.

Trendlines

A chart feature that displays a line showing the progression of value change over time.

Try It!   Adding and Modifying Trendlines

1 Start PowerPoint, and open **P43Try** from the data files for this lesson.

2 Save the presentation as **P43Try_xx** in the location where your teacher instructs you to store the files for this lesson.

3 Click slide 3 and click in the chart to select it.

4 Click the Chart Elements button ⊞ to display the pop-out menu of chart elements.

5 Click the Trendline check box to display the trendline. A default linear trendline appears on the chart.

6 With the Chart Elements menu still displayed, move the pointer to the right of Trendline to display the right-pointing arrow, and then click the arrow to display a menu of further options.

7 Click More Options to open the Format Trendline task pane.

8 In the Format Trendline task pane, click Moving Average.

9 Click the Fill & Line icon ◇ and select Solid Line.

10 Click the Color down arrow and choose Gold, Accent 5.

11 Click the Width up arrow until 3 pt appears.

12 Click the Begin Arrow type down arrow and select Diamond Arrow.

13 Click the End Arrow type down arrow and select Diamond Arrow.

14 On the chart, click the original linear trendline and press DEL to remove it.

15 Save the **P43Try_xx** file, and leave it open to use in the next Try It.

A trendline in a chart

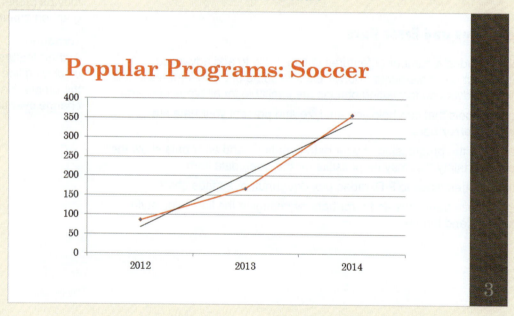

Popular Programs: Soccer

Try It! | **Adding Error Bars**

1 In the **P43Try_xx** file, click slide 4 and select the chart.

2 Click the Chart Elements button ➕ to display the menu of chart elements, and then click the Error Bars check box.

3 Click the right-pointing arrow to the right of Error Bars and then click More Options.

4 In the Add Error Bars dialog box, make sure 2012 is selected, and then click OK.

   ✓ *If the Add Error Bars dialog box does not appear, you have added error bars to only one series. Click Undo, select the outside border of the chart, and repeat steps 2 and 3.*

5 In the Format Error Bars task pane, click the Fill & Line icon ◊ and then click Gradient line.

6 Click the Preset gradients down arrow and select Medium Gradient – Accent 6.

7 Click the Width up arrow until 2.5 pt appears.

   ✓ *Note that the changes are applied only to the data series currently selected. To modify another set of error bars, choose the data series by clicking on the chart.*

8 Close the Format Error Bars task pane.

9 Save the **P43Try_xx** file, and leave it open to use in the next Try It.

The chart with formatted error bars

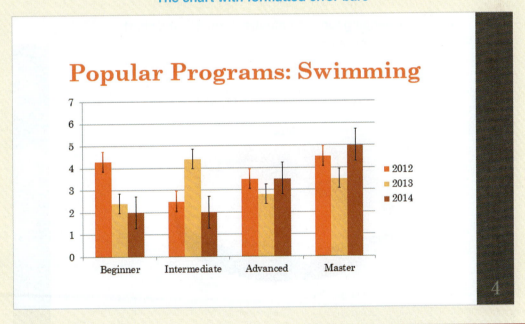

Formatting Chart Text

- You can change formats for any text that appears on a chart. Adjust font, font size, font style, or font color to emphasize text.

- By default, numbers that appear on chart axes use the General number style, unless you have applied number formatting in the data sheet used to create the chart.

- In the Format task pane, you can adjust number formatting for the specific chart element.

- To fine-tune the appearance of axis labels, you can adjust alignment and text direction. You can also specify an angle on which to set labels, which can be helpful when you have a number of axis labels that would otherwise crowd each other.

Try It!   **Formatting Chart Text**

1 In the **P43Try_xx** file, display slide 2.

2 Click the legend to select it.

3 Click HOME > Font Size > 14, and then click Bold **B** .

4 Click the Chart Elements button **+** , point to Data Labels, click the right-pointing arrow, and select More Options.

5 In the Format Data Labels task pane, with LABEL OPTIONS selected, click Inside End in the Label Position options.

6 Click NUMBER to expand those options.

7 Click the Category down arrow and click Currency.

8 In the Decimal places box, type **0**.

9 Click TEXT OPTIONS. In the TEXT FILL area, click the Color down arrow and select Black, Text 1.

10 Display slide 4 and click the horizontal axis to select it.

11 In the Format Axis task pane, click TEXT OPTIONS and then click the Textbox icon.

12 Click the Custom angle box and type **-20**.

13 Close the Format Axis task pane.

14 Save the **P43Try_xx** file, and leave it open for the next Try It.

Changing font and number formats on a chart

Fine-Tuning Chart Appearance

■ PowerPoint offers many ways to customize the appearance of charts.

- You can choose to start numbering on an axis from a particular value, and select numbering intervals.

- You can add axis labels to provide more information about the data.

- For column and bar charts, you can adjust the gap and overlap of series columns and bars.

- You can change the appearance of a specific data series with a new fill. For a line chart, you can format the markers to make them stand out more.

- You can customize the plot or chart background to improve appearance.

■ When applying a number of different formats to a chart, you can save time in selecting the element to format by clicking the down arrow next to the currently selected element in the Format task pane to display a drop-down list of other elements.

■ Clicking an element in this list displays the task pane options for that element.

Try It!   **Changing Axis Formats**

① In the **P43Try_xx** file, display slide 3 and click the chart to select it.

② Click the Chart Elements button ⊞ and point to Gridlines. Click the right-pointing arrow and then click Primary Major Vertical to add vertical gridlines to the chart.

③ With the Chart Elements menu still displayed, click the Axis Titles check box, click the right-pointing arrow, and deselect Primary Horizontal.

④ With the default axis title displayed on the vertical axis, type **Participants**.

⑤ Right-click the vertical axis and click Format Axis to display the Format Axis task pane.

⑥ Under Units, change Major to 25.0.

⑦ Under Bounds, change Minimum to 75.0 and press ENTER .

⑧ Save the **P43Try_xx** file, and leave it open for the next Try It.

Try It!   **Changing the Appearance of Data Series**

① In the **P43Try_xx** file, click the orange data series line on the chart to display the Format Data Series task pane.

② Click the Fill & Line icon ◇. In the LINE settings, click the Width up arrow until 4 pt appears.

③ Click MARKER to display the settings for the data markers, and then click MARKER OPTIONS to expand those settings.

④ Click Built-in, click the Type down arrow, and click one of the large square shapes. Then click the Size up arrow until 16 appears.

Line chart formats

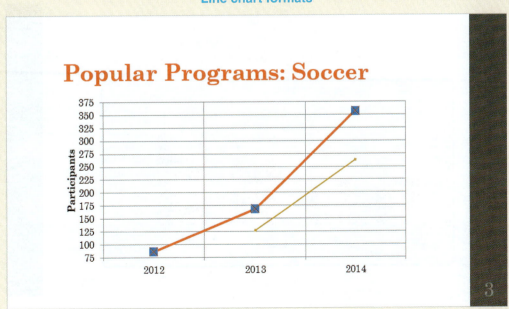

Popular Programs: Soccer

(continued)

Try It!   **Changing the Appearance of Data Series** (continued)

5 Display slide 4 and select the chart by clicking its outside border. The task pane should be Format Chart Area.

6 In the task pane, click the down arrow to the right of CHART OPTIONS to see a list of chart elements.

7 Click Series "2013" to select that data series on the chart and display series options in the task pane.

8 In the FILL settings, click Gradient fill and then apply the Bottom Spotlight – Accent 2 preset gradient.

9 Click the Series Options icon ▮▮.

10 Click the Series Overlap down arrow until -10% appears.

11 Save the **P43Try_xx** file, and leave it open for the next Try It.

Try It!   **Formatting a Chart Background**

1 In the **P43Try_xx** file, click the down arrow next to SERIES OPTIONS in the task pane and click Chart Area.

2 Click the Fill & Line icon ◇, and then click Picture or texture fill in the FILL settings.

3 Click the Texture down arrow and then click the Water droplets texture.

4 Change the transparency setting to 30%.

5 Scroll down in the task pane to display the BORDER settings.

6 In the BORDER settings:

    a. Click Solid line.

    b. Click the Color down arrow and click Blue from Standard Colors.

    c. Click the Width up arrow until 3 pt appears.

7 Click the Rounded corners check box at the bottom of the task pane, and then close the task pane.

8 Close the **P43Try_xx** file, saving changes, and exit PowerPoint.

Column chart formats

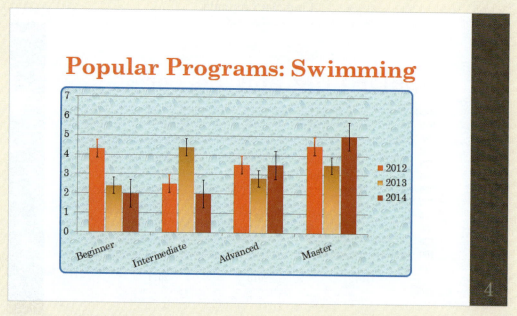

Lesson 43—Practice

Jones & Madden Realty is preparing a presentation on housing sales and trends in a city neighborhood. In this project, you work on the charts included in the presentation to improve their usefulness and appearance.

DIRECTIONS

1. Start PowerPoint, if necessary, and open **P43Practice** from the data files for this lesson.

2. Save the presentation as **P43Practice_xx** in the location where your teacher instructs you to store the files for this lesson.

3. Display slide 3.

4. Click one of the **Single-Family** bars to select that data series.

5. Click the **Chart Elements** button ➕ and then click **Trendline** to add a trendline for the Single-Family series.

6. Right-click the trendline and select **Format Trendline**.

7. Click the **Fill & Line** icon ◇, click the Color down arrow and select **Tan, Accent 6**, click the **Width** up arrow until **3 pt** appears, and apply the **Oval Arrow** beginning and ending arrows.

8. Click the down arrow next to TRENDLINE OPTIONS in the Format Trendline task pane and click **Horizontal (Value) Axis**.

9. Click the Axis Options icon ▮▮▮. In the AXIS OPTIONS settings, click the Display units down arrow and select **Millions**.

10. Click **NUMBER** to expand those settings. Click the **Category** down arrow and select **Number**, and then click in the Decimal places box and type **1**.

11. Display slide 5 and click the chart title to select it.

12. Click **HOME** > **Font Size** > **20**, and then click **Bold** B .

13. In the Format Chart Title task pane, click the down arrow to the right of TITLE OPTIONS and select **Plot Area**.

14. Click **Gradient fill**, then click the **Preset gradients** down arrow and select **Medium Gradient – Accent 6**.

15. Click the **Direction** down arrow and click **Linear Diagonal – Bottom Right to Top Left**. Your slide should look similar to Figure 43-1 on the next page.

16. Preview the presentation to see your chart formats. Then insert your name, slide numbers, and the date on all slides.

17. **With your teacher's permission,** print the presentation as handouts with 6 slides per page.

18. Close the presentation, saving changes, and exit PowerPoint.

Figure 43-1

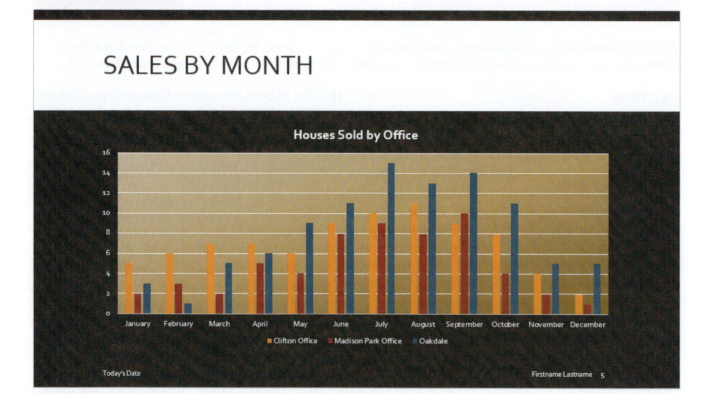

Lesson 43—Apply

In this project, you continue working for Jones & Madden to customize charts for the sales presentation.

DIRECTIONS

1. Start PowerPoint, if necessary, and open **P43Apply** from the data files for this lesson.

2. Save the presentation as **P43Apply_xx** in the location where your teacher instructs you to store the files for this lesson.

3. Display slide 3. Right-click the trendline and click **Delete** to remove it.

4. Add error bars to the chart on slide 3. On the submenu, choose **Percentage**.

5. Choose to format the error bars for the Single-Family series. Change the color to **Tan, Text 2** and the width to **2.5 pt**.

6. Display slide 4. Display the primary major vertical gridlines.

7. Change the units of display for the vertical axis to **Thousands**, then apply **Number** formatting with **1** decimal place.

8. Change the Minimum under Bounds to **6000.0**.

9. Increase the font size of the text for both axes to **16**.

10. Apply different line markers for each line on the line chart and adjust the line weight to show up more clearly.

11. Add a fill of your choice to the chart's plot area. Your slide might look similar to Figure 43-2 on the next page.

12. Display slide 5. Click any column for the Oakdale series. In the Format Data Series task pane, change Series Overlap to 0%. Change Gap Width to 100%.

13. Preview the presentation and make any necessary adjustments. Then insert your name, slide numbers, and the date on all slides.

14. **With your teacher's permission,** print the presentation as handouts with 6 slides per page.

15. Close the presentation, saving changes, and exit PowerPoint.

Figure 43-2

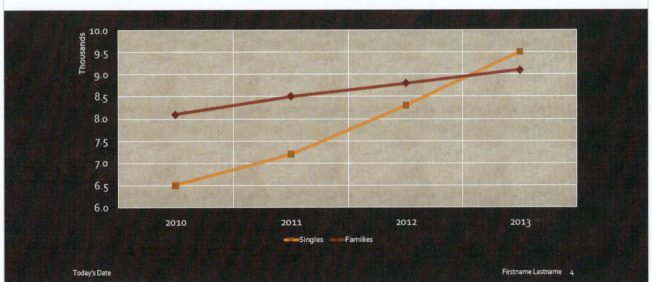

End-of-Chapter Activities

➤ PowerPoint Chapter 6—Critical Thinking

Analyzing Data and Preparing a Multimedia Presentation

You work for Harris Inc., a marketing firm that has been hired by your local chamber of commerce to prepare a presentation on tourism in your city. The chamber of commerce wants to see some information on top attractions in your area and has asked Harris to focus on the most popular destination.

In this project, working alone or in teams, you will research on the Internet to find information on what attractions in your area are considered the most popular by travelers and travel guide Web sites. (If you live in a small community, research attractions in a nearby city or in a city you would like to visit.) You will use a table to list the top five attractions and a chart to rank them by popularity. You will use several slides to concentrate on the most popular attraction, giving information about the attraction and including pictures and, if available, a video that relates to the attraction. You will apply advanced animation effects to give the presentation additional visual interest.

DIRECTIONS

1. Start a new presentation, and save it as **PCT06_xx** in the location where your teacher instructs you to store the files for this chapter.

2. Insert the title **Top Attractions in** and add the name of your city or the city you would like to research. In the subtitle placeholder, type **A Presentation by** and then insert your first name and last name.

3. Apply a theme and variant of your choice.

4. Add a slide that gives some basic information about your chosen city.

5. **With your teacher's permission**, use the Web to research the topics listed above. Use valid and reputable sites for your research and make a rough table of the most popular attractions in your city. You should try to find information from at least three travel information sites, and you should try to rank the sites according to how often they are mentioned first, second, third, and so on.

6. Add a new slide and draw a table to organize the information on which attractions in your area are listed most often by travel writers. In the first column, list as many attractions as you have room for on the slide. In the other columns, type the names of the Web sites as the column headers. Use a simple X to indicate which Web site mentioned each location.

7. Apply advanced table formatting to improve the appearance of the table: apply and adjust a table style, apply additional shading and border formats, and adjust cell widths and table size to present the information clearly. If you have an appropriate image of your city, you may want to use it as a background image for the table. Or, you may search for an image online.

   ✓ Be sure to supply a credit line for the location where you find the image.

8. Work out a system you can use to create number values for each attraction; for example, each instance where an attraction is ranked first is 5, each instance where it is ranked second is 4, and so on. Add up all of the rankings for each attraction.

9. Add a slide and create a column chart that shows the rankings of the top destinations. You may not want to use all the attractions listed in the table on slide 4—only the most popular.

10. Apply advanced chart formatting to improve the appearance of the chart: add or remove chart elements, adjust text formatting, change the appearance of the data series, apply a plot or chart background, and so on.

11. Add a slide that lists the top destination, as determined by your chart. If you have pictures of the attraction, add them to this slide, or search online for suitable pictures.

✓ *If you find pictures online, be sure to supply a credit line for each image.*

12. Use advanced picture formatting to improve the images on the slide: apply corrections and effects, crop to a shape, or use a picture as a fill for a shape.

13. Search for sounds or music appropriate to your top attraction and add one to the slide with the pictures. Adjust audio formats as necessary.

14. Search for online video that relates to your top attraction. If any video clips are available, add one to a slide with an appropriate slide title. Make any necessary adjustments to the video using advanced video settings.

✓ *Be sure to supply a credit line for the video, if appropriate.*

15. Check spelling.

16. Animate the chart to have each column fly in separately. Then add an emphasis effect to only the column of the most popular attraction. Using the timeline, adjust timing to allow viewers enough time to understand the importance of each column before the next one appears.

17. Animate the pictures you inserted, using a variety of animation effects. Insert a text box with text such as *Click here* that will act as a trigger to animate the images. At least one animation should use a motion path.

18. Preview the presentation and then make any necessary corrections and adjustments. Insert your name and the date on all slides.

19. Deliver the presentation to your class. Ask for comments on how the presentation could be improved.

20. **With your teacher's permission**, print the presentation as handouts. Then compress and optimize all media in the presentation.

21. Close the presentation, saving changes, and exit PowerPoint.

➤ PowerPoint Chapter 6—Portfolio Builder

Glacier National Park Presentation

Voyager Travel Adventures is finalizing a presentation on its newest adventure location, Glacier National Park. In this project, you complete some final tasks on the presentation, including applying advanced image formats, improving the appearance of a chart, creating and formatting a table, and adding animations.

DIRECTIONS

1. Start PowerPoint, if necessary, and open **PPB06A** from the data files for this chapter.

2. Save the presentation as **PPB06A_xx** in the location where your teacher instructs you to store the files for this chapter.

3. On slide 1, insert **PPB06B_picture.jpg** as a fill for the mountain shape. Adjust the saturation of the picture to **200%**.

4. Animate the title to **Fade** in by word, with a **35%** delay between words. Set the animation to occur **After Previous**.

5. Animate the subtitle to **Float In** and then change color to black. Set the animation to occur **After Previous**.

6. On slide 3, modify the chart as follows:

   a. Change the display units for the vertical axis to **Millions**. Change the Minimum under Bounds to **1500000.0**.

   b. Insert a Linear trendline and format it to stand out on the chart.

   c. Change the title to **Visitors per Year**, and remove the legend.

   d. Format all chart text as boldface, except for the *Millions* label. Format *Millions* in italic.

   e. Apply a fill of your choice to the chart area, and then change the color of gridlines if necessary to show up well.

7. On slide 4, apply the **Float In** animation effect to the SmartArt diagram. Use the **After Previous** start option, and animate each element of the graphic so that the picture and the description appear at the same time. Use the timeline to create **2.5** second delays to adjust the appearance of each element.

8. On slide 5, insert an online audio clip of a train. Set the sound to play across slides if it is fairly long, set the volume to medium, and choose to hide the clip during the presentation. Set it to play automatically.

9. On slide 7, select the leftmost image in the top row and use the Corrections button to increase sharpness by **25%** and contrast by **20%**.

10. Select all of the images on the slide and apply the **Simple Frame, White** picture style. Then use the Picture Border button to change the border color to **Olive Green, Accent 3, Lighter 40%**.

11. Animate the images by using the **Zoom** effect, from **Slide Center**, **After Previous**. Use the Animation Painter to apply the same effect settings to each image in whatever order you wish. Use the timeline to adjust timing. Adjust the rotation of the images to make a more interesting display.

12. On slide 8, make the following changes.

    a. Apply one of the soft edge picture formats to each image and change the size of each image to approximately 3.0 wide.

    b. Stack the images so they are centered on each other in the middle of the slide.

    c. Use motion path settings to move each picture to a new location on the slide. Make sure each starts **After Previous**.

13. Add a new Title Only slide at the end of the presentation and insert the title **Adventure Packages**.

14. Draw a table on slide 10 into which you can copy the information from the content area of slide 9. Format the material as follows. (See Illustration 6A on the next page.)

    a. Place the text *Short Tours* and *Full Tours* in a column to the left of the tabular information and change text rotation to **270°**.

b. Center the rotated text vertically and horizontally, and center the remaining table text vertically.

c. Apply shading colors and fills to make it easy to differentiate the short tour and full tour information.

d. Apply formatting such as gradients to improve the visual appearance.

e. Apply an effect such as Shadow to the table.

15. Delete slide 9.

16. Insert the date, slide number, and a footer with your full name on all slides.

17. Preview the presentation and then make any necessary corrections and adjustments to transitions and other effects.

18. Deliver the presentation to your class. Ask for comments on how the presentation could be improved.

19. **With your teacher's permission,** print the presentation.

20. Close the presentation, saving changes, and exit PowerPoint.

Illustration 6A

Adventure Packages

	Days	Lodging	Meals Provided
Short Tours	4	Glacier Park Lodge	Breakfast, Dinner
	4	Village Inn at Apgar	None
	4	Rising Sun Cabin	Breakfast
Full Tours	Days	Lodging	Meals Provided
	6	Swiftcurrent Inn, Lake McDonald Lodge	Breakfast, Dinner
	6	Many Glacier Hotel, St. Mary Lodge	Breakfast, Dinner

Today's Date
FIRSTNAME LASTNAME

9

Chapter 7

(Courtesy Konstantin Chagin/Shutterstock)

Finalizing and Sharing a Presentation

Lesson 44

Making a Presentation Accessible to Everyone

> ## ➤ What You Will Learn
>
> **Adding Narration to a Presentation**
> **Working with Advanced Accessibility Options**

WORDS TO KNOW

Alternative text
Text associated with a picture or other object that conveys in words what can be seen in the object.

Software Skills   Add narration to a presentation to allow people with visual challenges to hear your content. Supplying accessibility information such as alternative text descriptions of pictures and other objects can also help a viewer to understand your presentation.

What You Can Do

Adding Narration to a Presentation

- One way to ensure that your presentation is accessible is to add narration to the presentation. Narration can help those who have visual impairments to understand your points.

- Narration can also be helpful in a self-running slide show to explain or emphasize your points to viewers. Narration takes precedence over all other sounds on a slide.

- To record narration, your computer must have a microphone, speakers, and sound card.

- Before you begin adding narration to slides, make sure your microphone is working correctly.

- To record narration, use the Record Slide Show button on the SLIDE SHOW tab.

- When you select whether to start at the beginning of the presentation or at the current slide, the presentation begins in Slide Show view so you can match your narration to each slide.

- You also have the option to record timings and narration or just narration.

■ You will see that each slide to which you added narration has a sound icon displayed in the lower-right corner. Viewers can click the icons to hear your narration, or you can use the AUDIO TOOLS PLAYBACK tab to specify that the narration will play automatically.

■ Before you begin, remember these tips.
- Click through the entire presentation at least once, reading each slide's content.
- Don't begin reading until the timer indicates 0:00:01.
- If you make a mistake, keep reading (especially if you're also recording timings). Remember you can always go back and redo a single slide.

Try It!   **Adding Narration to a Presentation**

1 Start PowerPoint, and open **P44Try** from the data files for this lesson.

2 Save the presentation as **P44Try_xx** in the location where your teacher instructs you to store the files for this lesson.

3 On the SLIDE SHOW tab, click the Record Slide Show down arrow.

4 Click Start Recording from Beginning.

5 If you have a microphone attached to your computer, select both options in the Record Slide Show box. If you don't have a microphone set up, you may not have the option of selecting Narrations and laser pointer. Click Start Recording.

6 When the slide show opens, read the text on the slide as clearly as possible. Be sure to time your reading with the way the text appears on screen.

7 When you've finished with slide 1, click the screen to move to the next slide.

8 Continue recording the slide text until the end of the presentation.

9 Save the **P44Try_xx** file, and leave it open to use in the next Try It.

Record Slide Show dialog box

Working with Advanced Accessibility Options

■ Ensuring that presentations are accessible to all viewers can require you to do some behind-the-scenes work.

■ Use the Accessibility Checker to identify issues that could make the presentation difficult to understand for persons with disabilities.

■ You will remember that the Accessibility Checker task pane divides issues into three categories.
- Errors are issues you should definitely fix if you want all viewers to be able to understand content.
- Warnings are issues you do not necessarily have to fix but could fix for best comprehension by all viewers.
- Tips give you suggestions for ways to improve content.

■ Use the instructions in the Accessibility Checker task pane to help you make the necessary corrections.

■ Missing Alt Text is a very common accessibility error, especially in presentations that contain pictures and other graphics. You provide **alternative text** to describe images for viewers who cannot see them.

■ The Accessibility Checker will also always prompt you to check reading order—to make sure a screen reader will read content in the order you want. You will usually want the slide title to be read first, followed by text in the content placeholder.

■ If you have added sounds or narration to a presentation, you may also be prompted to supply captions for the audio content to meet the needs of those with hearing challenges.

Try It!   **Working with Advanced Accessibility Options**

1 In the **P44Try_xx** file, display slide 1.

2 Click FILE > Check for Issues ⚇ > Check Accessibility. The Accessibility Checker task pane opens with a list of issues to check and correct.

3 View the Missing Alt Text errors. You do not need to supply alternative text for the Audio objects, but you should supply alternative text for the images and the table.

4 On slide 3, right-click the butterfly image, and then click Format Picture. In the Format Picture task pane, click the Size & Properties icon 🖃.

5 Scroll down, if necessary, and expand the ALT TEXT heading.

6 In the Title box, type **Butterfly Image 1**. In the Description box, type **Butterfly shape filled with a picture of an orange flower**.

> ✓ *Notice that as you supply alternative text, the error is removed from the Accessibility Checker list.*

7 Display slide 4 and select the butterfly image. Supply the alternative text title **Butterfly Image 2** and the description **Butterfly shape with a green floral fill**.

8 Display slide 5 and select the table. Supply the alternative text title **Thorn Hill Workshops** and the description **Information about workshops at Thorn Hill Gardens, including programs for water features, perennial gardening, annuals, pruning, and shrubs and trees**.

9 In the Accessibility Checker task pane, view the suggestions under TIPS. You do not need to supply captions for the audio files, because they consist of narration you read directly from the slides. Under Check Reading Order, click Slide 1 to go to that slide.

10 To check reading order, click HOME > Select ▷ > Selection Pane. Objects are read from the bottom of this pane to the top. Content on slide 1 is in the correct order, with the title at the bottom, the subtitle next, and then the narration audio object.

11 Check the reading order for the remaining slides. On slide 4, move the TextBox 4 object to be the third object from the bottom of the list. Then close the Selection and the Accessibility Checker task panes.

12 Close the **P44Try_xx** file, saving changes, and exit PowerPoint.

Checking reading order for slide content

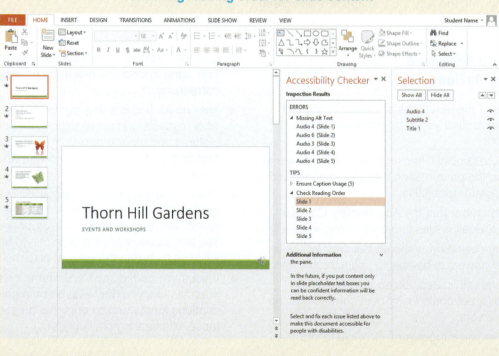

Lesson 44—Practice

Peterson Home Healthcare is preparing information for its annual board meeting. Several of the board members have physical challenges that you need to address as you are preparing presentations. In this project, you add narration to a presentation about options for upgrading IT equipment throughout the company.

DIRECTIONS

1. Start PowerPoint, if necessary, and open **P44Practice** from the data files for this lesson.

2. Save the presentation as **P44Practice_xx** in the location where your teacher instructs you to store the files for this lesson.

3. Create a footer with your name in it.

4. Click **SLIDE SHOW** > **Record Slide Show** > **Start Recording from Beginning**.

5. If you have a microphone attached to your computer, select both options in the Record Slide Show box.

6. Click **Start Recording** to begin.

7. Read the contents of each slide until you reach the end of the presentation.

8. Click **SLIDE SHOW** > **From Beginning** to listen to your narration.

9. Select slide 4 and in the Stage 2 box, place the insertion point at the beginning of the bullet point. Type **Hire a contractor** and press ENTER .

10. Click **SLIDE SHOW** > **Record Slide Show** > **Start Recording from Current Slide**.

11. Select the same options in the Record Slide Show box that you chose for the initial recording and click **Start Recording**.

12. Read the entire slide and then close the recording box.

13. **With your teacher's permission**, print slide 4. It should look like Figure 44-1.

14. Close the presentation, saving changes, and exit PowerPoint.

Figure 44-1

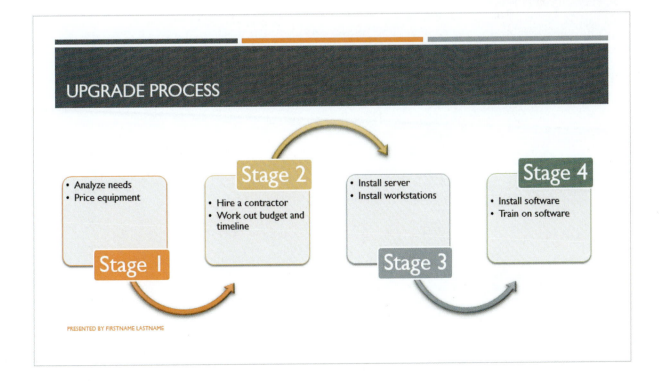

UPGRADE PROCESS

- Analyze needs
- Price equipment

Stage 1

Stage 2
- Hire a contractor
- Work out budget and timeline

- Install server
- Install workstations

Stage 3

Stage 4
- Install software
- Train on software

PRESENTED BY FIRSTNAME LASTNAME

Lesson 44—Apply

In this project, you continue to work on the presentation for Peterson Home Healthcare. You check accessibility for the slides and make the necessary corrections to ensure that all viewers will be able to understand the presentation.

DIRECTIONS

1. Start PowerPoint, if necessary, and open **P44Apply** from the data files for this lesson.

2. Save the presentation as **P44Apply_xx** in the location where your teacher instructs you to store the files for this lesson.

3. Create a footer with your name in it.

4. Run the Accessibility Checker, and review the errors and tips listed in the Accessibility Checker task pane.

5. On slide 1, provide alternative text for the clip art image, supplying both a title and a description.

6. On slide 2, provide alternative text for the photo, supplying both a title and a description.

7. On slides 3 and 4, provide alternative text for the SmartArt diagrams.

8. Check the reading order on each slide and correct the order if necessary. Make sure the narration always appears just below the footer placeholder in the list of items that will be read.

9. Close the presentation, saving changes, and exit PowerPoint.

Lesson 45

Saving a Presentation in Other Formats

➤ What You Will Learn

Saving Slides As Pictures
Creating a Picture Presentation
Saving a Presentation in PDF or XPS Format

Software Skills   Save slides or a presentation in a picture format so the slides can be used in other applications. You can save a presentation in other formats that make it easy to share the presentation with colleagues or clients.

What You Can Do

Saving Slides As Pictures

- You can save a single slide or an entire presentation in a graphic file format that allows you to insert the slides as pictures in other applications, such as Word documents.

- By saving a slide or presentation as a picture, you can ensure that it is viewable by anyone with a computer regardless of whether they have a Mac or PC computer or what version of software they are using.

- Use the Change File Type option on the Export tab in Backstage view to save a slide or presentation as a picture.

- You can choose among four picture file formats.
  - PNG and JPEG are listed on the Change File Type tab.
  - If you prefer GIF or TIFF, you can use the Save As button at the bottom of the tab and choose either option in the Save as type list.

- Once you have provided a name for the new file, selected a format, and issued the Save command, PowerPoint displays a dialog box to ask if you want to save only the current slide or every slide in the current presentation.

- The resulting files can be used just like any other picture file.

Try It!   **Saving Slides As Pictures**

1 Start PowerPoint, and open **P45TryA** from the data files for this lesson.

2 Save the presentation as **P45TryA_xx** in the location where your teacher instructs you to store the files for this lesson.

3 Display slide 3.

4 Click FILE > Export > Change File Type.

5 Click JPEG File Interchange Format and then click Save As.

6 Change the file name to **P45TryB_xx** and make sure the file location is the folder where you are storing files for this lesson.

7 Click Save.

8 Select Just This One at the prompt.

9 In Word, open **P45TryC** from the data files for this lesson.

10 Position the insertion point on the blank line following the first paragraph of the memo, and then click INSERT > Pictures.

11 Navigate to the location where you are storing files for this lesson, click **P45TryB_xx.jpg**, and click Insert.

12 Resize the inserted picture to 5" wide, center it, and use PICTURE TOOLS FORMAT > Picture Border to apply a Lime, Accent 1 border.

13 Save the document as **P45TryC_xx** in the location where your teacher instructs you to store the files for this lesson.

14 Close the document and Word. Leave the **P45TryA_xx** file open in PowerPoint for the next Try It.

A slide used as an illustration in a document

Thorn Hill Gardens

5656 Winston Pike
Oxford, OH 45056

To: All Staff

From: Rachel Cummins

Subject: Upcoming Events

Date: March 21, 2015

Greetings, all. The new presentation covering events and workshops has been uploaded to the kiosk in the main lobby. I think you'll like the new, clean, bright PowerPoint 2013 formats. See the picture below of the slide advertising the Butterfly Show.

Butterflies in the Garden

Join us at Thorn Hill Gardens for the Tenth Annual Butterfly Celebration
· May 1 through July 31
· Open every day in the Arboretum
· 9:00 a.m. – 5:00 p.m.

The Communications Staff will continue to create and upload presentations for upcoming events as the need arises. We welcome input from all staff members. If you know of information that should be added to our slides, let us know.

Creating a Picture Presentation

- When you save slides as pictures using a picture file type, you create separate graphic files. This is the option to use if you need to insert a picture of a slide in a standard graphic format.

- You have another option for saving a presentation so that its slides become pictures.

- The PowerPoint Picture Presentation format, which can be selected from the Save as type list, transforms each slide in the presentation to a picture.

- You might use this option if you want to share a presentation but you do not want the recipient to be able to edit the presentation.

- Because all objects on a slide become part of a single picture, the presentation's file size may be smaller than the presentation from which it was created. This is often helpful when you are sharing a presentation via e-mail.

- A picture presentation uses the same .pptx extension as a default PowerPoint presentation.

Try It!   Creating a Picture Presentation

1. In the **P45TryA_xx** file, click FILE > Export > Change File Type > Save as Another File Type, and then click Save As.

2. Change the file name to **P45TryD_xx**.

3. Click the Save as type down arrow and select PowerPoint Picture Presentation.

4. Click Save, and then click OK when you see the information box about how the presentation has been saved.

5. In File Explorer, navigate to the location where you are saving files for this lesson.

6. Position the pointer over the **P45TryA_xx** file to see a ScreenTip with properties, including the file size.

7. Now point to the **P45TryD_xx** file and compare the size of the file to that of the original PowerPoint presentation.

8. Double-click **P45TryD_xx** to open it.

9. Click on the first slide to see the selection box that surrounds the entire slide, indicating that it is a single picture.

10. Close the **P45TryD_xx** file. Leave the **P45TryA_xx** file open to use in the next Try It.

Saving a Presentation in PDF or XPS Format

- Another way you can prepare a presentation for sharing with others is to save it in PDF or XPS format.

- PDF, or Portable Document Format, is a format that preserves the look of a page or a slide so that a viewer can see the content without being able to edit it.

- XPS, or XML Paper Specification, is a Microsoft document format that preserves page content as PDF does.

- When you choose to save as PDF or XPS, by default PowerPoint will save the presentation as slides, with the slides proceeding one after another in the document.

- If you choose the Options button in the Publish as PDF or XPS dialog box, you can choose to save the presentation as handouts or notes pages, or in outline view. You can choose which slides to publish and choose among other options such as whether to apply a frame to slides or include comments and markup.

- Your PDF or XPS reader opens by default after you publish the presentation to enable you to review the presentation in its new format.

Try It!   Saving a Presentation in PDF or XPS Format

1   In the **P45TryA_xx** file, click FILE > Export > Create PDF/XPS Document, and then click the Create PDF/XPS button.

2   In the Publish as PDF or XPS dialog box, change the file name to **P45TryE_xx**, and then click the Options button.

3   In the Options dialog box, in the Publish options area, click the Publish what down arrow and select Handouts. Then click the Frame slides check box.

4   Click OK, and then click Publish.

5   Your PDF or XPS reader opens to display the published handouts.

6   Navigate back to the presentation.

7   Close the **P45TryA_xx** file, saving changes, and exit PowerPoint.

Handouts published to PDF

1

Lesson 45—Practice

Planet Earth is preparing materials for a presentation at the Civic Garden Center on what every homeowner can do to promote a healthy natural environment. In this project, you save a slide as a picture and then insert it in an Excel worksheet. Then you save the presentation in picture format to archive the presentation in a smaller file size.

DIRECTIONS

1. Start PowerPoint, if necessary, and open **P45PracticeA** from the data files for this lesson.

2. Save the presentation as **P45PracticeA_xx** in the location where your teacher instructs you to store the files for this lesson.

3. Display slide 4.

4. Click **FILE** > **Export** > **Change File Type** > **JPEG File Interchange Format**, and then click **Save As**.

5. Navigate to the location where you are storing files for this lesson, and change the file name to **P45PracticeB_xx**.

6. Click **Save**.

7. Click **Just This One**.

8. Start Excel, and open **P45PracticeC** from the data files for this lesson.

9. Save the worksheet as **P45PracticeC_xx** in the location where your teacher instructs you to store the files for this lesson.

10. Click cell A3, and then click **INSERT** > **Pictures** 🖾.

11. Navigate to the location where you are storing files for this lesson, click **P45PracticeB_xx**, and then click **Insert**.

12. Resize the picture to **5"** wide, and adjust its position to fit in the blank rows between the *Compost Initiative* heading and the worksheet data.

13. With the picture still selected, click **PICTURE TOOLS FORMAT** > **Picture Border** 🖉 and select **Green, Accent 1**.

14. **With your teacher's permission,** print the worksheet. Your printout should look similar to Figure 45-1.

15. Close the **P45PracticeC_xx** file, saving changes, and exit Excel.

16. In the **P45PracticeA_xx** file, click **FILE** > **Export** > **Change File Type** > **Save as Another File Type**, and then click **Save As**.

17. Change the file name to **P45PracticeD_xx**, click the **Save as type** down arrow, and click **PowerPoint Picture Presentation**.

18. Click **Save**, and then click **OK**.

19. Close the presentation, saving changes, and exit PowerPoint.

Figure 45-1

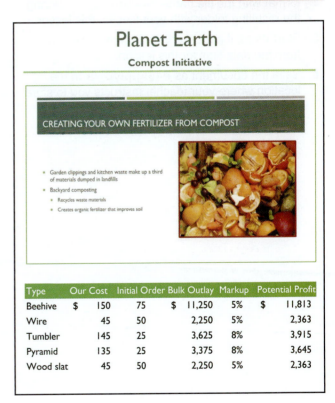

Lesson 45—Apply

In this project, you continue working with the Planet Earth presentation. You save all slides as pictures so that you can insert them in a Word document you have prepared to help you deliver the presentation. Then you save the presentation as a PDF so that you can easily e-mail it to the Planet Earth communications coordinator for approval.

DIRECTIONS

1. Start PowerPoint, if necessary, and open **P45ApplyA** from the data files for this lesson.

2. Save the presentation as **P45ApplyA_xx** in the location where your teacher instructs you to store the files for this lesson.

3. Insert your name and the date on all slides. For notes and handouts, insert your name and the date in the header.

4. Export all slides in the presentation in JPEG format with the file name **P45ApplyB_xx**, storing the resulting folder with your files for this lesson.

5. Start Word, if necessary, and open **P45ApplyC** from the data files for this lesson.

6. Save the document as **P45ApplyC_xx** in the location where your teacher instructs you to store the files for this lesson.

7. Click in the first cell under the Image heading, and then choose to insert pictures and navigate to the **P45ApplyB_xx** folder. Open the folder and select **Slide1.JPG**.

8. Resize the picture to **3.5"** wide.

9. Insert the remaining three slides in the appropriate table cells.

10. **With your teacher's permission,** print the Word document. The first page should look similar to Figure 45-2 on the next page.

11. Close the **P45ApplyC_xx** document, saving changes, and exit Word.

12. In the **P45ApplyA_xx** file, save the presentation in PDF format with the name **P45ApplyD_xx** as handouts with 4 slides per page, and frames around the slides.

13. Close the presentation, saving changes, and exit PowerPoint.

Figure 45-2

Saving the Earth:
What Can You Do in Your Own Back Yard?

Presentation Script

Slide	Remarks	Image
1	Introduce Planet Earth and the topic of the current presentation: what every homeowner can do at his or her residence to promote green initiatives and a healthy ecosystem.	
2	Discuss landscaping and point out how healthy and attractive plantings can not only add value to a home but can also provide important habitat areas for wildlife Define hardscaping and point out that paths should be in good repair and in scale with both the garden and the house.	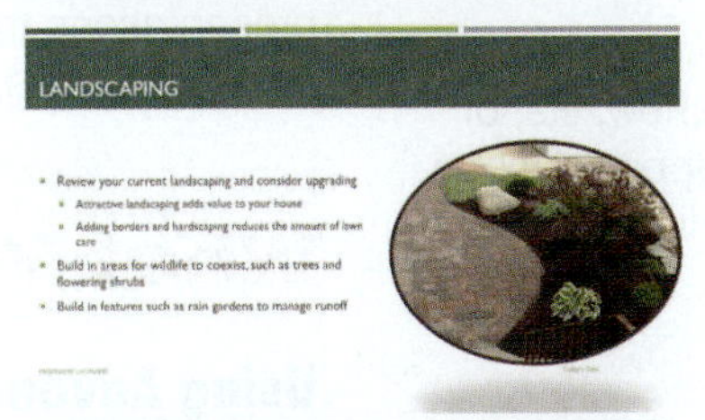
3	Why plant native species? Point out that they have had a very long time to adapt to the climate and can thus be hardy and untroubled by pests. Organic fertilizing and pest control is particularly important for homes with pets and children who spend time on the lawn.	

Lesson 46

Working with Links and Actions

> ## ➤ What You Will Learn

Using Advanced Link Settings
Working with Advanced Action Settings

Software Skills   Links and action settings can be used to create interactive presentations that allow viewers to jump to different locations in the presentation, open other files, run programs, or interact with objects on the slide.

What You Can Do

Using Advanced Link Settings

- You can use links to move from a presentation to another application to view data in that application. For example, you could link to a Microsoft Excel worksheet during a presentation.
- If the computer on which you are presenting the slides has an active Internet connection, you can also use a link to jump from a slide to any site on the Web.
- You can set up a link using text from a text placeholder or any object on the slide, such as a shape or picture.
- You have four **target** options to choose from.
  - Existing File or Web Page lets you locate a file on your system or network. Use the Browse the Web button to start your browser so you can locate the page you want to use as a target.
  - Place in This Document lets you select a slide or custom show from the current presentation. When you click a slide for the target, it appears in the Slide preview area.
  - Create New Document allows you to specify the name of a new document and link to it at the same time. If you create a file with the name Results.xlsx, for example, Excel opens so you can enter data in the Results workbook.
  - E-mail Address lets you set up a link that will open a new e-mail message to send to the address you specify.
- If you want to provide a little extra help to a viewer about what will happen when a link is clicked, you can provide a ScreenTip. The ScreenTip will appear when the presenter or viewer moves the mouse pointer over the link.

Try It!   **Creating Links to External Documents**

1 Start PowerPoint, and open **P46TryA** from the data files for this lesson.

2 Save the presentation as **P46TryA_xx** in the location where your teacher instructs you to store the files for this lesson.

3 Start Word, and open **P46TryB** from the data files for this lesson.

4 Save the document as **P46TryB_xx** in the location where your teacher instructs you to store the files for this lesson. Close the document and exit Word.

5 Start Excel, and open **P46TryC** from the data files for this lesson.

6 Save the workbook as **P46TryC_xx** in the location where your teacher instructs you to store the files for this lesson. Close the workbook, and exit Excel.

7 On slide 1, click the earth in the Planet Earth logo.

8 Click INSERT > Hyperlink 🌐.

9 In the Insert Hyperlink dialog box, make sure Existing File or Web Page is selected.

10 In the Look in box, navigate to the location where you are storing files for this lesson, select **P46TryB_xx**, and click OK.

11 Display slide 10 and click the Discussion shape to select it.

12 Click INSERT > Hyperlink 🌐.

13 In the Current Folder list, scroll down and select **P46TryC_xx**, then click OK.

14 Save the **P46TryA_xx** file, and leave it open to use in the next Try It.

Insert Hyperlink dialog box

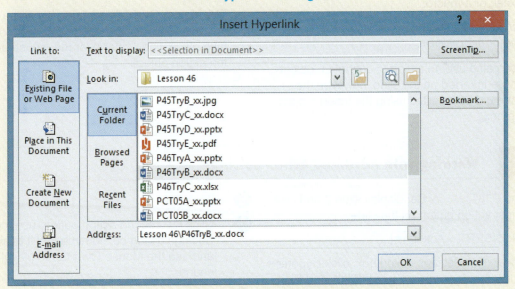

Creating a ScreenTip for a Link

1 In the **P46TryA_xx** file, display slide 1 and right-click the earth in the Planet Earth logo.

2 Click Edit Hyperlink to open the Edit Hyperlink dialog box.

3 Click the ScreenTip button.

4 In the Set Hyperlink ScreenTip dialog box, click in the ScreenTip text box and type **Click here to learn more about Planet Earth**.

5 Click OK twice.

6 Save the **P46TryA_xx** file, and leave it open to use in the next Try It.

Working with Advanced Action Settings

- Like links, actions allow you to link to a slide in the current presentation, a custom show, another presentation, a Web page URL, or another file.

- Actions are most commonly associated with action buttons, shapes you select from the Shapes gallery and draw on a slide to perform specific tasks.

- You have a number of other options for applying actions, however.

  - You can use an action to run a program, such as Excel, or a macro.

    ✓ *You may have to respond to a security warning the first time you run a program.*

  - You can also use an action to control an object you have inserted on the slide; however, the object must be inserted using the Insert Object dialog box.

    ✓ *If you use an existing file, you can choose in the Insert Object dialog box to display the object as an icon on the slide.*

  - You can use an action setting to play a sound effect or sound file.

- Use the action options, such as Hyperlink to, Run program, or Play sound, in the Action Settings dialog box to set the target for the action.

- By default, you set actions on the Mouse Click tab, which means that the action takes place when you click on the action object during the presentation.

- The Mouse Over tab contains the same options as the Mouse Click tab. Actions you set on this tab will take place when you hover the mouse pointer over the action object.

Working with Advanced Action Settings

1 In the **P46TryA_xx** file, display slide 2 and click the first action button on the slide.

2 Click INSERT > Action ⭐.

3 In the Action Settings dialog box, click Hyperlink to, click the down arrow, select Slide, and then select 3. Project Overview.

4 Click OK.

5 In the Action Settings dialog box, click the Mouse Over tab, click the Play sound check box, click the down arrow, and click Chime.

6 Click OK.

7 Click the second action button, use the Action Settings dialog box to hyperlink it to slide 7, and use the Mouse Over tab to play the Chime sound.

8 Continue setting actions for the next two buttons, linking to slide 12 and slide 16, and playing the Chime sound.

9 Display slide 9 and click the action button in the lower-right corner.

(continued)

Try It!   **Working with Advanced Action Settings** *(continued)*

Specify actions in the Action Settings dialog box

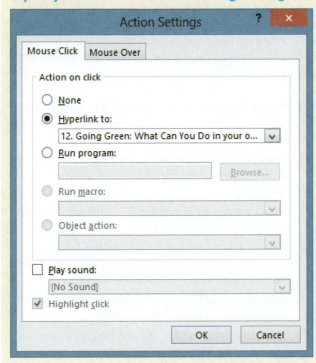

10. Click Insert > Action ★.

11. Click Run program and then click Browse.

12. Click Desktop in the left pane and select one of the shortcuts on the Desktop.

13. Click OK twice.

14. Click SLIDE SHOW > From Beginning 📺 and watch the slide show, clicking all the links and action buttons as they appear. On slide 2, move the mouse pointer over the action buttons to hear the chimes and then click the button to jump to a new slide. When you jump to an external document, view the content, then close the document and its application and return to the presentation.

    ✓ *If you receive a security warning when you click the action button on slide 9 to run a program, click Enable.*

15. Close the **P46TryA_xx** file, saving changes, and exit PowerPoint.

Lesson 46—Practice

Peterson Home Healthcare is starting the process of training employees on Microsoft Office 2013 after the installation of the new network and workstations. In this project, you begin work on a presentation that employees can access from their own computers to learn more about Microsoft Office 2013. You create links and action items to make it easy for employees to interact with the training materials.

DIRECTIONS

1. Start PowerPoint, if necessary, and open **P46PracticeA** from the data files for this lesson.

2. Save the presentation as **P46PracticeA_xx** in the location where your teacher instructs you to store the files for this lesson.

3. Start Word, if necessary, and open **P46PracticeB** from the data files for this lesson.

4. Save the file as **P46PracticeB_xx** in the location where your teacher instructs you to store the files for this lesson.

5. Display slide 2 and select the first bullet item.

6. Click **INSERT** > **Hyperlink** 🌐 > **Place in This Document** and select the **Introduction** slide. Click **OK**.

7. Repeat this process for each of the other bullet items on slide 2, linking them to the corresponding slide.

8. Select the *Test Your Knowledge* object on slide 6. Click **INSERT** > **Hyperlink** 🌐 > **Existing File or Web Page**.

9. Select the file **P46PracticeB_xx** from the solution files for this lesson. Click **OK**.

10. Preview the presentation, testing the links you inserted on slides 2 and 6. Then insert your name, the date, and slide numbers on all slides.

11. **With your teacher's permission,** print slide 2. It should look similar to Figure 46-1.

12. Close the presentation, saving changes, and exit PowerPoint. Close the Word document and exit Word.

Figure 46-1

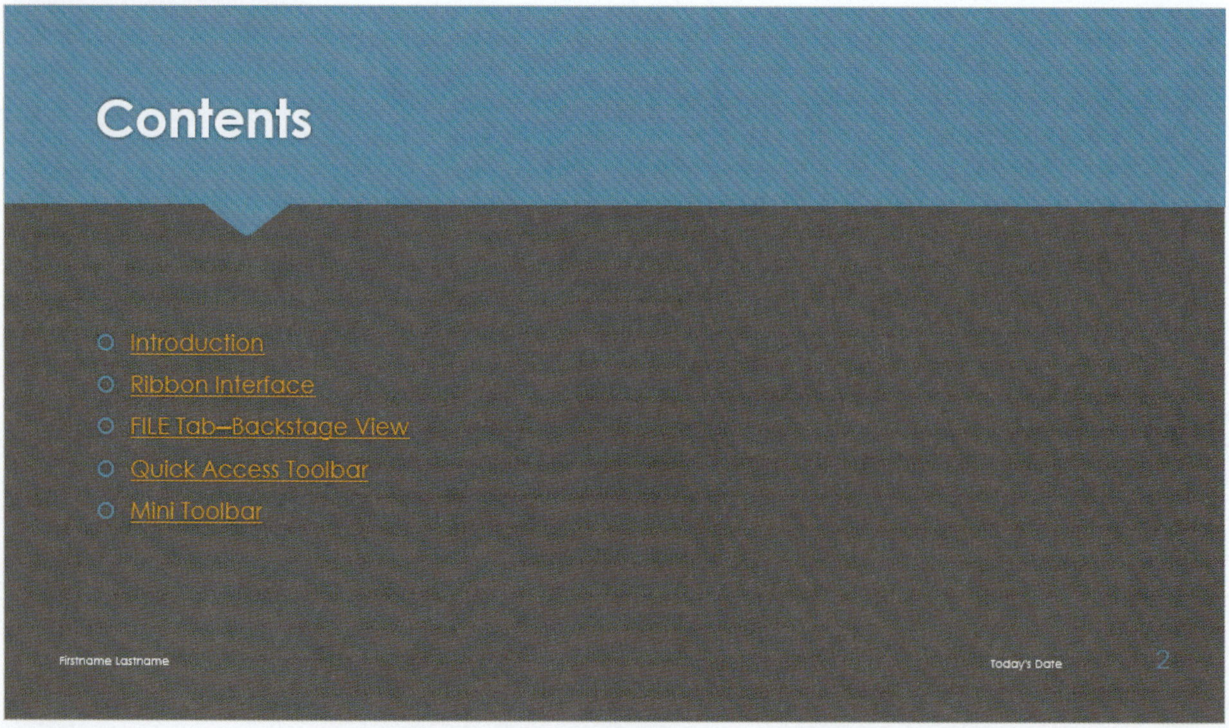

Contents

○ Introduction

○ Ribbon Interface

○ FILE Tab—Backstage View

○ Quick Access Toolbar

○ Mini Toolbar

Firstname Lastname   Today's Date   2

Lesson 46—Apply

In this project, you continue to work on the Peterson Home Healthcare interactive presentation. You add action settings to allow viewers to open other applications and links to make it easy to navigate the materials.

DIRECTIONS

1. Start PowerPoint, if necessary, and open **P46ApplyA** from the data files for this lesson.

2. Save the presentation as **P46ApplyA_xx** in the location where your teacher instructs you to store the files for this lesson.

3. Insert your name, slide numbers, and the date on all slides.

4. Open **P46ApplyB** from the data files for this lesson.

5. Save the presentation as **P46ApplyB_xx** in the location where your teacher instructs you to store the files for this lesson.

6. Select the shape at the upper-right corner of the first slide in **P46ApplyB_xx** and create a hyperlink to **P46ApplyA_xx**. Then save and close **P46ApplyB_xx**.

7. Select the word *here* in the last bullet item on slide 8 and link it to **P46ApplyB_xx**.

8. Open Slide Master view. On the Title and Content layout (not the slide master), select the **Questions** text box and create a link to an e-mail address. Use the following address: **jpeterson@petersonhomehealth.com**

   ✓ *This e-mail address is a dummy for setup purposes only.*

9. Select the **More Info** box and create a link to the Office Online home page at **http://office.microsoft.com/en-us**.

10. Add the following ScreenTip to the More Info link: **Visit Microsoft Office Online**.

11. Insert a Custom action button from the Shapes gallery below the More Info box and link the button to slide 2. Type **Contents** on the action button, and format the button with the same Quick Style as the text boxes but a different color, as shown in Figure 46-2 on the next page.

12. Make sure all three boxes are the same shape, width, and height. Align left and distribute the three boxes vertically. Then select the boxes, copy them, and paste them on all slide layouts except the title layout, section header layout, and picture layouts. Exit Slide Master view.

13. Display slide 4 and select the *Open Word* shape. Apply an action setting that will run Microsoft Word: Click **Browse** and navigate to the location where Office 15 program files are stored.

    ✓ *On a Windows 8 computer, your path may be similar to C:\ Program Files\Microsoft Office 15\root\office15\WINWORD.EXE.*

14. Select the *Open Excel* shape and browse to the same location, but select **EXCEL.EXE** in the office15 folder.

15. You are ready to test your interactive presentation. Follow these steps in Slide Show view:

    a. On slide 2, test each of the links to slides, using the **Contents** action button to return each time to slide 2.

    b. Test the **Questions** and **More Info** buttons. Close the e-mail message window without creating a message, and close the Web page after you are done viewing it.

    c. On slide 4, click the **Open Word** shape, and then click **Enable** when alerted to the potential security risk. Close Word. Click the **Open Excel** shape, click **Enable** if necessary, and close Excel.

    d. On slide 6, click the **Test Your Knowledge** object to open the Word document with three questions. For extra credit, answer the questions and then save the document with a new name such as **P46ApplyC_xx**. Close the document to return to the presentation.

       ✓ *If you get an error message when you click this link, adjust the link target in Normal view and then return to the slide show.*

    e. On slide 8, click the link that takes you to **P46ApplyB_xx**. Use the link to navigate to the information on customizing the Quick Access Toolbar, then use the action button to return to the first slide. Use the button at the upper-right corner of the slide to return to **P46ApplyA_xx**.

16. **With your teacher's permission,** print slide 8. It should look similar to Figure 46-2 on the next page.

17. Close the presentation, saving changes, and exit PowerPoint.

Figure 46-2

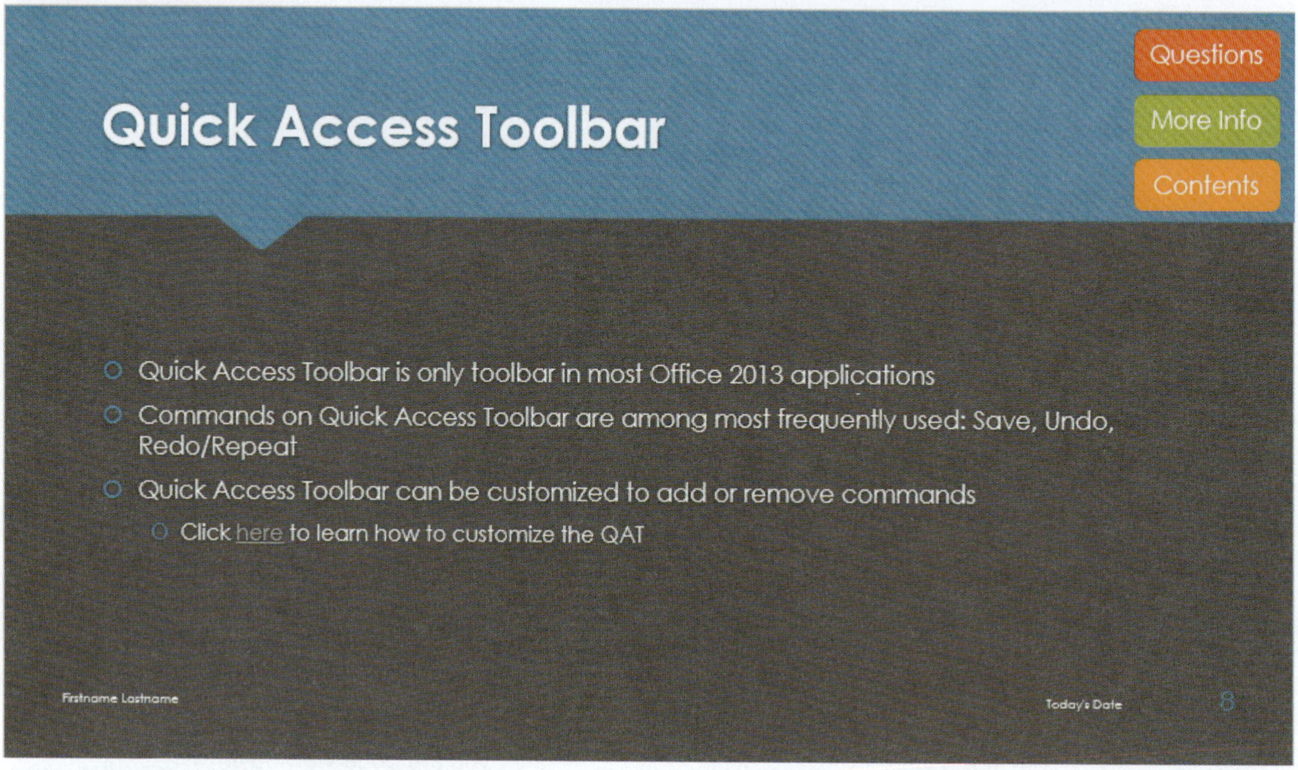

Quick Access Toolbar

Questions

More Info

Contents

- Quick Access Toolbar is only toolbar in most Office 2013 applications
- Commands on Quick Access Toolbar are among most frequently used: Save, Undo, Redo/Repeat
- Quick Access Toolbar can be customized to add or remove commands
  - Click here to learn how to customize the QAT

Firstname Lastname

Today's Date

8

Lesson 47

Working with Online Presentations

➤ What You Will Learn

Working in the SkyDrive

Editing a Presentation in the PowerPoint Web App

Sharing Online Files

Working with Co-authors

Supporting and Maintaining Web-Based Presentations

Software Skills   Teamwork really is the name of the game for many people who work on presentations today. Often more than one person is responsible for content, another works on the design, another prepares the photos, and someone else gathers the video and audio clips. The PowerPoint Web App enables a team to work together on a presentation that is stored on the SkyDrive. You can set options to share documents so that your team members can easily participate in a joint project.

WORDS TO KNOW

Co-authoring
A form of teamwork when more than one author can work on a file at the same time.

What You Can Do

Working in the SkyDrive

- Working on a presentation with a team can be a simple process when you post a file to an online location such as a SharePoint team site or your Windows SkyDrive account.

- A presentation stored on your SkyDrive is accessible from any location where you have Web access.

- The SkyDrive offers several default folders, such as Documents and Pictures, in which you can store your files. You can also create your own folders.

- Creating your own folders makes it easy to share some files without giving others access to all of your documents.

- You can save files to the SkyDrive from within any Office 2013 application. The files can then be accessed not only from your desktop but also from the SkyDrive.

■ You can also upload files from your computer to the SkyDrive using the SkyDrive's Upload option.

■ In the SkyDrive, folders are represented by tiles. You can select folders by clicking check boxes and open them by clicking or tapping on a touch screen.

■ You can change the SkyDrive display to see folders in a hierarchy.

■ Use the Properties pane to see more information about a folder.

Try It!   **Creating a SkyDrive Folder and Saving a File to the SkyDrive**

1 Start PowerPoint, and open **P47Try** from the data files for this lesson.

2 Click FILE > Save As, and then click your SkyDrive in the Save As list.

3 Click the Browse button. The Save As dialog box opens.

4 Click the New folder button in the menu bar and then type **Presentations** as the new folder name. Press [ENTER] .

5 Double-click the Presentations folder to open it.

6 Change the file name to **P47TryA_xx** and then click Save. Notice that the renamed file is now open on your desktop, and the Save button in the Quick Access Toolbar has changed to show the link symbol 🔁 that means you can refresh the file to show any changes others have made to the file.

7 Close the **P47TryA_xx** file, and leave PowerPoint open to use in the next Try It.

Try It!   **Working with Folders in the SkyDrive**

1 Start your Web browser, and type **http://skydrive.live.com** in the address bar.

2 If necessary, sign in with your Microsoft account name and password. Your SkyDrive appears with three default folders (Documents, Pictures, and Public) and the Presentations folder you created in the last Try It.

3 Click in the upper-right corner of the Presentations folder tile to display a check box, and then click the check box to select the folder.

4 Click the Properties icon ⬚ to open the Properties pane and display the sharing status and other information for the Presentations folder.

5 Click the Properties icon ⬚ to close the Properties pane.

6 Click the check box on the Presentations folder to deselect it, then click the Presentations folder to open it and display the tile for the **P47TryA_xx** file you saved to the SkyDrive.

7 Click the **P47TryA_xx** tile to open the presentation in the PowerPoint Web App.

8 Leave the **P47TryA_xx** file open in the SkyDrive to use in the next Try It.

(continued)

Try It!   **Working with Folders in the SkyDrive** *(continued)*

Viewing properties for a SkyDrive folder

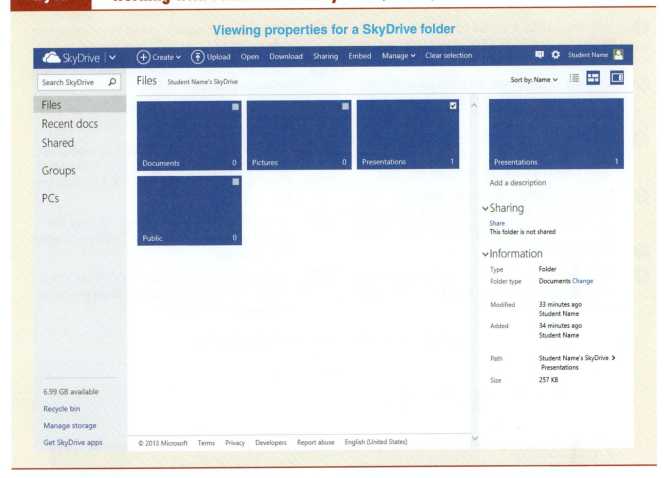

Editing a Presentation in the PowerPoint Web App

- You have two options for editing a presentation stored on the SkyDrive. You can edit it in the PowerPoint Web App, or you can open the file in your desktop version of PowerPoint.

- The PowerPoint Web App offers many of the same commands you find in your desktop PowerPoint.

- You can modify text; insert objects such as pictures, shapes, or SmartArt diagrams; change the theme or variant; apply some animation and transition effects; and view the presentation in Reading or Slide Show view.

- You can also insert and work with comments, a valuable tool when you are working on a presentation with a team.

- You can click OPEN IN POWERPOINT at any time to open the presentation in your desktop version of PowerPoint. You might do this to use tools or features that aren't available in the PowerPoint Web App.

- Microsoft presents a warning about opening the online version. If you are not sure about the security of the SkyDrive site or the file you want to open, you may not want to open it on your desktop.

- Whenever you open and edit the online version in PowerPoint, saving your changes updates the version stored on the SkyDrive.

Try It!   **Editing a Presentation in the PowerPoint Web App**

1 With the **P47TryA_xx** file open in the PowerPoint Web App, click EDIT PRESENTATION and then click Edit in PowerPoint Web App.

2 Click the DESIGN tab, click the More Themes arrow, and click Metropolitan to change the theme.

3 On slide 1, click the title placeholder, click the ANIMATIONS tab, and click the Fly In animation. Click Effect Options ⭐ and click From Top.

4 Click the subtitle placeholder, click the ANIMATIONS tab, and click the Fly In animation. Click Effect Options ⭐ and click From Bottom.

5 Display slide 5.

6 Click INSERT > Clip Art 🖼️. In the Clip Art dialog box, type **cleats** or **soccer** in the search box and then click Search 🔍.

7 Click a search result of a foot in cleats kicking or resting on a soccer ball. Click Insert.

8 Move the picture to the lower-right corner and increase its size.

9 On the PICTURE TOOLS FORMAT tab, click the Drop Shadow Rectangle picture style.

10 Click OPEN IN POWERPOINT to save changes and open the file in your desktop PowerPoint. Click Yes when asked if you want to open the file.

11 Click the ANIMATIONS tab and display the Animation Pane. Set both animations to occur After Previous.

12 On the DESIGN tab, click the Variants More button ⏷, click Colors, and change the color scheme to Red Orange.

Applying an animation to a slide in the Web App

(continued)

Try It! Editing a Presentation in the PowerPoint Web App *(continued)*

13 Click Save 🖫 on the Quick Access Toolbar to save changes and update the presentation on the SkyDrive.

14 Click FILE > Save As, and then save the presentation with the same name in the location where your teacher instructs you to store the files for this lesson.

15 Close the presentation in PowerPoint, make the Web browser active, and open the **P47TryA_xx** file in the PowerPoint Web App.

16 Click START SLIDE SHOW to view the presentation as a slide show. Notice that the changes you made in PowerPoint to animations and colors are present in the online presentation.

17 Close the **P47TryA_xx** presentation, and leave the SkyDrive open for the next Try It.

Sharing Online Files

■ When you are working with the PowerPoint Web App, you can share the presentation and work in the same file with other editors at the same time. This feature is known as **co-authoring**.

■ If you have stored your files in the default Documents folder, you can choose to make this folder public, allowing anyone with a Microsoft account to access the folder. You would not want to share files in this way if they contained sensitive information.

■ A much safer option is to create your own folders and then choose who can share the files in those folders.

■ You set sharing options by selecting the folder or file you want to share and then sending a link to the folder or file via e-mail to your colleagues.

■ You can choose whether team members can edit the file and whether anyone with access to the folder has to first sign in.

Try It! Sharing Online Files

1 In the SkyDrive, in the Presentations folder, click the **P47TryA_xx** file tile to select it.

2 In the SkyDrive toolbar, click Sharing.

3 In the To box, type the e-mail address of a fellow student or your teacher.

✓ *If you have another e-mail account, you can send the sharing invitation to yourself and play the role of team member in the next Try It.*

4 In the *Include a personal message (optional)* box, type **Please view the P47TryA_xx file in this folder.**

5 Click Share. You will then see information on the name and e-mail address of the person with whom you are sharing the folder. Click Done.

6 Have your teammate open his or her e-mail account. Your teammate should see a new message with a link to the file.

7 Leave your browser open to use in the next Try It.

(continued)

Try It!   **Sharing Online Files** (continued)

Invite a colleague to share a SkyDrive folder

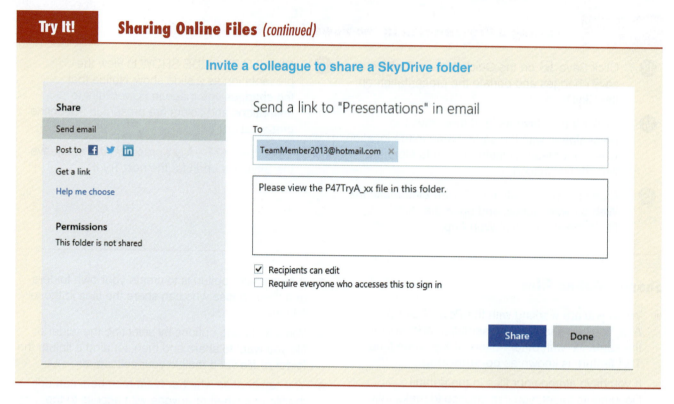

Working with Co-authors

- When you're working in the PowerPoint Web App, you can work with co-authors on the same file at the same time.

- While you're working in the file, your co-authors have the option of opening a read-only copy or editing the file and then synchronizing the file with the presentation on the SkyDrive.

- If a co-author makes a change to the presentation, the changes will be added to the presentation when you close the file.

- To avoid confusion when several authors are working on the same file at the same time, co-authors should make a point of using positive communication skills.

  - When a group is working on a single project, they should appoint a team leader who can be responsible for establishing procedures that all group members can understand and follow.

- Communication pathways should be established so that all participants know the best ways to contact each other to obtain and convey information. A team with good communication skills is better able to identify and resolve issues that would otherwise become problems.

- Objectives for the project should be clarified so that all participants know the scope of work and the kinds of changes they can make. For a presentation, team members should also understand what audience the presentation is intended to reach.

- One issue that should be resolved when co-authoring is how changes are to be made. Can each reviewer make changes independent of others, or should reviewers use comments to suggest changes?

- In the latter case, one team member or the team leader would then be designated to respond to all changes and reconcile edits.

Try It!   Working with Co-authors

✓ *The first five steps are instructions for your teammate. If you are using an alternate e-mail account to act as a co-author, perform these steps yourself.*

1 Your teammate should click Show content in the warning message to enable the link, then click the link to the presentation file that is included in the message from you. The presentation file opens in the PowerPoint Web App.

2 Click EDIT PRESENTATION > Edit in PowerPoint Web App. If you see a confirmation message, click Continue to confirm that your account will be used to access the document.

3 Display slide 5. Notice the second subbullet below the last bullet item refers to Adidas TS Bound. The shoe name should be TS Bounce.

4 Click INSERT > Comment 🗒. Click in the box with your login name in the Comments pane and type: **Notice name of Adidas TS shoe is wrong. It should be Bounce.**

5 At the upper-right side of the Web App window, click Sign Out. The Web App window reappears, with an option to sign in.

6 Sign in as yourself.

7 Click **EDIT PRESENTATION > Edit in PowerPoint Web App**. Display slide 5 and click the comment marker at the upper-left corner of the slide to read the comment from your co-author.

8 In the Reply box, type **Oops!**

9 Correct the word *Bound* to **Bounce**, and then close the Comments pane.

A message shows that a team member is now editing the presentation

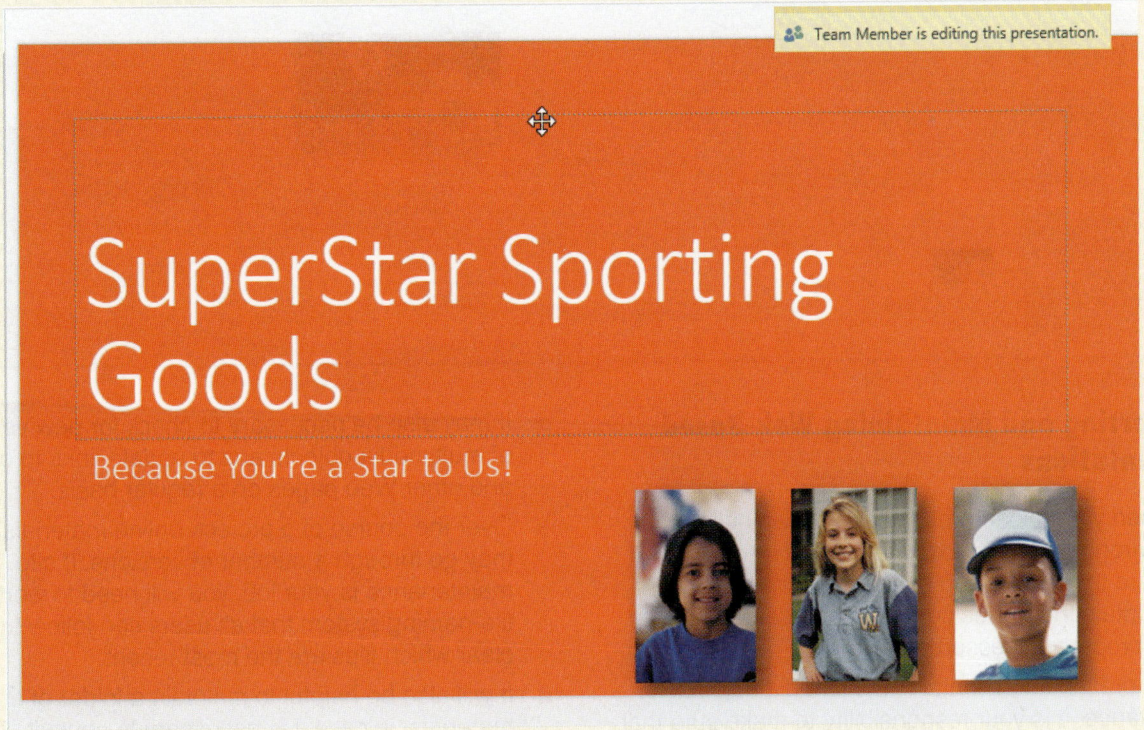

👥 Team Member is editing this presentation.

SuperStar Sporting Goods

Because You're a Star to Us!

(continued)

Try It!   **Working with Co-authors** *(continued)*

10 Click the OPEN IN POWERPOINT icon and click Yes.

11 Save the presentation as **P47TryB_xx** in the location where your teacher instructs you to store the files for this lesson.

12 Close the **P47TryB_xx** file, and exit PowerPoint. Exit your browser.

Comments in the PowerPoint Web App

Supporting and Maintaining Web-Based Presentations

- When you upload presentations to an online environment in the expectation that others will share those files, you have a responsibility to maintain those files so that the presentations can be properly accessed and viewed.

- If a presentation contains multimedia objects, for instance, it is your responsibility to make sure that all objects play correctly on the slides when viewed. If supporting files are necessary, such as video or audio files that are linked to slides rather than embedded on them, you must make sure those linked files are available in the same folder with the presentation.

- It may also be necessary to check for new versions of multimedia objects and to update links to objects and other Web pages on a regular basis.

- Over the course of a project, online materials may go through a number of versions. If site maintenance is your job, you will need to work out a file-naming system that all users can follow to make clear which files are the most recent.

- It will also be helpful to maintain a folder of archive materials, in case it is necessary to consult a previous version.

Lesson 47—Practice

You are working with your local humane society to put together a presentation that showcases some of the animals currently available for adoption. Several of the other people working on the presentation are volunteers, and they will be working from home. You need to post the presentation to the SkyDrive, so that you can all work on it using the PowerPoint Web App. In this project, you post the file, invite a teammate to share it, and allow the teammate to edit and add comments to the presentation.

DIRECTIONS

✓ *Work with a teammate on this exercise, or use two e-mail accounts to do all steps yourself. Steps that should be done by your teammate are in the Teammate Actions section. You will perform these steps if you are someone else's teammate or if you are doing all steps yourself.*

1. Start PowerPoint, if necessary, and open **P47Practice** from the data files for this lesson.
2. Click **FILE** > **Save As** > [Your Name's] **SkyDrive**.
3. Click the **Browse** button to open the Save As dialog box.
4. Click **New folder** and type **Humane** as the new folder name.
5. Double-click the **Humane** folder to open it.
6. Save the presentation in the Humane folder as **P47Practice_xx**.
7. Start your Web browser and type **http://skydrive.live.com** in the address bar.
8. Sign in to the SkyDrive if necessary.
9. Open the Humane folder to display the **P47Practice_xx** file, and then click the file to open it in the PowerPoint Web App.
10. On the PowerPoint Web App menu bar, click **SHARE**.
11. In the To box, type the e-mail address of your teammate. Then in the *Include a personal message* box, type **Please review and add comments as necessary.**
12. Click **Share**, and then click **Done**.
13. Close your Web browser. Close the **P47Practice** file, and exit PowerPoint.

Teammate Actions

1. Start your e-mail program and choose to receive messages.
2. Open the message from your teammate that contains the link to the **P47Practice_xx** file. Click **Show content** to enable the link.

3. Click the link to open the file in the PowerPoint Web App.
4. Sign in with your account name and password.
5. Click **EDIT PRESENTATION** > **Edit in PowerPoint Web App**. If necessary, click **Continue** to confirm your access to the file.
6. With slide 1 displayed in the Web App, click **INSERT** > **Comment**, and then type the following comment: **I like the theme but not the colors. Can we change color scheme?**
7. Add a second comment to slide 1: **I've animated pictures for more visual interest. Please check settings.**
8. Select the left picture, click **ANIMATIONS** > **Fly In**, and then click **Effect Options** and click **From Left**.
9. Animate the center picture to **Fly In From Top**, and the right picture to **Fly In From Right**.
10. Display slide 5 and insert the following comment: **Let's change this content to a SmartArt diagram for visual variety.**
11. Click **FILE** > **Exit** to close the presentation and the PowerPoint Web App.

Update the Presentation

1. In your SkyDrive, with the **P47Practice_xx** file open, click **EDIT PRESENTATION** > **Edit** in PowerPoint.
2. Click **Yes**. The presentation should show the comments added by your teammate. (If it doesn't, click the **Save** button in the Quick Access Toolbar to refresh the presentation.)
3. Save the presentation with the same name in the location where your teacher instructs you to store the files for this lesson.
4. Close the presentation, and exit PowerPoint.

Lesson 47—Apply

In this project, you continue working with the humane society presentation. You work in the PowerPoint Web App and in PowerPoint on your desktop to respond to your teammate's comments and finalize the presentation.

DIRECTIONS

1. Start PowerPoint, if necessary, and open **P47Apply** from the data files for this lesson.

2. Save the presentation as **P47Apply_xx** in the Humane folder on your SkyDrive.

3. Open your browser and navigate to the SkyDrive site. Sign in if necessary.

4. Open the **P47Apply_xx** presentation in the SkyDrive and choose to edit it in the PowerPoint Web App.

5. On slide 1, view the comments by your teammate. Both of these issues need to be handled in the desktop version of PowerPoint, so you cannot address them now.

6. Display slide 5 and view the comment. Then close the Comments task pane.

7. On the HOME tab, click **New Slide** 🖼️. In the New Slide dialog box, click **Title and Content**. Click **Add Slide**.

8. Insert the title **The Adoption Process**.

9. Click in the content placeholder and then click **INSERT > SmartArt** 📊 and select the **Vertical Chevron List** layout.

10. Insert the SmartArt content as follows:

    a. Click in the first chevron shape to select it. When the diagram changes to a text pane, type **Step 1** in the first bullet item.

    b. Click next to the first subordinate bullet and type **Come to the shelter or visit our Web site**.

    c. Click in the second subordinate bullet and then click the **Promote** button ← on the SMARTART TOOLS DESIGN tab.

    d. Type **Step 2**, press ENTER , click the **Demote** button → , and type **Find your special friend**.

    e. Continue adding steps as shown in Figure 47-1.

11. Click outside the diagram and wait a few seconds for it to update. Then select it and change colors to the **Colorful – Accent Colors** option.

Figure 47-1

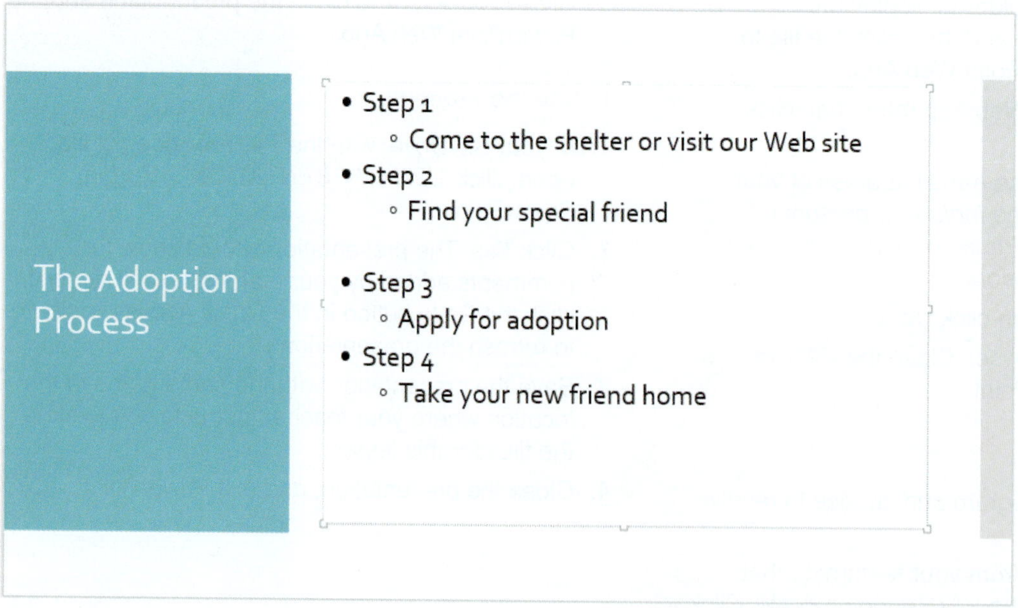

The Adoption Process

- Step 1
  - Come to the shelter or visit our Web site
- Step 2
  - Find your special friend

- Step 3
  - Apply for adoption
- Step 4
  - Take your new friend home

12. You no longer need slide 5, so click it and then click **HOME** > **Delete** ✕.

13. Open the presentation in PowerPoint. If you do not see the new slide 5, click **Save** 🔄 in the Quick Access Toolbar to refresh the presentation.

14. Address the first comment on slide 1 by changing the color scheme to **Paper**.

15. Address the second comment on slide 1 by previewing the animations, and then change the Start option to **After Previous** for each picture. Change the Duration to **01:00** for each picture. Apply a Delay of **00.50** to the center and right pictures.

16. Delete both comments on slide 1.

17. Preview the presentation and then save changes to update the SkyDrive version.

18. Save the presentation with the same name to the location where your teacher instructs you to store the files for this lesson. Then insert your name and the date on all slides.

19. **With your teacher's permission,** print slide 5. It should look similar to Figure 47-2.

20. Close the presentation, saving changes, and exit PowerPoint. Close your browser.

Figure 47-2

End-of-Chapter Activities

➤ PowerPoint Chapter 7—Critical Thinking

Developing a Professional Digital Portfolio

You work for Sinclair College in the Student Affairs office. Sinclair encourages students to develop a professional digital portfolio that they can present to graduate schools and prospective employers.

In this project, you create a sample digital portfolio to help students design their own. You research on the Web to determine what kinds of content a digital portfolio should contain, and then you develop some of that content in the form of *artifacts* such as descriptions of technical skills that have been attained, certifications, awards, community service projects, membership in organizations, a resume, sample professional documents such as application and follow-up letters, samples of project work, and evaluations of work.

DIRECTIONS

1. Start a new presentation, and save it as **PCT07_xx** in the location where your teacher instructs you to store the files for this chapter.

2. Apply a theme and variant of your choice. You may also want to change the orientation to Portrait and change the slide size to Letter Paper.

3. On slide 1, insert the title **Digital Portfolio** and use your name as the subtitle.

4. **With your teacher's permission,** research online what a digital portfolio is. View samples of digital portfolios and identify the categories of content a professional digital portfolio should include.

5. On slide 2, create a table of contents for your presentation. The contents entries should be the types of content included in a digital portfolio, as listed above.

6. Create one or more slides for each contents item. For each category of portfolio information, provide specifics of your achievement in that category. For a category such as Awards and Scholarships, for example, list awards and scholarships you have received in your educational career, or make up representative content.

7. For categories that require external documents, such as a resume or samples of application or follow-up letters, use documents you have prepared for this course or create sample documents. Save copies with appropriate names in the location where your teacher instructs you to store the files for this chapter.

8. Provide links or action buttons from the slide to those documents. Provide action buttons to return to the portfolio presentation from all external files.

9. For the project work category, select one of the Critical Thinking projects you have completed for this course. Save the title slide as a picture and use it on your portfolio slide as a link to the Critical Thinking file.

10. After you have created all the slides for the categories of the portfolio, return to slide 2 and create links from each contents item to the relevant slide.

11. For all slides except the title and the contents slide, insert a Return action button that links back to the contents slide.

12. Check the spelling and grammar in the presentation and correct errors.

13. Preview the slides and check all links and action buttons. Insert your name, slide numbers, and the date on all slides.

14. Deliver the presentation to your class. As part of your presentation, discuss the importance of digital portfolios and why a person would want to develop one. Ask for comments on how the presentation could be improved.

15. **With your teacher's permission**, print the presentation as handouts.

16. Close the presentation, saving changes, and exit PowerPoint.

➤ PowerPoint Chapter 7—Portfolio Builder

Glacier National Park Presentation

In this project, you do the final work on Voyager's Glacier presentation. You save a slide as a picture to use in a Word document, check and address accessibility issues, add links and action buttons to external content, and finally save the presentation in PDF format.

DIRECTIONS

1. Start PowerPoint, if necessary, and open **PPB07A** from the data files for this chapter.

2. Save the presentation as **PPB07A_xx** in the location where your teacher instructs you to store the files for this chapter.

3. Start Word and open **PPB07B** from the data files for this chapter.

4. Save the document as **PPB07B_xx** in the location where your teacher instructs you to store the files for this chapter.

5. In PowerPoint, open **PPB07C** from the data files for this chapter.

6. Save the presentation as **PPB07C_xx** in the location where your teacher instructs you to store the files for this chapter.

7. In the **PPB07A_xx** file, display slide 1 if necessary, and export only the current slide as a JPEG file with the name **PPB07A_slide 1**. Save the picture in the location where your teacher instructs you to store the files for this chapter.

8. Switch to the **PPB07B_xx** Word document, and insert the **PPB07A_slide 1** picture in the first blank paragraph.

9. Save the Word document and close it.

10. Check accessibility for the presentation. Address issues as follows:

    a. Supply alternative text for the shape on slide 1, for the chart on slide 3, for the SmartArt diagram on slide 4, and for all pictures in the presentation, including the pictures in the SmartArt diagram.

    ✓ For the pictures on slide 8, display the Selection pane and hide all pictures except Picture 2, create the Alt Text entry, and then display each additional picture to add Alt Text.

    b. Notice the warning about merged cells in the table on slide 9. Fix this issue by deleting the first column of the table (the one with the rotated text).

    c. Read the information on how to fix the No Header Row Specified error. Delete the third row from the bottom of the table and then fix the header row error as directed in the task pane.

    d. Add alternative text for the table.

    ✓ You don't have to worry about providing a caption for the audio file.

11. Display slide 2 and create a link from the phrase *Web cams* in the last bullet item to **http://www.nps.gov/glac/photosmultimedia/webcams.htm**.

12. Still on slide 2, insert actions as follows:

    a. Create a text box in the lower-left corner with the text **A brief look at . . . .** Add an action setting to the text box that links to the **PPB07B_xx** file in your solution folder.

    b. Draw a Custom action button about the same size as the text box and use the Mouse Over tab in the Action Settings dialog box to link to the first slide in the **PPB07C_xx** presentation.

    c. Format the text button and action button as desired, and position the action button behind and slightly below the text box, so that you can easily rest the mouse pointer on it during the presentation.

13. Check the reading order for all slides.

14. Insert a footer with the date and your full name on all slides.

15. Run the presentation to test your links and actions. Close the browser after testing the Web cams link; close Word after viewing the packages document; play the album slide show all the way through and then end it to return to your main presentation. Save your changes.

16. Deliver the presentation to your class. Ask for comments on how the presentation could be improved. Make any necessary changes.

17. Export the presentation in PDF format with the name **PPB07D_xx**. Select the Handouts option with 6 slides per page and frame the slides.

18. **With your teacher's permission,** print the PDF presentation.

19. Close the presentation, saving changes, and exit PowerPoint.

Illustration 7A

Index